From Children to Citizens

Francis X. Hartmann
Editor

From Children to Citizens

Volume II

The Role of the Juvenile Court

Springer-Verlag
New York Berlin Heidelberg
London Paris Tokyo

Francis X. Hartmann
Program in Criminal Justice Policy and Management
John F. Kennedy School of Government
Harvard University
Cambridge, MA 02138
U.S.A.

With 8 illustrations.

Library of Congress Cataloging-in-Publication Data
The Role of the juvenile court.
(From children to citizens ; v. II)
Includes index.
1. Juvenile courts—United States—Congresses.
2. Juvenile justice, Administration of—United States
—Congresses. I. Hartmann, Francis X., 1933–
KF9794.A2R64 1987 345.73'081 86-29724
347.30581

Softcover reprint of the hardcover 1st edition 1987

Typeset by TCSystems, Shippensburg, Pennsylvania.

9 8 7 6 5 4 3 2 1
ISBN-13: 978-1-4613-8703-9 e-ISBN-13: 978-1-4613-8701-5
DOI: 10.1007/978-1-4613-8701-5

To James Weissman,
a valued friend and colleague
who did justice to children
and their communities

Preface

The issues around which the juvenile justice system is centered frequently evoke anger and impatience. These emotions arise because the issues are so important and movement concerning them seems nonexistent. The persons who are involved with those same issues, however, elicit respect and, often, affection.

The Executive Sessions of the Kennedy School of Government combined the two elements—issues and persons—with the stated goal of advancing fruitful and effective public policy. The Executive Session on the Future of the Juvenile Justice System, over a period of almost two years, regularly brought to the same table people who understood the issues well, who were professionally and personally invested in certain positions on the issues, and who were willing to engage themselves fully in the exchange of ideas, both theoretical and practical, which an Executive Session demands. I had the privilege of chairing the meetings of the Session.

This book is one of the products of that process. As the editor, I take certain positions regarding the future of the juvenile justice system and what the system should look like ten years from now. Not every member of the Session will fully agree with what I see as the pivotal role of the court in that system. Part of that may be due to an inability to effectively communicate a new vision of the responsibilities of the court, leading to a version of the court different from that now in place. But part is undoubtedly due to the fact that, pure and simple, there was disagreement among those who participated in the Executive Session. But those in disagreement would still acknowledge that what we have written is quite different from what we would have written and espoused before the Executive Session began.

We heard, and continue to hear, the experienced voices of Ellen Schall,

Orlando Martinez, Sidney Dwoskin, Jim Rowland, and Ned Murphy, all of whom bear very real burdens for the day-to-day care of thousands of children. We heard the passion, around different positions, of Judges Gladstone, Quinn, White, and Milligan. Who could not but be moved by the reasoned, caring logic of Janet Fink and Barbara Flicker? And the thoughtful insights of Cathy Ryan and the late Jim Weissman and incisive comments of Mark Sidran showed us that prosecutors are very different from their stereotypes. The same should be said of Lee Brown and Hubert Williams, who, as chiefs of police, might have been expected to be hard-liners. Instead, they were statesmen. Jim Brown educated us about alternatives to the court; Donna Hamparian about violent offenders; Dick Barnum about responsibility; and Don McCorkell reminded us again of the breadth of vision achieved by responsible state legislators. Robbie Calloway was evidence of the strength of private nonprofit organizations. Michael Smith and Peter Greenwood each had a special way of thinking about issues and of sharing that gift with others. Phil Cook and Lloyd Ohlin, the latter the dean of academics addressing juvenile justice issues, brought imagination and intellect to the enterprise.

The Office of Juvenile Justice and Delinquency Prevention funded the Executive Session, and Alfred Regnery, Jim Wootton, and Pam Swain participated fully. It is a mark of their professionalism and competence that, while they demanded that the Session produce tangible results, they never attempted in any way to influence the character of those results.

Each member of the Session was carefully chosen, and the enterprise would have been diminished if any one had been absent. The loss of Jim Wiessman in mid-Session is evidence of that. We are in debt to those who gave generously of their time and talent.

Mark Moore's work, in a companion volume of this report, while clearly consisting of his own opinions, is informed by the other members of the Session. The same is true of my conclusion to this volume, as well as the chapters written by the other members of the Session. Each are different from what would have been written had the authors not been members of the Session. As a whole, then, this volume and its companions argue that, amidst the anger, impatience, respect, and affection, there is a hope for a new way to conceptualize the problem of juveniles at risk. There are new roles, especially for the court as it relates to and works with the community, and there is a need for further research on specific programmatic efforts.

Special thanks are due to my colleagues Mark Moore and George Kelling. Mark was a driving intellectual force in the discussions of the Session. George, too, played a critical and pivotal role in the discussions because, while better known for his creative work in the police field, he brought to the Session years of extensive and caring experience working with troubled children.

Mary Alice Sloan graciously organized Executive Session logistics.

Susan Michaelson flawlessly carried the burdens of coordinating the publication of the three companion volumes. Gaylen Moore was the thoughtful final editor of the papers. And Betsy Meinhold's calm efficiency in production was always more effective than my own excessive urgency.

Finally, I am impossibly grumpy while writing. My wife, Karen Goldthwaite Hartmann has been wonderfully patient and quietly supportive. Thank you Karen.

Acknowledgments and Notes

This book was prepared under Grant #85-JN-CX-0004 (S-1) from the Office of Juvenile Justice and Delinquency Prevention, Office of Justice Programs, U.S. Department of Justice.

The points of view or opinions in this document are those of the authors and do not necessarily represent the official position or policies of the U.S. Department of Justice.

FRANCIS X. HARTMANN

Contents

Contributors

Richard Barnum, Director, Boston Juvenile Court Clinic, 17 Somerset Street, Boston, Massachusetts 02108, U.S.A.

Thomas R. Bearrows, Attorney, Winston & Strawn, Chicago, Illinois 60603, U.S.A.

Jeffrey L. Bleich, Boalt Hall School of Law, University of California, Berkeley, California 94720, U.S.A.

Philip J. Cook, Professor, Institute of Policy Sciences and Public Affairs, Duke University, Durham, North Carolina 27706, U.S.A.

Janet R. Fink, Assistant Attorney-in-Charge for Legal Affairs, Legal Aid Society, Juvenile Rights Division, New York, New York, 10038, U.S.A.

Barbara Flicker, Consulting Director, The Institute of Judicial Administration, Inc., New York University School of Law, New York, New York 10012, U.S.A.

Peter W. Greenwood, The Rand Corporation, Santa Monica, California 90406, U.S.A.

Donna Hamparian, Co-Director, Ohio Serious Juvenile Offender Project, Columbus, Ohio 43212, U.S.A.

Francis X. Hartmann, Executive Director, Program in Criminal Justice Policy and Management, John F. Kennedy School of Government, Harvard University, Cambridge, Massachusetts 02138, U.S.A.

George L. Kelling, Professor, College of Criminal Justice, Northeastern University, and Research Fellow, Program in Criminal Justice Policy and Management, John F. Kennedy School of Government, Harvard University, Cambridge, Massachusetts 02138, U.S.A.

John H. Laub, Associate Professor, College of Criminal Justice, Northeastern University, Boston, Massachusetts 02115, U.S.A.

Don McCorkell, Jr., Representative, Oklahoma House of Representatives, State Capitol, Oklahoma City, Oklahoma 73105, U.S.A.

Martha Minow, Professor, Harvard Law School, Cambridge, Massachusetts 02138, U.S.A.

Edward M. Murphy, Commissioner, Department of Mental Health, Boston, Massachusetts 02114, U.S.A.

Lloyd E. Ohlin, Professor Emeritus, Harvard Law School, Rural Route 1, Box 180A, Pigeon Hill Road, Milbridge, Maine 04658, U.S.A.

Michael W. Oshima, New York University School of Law, Mercer Street Residence, #62, 240 Mercer Street, New York, New York 10012, U.S.A.

Catherine M. Ryan, Attorney, Ryan and Miller, 1 North LaSalle, Suite 2525, Chicago, Illinois 60602, U.S.A.

Ellen Schall, Commissioner, New York City Department of Juvenile Justice, New York, New York 10013, U.S.A.

Mark H. Sidran, Attorney, McKay and Gaitán, 701 Fifth Avenue, Seattle, Washington, 98122, U.S.A.

Saul N. Weingart, Research Fellow, Program in Criminal Justice Policy and Management, John F. Kennedy School of Government, Harvard University, Cambridge, Massachusetts 02138, U.S.A.

Executive Session on the Future of the Juvenile Justice System

Participants

Richard Barnum, Director, Boston Juvenile Court Clinic, Boston, Massachusetts

James W. Brown, Director, Community Research Center, Champaign, Illinois

Lee P. Brown, Chief of Police, Houston, Texas

Robbie Callaway, Director of Government/United Way Relations, Boys Club of America, Rockville, Maryland

Philip J. Cook, Professor, Institute of Policy Sciences and Public Affairs, Duke University, Durham, North Carolina

Sidney Dwoskin, Chairman, American Probation and Parole Association, Los Angeles, California

Janet R. Fink, Assistant Attorney-in-Charge for Legal Affairs, Legal Aid Society, Juvenile Rights Division, New York, New York

Barbara Flicker, Consulting Director, The Institute of Judicial Administration, Inc., New York University School of Law, New York, New York

William E. Gladstone, Judge, Family-Juvenile Division of the Circuit Court of the 11th Judicial Circuit, Miami, Florida

Peter W. Greenwood, The Rand Corporation, Santa Monica, California

Donna M. Hamparian, Co-Director, Ohio Serious Juvenile Offender Project, Columbus, Ohio

Francis X. Hartmann, Executive Director, Program in Criminal Justice Policy and Management, John F. Kennedy School of Government, Harvard University, Cambridge, Massachusetts

George L. Kelling, Professor, College of Criminal Justice, Northeastern University, and Research Fellow, Program in Criminal Justice Policy and Management, John F. Kennedy School of Government, Harvard University, Cambridge, Massachusetts

Orlando L. Martinez, Director, Division of Youth Services, Denver, Colorado

Don McCorkell, Jr., Representative, Oklahoma House of Representatives, Oklahoma City, Oklahoma

John Milligan, Judge, Court of Appeals, Fifth District, Canton, Ohio

Mark H. Moore, Daniel and Florence Guggenheim Professor of Criminal Justice Policy and Management, John F. Kennedy School of Government, Harvard University, Cambridge, Massachusetts

Edward M. Murphy, Commissioner, Department of Mental Health (formerly Commissioner, Department of Youth Services), Boston, Massachusetts

Lloyd E. Ohlin, Professor Emeritus, Harvard Law School, Cambridge, Massachusetts

Luke Quinn, Judge, Juvenile Division of Probate Court, Flint, Michigan

Alfred S. Regnery, President and Publisher, Regnery Gateway, Inc., Washington, D.C. (formerly Administrator, Office of Juvenile Justice and Delinquency Prevention)

James Rowland, Director, Department of Youth Authority, State of California, Sacramento, California

Catherine M. Ryan, Attorney, Miller and Ryan, Chicago, Illinois (formerly Assistant State's Attorney, Juvenile Division, Chicago)

Ellen Schall, Commissioner, New York City Department of Juvenile Justice, New York, New York

Mark H. Sidran, Attorney, McKay and Gaitán, Seattle, Washington (formerly Assistant Chief Deputy Prosecuting Attorney, Juvenile Division, Seattle)

Michael E. Smith, Director, VERA Institute of Justice, New York, New York

Pamela O. Swain, Director of Research and Program Development, Office of Juvenile Justice and Delinquency Prevention, Washington, D.C.

James Wootton, formerly Deputy Administrator, Office of Juvenile Justice and Delinquency Prevention, Washington, D.C.

James Weissman, formerly Chief Deputy of the Juvenile Division. Office of the District Attorney, Denver, Colorado

William S. White, Judge, Illinois Appelate Court, First District, Chicago, Illinois

Hubert Williams, President, The Police Foundation, Washington, D.C. (formerly Director of Police, Newark, New Jersey)

Section I
Socializing Children: The Community's Interest

1
The Public Duties of Families and Children*

MARTHA MINOW

Disappointment with legal treatment of children has been a recurring theme in legal and political circles for nearly 100 years in this country. Criticism spawned innovations like the juvenile court, yet some of the disappointment arises when experiments seem to fail on their own terms. The juvenile court, in particular, produced chaotic and bureaucratic environments with questionable ties to justice. Subsequent reforms introduced greater protection for rights of juveniles in the court, yet these too have been sharply criticized for failing to alter the perception—of both alleged offenders and victims of juvenile crime—that unfairness, routinization, and superficiality characterize the legal response to juvenile crime.

There is disappointment with legal treatment of children because problems recur even when sharply different alternatives are tried. One line of criticism charged that institutionalization of juvenile offenders yielded serious abuses of their dignity and failed to set these individuals on more constructive paths. The deinstitutionalization and diversion movements that followed, however, also triggered criticisms for failing both to protect the community and to assist the juveniles. Similarly, critics cite state procedures for handling child abuse and neglect for an insensitivity to parents' rights, for delays in protecting children regardless of their parents' rights, for producing unwieldy systems of foster care that become permanent rather than temporary settings, and for failing to strengthen the security and quality of foster care and the rights of foster parents.

Competing criteria may explain in part such contrasting criticisms. Some people think that the dignity accorded to juveniles by legal processes is more important than concerns about community safety; others disagree. Some charge racism and classism in the operations of law enforcement; others emphasize claims of bureaucratic ineptitude and inadequate resources. However individual critics order their criteria, collective debates about juvenile justice reveal a persistent sense of futility about

* Another version of this chapter appeared in 1986 as: Rights for the next generation: A feminist approach to children's rights. *Harvard Women's Law Journal, 9*(1).

reform efforts in any conceivable direction on behalf of children involved with the law.

Nonetheless, children continue to be both victims and threats to others. Legal frameworks for dealing with children as victims and victimizers have not stemmed these patterns. In this chapter, I seek to locate the sense of futility about reforming juvenile law within the general topic of legal treatment of children.[1] I will first suggest that an initial examination of the legal treatment of children exposes seeming contradictions and anomalies. The same child is often treated differently by different parts of law. Some of this confusion could be explained as the usual problem in drawing boundaries: there is no sharp cut-off that naturally divides childhood and adulthood. And some of the confusion could be explained as the residue of an incomplete transformation of the legal treatment of children and other non-standard adults from the rules prevailing in the past.

The inconsistencies in legal treatment of children, I will argue, arise not from anything intrinsic to children. Instead, the problems stem from legal conceptions affecting children—conceptions insensitive to the relationships children have and those they need. Finally, this chapter will conclude with an analysis of the ways that rights for adults are similarly problematic. This analysis will probe aspects of legal treatment of children beyond the juvenile court context; it will also suggest that the dilemmas we face with legal treatment of children highlight dilemmas we need to address for adults as well.

Contradictions in the Legal Treatment of Children

An initial view of the legal treatment of children reveals patterns of inconsistency. In many places, a 15-year-old may consent to her own abortion without telling her parents, but the truancy laws and school regulations require that she obtain parental permission to miss school to see the doctor. A 17-year-old may be treated as an adult on charges of committing a violent crime; he may even be subject to the death penalty; but the same person could well be treated as a child for purposes of employment and other contractual relations, including marriage. A 6-year-old may not consent to her own medical care, but she may be forced to testify in court against her parents. The law may compel the payment of child support for an individual past the age of 18 who is still attending school, but allow nonpayment if school attendance ceases.

A Problem of Drawing Lines?

Each of the inconsistencies could be attributed to the general problem of drawing boundaries; there seems no obvious line between childhood and adulthood. So perhaps it is not surprising that the law draws many—and many inconsistent—lines. The very characterization of an individual as child or adult is contestable as a definitional matter. This society has adopted varied and conflicting definitions over time, and even at the same time. Different conclusions could result from focussing on biological factors, indications of mental status, relationships between the individual and other persons, behavior, and age, not to mention any combination of such factors. As historians suggest, the very ideas of childhood and adolescence have specific historical and cultural origins, making visible the very mutability of these ideas in current policy debates.

A popular theory among historians today is that childhood was created by late Medieval society, and adolescence by industrial society. Preindustrial societies integrated children in the work and play of adults as soon as the individual was free from dependence on the nurse or mother.[2] To establish this theory, historians rely on external signs like dress and social roles. Some accounts suggest that life stages existed in earlier societies, but with less of the lock-step quality of advanced industrialized societies that use compulsory schooling and exclude children from the workforce. Adolescents in the early national period in this country, for example, appear to have moved in and out of the adult world and roles of economic independence; an individual might venture from home to try an economic venture, and return to home and a more dependent role if the effort failed.[3]

Recent historical work suggests that despite cultural changes over time, the transition between ages five and seven remains persistently significant. This two year period marked the time when an individual started to assume responsibilities in a pre-industrial society. In industrial society it also marked the First Communion in Roman Catholic ritual, compulsory schooling, and criminal responsibility in common law. Contemporary psychological theories also pinpoint the transition signaled by ages five to seven as the point when the individual's thinking processes may shift to enable the solving of concrete problems and the ability to organize basic concepts.[4] Perhaps, in cultures where the tasks of adulthood involved less abstract thought and management of complex problems, this point of transition was the important one in assuming "adult" societal roles.

Through compulsory schooling, child labor laws, and juvenile court reform, reformers in essence invented further stages of development after age seven that held individuals off from adulthood. Similarly, these reforms marked changed ideas about what adulthood means and about society's relationship to people who are not yet adults. The Progressive Era reformers offered a variety of reasons for their schooling, labor, and juvenile court reforms at the turn of the twentieth century. Some expressed revulsion at the risks to children in industrial labor settings; others identified the economic and political needs of an industrial society for people with formal educations, or, at minimum, literacy.[5] Contemporary commentators have observed that the child became the focus for humanitarian reforms that otherwise occupied the Progressives. Humanitarian concerns—and paternalist measures—were more palatable politically when focussed on children. The child in this sense "united the campaigns for health, education, and a richer city environment; and he dominated much of the interest in labor legislation."[6] Similarly, the child served as a symbol of the human who could be redeemed or changed, and who could then help change society.[7]

Notions of the child as a creature different from adults certainly occupied the inventors of the juvenile court, but the child's differences, according to reformers, ranged from the child's asserted innocence and impressionability to the child's alleged dangerousness to society. Thus, alongside an environmentalism that attributed children's crimes in the 1890s to their external conditions—inhumane treatment by parents and society—there arose a Freudian view of the child who internally seethed with tensions, impulses, and lacked moral sensibility.[8] Both environmentalism and psychological theories supported excuses for a child's deviant conduct and promoted social service programs to assist both child and family. Such developments, along with the social rules excluding children from adult activities, made ambiguous what exactly children were to be held accountable for, and what enforceable duties children should have. Social critics, especially in the 1960s, attacked the creation of adolescence in particular for stigmatizing and excluding young people from adult worlds and responsibilities.[9]

Competing theories about childhood do not resolve the practical – and political – issues about when to treat a given individual as a child or as an adult. Whether to treat an individual as a child or as an adult becomes a tough question when there are sharp differences in the treatment accorded to each. The differences in treatment may be diminishing in the criminal justice context, as juvenile court procedures and sanctions converge with those of the adult courts. Juveniles may now be tried in adult courts under some circumstances, and may receive adult punishments for crimes committed as juveniles.[10] Yet, many differences and ambiguities remain in the juvenile justice process. Fourth amendment protections, for example, have not conclusively been granted to minors.[11] In addition, because of their special commitments to understanding the defendants—and their unique institutional attachments to social and psychological service agencies—juvenile courts face unique problems. Unlike a juvenile court, an adult criminal court simply does not have to confront whether the defendant should have the right to refuse consent to a psychological evaluation, or to control whether parents, teachers, or employers should have future access to that evaluation or other court records. The law presumes that the adult defendant, unless charged with mental incompetence, is able to grant or withhold consent;[12] the adult defendant is also presumed to have less dependent relationships with other adults and less chance of changing in the future, making the problem of access to records appear quite differently. How the juvenile court officials answer questions about consent to psychological evaluations and access to records depends in part on what conception of childhood or adolescence they adopt, although their answer may well reflect other institutional interests as well. Yet since the choice of conception deeply affects the choice of treatment, there are no neat tests for determining what "childhood" means.

The legal lines drawn between childhood and adulthood express judgments about the different kinds of competencies demanded under different circumstances. Perhaps, then, the variations in legal treatment of the same person, for different purposes, reflect notions about the kinds and degrees of competence society deems relevant to a given task or responsibility. Variations could be justified on the basis that each individual progresses through stages of development, and at any given time in a child's development, he or she may be competent for some purposes and incompetent for others. Simply put, children need custody and care when they are incompetent, and rights and autonomy when they are competent. But the two conditions are not mutually exclusive, so the same child may need custody and care for one purpose, and rights for another.

The chief defect in this view, which carries some theoretical appeal, is that it fails to describe the current legal universe. It seems bizarre to justify the variable treatment of young people, currently manifested in the patchwork of legal regulations, as though it expressed careful judgments about their competencies for various tasks and responsibilities. Why would a 15-year-old be competent to consent to her own abortion but not to miss school to meet the doctor, without parental permission? Why would the 17-year-old be competent to be treated as an adult in criminal court but not competent to sign a contract at that age? A theory of variable competence may make theoretical or programmatic sense, but it does not supply the rationale for the particular choices the law has made up to this point.

An Incomplete March Toward Children's Rights?

An alternative explanation for the inconsistent treatment of children is that the current legal patterns reveal a partial, but incomplete, historical movement extending rights to children. Like the civil rights movements extending rights to blacks, women, and the handicapped, a deliberate movement to enunciate and implement children's rights has grown over the past several decades. And, as in those other civil rights movements, advocates push to expand the definition of who is a self-determining person, who can make claims recognized by law, and who can assert entitlements to change how he or she otherwise would be treated.

One conception of the history of Western civilization locates these civil rights movements in the deeper context of the liberal tradition. Challenging feudal hierarchies that established fixed patterns of social obligations and dependence, liberal ideology, it is claimed, introduced notions of individual autonomy, freedom, and equality through the vehicle of individual rights. The French and American Revolutions adopted such notions as their watchwords, but one historical narrative has located the liberal transformation even earlier.[13]

Whatever its deep sources, the civil rights movements of the mid-twentieth century proceeded on a conception of each individual's right to be treated the same as other individuals, and to be protected against unwarranted intrusions by the state. Often working through the courts, and sometimes through legislatures, the civil rights movements for blacks, women, and children produced landmark legal changes that can be described as critical moments in the march of legal progress.

Notable decisions in the field of children's rights can be fitted within such a narrative. Perhaps the initial point for children's rights converged with the movement for racial justice: *Brown v. Board of Education*[14] accorded equal treatment to children regardless of race, and in so doing, granted children the status of rights-bearing individuals. In 1967, the landmark juvenile justice case, *In re Gault,*[15] required that delinquency proceedings use certain procedural protections just as adult criminal courts do—notably, procedural rights to a hearing, cross-examination, and access to legal counsel. Besides requiring these procedures specifically, the decision announced children's entitlement to be treated as rights-bearing persons rather than subjects of paternalism—as persons entitled to liberty, not entitled only to custody. Even an institution ostensibly devoted to children's best interests could hurt them, and the Court concluded that for this reason, children need and deserve the kinds of rights against the exercise of state power that adults enjoy.

Similarly, the Supreme Court's decisions in *Tinker v. Des Moines Independent Community School District*[16] and *Planned Parenthood of Central Missouri v. Danforth*[17] recognized rights for children that approximated the rights of adults. In *Tinker,* the Court declared unconstitutional a school rule that prevented children from expressing their political views at school by wearing black armbands. Although the Court ruled that students' free speech rights are limited—their exercise cannot disrupt the school's daily operations—the Court announced that children enjoy rights and do not lose them when they enter the schoolhouse gate. Similarly, in *Danforth,* the Court rejected a statute requiring parental consent to a minor's abortion. The Court ruled that the minor has a right, just as an adult woman does, to determine in consultation with medical personnel whether to terminate her pregnancy, and this right permits autonomy from both state intervention and the intervention, or veto, of other persons. This right may have some basis in an asserted competence of the child: the Court suggested that any girl old enough to get pregnant is old enough to decide whether or not to continue the pregnancy.[18] Yet the basis for the minor's right has as much to do with a pragmatic view that the minor is in fact a separate person, and the state cannot expect to force the child's submission. The court reasoned that "where the minor and unconsenting parent are so fundamentally in conflict and the very existence of the pregnancy already has fractured the family structure," then "the veto power [would not] enhance parental authority or control."[19]

These cases suggest a legal march away from the conception of the child as a dependent person, toward the view of the child's independence and independent enjoyment of legal rights. And this march is founded as much in practical assessments of the abusive institutions and unrealistic hopes for parental authority as theories of individual competency. Rather than expressions of variable competence, remaining inconsistencies in the legal treatment of children show the incompletion of the march of children's liberation. Is this a sensible way to understand the patterns of legal treatment of children?

Persistent Counter-principles?

The narrative of the march of children's rights has a major flaw: it ignores some of the more recent legal developments that in fact curtail the rights of children and subordinate them to adults. A Supreme Court decision in 1971, 4 years after *Gault,* denied children in juvenile court the right to trial by jury assured to adults.[20] And in 1984, the Court decided that a state can authorize detention for juveniles who pose a serious risk of committing a crime, because "juveniles, unlike adults, are always in some form of custody."[21] Accordingly, reasoned the court, the state may subordinate whatever interests a child has in liberty to actions made in the name of the child's interests. Precisely opposite to the reasoning in *Gault,* the Court has revived a notion of custody, rather than liberty, as children's due, and has thereby legally enforced a difference between children and adults.

These are not simply a few aberrant decisions. The Court has also ruled that unlike adults, children are not entitled to an adversarial hearing when they face commitment to an institution for the mentally ill. Instead, the Court concluded that parents can be trusted to act in their child's interest when they seek such commitment decisions, and any doubt about this can be resolved by the admitting medical personnel, rather than by a legal proceeding.[22] The Court also countered an initial declaration of children's rights to hearings before facing school suspensions with a subsequent ruling that children have no right to a prior hearing when threatened with corporal punishment in the school setting.[23] Again, pitted against the rights theory is a view of children's essential difference from adults. They depend on adults, and adults are entrusted with their custody and with power to make decisions about them. Thus, children's liberty interests are subordinated to their legal relationships with adults.

These counter principles of child dependency and custody animate legislative as well as judicial action. Several states have enacted laws requiring minors who seek abortions to notify their parents, and the Supreme Court has approved at least one of these statutes.[24] Although this is not a reversal of the *Danforth* decision, which struck down a consent requirement for minors seeking abortions, it is a resurgence, at least in part, of children's custodial relationships with parents as a curb on children's rights. In another trend, many states recently have raised the legal age for drinking or driving, or both, to combat the high risks of drunk driving among teenagers.[25]

In each of these developments, state and parental interests in controlling and guiding children counter or constrict notions of individual rights for children. The inconsistent legal treatment of children from this perspective expresses the results of a contest between two competing principles: the principle of individual rights, and the principle that the care and custody of children by adults serves the interests of both. This second principle—shared interests—indeed suggests that individual rights are not just unnecessary but may actually damage the relationships between parent and child, teacher and child, and even judge and child, because children need authority, not rights.

How do the two principles cohabit in the law? They may relate chiefly through compromise, and compromise may explain the inconsistent and incoherent results. The Supreme Court's recent decision in *New Jersey v. T.L.O.*[26] is a case in point. There the Court faced the question, are public school students protected by the Fourth Amendment against unreasonable searches and seizures by school officials? A school official searched a student's handbag after accusing her of violating the school rule against smoking in the bathroom; the search unearthed a small amount of marijuana and evidence that the student had been selling drugs to other students.[27] Could the products of this search be introduced in a juvenile court proceeding initiated after school officials turned the student over to the police? The Supreme Court avoided this exclusionary rule question with their compromise decision. Yes, the Court ruled, the student does enjoy Fourth Amendment protections in the school context, but not according to the same standards that would apply to adults. Instead, school officials need no warrant and need only act reasonably under the circumstances to justify a search or seizure, and these circumstances include suspicion that the student violated a school rule, not the more restrictive suspicion of violation of public laws. Students do enjoy individual rights—but they also need and deserve the kind of authority that is manifested in school rules and in the enforcement practices deemed necessary by school officials. What we have here is not simply an incomplete march toward children's rights, but a contest between warring notions of children's legal due: rights versus custody.

It's Not About Children After All

It is possible that the legal treatment of children simply does not have children themselves as central concerns, but that children may be the instruments for fulfilling other social purposes.

Consider this example. Wisconsin treats as an adult any child 16 years or older who violates the motor vehicles rule that a driver involved in an accident must remain at the scene of the accident to provide information and assistance to the victim(s) and/or the police.[28] But Wisconsin also provides juvenile court treatment for any young person, up to age 19, who allegedly violates the criminal law, including the law against homicide.[29] The Wisconsin Supreme Court justified this apparently inconsistent treatment of young people by citing, as a rational basis, the seriousness of motor accidents and the state's need to deter bad conduct in that context.[30] The regulation of children pertains not to a conception of their right to be treated like adults, nor to a conception of their competency to be so treated, nor, still further, to a balance struck between rights and protections. Instead, the societal interest in regulating motor accidents is preeminent, and children happen to be affected in the process.

It could be that the inconsistent legal treatment of children arises because children simply are not the focus of the varied laws that affect them. Powerful social goals instead are the focus of these laws. Traffic safety, control of violent crime, and regulation of abortion, for example, are social goals in which children may have incidental roles, and the laws affecting children in these areas actually play out political and practical debates in which children are quite beside the point. Some concern for children may be mixed in with these other concerns. Yet it is noteworthy that laws against child labor, for example, did not pass legislatures until organized labor joined in their support—and claimed that child labor laws could improve the ability of adult workers to command higher salaries by constricting the available labor pool. Children here were only one of many social concerns, and perhaps not even a central one.

Put somewhat more contentiously, let me suggest that the inconsistent legal treatment of children stems in some measure from societal neglect of children. The needs and interests of children, difficult enough to discern, are too often submerged below other societal interests, and it is the dominance of these other interests that helps to explain the inconsistent treatment of children. It may seem odd to talk about societal neglect of children, given widespread claims that this is a child-centered culture, and given the occasional outpouring of outrage over particular problems confronting children.[31]

Yet here are some facts. Despite the wealth of this nation, 12 countries do better than we do in keeping their infants alive.[32] Over 20% of all children in this country live in families whose incomes fall below the poverty line.[33] The same point put another way: 40% of the people living in poverty in this country are children.[34] Over 1 million children come to the attention of public authorities each year as victims of serious abuse by adults—and these are just the children whose abuse becomes known by others.[35] The typical state budget spends about the same daily fee for a child in foster care as a kennel charges per day to house a dog.[36] Only 35% of all mothers raising children alone receive any child support from fathers.[37] Nearly 1 million children under 5 have no adult supervision during the day.[38]

Adolescent suicide for children aged 15–19 increased from 3 out of 100,000 in 1950 to 10 out of 100,000 in 1977.[39] The risks of injury and violence for 15–24-year-olds has grown more serious in recent years. The issues for children in this country are especially severe for racial minorities. About 15% of white children suffer some nutritional deficit—compared with about 33% of all black children.[40]

Why do children face such problems—and why do their problems seem so unfamiliar in public debate? Here, the basic legal framework governing children deserves attention. That basic framework assigns child-care responsibilities to parents, and thereby avoids public responsibility for children. Public power becomes relevant only in exceptional circumstances, when parents default. The government is not supposed to "intervene" in the private realm of the family, where children's needs and interests are managed by their parents.[41]

Children's rights represent a challenge to this pattern of societal neglect, or, put less contentiously, the pattern of governmental assignment of child-care responsibilities to the parents. The arguments on behalf of rights for children seek to secure direct governmental attention to allow children to say what they want for themselves, or specific governmental rules restraining parents, teachers, and other authority figures from imposing their wills on children. The confused legal treatment of children arises in large measure because the notion of children's legal rights challenges traditional allocation of responsibility that minimizes public responsibility for children; rights for children could also challenge the adults entrusted with the individual's care. In the next section, I will suggest that the idea of rights for children produces confusion because children lack the autonomy often assumed by a framework of rights, and the grant of rights to children opens rather than closes questions about responsibilities and duties for children. Further, rights for children raises the important issue of responsibilities children themselves could or should have.

Rights, Duties, and Responsibilities

Let us suppose we could muster the political and moral will to put children higher on the agenda of public policy, rather than treating only the aberrant case as a public concern. I suggest we would still be plagued by conceptual confusion about the meaning—or meanings—of children's rights. This confusion, I will argue, points to an underlying complexity in the meanings of rights for adults as well. In the hope that analytic clarity could sharpen the debate over children's rights, and pose more productive questions for the practical jurisprudence of children's rights, I offer the following analysis.

Conceptions of Children's Rights

Conceptual and practical difficulties in crafting rights for children reach beyond the problem of drawing an exact line dividing childhood and adulthood, and beyond delays in implementing a historical extension of rights to people who have not had them. The contest between the principle of rights and the principle of custody takes place as a deeper battle over rights for children. Also at work, as noted above, is the issue of societal neglect, presided over by sharp division between public and private responsibility for children, under a governmental allocation of power over children to their parents. In short, rights for children are problematic because the dominant conception of rights presumes a kind of autonomy and direct relationship between the individual and the state, while conceptually, and practically, children in our society are not autonomous persons but instead dependents who are linked legally and daily to adults entrusted with their care. Children's double dependency—dependency constructed by legal rules and by their living situation—places children outside the sphere of rights-bearing persons in a system that makes independence a premise for the grant of rights. And children's dependencies situate them within the sphere of the private family, where parents stand between children and the state.

Rights for children could take several forms. First, children's rights could be efforts by the state to protect children from the neglect or abuse of the adults entrusted with their care. Perhaps better named "child protections," such rights appear in state statutes defining child abuse and authorizing state proceedings to evaluate, help, or punish parents on this basis. Child protective rights also arise in rules restricting child labor, and even rules restricting drinking and driving by children. Although such rules cut in the opposite direction of adult rights that enable individuals to exercise autonomous choices, the rhetoric of rights can, and has, been applied to child protection because it penetrates the normally private sphere of the family and constructs a direct relationship between child and state, where the state has obligations that can be invoked by or in the name of the child.

Alternatively, rights for children could protect children from state power but do so in a way that reinforces the privacy of the family, and indeed, the authority of the parents. A hint of this possibility appears in *Gault,* where the Court articulated the child's right to consult legal counsel in the context of juvenile court proceedings as in fact a right of the child and parents together. Conceivably, the parents' exercise of this right could reinvigorate their authority over the child; in any case, the conception of the child's right here conjoins the child with the parent rather than stationing the state with the child against the parent, and rather than offering the child state assistance to pole-vault over parental authority. Another example is the standard law of child support that entrusts a custodial parent or guardian with the power to assert the child's right to support, whether or not such assertion is what the child wants, or is even fully in the child's interest.[42] A more direct example of this form of children's rights appears in cases like *Wisconsin v. Yoder,*[43] where the Supreme Court allowed Amish children to avoid the compulsory schooling requirement due to its asserted infringements on their religious beliefs and way of life. There, too, the Court's grant of protection to children from a state requirement strengthened parental authority, for it was the parents who asserted the children's claims; indeed, it was parents who faced sanctions for failing to assure their children's attendance at the public high school. On occasion, it might be fair to call this form of legal rule "family protection," but family protection itself is a particular conception of the best way to advance the rights of children.

Justice William O. Douglas' dissenting opinion formulated a contrasting, third form of children's rights by arguing that the children themselves should be allowed to voice their views about attending the public high schools.[44] Under this conception, children's rights could empower them to voice their own views and take their own actions, regardless of their parents' preferences. In this form, children's rights would involve the state in suspending its usual reinforcement of parental power, and indeed would involve the state in lifting children from their usual dependence on and subjection to parental authority. Thus, in *Danforth,* giving minors rights to consent to their own abortions involves the state in not only rejecting parental demands to have their power reinforced by the state, but also draws the state into authorizing doctors and other medical personnel to enter into treatment directly with the minor, without the parental consent customarily required.

These permutations of children's rights create considerable confusion in public debates on the subject. The same banner of children's rights can be raised by sharp opponents over the role of the child's own voice, the parents' authority, and the responsibilities of the state. Consider, for example, a case where parents oppose medical treatment for their child.

A state agency may bring suit to order such treatment over the parents' objections, and do so in the name of the child's rights. Yet a lawyer for the child, undoubtedly hired by the parents, may assert that the child has a right to determine whether he, himself, wants the medical treatment.[45] Both sides have a fair claim to the assertion of "rights" for the child, because rights represent the coinage of opposition to two kinds of power, the power of the parents and the power of the state. Freedom from parental power for the child could be achieved in some measure if the state asserted power over the child, but a very different sort of freedom would arise if the state accorded the child freedom to choose for himself. Even this latter form of freedom requires state involvement and state enforcement; and this latter form of freedom may be unimaginable or impossible in many situations facing children. Still, the double layers of parental and state control supply the basis for rights arguments on behalf of children that point in opposite, or contrasting, directions.

The Concept of Rights as Problematic for Adults Too

The roots of these contrasting rights arguments are not restricted to the situation of children. Rights represent both the reaction of a liberal state to the feudal state, on the one hand, and enduring conceptions of human relationships facilitated by rights, on the other. In a liberal state, persons under the law may be treated either as separate, autonomous, and responsible individuals entitled to exercise rights and obliged to bear liabilities for their actions, or else as dependent, incompetent, and irresponsible individuals denied rights and removed from liabilities, subjected instead to the care and protection of the state or a guardian. In a sense, these two tracks of legal treatment for persons emerged when the modern state challenged traditional notions of a social organism submerging each individual in the community and obliging obedience by each individual to the authority of the religious and political authorities. The modern state, at least according to some accounts, introduced ideas of the consent of the governed, and, therefore, the autonomy of individuals to grant or withhold consent. This new set of ideas thus created an opening wedge for what has become the dominant set of conceptions about the relationship between the individual and the society: notions according rights to autonomous individuals against a state and notions imposing responsibilities on individuals for their willed actions.

These ideas co-exist, however, with earlier and persistent uses of law to facilitate interpersonal relationships. Feudal relationships embodied a contractual dimension, a notion of chosen affiliation, permitted and enforced by law. The jurisprudential activities of liberalizing lawyers, like Blackstone, developed new rationalizing schemes to replace the feudal order of legally enforced, hierarchical relationships of mutual obligations. Legal rights articulated as the claims of autonomous, fungible individuals in this sense supplanted the feudal tradition of chains of relationships, but the purpose of liberal freedoms, in some measure, remained to enable affiliations between people. Freedom of association, freedom of religion, rights to marry, rights to procreate, and rights to retain contact with family members are all current versions of this kind of rights concept—one at odds with the claim that rights protect autonomy, not human relationships or connections.

Of course, for some individuals and some circumstances, the earlier feudal notions of status-based relationships and mutual obligation endured. Especially for people who continued to occupy special statuses even under the liberal order—persons like children, women, and mentally incompetent people—the dependency track of legal treatment remained in force. Yet rather than seeing these people in special statuses as solely the exceptions to the liberal legal order, it is possible to see them simultaneously as people for whom the law—including legal rights—engenders relationships with others, relationships of care, protection, and perhaps, at times, chosen affiliation. The tensions between rights to autonomy and rights to connection may seem most vivid and poignant with people like children, but these tensions arise for adults as well.[46] Relationships of responsibility and care for adults remain problematic in a regime of rights that emphasizes individual autonomy to the exclusion of duty and interpersonal connection. And adults who are accorded only rights of autonomy may be unable to create the kinds of environments children need to develop trust and a sense of personal responsibility.

The Dilemma for Juvenile Court

The history of the rise and fall of the juvenile court could be understood as an experiment in restricting the liberal rights tradition and reviving the dependency and care track for juveniles; in this light, it was an experiment tried and rejected. The initial effort called for carving out legal territory to remove juveniles from the realm of both rights and responsibility for their actions. The explicit rationale for this experiment drew from claims of children's incompetence and actual dependency, as well as optimistic predictions about their ability to learn and grow into responsible, autonomous persons if helped toward that end. Creating a set of institutions that looked to the juvenile's needs entailed denying juveniles rights accorded to those already autonomous and responsible. Instead, the juvenile would enter into a dependency relationship with the state, much like the feudal orders of guardian and ward, and other hierarchical relationships. And without the disciplining focus of individual rights rhetoric and procedures to enforce it, the needs of society and bureaucracy rather than the needs or obligations of the individual could take precedence.

The disillusionment with the results produced an obvious cure, the same cure developed for the defects of feudalism more generally: liberal rights to autonomy. Thus, *In re Gault* and subsequent developments prescribed rights for juveniles, in part to constrain the power of the state, and in part to fulfill the very educational function animating the initial juvenile court experiment. But this time, juveniles were to learn the norms of a liberal order that metes out justice through the interplay of rights and restraints on governmental power.

If the two tracks of legal treatment—the one based on rights and the one based on dependency—sound familiar, it is because they continue to frame debates over the treatment of juveniles. Current debates over whether juveniles should have the same rights regarding bail, searches, probation, and parole as adults deploy rights rhetoric in contrast to dependency rhetoric. Diversion of status offenses from the jurisdiction of the juvenile court in a sense marks a rights conception—juveniles should have the same rights as adults and be free from state coercion when adults would be free. But diversion programs carry with them a larger portion of dependency notions, offering the juvenile "care" or help in response to violations of standards of conduct. Thus, the rights for autonomous persons framework contrasts with but also may work in conjunction with the framework of care for dependent persons in the context of juvenile court jurisprudence.

A serious shortcoming in this rendition, however, is that it obscures the degree to which the juvenile court experiment borrowed only some features of the rights to care, connection, and, indeed, custody. The juvenile court offered rights in the form of child protection against parents in situations like charges of abuse; the juvenile court currently offers some forms of family protection against state power, and at times affords juveniles power to assert their own wishes. But it has not taken as its task the articulation or promotion of rights of care and connection, rights to affiliative relationships—or the preconditions for such relationships.

In part, this omission might have been cured had the juvenile court spelled out not just rights, but duties – including both the duties of adults upon whom the juvenile is dependent, and the duties of the juvenile to those entrusted with his care, to the state, and to the larger community as well.[47] The notion of duty at least introduces a bilateral dimension to rights that gives them content. Difficulties in articulating the duties of parents, children, and state officials would certainly arise, but at least the task of formulating these duties would direct people's attention to aspects of rights committed to facilitating interpersonal connections. In this sense, rights represent not only a social commitment to preserve individual freedom from the injuries and intrusions of others, but also individual freedom to form relationships with others. And the preconditions for relationships are not just bilateral, but also social; not just a subject for the parent and child, but also for the state and the community. Here the separation between public and private responsibility for children exacerbates the underlying problem of forging compatibility among the goals of protecting children, protecting families, and giving children their own increasing chances to speak.

The rhetoric of "duty" is problematic chiefly because it may hide the critical need for the juvenile court, and other institutions addressing children's rights, to focus on the preconditions for relationships. Treating children as though they already had working relationships with parents or other adults, and as though enforcing rights and duties alone would fix the problems brought to the court, could miss what those problems are truly about. Thus, in addition to articulating the duties that children, parents, state officials, and others owe one another if rights are to be meaningful, a jurisprudence of children's rights should probe more deeply into the preconditions for relationships among each of these actors. What legal rules governing child custody, education, and child support would promote the creation of settings where children thrive? Although questions like this would be difficult to address with practical detail. I suggest that pursuing this line of inquiry holds promise of breaking out of the patterns of disillusionment that have accompanied the reforms that at first treat children differently from adults, then treat them like adults, and in each instance, build bureaucratic institutions and a public sense of futility.

A Concluding Hope

Children lack the autonomy presumed under one version of what rights mean, but so do adults. Children need environments where they can learn what is just, learn what it means to have their needs met, and learn what it means to have and fulfill obligations and to meet the needs of others. Adults need this too—from other adults, and from children as well. Debating whether children should be treated like adults for one purpose but not for another misses these points. So does debating whether children are entitled to liberty or custody, although both of these norms contain hints of an important line of inquiry. That inquiry addresses the interrelationships and tensions between rights for children that constrain abuses of power by their parents and by the state, and rights for children that promote their abilities to form relationships of trust, meaning, and affection with people in their daily lives and their broader communities.

Can such an inquiry be more than an academic exercise? Can ideas do anything to connect the needs of children to the tasks of vast, bureaucratic institutions like juvenile courts, the inconsistent patchworks of laws governing children or the much frayed fabric of family and community ties? Perhaps efforts to bring the talk about children's rights in greater accord with the facts of children's double dependency, on parents and on the state, could begin to build a jurisprudence of children's rights of some use in current debate. Further, it is clear that there remains a role for an institution, perhaps still called a juvenile court, that engages in efforts to educate parents, children, and the broader community to their interdependent needs, duties, and, yes, rights. Someday, such a court could bear the role of mender of the social fabric in which it is safe for children and adults to craft trusting relationships. Meanwhile, a richer debate over the rights for children, a debate joining goals of autonomy and goals of affiliation, would expose how our society neglects children by treating responsibility for children as a private matter while failing to meet adequately the preconditions for that private responsibility.

Endnotes

1. I mean to focus on children and adolescents, but the analysis also bears on others who do not fit the assumptions of self-reliance and competence attributed to the adult contemplated by standard legal rules.
2. Aries, P. (1962). *Centuries of childhood: A social history of family life*. (R. Baldick, Trans.).

   Demos, J. (1970). *Little commonwealth: Family life in Plymouth colony*. Oxford University Press.

   Kett, J. (1977). *Rites of passage: Adolescence in America 1790 to the present*.

3. Kett, J. supra at 14–27.
4. Kagan, J. (1984). *Nature of the child* (pp. 76–86). New York: Basic.
5. Zelizer, V. (1985). *Pricing the priceless child: The changing social value of children*. pp. 56–137. New York: Basic. (Attitudes about work and education figure in the transformation of conceptions of a child's worth.)
6. Wiebe, R. (1966). *The search for order*. New York: Hill & Wang.
7. Wishy, B. (1968). *Child and the republic: The dawn of modern American child nurture*. Philadelphia, PA: University of Pennsylvania Press. See also, Skolnick. (1975). The limits of childhood. *Law and Contemporary Problems 39*, 39. (Contrasting ideas of child as innocent and child as evil.) See generally, Ryerson, E. (1978). *The best-laid plans: America's juvenile court experiment*. New York: Hill & Wang. (Rationales for juvenile court.)
8. Skolnick. (1975). The limits of childhood. *Law and Contemporary problems 39*, 39.
9. Goodman, P. (1974). *Compulsory miseducation*.

   Farson, R. (1974). *Birthrights*.

10. Killing young killers. (1986, January 9). *NY Times*, p. A–11, (1986, January 11). *NY Times*, p. 6. (A South Carolina case imposing capital punishment for crimes committed while the defendant was a juvenile.)
11. *New Jersey v. T.L.O.*, 105 S. Ct. 733 (1985).
12. Ongoing debate over the insanity defense and diminished capacity defenses for adults in a sense opens the characterization problem from the other side: When is an adult like a child, or otherwise characterizable as someone not responsible, or less responsible, for his actions? Yet, even putting aside these more extreme cases where medical testimony about mental states becomes critical to the determination, the line-drawing problem to divide childhood and adulthood has come to trigger more debate, rather than less, over time.
13. See generally, Kennedy. (1979). *Blackstone's commentaries*.

Buff, L. Rev., 28, 209 (1979); Seidman, S. (1983). *Liberalism and the origins of European social theory*. Berkeley, CA: University of California Press. (Assessment of enlightenment's consequences of liberalism).

14. 347 U.S. 483 (1954); 349 U.S. 294 (1955).
15. 387 U.S. 1 (1967). The reasoning in this decision has little to do with any assessment of a juvenile's actual competence. Rather, it grew from a critique of a kind of institution that the juvenile court had become—an institution marked by abusive discretion. Justice Fortas concluded that "the condition of being a boy does not justify a kangaroo court."
16. 393 U.S. 503 (1968).
17. 428 U.S. 52 (1978).
18. 428 U.S., at 75.
19. 428 U.S., at 75.
20. *McKeiver v. Pennsylvania,* 403 U.S. 528 (1971).
21. *Schall v. Martin,* 104 S. Ct. 2403 (1984).
22. *Parham v. J.R.,* 442 U.S. 584 (1979).
23. Compare *Goss v. Lopez,* 419 U.S. 565 (1975) with *Ingraham v. Wright,* 403 U.S. 651 (1977).
24. *H.L. v. Matheson,* 450 U.S. 398 (1981).
25. See: Drinking limit - State impact. (1984, July 9). *U.S. News & World Report,* p. 14. Ahead: Minimum drinking age of 21. (1984, June 25). *U.S. News & World Report,* p. 8.
26. 105 S. Ct. 733 (1985).
27. *Ibid.,* at 737.
28. Wis. Stat. Ann. §48.17(1) (1979).
29. Wis. Stat. Ann. §48.12 (1979).
30. *State of Wis. v. Hart,* 89 Wis.2d 58, 277 N.W.2d 843 (1979).
31. See Recent Development, The Insurance Crisis: Who's looking after day care? *Harv. Women's L.J. 9,* 199 (1986) (Discussing magnitude of response to child abuse in day-care centers).
32. *A children's defense budget: An analysis of the President's FY 1986 Budget and Children.* (1985). p. 4.
33. *A children's defense budget.* p. 18.
34. My calculations from *A children's defense budget,* p. 33, make it approximately 37.7% (13.3 out of 35.2).
35. Burke, S., Peck, M., and Gardner, J. (Eds.). (1982, April 17). Better health for children. *Proceedings of the Harvard School of Public Health Conference,* p. 76. *A Children's Defense Budget* says 1.5 million (p. 38).
36. Vorenberg, E. (Ed.) Schreiber, M. (research). (1982). *Massachusetts: The state of the child.* Massachusetts Advocacy Center. p. 82.
37. Levitan, S. A., and Belous, R. S. (1981). *What's happening to the American family* (p. 73). Baltimore, MD: The John Hopkins University Press.
38. U.S. Committee on Civil Rights. (1983, May) *Disadvantaged women & their children.* p. 13. (32,000 preschoolers are caring for themselves; two million between the ages of 7 and 13 are unsupervised.)
39. *Better health for children,* p. 75.
40. *Better health for children,* p. 76.
41. From another vantage point, however, the state is always "intervening" in the sense that its noninvolvement in family matters expresses its approval, or at least its non-disapproval, of what goes on in the private realm. Further, public norms governing compulsory schooling, child employment, and indeed, marriage, child support, and child abuse establish governmental rules

about what children need and deserve. See generally, Minow (1985). Beyond state intervention in the family: for Baby Jane Doe. *Journal of Law Reform, 18,* 933.

42. See Sugarman. (1985). Norton: Coerced maternal cooperation. In R. Mnookin et al. *In the interests of children: Advocacy, law reform, and public policy* (pp. 366–447). New York: W.H. Freeman.
43. 406 U.S. 205 (1972).
44. *Ibid.*, at 241–249.
45. See *In re Green,* 448 Pa. 338, 292 A. 2d.387 (1972). (Remand for determination of child's wishes regarding medical treatment for curvature of the spine.)
46. This may be why the legal framework often seems inadequate for dealing with questions of inclusion and exclusion in group membership. The problem of inclusion and exclusion has come before the Supreme Court recently. See *Roberts v. U.S. Jaycees,* 468 U.S. 609 (1984).
47. To some extent, the general substantive law defining offenses for which a juvenile could be punished defines such duties, but perhaps too generally and with too little immediate demonstration.

2
The Politics of Juvenile Justice in America

DON MCCORKELL, JR.

With the hundreds, in fact thousands, of state and local governments sharing the responsibility for juvenile justice in America, it is difficult to discuss the politics of juvenile justice without tending toward oversimplification. There are, however, some themes that transcend the peculiar politics of each of the states, cities, counties, and courts that share the responsibility for and power to define the nature and character of our juvenile justice system.

Before we devote our attention to identifying those themes, we must deal with some basic concepts that will help define the scope of our inquiry. First, we define the juvenile justice system as the amalgamation of those systems, institutions and activities which are used by our society to cope with the child who is at risk or who poses a risk. Second, we must define and come to terms with the concept of politics. By politics, we mean that process which we use to make public policy and the various interests, philosophies, personalities, which must be sorted out in that process.

We should also consider the present and potential roles of the various levels of government in addressing juvenile justice issues. State governments have traditionally held the primary responsibility for policy-making in juvenile justice, and share or delegate the responsibility for implementation of policy to local governments in varying degrees and patterns, depending on the state. With a few dramatic exceptions, the federal government, to date, has played a limited role in determining juvenile justice policy. The federal role has been essentially that of a catalyst, supporting its efforts through financial incentives or controls.

One of the first lessons one learns in politics is that the most powerful force in government is inertia. Therefore, it is unlikely that the traditional roles of local, state, and federal government will change in any fundamental way in the near future. Under normal conditions, juvenile justice has been low on the agenda of each of these levels of government. Unless one is satisfied with the juvenile justice system as a whole (not just its structure and policy, but also how that policy is implemented), this raises a really important question: Can the political system respond to the needs of juvenile justice, the needs of children? Will it? Well, there are several forces at work, both for and against any dramatic change in resources and policy.

For one thing, assuming that the primary responsibility for juvenile justice policy remains at the state level, we have to recognize at least two major limitations: (1) Most states are facing major financial problems and are in a period of retrenchment and disengagement rather than expansion, although there is some movement toward expanded commitments to education which offers some hope for juvenile justice programs as we shall discuss later; (2) With the exception of a few states, state legislatures are part-time bodies faced with enormous agendas, and it is difficult to get juvenile justice high enough on the agenda for thoughtful and deliberate consideration.

On the other hand, perhaps simply because of the smaller scale of state government, major fundamental policy shifts are often proposed, considered, and adopted within less than a year. This is, to say the least, highly unusual at the federal level. This can be considered either a positive or negative aspect of state government, but more likely it is sometimes one and sometimes the other.

The degree and speed of responsiveness of the various levels of government may be a legitimate consideration in assigning responsibility for juvenile justice, particularly in light of the public's notoriously short attention span to specific issues.

The role of the media in the making and unmaking of issues in our political system is critical in this regard. An issue or concern which, for all practical purposes, did not exist last week can be this week's number one story and the next month return to oblivion. If the media focuses attention on any particular issue for a long enough period of time, a window of opportunity is often opened. Consider the example of the Ethiopian famine. With massive media exposure, the public response was overwhelming, and government responded quickly as a result.

The same will probably be true in the area of child abuse and neglect (a major portion of the juvenile justice system) because the media has picked up the issue and given it major nationwide coverage. It would be safe to bet that the number of bills introduced this year in state legislatures on child abuse will dramatically increase. There *will* be a response. Contrary to opinion in some circles, government is highly responsive and sensitive to even the slightest pressure. However, whether that response is appropriate or effective will depend on the particular politics involved.

There are several major issues or themes which will continue to play a major role in determining public policy in the area of juvenile justice. One of these is the values held by our society. As we shall see, many of these deeply held values drive some of the policy decisions made in this area, yet they often seem ambiguous and uncertain when applied to a specific issue.

One area that comes into contact with these basic beliefs is the area of the family and the notion of individual integrity versus the right of the state to intervene in the affairs of the family or individual. It would be fair to say, I think, that most Americans share a belief in limited government. How we define that, though, varies dramatically from individual to individual. We also strongly value individualism and the integrity of the family. All these values come into play when we consider the question of state intervention in the life of the family, particularly in the case of children who are considered deprived, abused, or neglected; those whom we earlier defined as children at risk. How we define and limit the right of the state to intervene depends in part, I believe, on the character of that intervention. If that intervention is confined to punitive use of the criminal code and court sanctions, then we have a situation in which stringent limitations must be considered to protect the rights of the family and family members.

A different situation is presented to us, though, when we consider the newer models for handling abuse and neglect. They are basically non-punitive or service models. The currently held popular view among professionals is that the issue in neglect cases is seldom bad parents versus good parents, but rather the character and quality of parenting. This makes the state's decision-making process much more complex. This public policy dilemma can be compared to the recent period in the field of mental health when we went from an understanding of mental illness as a black or white dichotomy in which one was either ill or healthy, to the idea that mental health is a continuum; no one is perfectly healthy, and probably no one is totally unhealthy. The same is true in the area of child abuse when we come to the conclusion that abusive or neglectful parents are not necessarily bad parents, but parents in need of assistance. Helping them become effective parents who will be able to build a strong family is a more effective strategy than removing children from bad parents, except in the most extreme circumstances.

The issues of child abuse and neglect, presented to the state in this context, are therefore quite different. It is in some sense easier to deal with protecting the rights of parents and families in extreme cases, and requiring certain proof before removing the child, than it is to deal with these issues in less serious cases. But that model greatly limits our ability to deal with the very real problems that we know exist in child neglect. It also may prevent us from having a positive effect on parents and families who could be significantly aided by a non-punitive service model which does not require a ruling that the parents are unfit and the child should be removed.

The result of this new way of thinking about child abuse is a series of codes adopted in many states which allow for state intervention when a child is considered deprived. An examination of the definition of deprived in various state jurisdictions, however, reveals an extremely general and ambiguous statement of the conditions that must exist in the family before such a ruling can be rendered. These codes often come up for criticism when the state has changed the language of its model to be more in tune with modern concepts of parenting and mental health, but has not yet changed its service delivery model from the old punitive model. This results in an expansion of the state's power to intervene in the lives of the family in a punitive fashion when that was not the intent of those seeking the broader statuatory language. Rather their intent was, and I think still is, to provide a mechanism whereby families with very serious problems can get help in a positive fashion without necessarily removing the child or terminating parental rights.

We also come into conflict with the issue of religion in the area of juvenile justice and child neglect and abuse. One illustration is a situation which has received considerable media coverage in recent years. An individual family, by virtue of its religious beliefs, does not provide medical attention to a child whose life is in danger or who may be permanently impaired if he does not receive it. In this case, the issue is: Does the state have a right to intervene in this family's decision, and to what extent should that right be limited? For instance, should the state have the right to take the child away from the family and provide medical attention, but not have the right to take punitive action against the parents?

In this country, up until the twentieth century, children were considered to be the property of adults. We have seen that ideas have changed dramatically in this century toward an expansion of children's rights. Yet the courts have recognized that children are not little adults with exactly the same rights, privileges, and responsibilities as adult citizens. Thus an extremely complex and difficult situation is presented to the courts and to the legislatures in their decision-making process because the ambiguity of childhood and adolescence must somehow be confronted in determining what are the rights of the child, what are the rights of the family, and what are the rights of the state. Contradictions emerge here as well. We see individuals arguing that the unborn child has a right to life which must be protected by the state, and then see these same people also arguing that after the child is born, the child's rights and responsibilities are to be protected solely by the family, and the state has no right to intervene to protect that child's interest (i.e., medical care, etc.). Conversely, of course, we see the situation in which the individual considers the state to have no right to intervene or protect the interests of the unborn child, but has extensive rights to protect the child after birth.

Clearly all of this presents an extremely complex and highly emotional set of issues for policymakers in determining the direction of juvenile justice and the state's power in this regard. Perhaps one of the basic issues we have to consider is that raised in the *Gault* decision in this area, as well as in the area of juvenile delinquency. The state's intervention in the lives of families, even when made ostensibly in the best interests of the family or child, is often punitive and sometimes contrary to these interests. Therefore the courts and other policymakers must provide extensive protection to see that services and other state programs which are provided to an individual or family are not simply new versions of control without adequate due process protections for the rights of the family.

There is no easy answer. If we are to provide the services we know can help families in trouble and prevent the children's problems from being exacerbated, we must have a model that will work effectively in getting these services to them. When a family resists those services, we have to face the question of whether the state's services are going to be effective when not wanted in each given instance, and whether or not the state intervention is, in fact, going to be disruptive and cause more harm than good.

Part of the answer to that question, of course, lies in the quality and design of services to be provided by the state. There have been many cases of the state intervening in a family in which problems exist, removing the child, and then placing the child in a more damaging environment than he was in previously. On the other hand, there have been some very positive cases in which the state has provided services which have strengthened the family and helped parents develop the skills necessary to keep the family together. If the state can articulate as a fundamental principal the importance of keeping the family together and strengthening the family whenever possible in statuatory language (as has been done in the state of Oklahoma and a few other jurisdictions), then some protection is provided against excessive state intervention and excessive use of the punitive removal of children from the family.

The federal and state governments are all, by and large, experiencing a period of fiscal restraint and retrenchment rather than a period of expansion and experimentation. This has an impact on a number of issues which have been with us for a long time but are coming more sharply into focus as a result, particularly in the definition and clarification of the roles of some of our social institutions, such as the schools and the courts. We see indications that both of these institutions are attempting to limit their roles, thus leaving some public policy areas untouched by the very institutions that are best equipped to deal with them.

The view that the schools should be limited in their interest to the curriculum alone significantly restricts one of the primary institutions that touches the lives of children. Such limitation often results in some children falling between the cracks. This is the child not being served by the school and not being served by the courts; he remains in that category of a child regarded as too difficult for the school to deal with because it means addressing issues and concerns that the school does not wish to address. As a consequence, this child may be expelled from the school system. But this does not mean that the child will fall within the jurisdiction of the court. The court is seeking to limit its involvement with children to those who are clear-cut cases of delinquency, i.e., children who have committed adult offenses.

This retrenchment of the school's involvement in the lives of children should be a major concern to public policymakers, particularly when the education system has been successful in dealing with non-traditional areas of responsibility. One of these is special education for children with physical, mental, or learning disabilities. This effort was federally mandated and, in spite of all its problems, has resulted in a dramatic change in the quality of education provided to these children and their ability to cope successfully with life. Second, although not directly operated by the education system in some instances, Headstart programs clearly made a dramatic impact upon the lives of the children they served. These children when followed up at a later date were found to have dramatically reduced experience with delinquency or criminal behavior, joblessness, etc. In addition, there is growing evidence that a substantial number of children showing up in the juvenile justice system in later years are children with learning disabilities that have never been diagnosed or treated.

Thus it would seem that there are several reasons to consider an expansion of the education system's involvement with the child—providing early childhood education, adequate testing and evaluation at an early age to identify children with special problems, and coordination with other social services as well as the courts in dealing with the specific needs of specific children. There is some reason for hope in education because it is the one area in which state governments have expanded their financial committment in recent years. It is an opportunity for those concerned with children who are at risk or pose a risk to see those children's needs met, at least in part, through that system.

Another factor that influences public policy in juvenile justice is the prevailing mood of the public. As we look back over the last twenty years, we see periods of extensive experimentation in an attempt to improve society, and periods when the prevailing view was that nothing new will make a difference in social conditions. These shifts in public opinion relate somewhat to the crosscurrents of pragmatism and other ideologies in American history. Pragmatism is one of the dominant themes of American politics and one of the themes that supports experimentation and change. It is grounded in a fundamental optimism that a desired outcome can be achieved by taking specific actions. This idea often comes into conflict with a variety of ideologies, some of which are less optimistic about the potential of either dealing effectively with the family of a neglected or abused child, or rehabilitating a child who is a delinquent offender.

One of the most basic issues which has dominated juvenile justice for the past few years is the issue of how to deal with the status offender. For some, the status offender is the child who falls somewhere between the child at risk and the child who poses a risk. Because he is beyond the control of his parents or is a runaway, etc., he is in their view not an appropriate subject for state intervention. Others, however, see this child as perhaps both at risk and posing a risk, and as a result, they would support extensive state intervention.

There is a substantial amount of pressure on the state from some parent support groups such as "Toughlove" and others to renew its interest in this type of child, and renew state intervention and control as an extension of the family's authority. This would put the state in the role of acting as a representative of the family to carry out and enforce the family's rules and policies. (This is the model requested by some families who seek the state's assistance.) Many professionals in the field are resisting this notion on the basis that such intervention has been counter-productive in the past.

Yet, despite the rather dramatic changes in juvenile codes in recent years to remove status offenses from the jurisdiction of the court or limit the court's power regarding status offenders, we often see these policy changes circumvented by those in the system who bring status offenders to court under other allegations. There are several reasons for this, but at least three are readily apparent:

1. The basic inertia in all systems. As we mentioned earlier, this is the most powerful force in our government, and although it provides a basic stability to our system, it also frustrates the intent to change. For this reason, and since those who implement policy interpret it on the basis of their past expectations, the most dramatic policy changes at the leadership level often are whittled down to minor adjustments at the implementation level.

2. Substantial public pressure is exerted at the local level to deal with the status offenders who are often a much greater cause for public dissatisfaction with the system than either the deprived or delinquent child, pressure to which local officials are naturally sensitive.

3. Once again, when the system disengages from a responsibility without adequate direction and support for those who should pick up that responsibility, a political vacuum is created which exerts pressure to revert to old patterns if new proposals are not quickly provided.

Again we seem to be at risk of falling into the same pattern we have fallen into in the mental health area. We determined that a lot of people in mental health institutions did not deserve to be deprived of their liberty and should not be institutionalized, and then we dumped those people on the street with no support. We are perhaps at a risk of doing that, and have already done that to a certain degree, in the juvenile justice system. While deciding rightfully that the way we were dealing with a number of youths was inappropriate—that institutionalization was indeed bad for the status offender—we should not in response completely disengage from that issue. This prevents us from serving the very real needs of the status offender. A new focus and new design of services would be a more appropriate response.

But as the experience in mental health has shown us, the previous design of services in terms of an institutional model was inappropriate. The plan was to shut down the mental health institutions and shift that money into more appropriate services with less punitive components, the goal being to help the mentally ill develop to the point of being able to exercise their responsibilities as adult citizens. However, we came face to face with the fact that funds were not available to implement this policy due to fiscal shortfalls; the money was needed in other areas. One of the basic issues in juvenile justice is resources. No matter what the model is, if the resources and the personnel are not available, the services will not be available, and we will not be able to produce the desired results for any of the population that we are concerned with.

This leads us to a discussion of some of the political ramifications of deinstitutionalization. Anyone who has gone through the process of shutting down institutions and trying to shift the focus of either a juvenile justice system or a mental health system or any other system to community and family-based services knows the political problems and pitfalls involved. The institutions often have a very strong political base and are well entrenched in the political system. In addition, the communities have not been significantly involved in the provision of services to these populations for generations. Since the industrial revolution, when society decided that we could take better care of those individuals in institutions than the community, the community has disengaged itself from that responsibility. Now we see communities which for generations have had no responsibility to provide for the needs of abused, neglected, or delinquent children discovering that they will have to provide for things like appropriate zoning for group homes, and being told it is a community responsibility. That message is met with considerable resistance, understandably, not only because of the natural emotions and fears of the average citizen, but because of the community's long period of disengagement from that responsibility. In addition, communities are not now what they used to be, a homogeneous stable environment in which there is a sense of relatedness and participation on the part of the people who live there, except in some areas of rural America and perhaps some older urban areas. Communities today are often transient neighborhoods in which people do not know or feel responsibility for their neighbors. Some of the communities to which individual juveniles are being returned are subcultures which will reinforce the very behavior we are trying to change. Nevertheless, community treatment for juvenile offenders is essential for effective treatment, but implementing it as policy is a major challenge.

Another hot political issue is the fight over direct provision of services by the state versus contracting with private providers for services. There are strong arguments for shifting from direct provision of those services to contracting for them. In the first place, there tends to be great public resistance to such change in services, and this resistance is a strong political force. Second, the contracting system offers a system more attuned to experimentation and fairly quick changes in policy direction due to the ability of the state to terminate the contract when services are considered inadequate.

But a private contracting model does not solve all problems. In fact, as with any shift in design, new problems are created by the new solution. Anyone who has examined the history of nursing homes in the United States as a model for the care of the elderly cannot help but be concerned about a shift to a wholly private provider model in the juvenile justice system. Such a shift creates new political forces, and at the same time it tends to reduce or eliminate other political forces. Unless the shift to private contracting is accompanied by skillful design and oversight, the new problems may be as great or greater than the problems in the old system. The opportunities, however, given successful controls and design, are significant enough to encourage further movement in this direction.

As we have seen, there are many dramatic political forces that affect the direction of juvenile justice in America. There is much room for concern, and yet there is significant reason for hope. The political landscape in juvenile justice is covered with pitfalls, traps, crosscurrents, and problems, and yet significant opportunities. The American public is not locked into a clear-cut ideology on the issues of the juvenile justice system. Our history of pragmatism, innovation and optimism is one which provides a sound basis for progressive change in the juvenile justice system, and for placing the concerns of children much higher on the country's agenda. That is particularly important when one realizes that the potential success of new designs and new directions for the juvenile justice system is limited by the resources given to that system.

Appendix to Chapter 2: Legislative Trends

JEFFREY L. BLEICH

Recent studies of juvenile courts and juvenile justice operations have concluded that there is no general philosophy or common purpose to America's juvenile justice system.[1] Philosophies appear to vary greatly across states and over time. Moreover, court operations and justice systems differ markedly from state to state. In response, some juvenile justice officials have wondered whether these regional differences are due to variations in how juvenile courts interpret their mandate or variations in the legislative mandates themselves. In order to explore this question, I have reviewed the enabling legislation for the juvenile justice system in each of the fifty states.

From the outset, I recognized that statutory language is, at best, a piecemeal approximation of a legislature's intent. Thus, rather than attempting to infer too much from the vagaries of statutory language, I concentrated solely upon the philosophical statements offered in each statute's preamble. The purpose was simply to uncover any general philosophical concensus and identify any emerging trends in that legislation.

However, during the course of my investigation, I discovered a striking similarity between nearly all of the statutes. Apparently, it is common practice among legislators to pattern bills after the statutes of other states. In the case of juvenile justice statutes, virtually every state's standard was based upon the language originally developed by the Illinois State Legislature in 1896. Of the 40 state preambles reviewed, 28 were based upon the Illinois statutory preamble.[2] This Illinois standard (or template) of juvenile court statutory preamble reads:

> The purpose of this statute is to secure . . . such care and guidance, preferably in the minor's own home, as will serve the . . . welfare of the minor and the best interests of the State. . . .
>
> . . . to preserve the unity and welfare of the family wherever possible . . . and to remove the child only when his welfare or the protection of the public would be endangered. . . .
>
> . . . and when the child has been removed to provide care, custody and discipline as shall approximate as nearly as possible that which should be given them by their parents.

This simple template reveals the three basic competing interests which the juvenile justice system must address. Specifically:

1. Recognition that youths are qualitatively different—requiring guidance and protection to aid their proper development;
2. Protection of society from delinquent criminality; and,
3. Respect for, and protection of, the integrity of the family.

Obviously, these objectives are interrelated and not always mutually obtainable. For example, promoting a youth's individual development frequently requires providing community care and interaction in lieu of harsh or retributive sanctions. Yet, releasing delinquent youths into society may place the community in jeopardy. Moreover, releasing the youth back to his family home may require state interventions which intrude into the family's privacy. Thus, while every state may wish to satisfy all three values, they inevitably are forced to make choices regarding the emphasis and preference they attach to each value. States, then, strike a balance which reflects their legislatures' sense of social priorities. Consequently, the 28 fundamentally similar state statutes have taken on profoundly different appearances.

Our analysis investigates how states balance the competing interests of protecting the community, preserving the integrity of the family, and providing nurturing, rehabilitative services to troubled youths. Moreover, we consider how the subtle changes which legislatures have made in the statutory template reveal changes in the public's view of juvenile justice.

Analysis of Statutes—Changes in Emphasis

A somewhat crude but effective means of differentiating the various statutes is to simply classify how they rank each of the objectives of juvenile justice relative to one another. These determinations can be drawn either by statements in the preamble explicitly giving precedence to one interest or by observing where legislatures have conspicuously omitted or diminished the importance of one or more interests. In general, this second technique (drawing inferences from a statute) might be inappropriate without first thoroughly examining the legislative proceedings and other indications of the legislature's intent. However, in this instance, the legislatures have clearly expressed their intent by consciously altering the standard template to accommodate different preferences and objectives.

To illustrate how various states emphasize the divergent goals of juvenile justice, we have created a simple table presenting all of the possible combinations of priorities—ranging from placing emphasis on all three objectives to emphasizing only one.

Explicit Statutory Emphasis

A few state statutes have been amended to explicitly grant precedence to one or more objectives of the juvenile justice system. For example, Massachusetts General Statutes Annotated, Chap. 119, Sec. 1, states:

TABLE 2.1. Areas of emphasis.

	No emphasis	Community youth	Community family	Youth family	Community	Family	Youth
Protection of community	No	Yes	Yes	No	Yes	No	No
Individual development of youth	No	Yes	No	No	Yes	No	Yes
Respect for family autonomy	No	No	Yes	No	Yes	Yes	No

It is hereby . . . the policy of this commonwealth to direct its efforts, first, to the strengthening and encouragement of family life for the protection and care of children.

Nebraska's General Laws, Chap. 43, Sec. 201.01, however, emphasize community protection:

. . . The responsibility of the juvenile court [is to] act to preserve the public peace and security.

And Alabama's Youth Services Act, Chap. 44, Sec. 1-1, focuses court attention upon the proper development of the youth, instructing court officers:

to promote and safeguard the social well-being and general welfare of the youth of the State.

Of the 40 state preambles considered, 8 states explicitly granted precedence to one specific set of objectives.[3] Of these, 2 emphasized community protection,[4] 1 emphasized the individual development of the child,[5] 3 stressed the family's and the youth's interests,[6] and 2 emphasized the state's and the youth's interests.[7] No statutes emphasized either the family's interests alone or the family's and community's common interests.

Modifications in the Template—Re-Writing the Clauses

The first clause of the standard juvenile justice preamble begins:

The court shall secure such *care* and *guidance, preferably in the minor's own home,* as will serve the . . . *welfare of the minor* and the *interests of the state.* (emphasis added)

In its standard form, this clause neatly summarizes the various interests involved. "Care," "guidance," and "welfare of the minor" each suggest a solicitous regard for individual development. "Preferably in the minor's own home" reflects a concern for preserving family integrity. And "the interests of the state" grants the state leeway in asserting its obligation to protect the community. However, throughout the various state statutes, these specific terms have been manipulated, omitted, and reconstructed to produce wide variations in the priority these values actually receive.

Individual Development and Community Protection

"Care, guidance, and welfare of the minor." The term "care and guidance" has been modified by 22 of the 28 states.[7] On its face, this term seems to emphasize nurturing of individual growth, and by its absence, rejection of retributive sanctions. As a result, it appears that several states have altered this language ostensibly to expand the state's capacity to protect the community. By the same token, several other states have read the term "guidance" to allow too much state coercion and have thus altered this passage to more clearly express the state's interest in protecting and nurturing the child.

Eleven states have modified the passage "care and guidance" to include more retributive or coercive language. For example, the Arkansas General Codes, Chap. 45, Sec. 402, replaces the term "guidance" with the terms "custody" and "discipline."

> The purpose is . . . [to secure] the care, *custody,* and *discipline* of juveniles . . . [that] approximates as nearly as possible that which should be given them by their parents.

Ten other states have added the terms "custody, discipline, and control" to this clause, ostensibly to assert the state's coercive or retributive powers.[8] Some states, such as Florida, include all of these terms, vesting the state with assuring "care, guidance, custody, control, and discipline."

In addition, 13 states have adopted an alternative set of court objectives which ostensibly clarify the state's guiding role—emphasizing the youth's protection and development.[9] The Montana Statutes, Chap. 41, Sec 5-101, reads:

> "The act shall be interpreted to . . . provide for care, protection, and wholesome mental and physical development of . . . youth."

This alternative construction, especially when viewed in the context of the other changes made by these states, appears to *de-emphasize* the court's coercive authority.

Thus overall, states seem to be split evenly in their desire to emphasize the youth's development and the community's protection.

"Welfare of the minor and best interests of the state." The terms "welfare of the minor" and "best interests of the state" are used both to describe the goals of the court and to define the preconditions for removing the child from his home. Specifically, the template prohibits removal unless it is necessary to the "welfare or safety of the child or the protection and safety of the community." These passages imply that the youth's

welfare and the state's interests are equally important. They further imply that the child's welfare involves more than his own safety and that the public's welfare consists, at least in part, of safety and protection. Moreover, these passages set conditions governing the use of the court's most extreme weapon—removing children from their homes.

In altering these parallel passages, states therefore re-weigh the importance of the state's and the youth's interests, redefine the scope of those interests, and expand or contract the court's power to exercise its most intrusive (i.e., coercive) powers.

Five states have entirely omitted the passage stating that the court's objective is to promote the welfare of the minor and the interests of the state.[10] Twelve other states have retained these goals but eliminated or altered the conditions for removal. Minnesota sets the most restrictive standard, allowing removal only if the minor's "welfare or safety cannot be adequately safeguarded without removal." By contrast, Indiana bases removal on the broader "best interests of the minor and the public." Kentucky's statute is even more vague—providing for removal of the child when "it is necessary." And Kansas, New Jersey, and Texas eschew setting any conditions which interfere with the court's powers as *parens patriae* (although this may simply be the result of non-innovation by these state legislatures). The remaining six states simply avoid specifying any pre-conditions to removing a child from his or her home.[11]

In addition, recent social changes have prompted some states to reaffirm their commitment to community protection. During the 1970s, when juvenile crime rates were on the rise, 9 legislatures added additional clauses specifically demanding adequate deference to public safety. California, Minnesota, and Virginia each added sections instructing officers to "take account of protection of the public in their determinations" and "protect the community against those acts of its citizens which are harmful to others."

In general, these alterations reflect a movement by the state legislatures to broaden statutory language to reduce conflict between the goals of promoting youth development and protecting the community. The vague statutory construction tends to grant broader powers to the court to set its own priorities and exercise its coercive powers.

The Family

The statutory template refers to the rights and interests of the family in each of its three clauses. Courts are admonished to give preference to treating the youth "in his own home," to preserve the "unity and welfare of the family wherever possible," and to provide youths with "care that approximates that which should be given them by their parents." Thus, the statutes, in essence, instruct the courts to consider treatment in the home first, to provide services which will strengthen the family's ability to fulfill its responsibilities second, and, if these efforts prove unsuccessful, place the child into another family-like environment.

The family-promotion clauses appear to support two different goals. On one hand, the clauses establish state deference to the integrity and dignity of the family. However, on the other hand, they also promote a functionalist goal—using families to socialize children cheaply and without the investment of court resources.

How states have modified these clauses provides some insight into the emphasis they place upon the family's interests and the objectives which deference to the family serves. Of the 28 states which possess these three clauses, only 5 have retained this original language.[12] Three others have altered the structure of these phrases but kept the principles essentially intact.[13] The remaining 20 states have effected substantial changes in the court's responsibility to the family.

The term "preferably in the minor's own home" suggests two possible objectives—deference to the family or deference to the rights of individuals to be rehabilitated in the least coercive and destructive manner available. Unless it is accompanied by instructions to protect the "unity and welfare of the family," this phrase may not reflect any special deference to the integrity of the family. Thus, "unity and welfare of the family" provides a more useful barometer of legislative intent regarding this value. Of the 30 states evaluated, 17 either retained the phrase "unity and welfare" or substituted roughly synonymous terms such as "strengthen family life," "strengthen family ties," and "preserve the privacy and unity of the family."[14] The rewordings in particular emphasize the state's interest in preserving family integrity and dignity for its own sake. Rather than focusing upon the broader notion of family welfare, these statutes suggest that the true state interest in families is in allowing them the privacy and intimacy to perform their social function. Moreover, by adding the word "strengthen," these statutes suggest active government assistance to families as a whole, rather than providing family services solely as a means to controlling the child.

On the other hand, 11 states consciously omitted any mention of protecting the families' interests.[15] The omissions suggest that these states are less concerned with preserving the family as a whole than with protecting the youth from any interventionist instincts. Moreover, they indicate a de-emphasis of family integrity interests.

Finally, 13 of the 30 states have dropped the instructions to courts to provide services which roughly approximate the care a youth would receive from a functional family. Eleven of these thirteen changes appear to be directed towards eliminating the notion of family as a conduit to youth development.

Six states have completely eliminated any reference to the type of facilities the court should provide.[17] Another state replaced the requirement for family care with "adequate care."[18] Oregon requires that the courts provide care which "best meets the needs of the child." And Utah, Colorado, and Maine each require only that the services provided "assist the minor in becoming a responsible and productive member of society." Interestingly, the states which eliminated this clause simultaneously retained the section emphasizing the unity and welfare of the family. Thus, the states which employed these modifications appear to be de-emphasizing the state's reliance upon family structures to produce proper socialization *and* suggesting that the court's true interest in family is in maintaining family integrity.

Thus, there appears to be fundamental shifting in the court's perception of the family's function in the juvenile justice system. While 11 states appear to be placing less emphasis upon the integrity and dignity of the family, 11 states have placed greater emphasis upon this value. Eight states have not effected any change in this balance. At the very least, it appears that states are struggling with the role of the family in the juvenile justice system. Current statutes now run the gamut from Pennsylvania (which makes no mention whatsoever of the family) to Virginia (which places the protection of family and youth autonomy first).

The Emergence of Alternative Statutes

The most obvious way in which states have varied from the statutory template, of course, is by rejecting it. Of the 40 states with juvenile justice preambles, 11 have replaced the standard format with entirely unique language which reflects both contemporary concerns and the perceived shortcomings of the original template.

The due process revolution of the 1970s (characterized by the *Gault, Kent,* and *Winship* decisions) appears to have prompted a few states to abandon specific references to statutory goals or objectives. Arizona, the state in which the *Gault* case originally arose, has replaced its traditional template with one requiring juvenile courts to provide a fair and comprehensive hearing. Similarly, Michigan's new preamble provides only procedural goals. Both of these amendments were passed in the early 1970s.

Other states have responded to the due process revolution by crafting statutes which reduce the state's coercive (community-protection) powers. South Dakota and West Virginia each crafted child-based standards, whose primary emphasis was the "protection of the child," "the welfare of the child," and "the rehabilitation of delinquent children."

Another attempt to protect children has been to re-establish the family as the central mediating body in promoting juvenile interests. Kentucky's 1980 amendments call for "recognition of the interests of all parties—including the parents." Massachusetts, Hawaii, and New York have gone further, creating entirely family-based courts. Massachusetts law directs its efforts "first, toward the strengthening and encouragement of family life . . . [and to] assist and encourage the use by famil[ies] of all available resources." The Massachusetts standard also explicitly rejects the notion of *parens patriae*. Similarly, New York's juvenile court was intended as "a special agency for the care and protection of the young and the preservation of the family."

Finally, Hawaii's and Indiana's statutes appear to reflect the whole range of new concerns driving juvenile justice legislation. Indiana's statute, passed in 1978, contains language referring to each of the interests raised in juvenile care:

> (1) To provide a juvenile justice system that protects the public by enforcing the legal obligations children have to society;
> (2) To provide a judicial procedure that insures fair hearings . . . ;
> (3) To insure that children . . . are treated as persons in need of care, treatment, rehabilitation, and protection;
> (4) To utilize diversionary programs which are consistent with public safety;
> (5) To strengthen family life by assisting parents to fulfill their parental obligations;
> (6) To remove children from their families only when it is in the child's best interest or in the best interest of public safety.

Hawaii's statutes neatly summarize these duties by directing courts to avail themselves to "children and families whose rights and well-being are jeopardized" and to "formulate a plan adapted to the requirements of the child and his family and the necessary protection of the community."

Emphasis of Juvenile Justice Statutes

As noted, juvenile justice statutes are designed to protect and promote a variety of competing interests. Clearly no state can promote one interest to the exclusion of others or strike a perfect balance among all three. Rather, the interests must constantly be juggled. However, the foregoing analysis provides a snapshot of where juvenile justice stands—and offers some insight into the goals currently emphasized by the various states.

Using the matrix constructed earlier, it appears that the states have distributed their emphasis in the following way.

As might be expected in choosing among difficult trade-offs, most states either have not adjusted their statutory language to reflect a specific preference of interests, or have gradually added emphasis to each interest until ultimately all interests have assumed equal weight. However, a surprising number of states (twenty-one), have modified their preambles to reflect an emphasis on one or two of the values.

Protecting family integrity appears to be an important *contributing* factor to the public interest and the youth's proper development rather than an independent objective of the courts. However, family unity is only included in statutes which emphasize all values or which emphasize youth development. No state emphasizes strengthening the family unit as the

TABLE 2.2. Areas of emphasis.

No emphasis	Community youth	Community family	Youth family	Community	Family	Youth
Arkansas	Connecticut	None	Kentucky	Nebraska	None	Alabama
California	Delaware		Massachusetts	New Jersey		West Virginia
Colorado	Florida		Montana			
Hawaii	Georgia		New Hampshire			
Idaho	Kansas		New York			
Illinois	Missouri		Virginia			
Indiana	Oregon					
Maine	Pennsylvania					
Michigan	Tennessee					
Minnesota	Texas					
Mississippi	South Dakota					
Nevada	Washington					
North Dakota	Wisconsin					
North Carolina						
Rhode Island						
Utah						
Vermont						
Wyoming						

most important court responsibility or allow it to supercede the proper protection and nurturing of youth.

Lastly, four states have chosen to emphasize only one of the three basic interests. The two statutes which stress the public's right to protection are older statutes which reflect the earlier notion of *parens patriae*. The other two, which emphasize youth development, are more recent—drafted in 1973 and 1980—and reflect more current trends.

Trends Over Time

The most useful aspect of any snapshot is as a reference point. Thus, one valuable product of this analysis is that it allows us to consider trends in juvenile justice over time.

Most obviously, legislatures have taken an active interest in juvenile justice statutes. Over 67% of the statutes reviewed have been amended in the last 20 years, and over 47% have been changed since 1975. Thus, it appears that juvenile justice remains a dynamic and current topic of legislative scrutiny.

The fact that 19 states have not clearly emphasized one of the three fundamental values of juvenile justice does not reflect inactivity by a majority of the states. On the contrary, over half the states in that category have amended their preambles within the past 10 years. In fact, one-third of those states have crafted new sections reflecting concern for due process protection, increased family participation, and redefinitions of the court's coercive powers. In some cases, it appears that preambles have been amended to correct perceived "imbalances" in the weighting of court priorities. And in three cases, states have created an entirely new format to ensure that the three interests receive unambiguously equal weight.

The key result which emerges from considering the statutes' timeliness is that family integrity, while not the predominant concern, is the fastest growing concern. Eight of the thirteen states which emphasize public order or public order and youth development were drafted before 1959.[19] By contrast all eight statutes which stress family integrity and/or youth development were drafted *after* 1969.[20] Thus, the fundamental ambiguity over the role of family integrity noted earlier is more understandable in light of its emerging role. Furthermore, this time trend indicates that legislatures are gradually moving from a public order/youth development model to one which includes family integrity and de-emphasizes community security.

Regional Distribution

State legislatures frequently borrow statutory language from their neighboring states in drafting bills. Moreover, neighboring states frequently have fairly similar values. Thus, it is not surprising that the various combinations of emphases are clustered regionally.

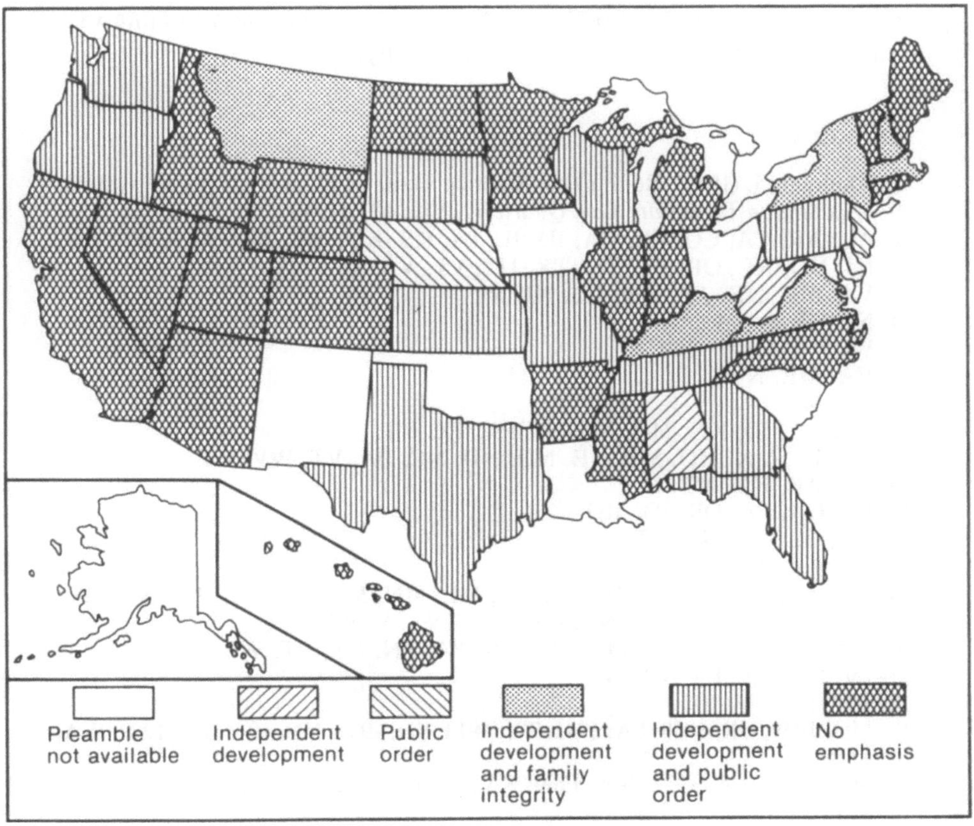

States which emphasize public protection and youth development appear to be located primarily in the south and midwest and Pacific northwest. This may be the result of less active legislatures in those portions of the country, since most of the statutes effecting this policy are over twenty years old. As might be expected, the more innovative or recent amendments—emphasizing youth development and/or family integrity—occurred in the east and northeast where legislatures tend to be more active. Finally, the states of the west and north tend to avoid emphasizing any one of the three public values.

Conclusion

Based on this analysis, it appears that state legislatures are still actively struggling to balance the competing interests of juvenile justice. Eastern and northeastern states appear to be the most active states, driving more towards a court which emphasizes family values. Southern, midwestern, and the Pacific northwest state legislatures seem to be the least active, relying upon older state and youth focused constructions. The remainder of the states seem to be at odds with themselves, emphasizing all interests until they ultimately lose their relative priority.

Endnotes

1. Kaufman, I. (1983). Re-thinking America's crazy quilt juvenile justice system. *Washington University Law Quarterly,* Vol. 60, p. 743.
2. AL, AR, CA, CO, FL, GA, ID, IL, IN, KS, KY, ME, MN, MO, MT, NE, NJ, ND, NC, OR, PA, TN, TX, UT, VT, VA, WA, WI.
3. VA, ME, NE, AL, WV, WI, NJ, NY.
4. NJ, NE.
5. WI.
6. VA, ME, NY.
7. AL, WV.
8. FL, GA, ID, KN, MO, NJ, OR, PA, TX, UT.
9. AL, IN, MA, MO, MT, NE, NH, ND, NC, PA, VT, WV, WI.
10. AL, AR, KY, MT, IN.
11. FL, GA, PA, OR, ID, MO.
12. CA, IL, MN, NE, VT.
13. AL, AR, NC.
14. AL, AR, CA, CO, ID, IL, IN, KY, ME, MN, MT, NE, NH, UT, VT, WI.
15. FL, GA, KS, MO, NJ, ND, OR, PN, TN, TX, WV.
16. CO, ID, IN, KS, KY, ME, MT, OR, PA, TN, UT, VT, WI.
17. IN, KS, KY, PA, WV, WI.
18. ID.
19. MO, 1959; OR, 1959; PA, 1942; TX, 1913; SD, 1939; NE, 1914; NJ, 1929; WA, 1915.
20. MA, 1972; VA, 1977; NY, 1969; KY, 1980; MT, 1979; NH, 1975; AL, 1975; WV, 1979.

3
Toward a Jurisprudence of Children and Families

MICHAEL W. OSHIMA

Through much of its history, American society has had an ambivalent relationship with families and youths. On the one hand, society has endeavored to respect the privacy of the family and to allow parents to determine how they will raise their children. This conviction often has required that certain families be left alone, even when their political and religious beliefs differed from our own. On the other hand, society has an interest in how children develop, because someday they will become full adult citizens with all the rights and privileges which accrue to that status. State intervention in family life is often necessary when a parent has exceeded the boundaries of reasonable punishment or has failed to make proper investments in a child's welfare.

In short, state intervention in family life has come to be regarded as a necessary evil; there are circumstances in which society must interfere with the child's or the parent's liberty, but on the whole we have been reluctant to do so. Given our ambivalence about intervention, as well as the sensitive and emotional nature of family disputes, it is not surprising that courts face great difficulties in developing principled standards for adjudicating family disputes.

This essay does not purport to provide a definitive answer to this dilemma. There are, in truth, no simple solutions to this problem. However, by exploring the basis of our concerns and actions, this paper attempts to eliminate some of the confusion surrounding state intervention in family matters.

On the Special Obligations of Parents and Children

In *A Theory of Justice,* John Rawls (1971) describes what he calls "natural duties"—fundamental duties for which society holds all individuals responsible, regardless of their status or position. Among these is the duty to "comply with and to do our share in just institutions when they exist and apply to us" (1971, p. 334). In addition, we have a number of natural duties which we owe to individuals (e.g., the duty of rendering assistance to another when he is in need or in jeopardy; the duty to avoid harming or injuring another; and the duty to avoid causing unnecessary suffering). "The first of these duties, the duty of mutual aid, is a positive duty in that it is a duty to do something good for another; whereas the last two duties are negative in that they require us not to do something that is bad. The distinction between positive and negative duties is intuitively clear in many cases, but often gives way" (1971, p. 114).

These duties are natural, because we have them regardless of whether we explicitly have committed ourselves to these actions. They are also natural in that they have no necessary connection with institutions or social practices (i.e., they hold between all persons, irrespective of institutional relationships). "In this sense the natural duties are owed not only to definite individuals, say to those cooperating together in a particular social arrangement, but to persons generally. This feature in particular suggests the propriety of the adjective 'natural' " (Rawls, 1971, p. 115).

In contrast, but not in opposition to these natural duties, are "obligations" connected with offices and not owed to all persons generally. Unlike natural duties, these obligations arise as a result of voluntary actions, such as the assumption of an office or the voluntary acceptance of benefits from a given social arrangement. Obligations also differ from natural duties in that the content of the former is defined by the institution of which the office is a part; established rules and practices specify exactly what it is that one is required to do. Finally, obligations, unlike duties, are owed only to specific individuals, namely, those who are cooperating to maintain the institution in question (Rawls, 1971, pp. 108–114).

Rawls gives as an example the obligations that one incurs as a result of running for and (if successful) holding public office in a constitutional regime. Yet obligations exist even when the grant of power by the government is not so immediate. *Black's Law Dictionary* (1979) reminds us that an office is simply "a right, and correspondent duty, to exercise a public trust." As defined, the term may apply to a large number of social arrangements which are not "public offices" per se. One may point, for instance, to the office of the executor, who performs a duty and exercises a power which is derived not from the consent of the legatees, but rather from a superior authority. I argue that the term may also apply to the position that the parent and the child occupy in American society.

Parents are expected, first, to give the child nurturance and love, and to perform other acts which contribute to his emotional growth. We also require parents to provide material support and shelter for the child until such time as that child is able to provide for himself. Finally, parents are obliged to provide the child, by themselves and through schools, with information regarding the repertoire of actions and thoughts that the child must command if he is to attain a sense of virtue and competence.

At first glance these obligations may strike one as onerous, but they are not always regarded as such by those responsible for carrying them out. Indeed, William Blackstone (1765), writing at a time when children were valued less as objects of affection than as potential wage earners, went so far as to describe these obligations as arising out of a principle of natural law and as (to some degree) self-enforcing:

The municipal laws of all well-regulated states have taken care to enforce this duty [in this case, the maintenance and support of children]: though providence has done it more effectually than any laws, by implanting in the breast of every parent that . . . insuperable degree of affection, which not even the deformity of person or mind, not even the wickedness, ingratitude, and rebellion of children, can totally suppress or extinguish (1765, p. 435).

Moreover, if the obligations are in fact burdensome, they also carry with them significant benefits. The parent receives love and respect from the child, and is provided with an opportunity to serve a mission which transcends the self, that of raising the child. In addition, parents are presented with a chance to validate, through their children, the value system that they brought to adulthood: "Each parent has a chance to promote a hard-won set of ethics and to test the utility of standards that took many years to create" (Kagan, 1977, p. 34).

From these obligations is derived the authority of parents to direct the upbringing and education of their children. This authority is by no means absolute; parents no longer have the power of life and death over their children as they once did in ancient Rome. Authority is granted to the parent only to enable him to perform more effectively his obligations to the child. If he has abused it, he can be stripped of this authority.

Blackstone describes the authority of the parent in the following manner:

He may lawfully correct his child, being under age, in a reasonable manner; for this is for the benefit of his education. The consent or concurrence of the parent to the marriage of his child under age, was also *directed* by our antient [*sic*] law to be obtained: but now it is absolutely *necessary;* for without it the contract is void. And this also is another means, which the law has put into the parent's hands, in order the better to discharge his duty; first, of protecting his children from the snares of artful and designing persons; and, next, of settling them properly in life, by preventing the ill consequences of too early and precipitate marriages. (1765, pp. 440–441, footnotes omitted).

The parent's authority generally extends until the child has reached the age of eighteen but may be withdrawn earlier in cases in which the parent has neglected or abused his office.

The child, correlatively, is obliged to obey parental orders. He must also avoid immoral and unwholesome companions, as well as conduct which is legally proscribed. Moreover, because the child is as a learner who must make appropriate investments in himself, he is expected to accept advice, attend school, and engage in other activities which would contribute to his preparation for a productive adult life.

These obligations, according to Blackstone, also arise out of a principle of natural law:

For to those, who gave us existence, we naturally owe subjection and obedience during our minority, and honour and reverence ever after; they, who protected the weakness of our infancy, are entitled to our protection in the infirmity of their age; they who by sustenance and education have enabled their offspring to prosper, ought in return to be supported by that offspring, in case they stand in need of assistance. Upon this principle proceed all the duties of children to their parents, which are enjoined by positive laws (1765, p. 441).

Although the state in most instances allows parents and children to carry out their obligations with minimal interference, it will step in if it deems such intervention necessary. This generally occurs in cases in which there has been a serious breach, abuse, or nonperformance of one's office. A child who is not willing to take advice or attend school, for example, may be taken to court on a charge of "incorrigibility" or "truancy". Similarly, the parent who abuses the power granted him or fails to meet the obligations of his office may be accused of abuse or neglect. The obligations outlined above, then, are enforceable and often serve as grounds for legal action against the parent or the child.

Toward A Substantive Conception of the Office of the Child

All of this may seem clear in a general sense, and is not likely to arouse much protest. Where society often divides is on the questions of how exactly children and parents are to discharge their obligations and what exactly we want children to learn.

On these points, the traditional authorities are likely to provide little guidance. Blackstone, for one, was writing at a time when childhood, as we know it, was relatively short, and when youths entered the labor market at a much earlier age than they do now. In America through much of the nineteenth century, it was not unusual to find youths beginning apprenticeships at the tender age of twelve in preparation for the occupation they had chosen. As apprentices, they normally lived with the master who taught them their trade, allowing them to be much more independent of their parents than are children today. This does not mean, of course, that children at that time were free to do as they pleased; most, in fact, were supervised quite closely by their masters. Yet, the early separation from the home meant that these children were less subject to the direct control of their parents than are youths today (Kelling, 1984; Skolnick, 1979).

Much has changed since that time. The growth of compulsory education and the passage of child-labor laws in the late nineteenth century removed youths from the labor market and extended the period of their economic dependence on parents. "[By] the early twentieth century, the notion that a child upon reaching puberty could assume a status independent of his parents had virtually disappeared. The state compelled the extension of childhood—enjoining longer supervision, more protracted education, and the postponed assumption of adult economic roles" (Marks, 1975, p. 88).

More recently, as a result of the challenge to authority and traditional beliefs in the 1960s, the rules defining good conduct have become more vague, and many forms of behavior which were once prohibited are now tolerated (e.g., abortion, premarital sex between consenting adults, and cohabitation by unmarried couples). Indeed, there is a sense that many of the rules that formerly guided our society have become nullities.

Paradoxically, as youths have grown more dependent upon their parents for material support, they have become more autonomous. This is in part because the supervision that parents provide in most cases does not match that of the masters of an earlier age. However, the current autonomy of youths is also attributable to direct grants of liberties in recognition of their increased competence, as well as new rights which allow them to do such things as purchase contraceptives[1] and procure abortions[2] without the prior consent of their parents.

Under such circumstances, any attempt on the part of the state to control the lives of adolescents is likely to be a costly and difficult endeavor. Yet there is no reason why this should lead us to abandon the task of formulating guidelines for developing principled and effective responses to the special needs of children and families. While there may be disagreement on the means to achieve this end, we still have a general idea of what children should become. Moreover, given that someday they will become adult citizens, with all of the rights and privileges thereof, the stakes are simply too high to give up in our efforts.

Getting back to basics. At the foundation of many of the obligations of parents and children is the desire that children grow to become responsible, resourceful citizens. This desire certainly underlies the parental obligation to educate the child, and on a more basic level, the requirement that the parent provide the necessary material support and shelter to enable his offspring to grow into adulthood. This desire is also clear in the duty of the child to go to school, accept advice, and engage in other activities which will contribute to his preparation for a productive adult life.

However, the child is by no means a passive actor in this movement towards responsible, resourceful adulthood; he does not simply sit there and absorb the teachings of his parents and instructors. He also has the obligation to test empirically the information that he receives and to learn through experience what it takes to function in the real world. The youth will, no doubt, make many mistakes in the course of his experimentation. Yet he will do so, it is hoped, under the supervision of his parents, who can correct him and see that he learns from his mistakes, as well as repair some of the damage that the youth may have caused.

The law to some degree encourages this experimentation. In recognition of the child's status as a learner, the state grants him some measure of autonomy so he may better carry out the obligations of his office. Yet realizing that the child may err during the course of his experimentation, the state also seeks to protect the child from the full consequences of his mistakes. The state does this by providing the child with a set of legal immunities which, among other things, enable him to set aside contracts made during the period of his minority, and provide for a mitigation of penalties for acts which, if committed by an adult, would otherwise draw a stiff fine or deprivation of liberty. The autonomy is necessary, because we value creativity, independence, and initiative—qualities which can hardly be developed in a rigidly controlled social environment. In addition, legal immunities are granted because we believe that a child should be able to test his limits without having to bear the full penalties for his mistakes.

This dual grant of autonomy and immunity gives a youth what amounts to a "learner's permit".[3] Yet because no learning process is complete until the youth has acquired some measure of responsibility, he should recognize that he is growing into a role in which he will no longer be able to make excuses. The law accomplishes this by gradually stripping the youth of excuses and increasing the penalties for mistakes as he gets older or begins to repeat his mistakes. This not only teaches the youth that he needs to select a course of action with the probable consequence of that action in mind, but also leads him to realize that he too is subject to some very basic rules, such as not to give offense.[4]

On the Nature of State Intervention

Complicating this picture of the office of the child, however, are the many rights that we have extended to children in recent years. According to Franklin Zimring,

> Before 1966, the United States Supreme Court had never decided a case that could properly be filed under the rubric of "juvenile rights"; in the last fifteen years, adolescence has been a major concern of the Court. The United States Reports are filled with cases adjudicating the rights of adolescents in matters as diverse as abortion, school suspension, involuntary civil commitment, corporal punishment, jury trials in juvenile court, and political demonstrations (1982, p. 14).

Analyses of this growth of rights now fill the pages of scholarly journals, law reviews, and legal treatises, with some advocating that we go much further, to articulate in effect a new Bill of Rights for children.[5]

Little is said in these analyses about redefining the obligations of children and parents, although this is precisely what the growth of children's rights has done. It has altered the basic configuration of obligations and obscured the continuity of those which have remained unchanged.

Because of these new rights, children no longer are required to obtain their parents' consent before purchasing contraceptive devices.[6] Nor do children have to seek their parents' advice before procuring an abortion.[7] Moreover, although schools may subject children to corporal punishment,[8] they are no longer permitted to discipline students for protesting their government's war policy[9] or challenging the schools' authority to dictate what students can wear to school and how long their hair can be.[10]

Unfortunately, many of these new rights have been granted without a clear jurisprudence of children and families, thereby contributing to our confusion over the continuity of obligations. While at least part of the impetus for granting new rights to children has stemmed from a desire to protect them from such dangers as child abuse and neglect (Rosenheim, 1973), one now finds in the children's rights movement at least two somewhat contradictory thrusts. The first attempts to obtain rights for children on the basis of their special needs, and the second seeks to extend adult rights to children on the basis of their greater competency (Houlgate, 1980; Skolnick, 1979; Zimring, 1979). Although the Supreme Court has decided several cases challenging state actions under the *parens patriae* doctrine, it has not yet formulated a coherent rationale for the decisions (Burt, 1976, 1983). Taken together, the new rights appear to be intended to protect parents and children against "undue" state intervention, and to curtail the state's ability to override parental interests in order to "protect" the child.[11] Yet they fail to give us a sense of what kinds of actions of the child we should seek to promote, and do not provide any real guidelines for determining what the state should do when in fact it does intervene.

If we grant that the state must occasionally step in to protect or correct the child, however, we must decide then what the state should do and what guidelines the state should use in balancing the three sets of interests at stake: (1) the child's interests in autonomy and freedom; (2) the right of the parent to control the child's upbringing; and (3) the state's interest in obtaining a well-informed electorate, insuring public health and tranquility, and sustaining a sense of civic virtue among its citizenry.

The traditional justification for state intervention, and the original legal basis for the juvenile court, was based on the state's conception of its role as *parens patriae*. A Latin phrase which literally means "parent of the country", *parens patriae* refers to the belief that the state as the ultimate authority has both the right and obligation to ensure the well-being and maintenance of citizens who, because of some impediment—be it age, infirmity, mental incapacity, or immaturity—demonstrate a need for supervision and protection. The concept, which is derived from English common law, was first explicitly applied in the United States in the 1839 case of *Ex parte Crouse*.[12]

Cases based on this doctrine had a significant impact on the power that parents could exercise over their children, because the *parens patriae* doctrine was seen as giving the state the power to overrule the parents' interests in order to promote the child's proper development. Hence, parents who had failed to support, educate, and maintain their children often found themselves subject to criminal penalties as well as to the termination of parental rights (or, to use our metaphor, impeachment from the office of the parent). Moreover, parents who had opposed medical treatment for their child often were ordered to provide such treatment even when their opposition was based on religious grounds (Bane, 1976).

In its intrusions into family life, the state purported to act in the "best interests of the child". It is not exactly clear what this phrase meant, but the "best interests" doctrine reportedly stimulated two major developments in law. First, children came to be perceived as autonomous individuals with interests distinct from, and independent of, those of their parents. Secondly, childen came to be seen as requiring counsel of their own when future custody was at stake. This latter development may be seen in the current practice of appointing guardians *ad litem* to represent children in abuse and neglect actions (Baskin 1974).

In recent years, however, the *parens patriae* concept and the "best interests" doctrine have come under growing criticism from judges and legal scholars. The *parens patriae* concept has been attacked as paternalistic and overreaching, the "best interests" doctrine as offering judges vast opportunities to interject their personal values into custody decisions. Courts increasingly have displayed a willingness to discard these concepts in favor of more substantive doctrines. As an important example, the landmark case of *In re Gault*[13] in 1967 weakened *parens patriae* in the delinquency area in favor of procedural due process guarantees for the child.[14]

In an effort to restrict discretionary state intervention, scholars and jurists have undertaken the formidable task of developing new judicial standards for juvenile cases. These standards are intended to provide greater limitations on state intervention into family life and define more clearly the relevant criteria to be used in balancing the interests of the parties in conflict.

Perhaps the most ambitious endeavor to date in this regard is the Juvenile Justice Standards Project of the Institute of Judicial Administration (IJA) and American Bar Association (ABA). Issued in twenty-three volumes, the IJA-ABA standards cover every stage of the juvenile justice decision-making process, from the youth's first contact with the system to parole. Among other things, the standards advocate determinate sentencing, with sanctions proportional to the seriousness of the offense committed and not merely the court's view of the juvenile's needs. The standards also would grant juveniles all of the procedural protections afforded adults and eliminate status offenses from the jurisdiction of the juvenile courts (Flicker, 1981).

The new standards will, no doubt, make clearer the acceptable grounds for state intervention into a youth's life, facilitating attempts to predict when such intervention will occur. The new standards also will promote more consistent decision-making by the courts in matters involving juvenile delinquency. Finally, the new standards will do much to clarify how the various interests at stake—those of the child, the parent, and the state—are to be balanced.

However, the public interest might be better served by an institution or set of institutions which did more than simply adjudicate delinquents. Moreover, society might derive greater benefit from an institution or set of institutions which did more than simply articulate rights.

In accordance with our views of the office of the child we might propose instead an institution which focused on the creation of opportunities for youths. Such an institution may take any one of a variety of forms, but would have as its guiding principle that of child advocacy—assisting youths in obtaining necessary resources and gaining access to desired programs. Robert Coates, Alden Miller, and Lloyd Ohlin, (1978, pp. 178–182) suggest that child advocates can work on at least three levels. They can first attempt to determine what kinds of problems a youth is experiencing and meet with parents, teachers, and school officials in an attempt to resolve these problems.

> Advocacy as envisioned here does not remove responsibility from the youth, but provides the youth with a support system that helps the youth learn to manage that responsibility more effectively. The staff person becomes a resource who [*sic*] the youth can call upon in any situation; the actual action taken by staff would be negotiated between the youth and the staff person and would ultimately be negotiated with other significant persons. [1978, p. 179]

Secondly, advocates might seek to secure for youths access to necessary resources in a given community, or if these resources are lacking, to take the steps required to develop them. Finally, advocates may push for general changes in public policies which would help all youths.

Of course, such an institution would require a more proactive approach to youths and their problems, as well as heavier investments in training staff members to deal with youths and their problems on an individual basis. This institution I propose, however, is not one which necessarily requires us to do anything completely new; it requires only that we do what we are already doing more effectively. Two pilot programs for juvenile offenders, for example, suggest that these child advocacy efforts may be usefully combined with the probation function.

The Volunteer Probation Counseling Program in Lincoln, Nebraska, takes high-risk misdemeanants (i.e., those likely to commit another serious offense) and provides them with intensive counseling for the course of a year. During the first two months in the program, the youth is required to meet with a probation officer and attend court-run classes. In the remaining months, the youth is placed under the supervision of a volunteer who is carefully selected by a psychologist familiar with the youth. During the ten-month period in which the volunteer is responsible for the youth, he provides the youth with additional counseling outside the court setting and attempts to resolve any difficulties the youth may have with members of the community. Many of these problems are education- and employment-related in nature, and volunteers have been successful in finding employment for their charges (Trojanowicz and Morash, 1983, pp. 205–206).

Project CREST (Clinical Regional Support Teams) in Gainesville, Florida, assigns youth offenders (in this case, repeat misdemeanants and felons) to volunteers and probation officers simultaneously. The volunteers—students in a counselor education program at the University of Florida—attempt to develop supportive relationships and resolve the youths' problems, while the probation officers set limits on the youths' behavior and monitor their compliance. An evaluation of Project CREST indicates that the youths participating in the program are less likely to repeat their crime than other youths not enrolled in the program (Trojanowicz and Morash, 1983, p. 206).

What is particularly striking about both of these programs is their extensive use of volunteers. This participation is valuable in at least two respects. First, it makes these programs less expensive to administer while at the same time providing youths with a level of supervision not found in most probation departments. Secondly, it involves the community, making citizens more aware of the juvenile justice system and of their responsibility to help it run efficiently.

In saying all of this, I do not wish to imply that the state should go out and immediately arrest all of those youths whom it believes would benefit from such programs. Nor do I suggest that procedural standards be relaxed in the juvenile courts in order to make it easier to convict youths and refer them to such programs. Youths who have committed offenses must continue to be adjudicated with all of the due process guarantees that the Constitution requires.

What these programs suggest, however, is that more can be done than simply incapacitating youths so they no longer pose a threat to the community. Moreover, this can be done in a way which involves the community and reminds citizens that they have an interest in creating opportunities which will enable the young offenders to develop into responsible and resourceful citizens.

Conclusion

The traditional juvenile court came into existence through a movement which was very much focused on saving children and promoting their development into responsible citizens. Through relaxed procedural standards and a therapeutic orientation, this new court attempted to create a compelling social environment for wayward youths and encourage their rehabilitation. We have since come to regard the procedural informality as leading to manifest injustice and the therapeutic claims of the court as being largely unfounded.

For all of its faults, however, the traditional juvenile court was able to capture the conception of the child that existed at the time of the court's inception (Kelling 1984, pp. 20–25). As I imply above, we have since come to view the office of the child in a somewhat different light, but we have yet to develop an institution that symbolizes the office of the child as it exists today.

This is part of the challenge—to construct an image of an institution or set of institutions which symbolizes what the office of the child means today. This institution must do more than simply adjudicate delinquents and articulate rights. Rather, it must serve as a visible reminder of that great responsibility and stake that all of us have: ensuring that youths at risk and youths posing risks are given those opportunities that will enable them to develop into responsible and resourceful citizens—citizens with whom all of us will live.

Endnotes

1. *Carey v. Population Services International,* 431 U.S. 678 (1977).
2. "Any independent interest the parent may have in the termination of the minor daughter's pregnancy is no more weighty than the right of privacy of the competent minor mature enough to have become pregnant." *Planned Parenthood of Central Missouri v. Danforth,* 428 U.S. 52, 75 (1976). See also *Bellotti v. Baird,* 443 U.S. 622 (1979).
3. I am indebted to Franklin Zimring (1982) for this term. For an excellent (and more complete) discussion of this concept, see his recent book, *The Changing Legal World of Adolescence* (New York: Free Press, 1982).
4. Before concluding this section, I must note that I am not proposing that the state inculcate a prepackaged set of moral values. This is not properly a matter for the state in the absence of moral consensus, and the task is best left to parents. This is consistent with society's belief that the family is the preferred unit for socializing youths, since the state would be less efficient and less benevolent at that task. It is also in line with our wish that value differences be recognized and not merely suppressed.
5. See, for example, Foster and Freed (1972).
6. *Carey v. Population Services International,* 431 U.S. 678 (1977).
7. *Bellotti v. Baird,* 443 U.S. 622 (1979); *Planned Parenthood of Central Missouri v. Danforth,* 428 U.S. 52 (1976).

8. *Ingraham v. Wright,* 430 U.S. 651 (1977).
9. *Tinker v. Des Moines Independent Community School District,* 393 U.S. 503 (1969).
10. *Hatter v. Los Angeles City High School District,* 452 F.2d 673 (9th Cir. 1971).
11. See, e.g., *Wisconsin v. Yoder,* 406 U.S. 205 (1972), in which the Supreme Court upheld the right of Amish parents to direct the religious upbringing of their children. In its opinion, the *Yoder* Court cited a previous decision in which the high court had granted parents the right to establish and send their children to parochial schools: "The child is not the mere creature of the State; those who nurture him and direct his destiny have the right, coupled with the high duty, to recognize and prepare him for additional obligations." *Pierce v. Society of Sisters,* 268 U.S. 510, 535 (1925).
12. "The basic right of a juvenile is not to liberty, but to custody." 4 Whart. 9, 11 (Pa. 1839).
13. 387 U.S. 1 (1967).
14. "The Latin phrase proved to be of great help to those who sought to rationalize the exclusion of juveniles from the constitutional scheme: but its meaning is murky and its historic credentials are of dubious relevance." *Gault,* 387 U.S. at 16.

References

Bane, M. J. (1976). *Here to stay: American families in the twentieth century.* New York: Basic Books.

Baskin, S. J. (1974). State intrusion into family affairs: Justifications and limitations. *Stanford Law Review 26,* 1383–1409.

Benditt, T. M. (1978). *Law as rule and principle: Problems of legal philosophy.* Stanford, CA: Stanford University Press.

Black's law dictionary. (5th ed.). St. Paul, MN: West Publishing Co.

Blackstone, W. (1765). *Commentaries on the laws of England. Book 1.* Oxford: Clarendon Press.

Burt, R. A. (1976). Developing constitutional rights of, in, and for children. In *Pursuing justice for the child* (pp. 225–245). Edited by M. K. Rosenheim. Chicago: University of Chicago Press.

Burt, R. A. (1983). The Burger Court and the family. In *The Burger Court: The counter-revolution that wasn't* (pp. 92–112). Edited by V. Blasi. New Haven: Yale University Press.

Coates, R. B., Miller, A. D., and Ohlin, L. E. (1978). *Diversity in a youth correctional system: Handling delinquents in Massachusetts.* Cambridge, MA: Ballinger Publishing Co.

Flicker, B. (1981). Prosecuting juveniles as adults: A symptom of a crisis in the juvenile courts. In *Major issues in juvenile justice information and training: Readings in public policy (pp. 351–377).* Edited by J. C. Hall, D. M. Hamparian, J. M. Pettibone, and J. L. White. Columbus, OH: Academy for Contemporary Problems.

Foster, H. H., Jr., and Freed, D. J. (1972). A Bill of Rights for children. *Family Law Quarterly 6,* 343–375.

Houlgate, L. D. (1980). *The child and the state: A normative theory of juvenile rights.* Baltimore, MD: Johns Hopkins University Press.

Kagan, J. (1977). The child in the family. *Daedalus 106,* 33–56.

Kelling, G. L. (1984, January). Social responses to children: The American experience. Paper prepared for Executive Session on the Juvenile Justice System, Harvard University.

Marks, F. R. (1975). Detours on the road to maturity: A view of the legal conception of growing up and letting go. *Law and Contemporary Problems 39,* 78–92.

Rawls, J. (1971). *A theory of justice.* Cambridge, MA: Harvard University Press.

Rosenheim, M. K. (1973). The child and the law. In *Review of child development research. Vol. III: Child development and social policy* (pp. 509–555). Edited by B. M. Caldwell and H. N. Ricciuti. Chicago: Unviersity of Chicago Press.

Schultz, J. L., and Cohen, F. (1976). Isolationism in juvenile court jurisprudence. In *Pursuing justice for the child,* (pp. 20–42). Edited by M. K. Rosenheim. Chicago: University of Chicago Press.

Skolnick, A. (1979). Children's rights, children's development. In *The future of childhood and juvenile justice* (pp. 138–174). Edited by L. T. Empey. Charlottesville: University Press of Virginia.

Trojanowicz, R. C., and Morash, M. (1983). *Juvenile delinquency: Concepts and control.* (3rd ed.). Englewood Cliffs, NJ: Prentice-Hall, Inc.

Zimring, F. E. (1979). Privilege, maturity, and responsibility: Notes on the evolving jurisprudence of adolescence. In *The future of childhood and juvenile justice* (pp. 312–335). Edited by L. T. Empey. Charlottesville: University Press of Virginia.

Zimring, F. E. (1982). *The changing legal world of adolescence.* New York: Free Press.

4
Juvenile Court Jurisdiction: Intervention and Intrusion

CATHERINE M. RYAN

The juvenile justice system is a group of interdependent social and legal organizations which operate to offer services and to exercise control over particular proscribed conduct of parents toward their children and of children toward themselves or others.

Society has established juvenile justice systems throughout the United States for several reasons. One, society recognizes specific rights, (i.e., the legal capacity to act or to demand action or forebearance on the part of another person). The senior citizen who goes to the grocery store has a right to this walk without being knocked down and robbed by anyone, including a 14-year-old. The nine-year-old child has a right to an education and not be kept home from school every day by parents who want a babysitter.

Two, society defines express duties, (i.e., the legal obligation to act or to refrain from acting in a certain manner). The twelve-year-old does not have the right to set fire to the school even after receiving a poor report card. The parent has a duty to provide adequate food for the infant.

Three, society discerns that youth have unique needs and disabilities as well as a special value in the society. Young children in particular cannot protect themselves from uncaring or dangerous adults, even if those adults are their parents. Immature youth may rush into harmful acts without an appreciation of the risk to themselves or others. Daring adolescents acting with peers may attempt illegal activities which they would avoid when alone. The juvenile justice system responds to these problems with restraint on some occasions and with firmness at other times.

Established in an era of optimism in the nineteenth century, the juvenile justice system has endured no end of criticism in the last two decades. Whether it be the United States Supreme Court (in *In re Gault*), a Presidential Commission (cited in *In re Gault*), or writers such as Anthony Platt (*The Child Savers*), critics have argued that the system has failed. Whereas in the early twentieth century the juvenile justice system appeared to be a welcome diversion of children from the criminal justice system, the 1970s witnessed the diverting of juveniles from the one-time diversion but now established juvenile justice system. Intervention and intrusion by juvenile justice professionals became suspect.

This paper will use the terms intrusion and intervention interchangeably and without distinction. More importantly, the terms have neither positive nor negative connotations and merely convey the concept of the involvement of outside persons or organizations in the decision-making of a biological family.

Jurisdiction: Areas of Intervention

Each society defines for itself the areas of behavior in which it will intervene. Society puts its members on notice about these areas in statements called laws. The laws do not serve as a code of preferred behavior, but rather describe the minimum level of behavior which that society will tolerate. Murder provides one example of behavior society will not accept. Although the law cannot require that one neighbor like another, no person may kill another.

Society holds juveniles to these laws, even though it provides a different channel of intervention for failures. A minor may not commit crimes which adults may not commit. Society has determined it must protect the rights of victims of crime, no matter who is the perpetrator.

Society places specific legal obligations upon parents toward their children, even though other adults do not have these obligations to the children. Parents must provide food, shelter, clothing, and education for their minor children. The juvenile justice system does not intrude in how parents choose to raise their children, so long as they do not fall below this minimum standard.

The controversy of the current decade is whether society should intervene when juveniles choose proscribed activities which are not a crime for adults and seemingly cause no harm to anyone except (perhaps, not even) themselves. Does society or the parents have the right to keep juveniles at home, rather than allow them to run away from home, and under the parents' control? Do juveniles have a right to make the choice not to live at home and to go elsewhere without parental consent? Does society or the parents have an obligation to save minors from harm that may come to them from the street or from lack of education? Do juveniles have a right to make these choices unless some measurable harm occurs from the street or from truancy and the like? Do youths have an obligation to live the lifestyles their parents have chosen for them? Do they have an obligation to prepare themselves to succeed in the job market?

Diversion and Court: Levels of Intrusion

Even when behavior clearly calls for intervention, members of society may choose different levels of intrusion.

In the Family

A ten-year-old breaks a window; the parent scolds the child and then repairs the window. A parent fails to supervise toddlers, and the omniscient grandparent demands better child care from the parent. A thirteen-year-old runs away from home after an argument, then returns two hours later. The persons involved make demands upon each other and reach some accommodation. There is no state intrusion or formal hearing process.

In the Neighborhood

An eleven-year-old puts graffiti on a neighbor's garage. The neighbor catches the young culprit and either administers her own justice, or complains to the juvenile's parents who handle the problem. Or in another situation, a parent in a fit of anger strikes his six-year-old in the head in front of a family friend. The friend talks to the parent about better ways to discipline a young child. There is still no state intervention and no formal process. Perhaps more importantly, there is no expectation that this level of interference with another person necessitates formal procedures or state action.

Early State Intervention

The process of intervention may become more defined when there is state action, yet still remains an informal process. A youth officer may interview a fourteen-year-old accused of stealing a bicycle and decide that a community adjustment adequately deals with the problem. Here the state has intruded in the person of the youth officer who then exercises discretion regarding the use of the power of the state. The youth officer sets conditions for a diversion from court in return for which the officer foregoes the enforcement powers she would attain through the court process. There is no formal process or due process procedures, and the parents and child voluntarily cooperate with the police officer's demands.

Similarly, a protective services social worker may investigate a child abuse report and determine that the parents have disciplined their four-year-old far too harshly for not knowing arithmetic. If the parents seem to care for their child but lack insight into their child's developmental level, the social worker may decide that parent training classes will address the problem without the need for involvement of the court. Here again, the state has intervened, in the form of the investigating social worker. The protective services worker makes demands upon the parents, without formal procedures or due process, in return for which the social worker restricts the level of state intrusion to a low level.

In the Court System

The level of intervention by the state increases in situations in which such voluntary cooperation with the requests/demands of the state is not present. The parties move to a more formal process, a court process that is fact-finding, limit-setting, and enforcing. This legal process is the system best equipped to adjudicate when there is not agreement as to the nature of the conduct which necessitated intervention, and is the best equipped to arbitrate when there is not agreement as to the type of intervention needed in response to the harmful conduct. Once it makes these determinations, the court system is also the system best equipped to coerce the behavior it has ordered.

Consider a fifteen-year-old charged with stabbing another youth. The charged juvenile may argue self-defense, while the victim may argue that the attack was unprovoked. If this was an assault or battery upon the victim, society must protect the victim's right to be secure from such attacks and must enforce the duty of the attacker to forego such assaults. If self-defense, society must protect the accused's right to be secure from false charges and unfair punishments and to enforce the duty of the accuser to refrain from false accusations. In either case, society must perform this task in a manner that prevents further violence and harm. The court provides a forum, utilizing a formal process with clearly defined rules, to accomplish these responsibilities.

Similarly, picture the parent who brings an infant with a fractured skull to the hospital. If, as the parents claim, the injury was from an unavoidable accident, society should not interfere in the family unit. If the fracture resulted from an intentional injury, society needs to take action to prevent further harm to the infant. Once again, society has an interest in determining these facts in a process that is trustworthy and nonviolent. The court system provides the formal process to address this situation with authority and restraint.

Problems of Intervention: Layering

Diversion from the formal or most intrusive process, although intended to meet family problems at the least intrusive level, may create other tensions. Although professionals within the juvenile justice system may see the movement from informal to formal intervention as a logical progression, the victim of a first burglary may see diversion of the juvenile offender from court as doing nothing. The juvenile offender who is sent to an athletic program after a first car theft, and to a counselling program after a second car theft, may fail to recognize any escalation of response to the repeated offenses. There is the danger that the minor feels he is getting away with the delinquent behavior. Drug-abusing parents may not perceive any difference between the authority of the private agency social worker who first told them not to leave their infant home alone, and that of the protective services worker who warned them again after the third report of abandonment. Even if each neglect incident brings the parents closer to court, the movement from one social worker to another may well appear to be arbitrary and fragmented to the parents.

Consequently, although the development of additional alternatives may seem progressive, the indiscriminate use of these interventions with the juveniles and their families may result in a lack of continuity and in an unevenness of response by the juvenile justice system. When this occurs, neither parents, nor youth, nor the community take the juvenile justice system seriously.

Moreover, this layering may aggravate the already serious problem of the remoteness of the courts from the time and place of the events to be judged. By the time the family reaches the court's attention, the police and the social workers may have exhausted their services and will probably have exhausted their patience. Yet, the court is just beginning to work with the family and is likely to want to use its various alternative dispositions which are often similar or identical to the diversion alternatives already exhausted.

Problems of Intervention: Information

No decision can be better than the information on which it is based. In many systems, particularly those with high volume, the ability to acquire data is limited, and what data does exist is controlled by certain agencies.

Knowledge is power, or rather, lack of it is lack of power, because members of the juvenile justice system cannot even make a choice about intervention if they are *unaware* there is a problem. If the neighbor fails to report the delinquent act, no youth officer will confront the juvenile offender, much less make a decision about adjustments. If the grandparent fails to report the abuse, no social worker will investigate the living conditions of the child, much less make a decision about risk to the child.

Knowledge is power because professionals will make decisions based on the information *they do have*. The youth officer may provide a community adjustment for the youth caught shoplifting because the officer has not seen him in trouble previously. A different outcome would ensue if the youth officer knew this juvenile has been arrested for shoplifting twelve times in a neighboring town.

The social worker who is not worried by an "accidental" black eye on a one-year-old infant would be more concerned about it if he or she knew the parent had lost custody of another child for abuse in a different state.

A decision-maker may also lack information which mitigates the offense. The youth officer and prosecutor may make different choices if they find out that the juvenile killed a parent in response to the adult's frequent beatings. The social worker and prosecutor may not choose court action if they learn that the parents who stopped sending their child to school did so because of frequent attacks upon the child on the way to school. While problems exist, knowledge of the context of facts in which the conduct occurred affects the response of the juvenile justice system. Therefore, the decision to intervene depends upon the gathering of accurate and adequate information.

Problems of Intervention: Due Process Procedures

The authority to intrude in a family's life is awesome, and the juvenile justice system exercises this authority on behalf of the society only when it seems necessary to protect certain rights and enforce specific duties. Because juvenile justice professionals who make these judgments are human persons with human biases and frailties, they are held to particular requirements of due process even as they seek to do good. As the intrusion and coercion heightens, the process of fault-finding and the determination of dispositions becomes more formal, and due process protections become more essential. Due process is meant to protect against unjust actions, however well-intentioned.

Although the purpose of due process is to protect individuals and families, the procedures used to accomplish it may be painful. One instance arises in the court's attempt to serve notice to a child and both parents for any court proceeding. This may prove painful to a mother and child who endure probing as to the absent father's whereabouts so that the court can attempt to include him in the life of the family he has rejected.

A second instance occurs in the tension between legal procedures and conventional understandings of truth. The juvenile who is told to value honesty learns it is part of the due process game to deny charges of an offense he knows he committed. This youth often does not understand the lawyer's justification that it is not a lie but rather an adult way to make the state prove its case.

Three, the minor offender who should receive a court disposition proportionate to the offense, record, and situation discovers plea bargaining. At times, the outcome of the court case may have less to do with what is appropriate to this youth and more to do with what the market can bear (i.e. whether time allows for trials, whether the witness appears in court).

Four, studies of child development demonstrate that children have a different sense of time than adults. As a result, young persons need an immediate response to their behavior in order to learn that parents or society approve or disapprove of it. Yet, in the need to meet due process protections of notice to parties, discovery of evidence, and pre-trial motions, the juvenile justice system often extends these procedural steps over time, and the court response (disposition), when it takes place, is remote in time from the precipitating conduct.

Thus, due process in practice may become involved in protecting the juvenile justice system as much as in protecting the rights of individuals. Further, it may thwart the ultimate goals of the system, especially if not tempered by awareness of situations like the ones above.

Intervention with Status Offenders

In centuries past, the question of state intervention in families was not an issue. If a young person committed what was an unlawful act for an adult, the king/state/government punished the youth as it would an adult. Beyond this, the law/society endowed the father of the family with a *patria potestus*. The father could kill his children or sell them into slavery. His power was another form of his property rights, since his children were his property.

Eventually, English society developed a belief that the king should protect those who had no other protection, including children. Early English law reveals that this concept usually worked to the benefit of property-owning children when adults tried to cheat them. The United States embraced the general principle of the state as the child's protector when it adopted English law. This concept provides a basis for juvenile court jurisdiction over children who are believed to need protection.

Substantial agreement exists as to what constitutes child abuse and neglect and, consequently, what constitutes juvenile court jurisdiction in this area. Furthermore, it is possible to agree on the elements of delinquency which constitute juvenile court jurisdiction because society generally agrees as to what constitutes a crime.

It is the issue of status offenses which leads to extensive debate, not so much because definition is difficult as because philosophies of the state's protective role differ. Status offenses refer to conduct which is not a crime if committed by an adult yet which is proscribed for minors. The common examples are running away from home, being truant, and being incorrigible or beyond the parents' control. Until a relatively recent period, juvenile codes viewed this behavior as delinquent and treated it as such. Over the last several decades the codes have clarified this behavior as distinct from delinquency and from child neglect. Due process reforms in juvenile justice systems have been extended to status offenses, so that the degree of state intervention brings a parallel formality of procedure with due process protection.

This development has sharpened the issue in the controversy regarding status offenders: Should society proscribe behavior of youth which is not unlawful for adults? The question is not blurred by ambiguities in jurisdictional definitions, nor by deficiencies in due process. The answer depends upon whether society sees status offenders as a vulnerable population to whom it owes protection, and whether society believes it should assume a protective stance toward these youth even it the young persons do not want this protection.

Proponents of intervention on behalf of status offenders note that society often treats youth differently than adults in delinquency situations. Juveniles commit all manner of delinquent acts which would be crimes if committed by adults. Yet, the juvenile justice system, on behalf of society, gives many children a pass and refrains from any court action–unlike the response to adult crime. A significant proportion of juveniles involved in delinquency are processed through community adjustments and diversion programs rather than court action.

This same philosophy can justify treating youth differently when it results in legislation that makes certain conduct unlawful for them but not unlawful for adults. The society has not yet given up on the juvenile who stops attending school and, in a protective role, the society insists on this education which it knows the youth will need in order to attain a job and to function within the society. The society sees a responsibility to save minors who are on the run from the dangers of street crime, from deprivation that can result from having no funds, and from the physical and emotional damage of being involved in prostitution and other forms of child exploitation.

This philosophy is premised on the belief that minors do not yet have the maturity to make life decisions by themselves. Juveniles are not miniature adults who have only physical growth ahead, but rather are developing persons whose psychological and emotional, as well as physical, growth can be damaged and destroyed. Society, exercising its duty to protect the vulnerable, distinguishes the street smarts of some minors from the maturity youths need to develop in order to become adults. The juvenile's ability to avoid muggings and to survive on the street, while impressive, is not equivalent to the adult's maturity to make decisions about family, career, and life goals.

Opponents of intrusion in the lifestyle of status offenders argue that society has no protective role that permits it to *anticipate harm* to the status offender. This philosophy partially rests on the experience that some primary institutions—families and schools among them—have not benefitted some juveniles and may have even harmed them. Consequently, this philosophy places the burden of decision on the youth to decide whether the institution offers anything of value. Beyond this, opponents of intervention point out that some youth survive well on their own without their biological families and achieve a place in the job market without educational diplomas and degrees.

A difficulty in these conflicting positions arises from the potential time lag between the youth's behavior (running away, truancy, and the like) and the outcome. Although some of the results of child exploitation may become visible fairly quickly, the impact of the lack of a diploma or degree on the youth's ability to earn a living may not become evident for years.

Proponents of intervention would have society act immediately in anticipation of harm and in hope of prevention. Opponents of intervention would encourage restraint until there is evidence of harm. Clearly, the philosophies differ when there is no immediate evidence of harm.

Intrusion because of anticipated harm is consistent with the juvenile justice system as it has traditionally operated and does operate today. Society recognizes certain needs of children and thereby defines omission of their care as neglect. For example, it is not necessary to prove harm to the minor in order to show that a parent is neglectful for failure to have the child attend school. Society assumes this is harmful and so holds a parent responsible for denying education to the child.

Should society not be protective if it is the minor rather than the parent who fails to meet its demand for education? If society's responsibility is premised on *who* makes the decision, that is whether it is the parent or the child who is the actor, then society is not protecting the child in terms of his or her needs (in this example, education) but rather is protecting *who* makes the decision. The outcome then is that parents must provide education or other needs, but minors can refuse it. In contrast, if society has a duty to protect the child in terms of need for certain care, then the law must arrange for the provision of that care regardless of who the responsible person is.

Moreover, intrusion to protect persons from themselves is consistent with the justice system as it has and continues to operate toward adults. Society finds drug abuse harmful and prohibits the use of particular drugs by adults. In the mental health field, the law provides for intervention to protect adults from their own harmful conduct.

Therefore, the juvenile justice system fulfills a long-standing duty when it acts to protect juveniles from their own potentially harmful behavior. The challenge is to articulate the risk of harm to the juvenile, to determine whether there are less intrusive ways to protect this juvenile, and to measure the effects of intervention against the effects of non-intervention.

Conclusion

Each society defines for itself the areas of behavior in which it will intervene. In the juvenile justice system, society intervenes with the otherwise autonomous family in order to offer services and exercise control concerning youths who are abused, neglected, delinquent, or status offenders.

In deciding whether to intervene and when to intervene, society measures the problems created by intrusion against the effects of non-intervention. Yet, the ultimate evidence of whether intervention is successful may not be available until later in the child's life, after the determination about intrusion is inalterably made. Consequently, society may rely on measures of anticipated harm as well as actual harm to decide upon intervention.

Section II
Socializing Children: Abstract Conceptions of the Task

5
The Development of Responsibility: Implications for Juvenile Justice

RICHARD BARNUM

The result of successful socialization is the development of responsibility. Responsibility is a complex virtue with multiple aspects which develop in different ways. Professionals in juvenile justice activities, concerned with promoting successful socialization of children, need to understand the development of responsibility. They need to appreciate how various juvenile justice activities can affect it, and be able to develop programs which will help to foster it.

This chapter will explore the development of the different aspects of responsibility in childhood and adolescence, and will look at what happens when this development fails. It will address specifically the roles of punishment and treatment as responses to different failures of responsibility. Based on an understanding of the development of responsibility, it will explore the justification for a separate system of justice for juveniles, and will suggest proper ways for the special capacities of that system to be used.

Responsibility

Responsibility is a virtue made up of three aspects representing three different types of learning (Levinger, 1971). The first is related to a capacity to take responsibility for one's own actions. The second relates to a state of competence: being responsible enough to take care of something or get something done. The third refers to a state of investment in others: feeling and taking responsibility for the concerns and needs of other people. Each of these aspects represents different personal qualities, and each develops in response to different processes. Their development differs in the ages at which the developments take place, and in the relative importance to them of intrinsic and environmental factors.

Guilt

The first aspect is a capacity for *guilt,* and has two parts. When we say we want someone to take responsibility for his actions, we are asking two things. First, we want him to acknowledge that he has in fact done something and not to deny it or to blame someone else. Second, if what he has done is wrong, we want him to know that it is wrong, and to feel badly about it. The two parts of guilt are a *cognitive* part (admitting guilt) and an *emotional* part (feeling guilty).

The cognitive aspect of guilt develops most basically as a function of ordinary cognitive development, and is present in neuropsychiatrically normal children by age two or three. By this age children routinely have gained enough control and sense of their own bodies and of the environment to be able to recognize and even predict the relationship between what they do and what happens next (Piaget, 1954). A one-year-old child might drop and break a glass as an experiment, as part of learning what happens when he opens his hand from around the glass. A normal three-year-old doing the same thing would be understood to do it on purpose, because he has sufficient control and understanding to know what will happen when he opens his hand.

The emotional aspect of guilt—feeling guilty—does not develop as a result of the same sort of intrinsic cognitive development. Instead, it develops in response to socializing input from the environment, primarily in the form of punishment. Ideally, when a child is punished for doing wrong, he experiences some kind of pain which he then associates with the wrongdoing. After enough experiences of such punishment, he begins to experience the same pain even if he is not exposed to actual external punishment. Ultimately he anticipates the pain even before doing wrong. Then even without his being aware of it, the anticipated pain prevents him from doing wrong. A child who has experienced enough of the right kind of punishment for misdeeds, so that he is thus prevented by his own emotions from doing wrong, is said to possess *internalized,* or effective *inhibitory,* guilt. This development usually takes place by five to seven years of age.

The achievement of effective inhibitory guilt depends on exposure to the right amount of punishment. Too little punishment does not generate enough anxiety to be effective in inhibiting behavior. Too much punishment may cause a child to be too generally inhibited or angry. A child with too little guilt may suffer from getting into various kinds of trouble, while one with too much guilt may suffer from lost opportunities because of a lack of spontaneity or capacity for initiative or exploration. Because the emotional aspect of guilt develops primarily in reaction to socialization experience, there is much greater variability among individuals in this aspect than there is in the cognitive aspect.

There are some conditions of impaired socialization in which the cognitive development necessary to admitting guilt is present, but emotional features interfere. An offender may have such difficulty with the emotional aspects of feeling guilty that he may deny, forget, or blame others for his wrongdoing. In such conditions (including abnormal personality development and dissociative states), the requisite development for being responsible for one's own actions is present, but the impact of abnormal socialization works against the taking of responsibility in the emotional area.

Reliability

The second aspect of responsibility is being responsible enough to take care of things in an adequate way, or being *reliable*. This feature rests in large part on a person's competence, on what he is in fact able to do.

Intelligence is a major factor in many kinds of competence. There are wide individual differences in intelligence, affected by both intrinsic and environmental factors. Even at the same levels of intelligence (as measured by formal testing) there are major differences among individuals in areas of specific competencies. Some of these differences seem to stem from variations in intrinsic neuropsychological development, while others are the result of differences in education, experience, and practice. Different children, even of the same intrinsic abilities, are exposed to vastly different kinds of opportunities for learning, both formal and informal. One may become expert in mathematics, another in hunting and gathering, and a third in begging and stealing on the street. Even within similar cultures and classes, families differ widely in the amount of responsibility they give to children. Some children are asked to do a lot and may develop significant competencies as a result. Others are more protected and may be less competent in the same areas at the same age.

Since an individual's general competence develops in response to a complex variety of factors, both intrinsic and environmental, there is wide variation among individuals in this aspect of responsibility. However, as a general rule, age is considered an important indicator of this aspect of responsibility, as it is a convenient (though rough) marker for an individual's level of experience and maturity. The development of this aspect of responsibility continues throughout childhood and adolescence; young children are considered generally less responsible in this regard than adolescents, and adolescents less so than adults.

Caring

The third aspect of responsibility is what we mean when we speak of feeling and taking responsibility for others. It reflects a state of *caring,* an interest in the feelings and needs of others. It rests on the emotional capacity for empathy, or the ability to put oneself in another's place.

Of the three aspects of responsibility, caring is the one whose development is probably the least dependent on intrinsic cognitive processes, and the most dependent on the socializing emotional input from the environment. The socializing input in question here is not a specific one like punishment with the emotional aspect of guilt. Instead, it is the general emotional quality and tone of the child's important intimate relationships. If these relationships are warm, attentive, understanding, and caring, then the child will take those qualities into himself and become a person who is warm, attentive, understanding, and caring to others. If primary socializing relationships are cool and distant, the child's own emotional orientation will be distant and uninterested in others' needs. If a child's predominant emotional experience with others is of being treated harshly or abusively, then he will become a person who tends to feel angry and aggressive towards others in turn.

Since this aspect of responsibility depends more on experience and less on intrinsic development, it varies widely among individuals. Most importantly, its variation depends much more on socialization than it does on age. An eight-year-old who has been well loved and cared for will have more of this kind of responsibility than will a twenty-five-year-old who has been treated with nothing but anger and abuse.

Failures in Responsibility

The development of responsibility can fail in various ways. Failures of responsibility can lead to problems which come to the attention of the juvenile justice system. Understanding these failures can help determine the appropriate responses to those problems

In adolescence, the development of responsibility can fail in either of two ways. Adolescence is a period of life when some failures of responsibility are common because of the nature of adolescent development. Failures confined to adolescence are referred to as *simple,* because they result from a specific developmental stress and tend to be limited in duration. Failures that begin earlier in life are referred to as *compound,* because they tend to be exacerbated by the stresses of adolescence but outlive those stresses in more durable and malignant ways.

Simple Failures

Adolescence is a time of emotional separation between the child and family, and for the establishment by the child of a new capacity for individual autonomy (Blos, 1962; Erikson, 1950). This process can threaten each of the aspects of responsibility, at least in the short term.

The capacity for guilt can be undermined by the attenuation of emotional and physical involvement between parent and child which supports this capacity in childhood. As separation develops, the immediacy of physical surveillance of the child and emotional responsiveness to the child by the parents diminish. These changes leave the child to rely more completely on his own internalized guilt to inhibit bad behavior, and there is usually a period of adjustment before internal processes are completely equal to the task. Failure of responsibility in this situation affects the emotional aspects of guilt, but not the actual capacity to be responsible for one's actions.

Actual competence in a variety of areas tends to increase in adolescence with age. However, as the child feels an increasing drive to experiment and to manage more aspects of his own affairs, he may take on responsibility for more than he has yet developed the capacity to handle. This sort of experimenting, testing, and developing one's capacity for autonomy is a normal part of adolescence. It ultimately leads to an increase in responsibility in this sense, but usually only after some attempts to handle difficult problems without help have failed.

Finally, as part of the separation process, adolescents turn their emotional investment away from their parents and prepare to invest more in peers and in finding their own place in society. During this adjustment there tends to be an interim period of increased emotional involvement in the self. As adolescents tend to be more self-involved, they may tend to be less attuned to the states and needs of others. The caring aspect of responsibility is temporarily weakened until the adolescent finds out how and for whom he will want to care as an autonomous individual.

Compound Failures

The development of responsibility can be impaired by many problems occurring in early childhood. Basic cognitive deficiencies may interfere with developing competence or even with the capacity to understand the effects of one's actions (Wilson and Herrnstein, 1985, ch. 6). Hyperactivity and other emotional or behavioral disorders may interfere with a child's capacity to respond to normal punishment with the development of effective guilt (Patterson, 1982). They may also impair a child's capacity to respond to benign emotional caretaking and to learn from it to care for others. Even for an intrinsically normal child, poor parental practices can adversely affect responsibility (Wilson and Herrnstein, 1985, ch. 8). Punishment which is overly harsh, lax, or inconsistent can impair normal guilt. Lack of exposure to or support for appropriate educational experiences can interfere with developing competence. Neglectful or abusive practices may harm a child's ability to care about others.

When such general developmental failures have been present in early childhood, the problems caused by the developmental tasks of adolescence are compounded. Though the simple failures of responsibility in adolescence tend to be outgrown as the adolescent becomes comfortable with his adult autonomy, it is much harder to outgrow these problems when there is not a firm foundation of character development from earlier childhood on which further growth can rest.

Most of the problems presented to the juvenile justice system are antisocial offenses of various degrees committed by adolescents suffering from some failure of responsibility. The vast majority of these adolescents are experiencing simple, developmentally specific failures which lead to one or a few brushes with the law as part of normal adolescence. When the developmental tasks of adolescence have been firmly mastered, these youths tend not to continue in patterns of serious anti-social behavior.

A small proportion of adolescents have had significant problems with the development of responsibility from early childhood. Compounding these earlier failures with the stresses of adolescence tends to result in these adolescents committing larger numbers of more serious offenses (Farrington, 1986). Furthermore, the likelihood of becoming a serious criminal in adulthood is much higher for adolescents with compound failures of responsibility than it is for those with simple failures.

Jurisdiction

From this simple characterization of responsibility, what can be learned about the reasons for a system of justice for children and adolescents that is separate from that for adults?

There are three good reasons for a separate justice system for children and adolescents. They rest on an understanding of the nature of failures of responsibility in adolescence.

The first reason is that for most adolescent offenders their offenses do not have the same meaning that similar offenses committed by adults would have. They are results of simple failures of responsibility. They are likely to be isolated events, out of the ordinary, and not predictive of a long pattern of anti-social behavior. They are not likely to require the same intensity of public response that the same offenses committed by adults would. Therefore it would be impractical at least (and arguably unfair) to bring the same system of justice to bear on their offenses as for offenses by adults.

The second reason applies to the smaller portion of adolescent offenders who show compound failures of responsibility. For this group neither of the above justifications for a separate system of justice apply. In many ways they have more in common with adult criminals than with most delinquents, especially in terms of poor socialization experience and inadequate guilt and caring. What distinguishes them from serious adult criminals is only their age. In some cases this may be a distinction without much significance, but in many cases the very youth (and resultant plasticity) of the serious juvenile offender may offer more hope for a rehabilitative approach than one might have in dealing with adults. This second reason for a separate justice system for juveniles rests on the belief that even offenders with serious long-standing problems can be aided in significant ways if help is provided early enough. One goal of a separate juvenile justice system is to be able to provide that help.

The third reason to have a distinct justice system for juveniles relates to the second aspect of responsibility. Because of their youth, juveniles' competence to care for themselves and to make decisions about important matters cannot be assumed to be adequate to the degree that it may be for adults. Families may be reliable protectors and advocates for their child, but they may not be—especially when there is doubt about their capacity for and commitment to furthering their child's well-being. When the family is inadequate to provide for the child's needs, there is a need for some intervention on the child's behalf by an agency of the state which is both expert regarding children and their needs, and also has the legal structure to respect and protect the rights of both children and families.

From this perspective the juvenile court plays the role of society's agent in determining to what extent a child may be lacking in responsible caretaking and supervision, to what extent he may himself be adequately responsible to take up the slack, what degree of risk may be involved, and who else in the community may be able to take on responsibility for the child. It is important to recognize that with regard to this area of responsibility, the issue is not an offense having been committed but rather the existence of a state of unprotected incompetence representing potential risk. State involvement is aimed at protecting and fostering the child's development, and is required whether or not the child has committed an offense himself.

It is important to point out that one reason which is sometimes offered for a separate juvenile justice system is not a good one. This is that children and adolescents, by virtue of their age or lack of maturity, are not as responsible for their acts as are adults (Weissman, 1983). This reasoning suggests that normal children and adolescents are similar to adults with severe mental illness or mental retardation (referred to as "mental disease or defect" in discussions of criminal responsibility). In this view the process of normal child development does not enable children to appreciate what they are doing or what effect it will have. However, we have seen that normal intrinsic cognitive development is sufficient for this capacity to be present by age two or three. It is a mistake to justify a separate legal approach for all children and adolescents on the basis of a developmental difference which applies only to very young or very disturbed children.

The relevant intrinsic developmental differences which do distinguish children and adolescents from adults are only two: the presence of simple developmentally specific failures of responsibility in adolescence, and the generally reduced competence and reliability of adolescents and children. Other failures of responsibility seen in children and adolescents—longstanding deficits in the emotional capacity for guilt and in caring for others—are not developmentally normal in children. They are abnormal in children just as they are in adults. In both cases they result from impaired socializing input rather than from intrinsic developmental differences between adults and children.

Responses

Given the appropriateness of a separate system of justice for juveniles, what should it do? The major task of the juvenile justice system is to respond to the offenses of juveniles. There are a variety of potential goals for this response, ranging from retributive to rehabilitative. *Punishment* and *treatment* are two alternative types of responses available to the system, which may be applied in pursuing one or more of these goals. Many serious arguments have been waged regarding the relative merits of these goals, and of these two specific responses to juvenile offenses. In these arguments punishment tends to be seen as an appropriate response to retributive goals, and treatment as fitting rehabilitative goals. It is useful to have a clear understanding of what each of these responses is, what their similarities and differences are, and how they interact with the development of the different aspects of responsibility. With such an understanding we will be able to see that when used properly, punishment and treatment both support the development of responsibility, and do not in fact represent conflicting goals at all.

Punishment

Punishment is the application of some pain or loss to a wrongdoer by someone in a position of authority. It is used in a very wide variety of contexts with various degrees of fairness and expertise. Its purposes may vary with its context. Among its common respected purposes are to educate a wrongdoer about what is wrong and right, to focus his attention on his responsibility for having done wrong, to underscore lessons previously taught, and to deter him from doing wrong again (Wilson and Herrnstein, 1985, ch. 19).

Its most widely accepted use is by parents of young children as part of instilling discipline (along with other means such as teaching rules and providing rewards for doing well). It is fairly clear that in this context properly applied punishment is not only a benign influence, but an essential experience for the development of appropriate guilt and inhibition of misbehavior (Hirschi, 1983; Patterson, 1982).

It is less clear what the effects of punishment might be in the juvenile justice system. At worst, it would likely be applied slowly and clumsily to older individuals in non-intimate contexts by authorities whose legitimacy was denied by those punished. Under such circumstances it is doubtful that punishment would accomplish much in the way of instilling new internalized guilt. However, if applied fairly, it would still inform the offender of the wrongfulness of his action and underscore his responsibility for it.

Treatment

Treatment is the provision of some service to remedy a disorder. It is provided to someone suffering from manifestations of the disorder by someone skilled in the application of the treatment as a result of the sufferer seeking help. In general, treatments may take many forms, including surgery, medicines, and various psychosocial interventions such as counselling or intensive residential rehabilitation. Among factors affecting their usefulness are the severity of the disorder, the power of the treatment, the accuracy of the diagnosis and specific treatment prescription, the skill of the treater, and the capacity of the sufferer to take part in the treatment process.

There are many conditions affecting children and families involved in the juvenile justice system for which various treaments might be useful (Barnum, 1986; Lewis, 1981; Lewis and Balla, 1976). They range from fairly specific treatments and disorders (such as taking anticonvulsant medicines to control seizures) to more vaguely defined ones (such as social skills training to improve aspects of impaired or undeveloped social competence). Most general discussion of treatment as a juvenile justice activity refers to vaguely defined psychosocial activities prescribed nonspecifically to address problems of emotional and social development.

Uses of Punishment and Treatment

There are two irrational traditions in juvenile justice related to punishment and treatment. The first of these traditions is the deletion of punishment from the public response to juvenile offenses. Punishment is a useful activity for fostering in children a sense of taking responsibility for their actions (though probably not for fostering other aspects of responsibility). It is likely to be more useful the younger its object, the more intimate its context, and the more rapid and consistent its application. For the vast majority of delinquents, offenses represent simple failures of responsibility specific to the stresses of adolescence. In such cases, punishment would be the most specific and useful response. It should be fair and relevant to the offense. It should be severe enough to remind the offender of his responsibility for the offense and to reinforce whatever feelings of guilt he may already have developed, but not so severe as to disrupt normal development. Concretely such punishment would likely rely heavily on programs such as fines, restrictions, restitution, and victim confrontation, rather than on incarceration. The youth of the offender and the informality of the context would make such programs *more* useful than punishment tends to be in courts for adults, rather than less.

The second irrational tradition regarding punishment and treatment is that in the place of punishment juvenile justice has tried to substitute treatment. This tradition of providing treatment for delinquency is associated with the medical model of delinquency. It rests on the understanding of delinquency as a disorder for which treatment can be expected to help. As a therapeutic approach, it tends to be non-specific about diagnosis and treatment prescription, applying global psychosocial interventions to delinquency as the disorder.

There are many problems with this tradition. First, delinquency is too broad a category to be thought of usefully as a disorder in itself. In fact, there are many different problems which may from case to case be part of delinquent activity. For some of these problems effective treatments are clearly available, but for others the evidence of treatability is uncertain. Furthermore, the difficulties of actually providing effective treatment under this model have been greater than most juvenile jurisdictions have been able to master. As a result, much of what may be called treatment is in fact non-specific custodial care.

More basically, when treatment is offered *instead* of punishment in response to a misdeed, it implies that the offender is not responsible for the misdeed. The substitution of treatment for punishment undermines whatever tendency the offender may have to take responsibility for what he has done, and fosters the offering of some illness or disorder as an excuse for the action. This may be appropriate in the rare cases of mental diseases or defects that truly interfere with the capacity to be responsible for one's actions. In most cases, however, it is confusing and disabling to the development of this aspect of responsibility.

A final problem with this tradition is that most people have a legitimate expectation of being punished if they are caught doing wrong. If punishment is not provided, and treatment is substituted, it is likely that the offender will interpret the treatment as punishment. This interpretation is more likely to the extent that the treatment is general rather than aimed specifically at a well-defined problem. It is also more likely if the treatment is coerced, especially if it is coerced without having explored the potential for voluntary contracting for treatment. When treatment is experienced as punishment for these reasons, the necessary formation of a cooperative alliance between therapist and client for addressing problems becomes very difficult. The resulting impairment of therapeutic alliance often interferes with the potential usefulness of treatment.

Solutions

The traditions of deleting punishment for juvenile offenders and providing treatment instead have caused serious problems for the juvenile justice enterprise. The resulting confusion about the purposes and justifications for interventions with juvenile offenders has been demoralizing both to those in the system and also to the community at large. One proposed solution with recent popularity has been to shrink the juvenile jurisdiction or do away with it altogether (Flicker, 1981). This would enable a return to a more forthright reliance on punishment as the appropriate public response to failures of responsibility regardless of age. We have seen in fact that age is not the important factor in determining the capacity to be responsible for one's actions, so there is some wisdom in this solution. But it is not sufficient, as it neglects the need to foster the other aspects of responsibility.

The right solution to the confusion about punishment and treatment is to use both. Punishment is useful in reminding an offender of his responsibility for his actions, but not usually very helpful in developing reliable competence or caring for others. Various forms of treatment are likely to be much more successful in helping to redress failures in these aspects of responsibility. If punishment is the sole response, and failures of responsibility in these other areas are neglected, the offender may in fact feel more responsible and might even be more inhibited from offending. But he would still often lack the caring for others that might motivate non-offensive choices, and the social and personal skills to enable him to carry out such choices effectively. Caring and especially social competence are aspects of responsibility which can in fact improve with treatment (Rutter and Giller, 1984). If fostering responsibility in general is a goal of the response to juvenile offenses, it would be wrong to neglect treatment as part of that response.

Good professional practice in responding to juvenile offenses would require an assessment of an offender's development in all aspects of responsibility. Punishment would be provided in fair proportion to the offense and in a manner which would be most effective in underlining the offender's responsibility for his action. Treatment would be provided in addition, specifically addressed to whatever disorders or developmental inadequacies were present. The offender and his family would be given as much opportunity as possible to contract autonomously regarding the details of the treatment in order to maximize their competent involvement in the treatment process. Treatment would not be forced unless there were a finding that refusal of treatment was incompetent. Even then it would only be forced if there were good reason to expect that the forcing of treatment would be useful.

Summary

Exploring the development of responsibility shows that normal children are responsible for their actions from very early childhood, and that adequately socialized children experience guilt and caring for others by early school age. It is developmentally normal for adolescents to experience transient failings in all aspects of responsibility, and for children and adolescents to be generally less able to be responsible for themselves than are adults. However, for children to lack feelings of guilt or caring for others is not developmentally normal. Instead, as with adults, such failings usually result from inadequate socialization.

A separate system of justice for juveniles is justified by the developmental differences between children and adults: that children are less able to be responsible for themselves, that adolescents normally experience transient irresponsibility, and that even poorly socialized children may have a better prognosis for rehabilitation than do poorly socialized adults. A separate court system cannot be justified by the proposition that children are less responsible for their actions than adults, since this is a false proposition. However, removing punishment as a response to juvenile offenses and replacing it with treatment fosters this proposition. It undermines the taking of responsibility for one's own actions by implicitly seeing offensive behavior as the result of some incapacity, disorder, or illness, thereby excusing it.

Children and adolescents who offend need some punishment as a reminder of their responsibility for what they have done. However, especially when they have serious long-standing problems, they also need much more. Punishment cannot be expected to be enough to foster a sense of caring for others or the competence to be responsible for oneself. But for these problems there are treatments that can make a significant difference. Relying on punishment alone without such treatment will have only a minor impact on an offender's general development of responsibility. As an enterprise rooted in the need to provide for the well-being of children, juvenile justice needs to embrace both punishment and treatment. Neither alone is sufficient to foster the full development of all aspects of responsibility.

References

Barnum, R. (1987). Biomedical problems and juvenile delinquency: Issues in diagnosis and treatment. In Wilson, J. Q. & Loury, G. C. (Eds.). *From children to citizens: Vol. III. Families, schools, and delinquency prevention*. New York: Springer.

Blos, P. (1962). *On adolescence*. New York: The Free Press.

Erikson, E. (1950). *Childhood and society*. New York: Norton.

Farrington, D. (1987). Early precursors of high rate offending. In Wilson J. Q. & Loury G. C. (Eds.). *From children to citizens: Vol. III. Families, schools, and delinquency prevention*. New York: Springer.

Flicker, B. (1981). Prosecuting juveniles as adults: A symptom of a crisis in the juvenile courts. In Hall, J. (Ed.). *Major issues in juvenile justice information and training: Readings in public policy*. Columbus, OH: Academy of Contemporary Problems.

Hirschi, T. (1983). Crime and the family. In Wilson, J. (Ed.). *Crime and public policy*. San Francisco: ICS Press.
Levinger, J. (1971). Patterns of parenthood as theories of learning. In Skolnick, A. and Skolnick, J. (Eds.). *Families in transition*. Boston: Little-Brown.
Lewis, D. (1981). *Vulnerabilities to delinquency*. New York: SP Scientific Books.
Lewis, D. & Balla, D. (1976). *Delinquency and psychopathology*. New York: Grune and Stratton.
Patterson, G. (1982). *Coercive family process*. Eugene, OR: Castilia Publishing Company.
Piaget, J. (1954). *The origins of intelligence in childhood*. New York: International Universities Press.
Rutter, M. & Giller, H. (1984). *Juvenile delinquency: Trends and perspectives*. New York: Guilford Press.
Weissman, J. (1983). Toward an integrated theory of delinquency responsibility. *Denver Law Journal 60*, 3.
Wilson, J. & Herrnstein, R. (1985). *Crime and human nature*. New York: Simon and Schuster.

6
Care and Discipline: Their Contribution to Delinquency and Regulation by the Juvenile Court

PETER W. GREENWOOD

Commentaries on the juvenile law or analyses of juvenile justice practices generally make a clear distinction between two types of cases: those involving abuse or neglect of the child, usually by the parents; and those involving criminal behavior on the part of the child. In abuse and neglect cases the predominant interest is the immediate and future welfare of the child. It is the parents' behavior that is on trial. In delinquency cases that are serious enough to make it to court the welfare interests of the child are balanced against the community's interests in avoiding future crimes. The child's behavior is on trial and provides the basis for imposing coercive controls.

This paper will argue that this distinction, between abuse and neglect cases on the one hand and delinquency cases on the other, is overly simplistic. The same basic issues of "quality of care" and "power to discipline" underlie both types of cases. In fact, many juvenile cases are a mix of abusive behavior by parents and delinquency by the child. Abused and neglected children have a much higher than average risk of becoming delinquent. The most violent or chronic delinquents have usually experienced abuse and neglect. Recognition of the linkages between abuse and delinquency is necessary to evaluate reform proposals that would handle these two types of cases in different courts or use different criteria to decide how the case should be handled.

One of the principle factors that distinguishes juveniles from adults, at least in the eyes of the law, is the presumption that juveniles are in the care of, and under the control of, some responsible adult. Disposition decisions for juveniles involve choices between alternative methods of care and supervision: remaining at home under the supervision of parents, or moving to the home of another family member; placement in a foster or group home; or placement in a 24-hour school or secure institution. In comparing the merits of these alternatives, the court (and probation department pre-sentence report investigators) must inevitably consider both the type of care and discipline the juvenile seems to require and the type of each he is likely to receive in the alternative placements.

Our expectations of justice for an adult are much more simple. If the defendant is found to have committed a crime, and was not certifiably crazy at the time, then the severity of the sentence imposed reflects primarily the punishment that is deserved for the crime and, if the defendant is incarcerated, some degree of protection against future crimes.

Let's compare typical cases in each of the systems: A 16-year-old and a 21-year-old with similar backgrounds and records are both found to have committed armed robbery. Sentencing options for the adult are usually limited to probation, probation and jail, or commitment to state prison. The choice in this case will depend on the seriousness of the charged offense (type of weapon, injury to victims, etc.) and the defendant's prior record. If the defendant has been convicted of a prior felony, he is likely to go to prison. We don't expect the court to pay very much attention to his family background or current living situation. If he is not incarcerated, we do not expect him to be under the control of anybody else even though he may be on probation. Once a month visits are not what we normally mean when we think of supervising a person's behavior.

Our concerns for the juvenile will be quite different, particularly if his record of placements is not extensive. Even if he is placed in a secure facility, the stay will probably be short. We will want to know about his home, what his parents have been doing to deal with his behavior in the past, and what changes they will make to do a better job in the future. We will want to know about any special problems he may have (health, drugs, learning disability, etc.) that may need looking after. And no matter what the research says about the limited overall effect of intervention programs, most of us are concerned about and try to anticipate the effects of a disposition on the juvenile's subsequent behavior.

Abuse and neglect appear to be primary causal factors in chronic delinquency. For that reason information about prior abuse or neglect is relevant to predicting future behavior as well as the suitability of the juvenile's home. Can the abuse or neglect be stopped? Has it caused the juvenile to require special treatment? Should prior abuse or neglect be considered a mitigating factor, and if so, for how long?

Subsequent sections of this paper will examine evidence concerning the effects of parental care and disciplinary measures on juvenile delinquency, what we know about remedial approaches to inadequate parenting, and the juvenile court's role in enforcing minimum standards of care and maximum limits on punishment.

Predictors of Chronic Delinquent Behavior

Causal Theories

Over the years there have been many different theories offered to explain delinquent and criminal behavior (see Empey, 1981 for a review of these theories). Some of the earliest postulated pure genetic or biological bases

(Lombroso, 1918; Goddard, 1914; Goring, 1913). Later theories focused on the criminogenic conditions of lower class life (Shaw and McKay, 1931, 1942, 1969; Sutherland and Cressey, 1955; Miller, 1958) and the consequences of impaired economic opportunity (Cohen, 1955; Cloward and Ohlin, 1960; Quinney, 1974). The theories that are most popular today tend to focus on specific developmental and socializing experiences (Bandura, 1977; Hirschi, 1969; Patterson 1982) and biological deficits (Mednick and Volavka, 1980) that may impede social development.

Although this is not the place for a detailed examination of these theories, it is necessary for the reader to have some understanding of the basic causal mechanisms that are thought to be responsible for criminal behavior in order to appreciate what prevention or rehabilitation programs must overcome. The six theories described here all offer different but useful insights into how criminal behavior develops.

Strain Theory (Cohen, 1955) holds that while lower-class males embrace middle-class goals and aspirations, their inability to effectively compete in school and for jobs, because of their inadequate socialization, leads to loss of self-esteem and delinquent drift. One of the reasons that lower-class youths are inadequately socialized to compete in a world of middle-class institutions is that their parents tend to be more permissive in controlling their behavior.

Control Theory (Hirschi, 1969) holds that humans are naturally antisocial, and that it is a failure of the socialization process (primarily in families) which leads to delinquent behavior. This failure in turn leads to lack of social competence and achievement and contributes to strain and frustration on the part of the juvenile who is unable to achieve his social and economic goals. Socialization is facilitated by bonds which exist between individuals and society. The four elements of these bonds are: attachment, commitment, involvement, and belief.

Social Learning Theory (Bandura, 1968, 1977) suggests that behavior is acquired and maintained through processes of direct observation, experimentation, and reinforcement, both positive and negative. Behaviors are copied and then encouraged or discouraged by whether they result in positive or negative reinforcement. Social learning theory provides another explanation of how inadequate or incompetent parenting contributes to later delinquency.

Psychoanalytic Theory (Freud, 1963) suggests that parental behavior during the earliest stages of the child's development can lead to apparently aberrant behavior. It emphasizes the continuing effects of stressful incidents or trauma experienced in early childhood on the unconscious mind.

Biological Theories (Mednick and Volavka, 1980) describe how various physical endowments or deficits may interfere with normal socialization or learning processes. To some extent, the biological and physical endowments of an individual are inherited from the parents and further influenced by prenatal and perinatal conditions. The relative strength of these influences has not yet been determined, but it has been shown for instance that:

1. The male offspring of fathers with criminal records, who are adopted at birth, are more likely to have criminal records in later life than adopted children whose fathers have no criminal records (Mednick, et al, 1984).
2. Low birth weight is associated with a higher risk of neurological disorders and low academic performance (Harmeling and Jones, 1968).
3. Malnutrition during early stages of fetal development produces a 60 percent deficit in the number of brain cells (Winick, 1971).

Criminal Personality Theory (Yockelson and Samenow, 1976, 1977) offers a description of the cognitive processes which may contribute to continuing criminal behavior and which are clearly influenced by the preceding theories.

Since none of the theories that assign the cause of crime to early socialization processes or physical endowments comes near to explaining all of the variance in criminal behavior across individuals, it seems clear that individual cognitive processes must play an important role in the continuation or cessation of criminal activity.

The developmental picture that emerges from the intersection of these theories is consistent with the data presented later. All of them help explain how particular physiological characteristics and parental behavior more likely found in low income families lead to early antisocial behavior. This in turn leads to rejection by conventional peers and poor achievement in school, supporting the drift toward more serious delinquent behavior.

Predictor Categories

There are five basic sets of factors which have been consistently found correlated to chronic delinquency among urban males.[1] They are, in the chronological order in which they tend to appear: (1) family characteristics, (2) biological or physical endowments, (3) familial experience, (4) pre-delinquent behavioral flags, and finally (5) criminal acts. Figure 6-1 shows how these five categories are interrelated with a sixth category that is much more difficult to measure and whose specific effects are largely unknown. This is the collection of experiences, peer relations, and opportunity structures that either reinforce or discourage whatever delinquent tendencies have developed.

Family Characteristics

Starting at the top of Figure 6-1 and working down, we begin with family characteristics that are more likely to produce delinquent boys. They are:

(1) low income, (2) father with a history of criminal behavior or alcoholism, (3) mother with a history of mental illness, (4) a large number of siblings, and (5) siblings with criminal records. Rather than causing delinquency directly, these family characteristics can be thought of as leading to or influencing the next two categories which are more directly associated with delinquency: biological or physical endowments and early familial experience.

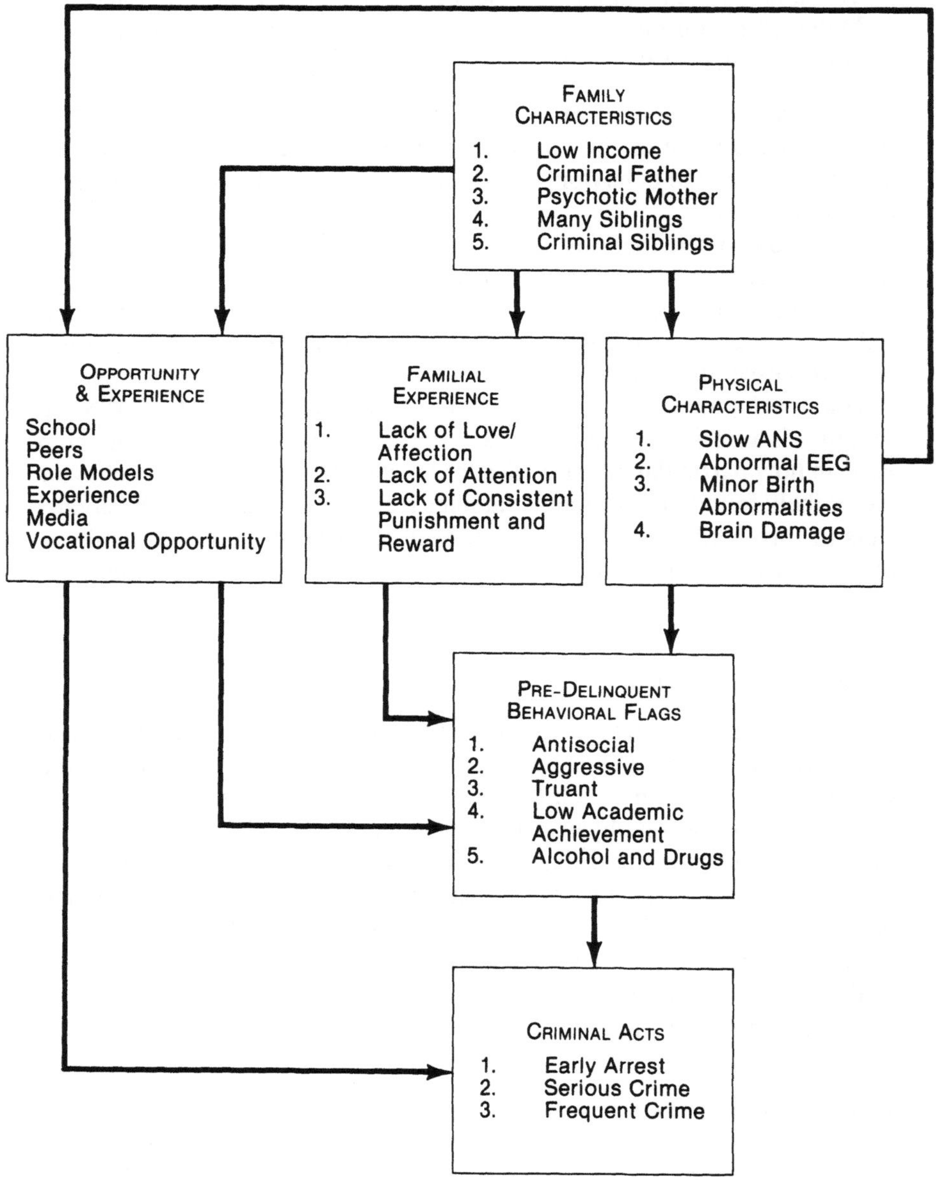

FIGURE 6.1. Delinquency predictors.

Biological or Physical Endowments

Theories concerning how criminal behavior may be influenced by genetic or physiological characteristics have had a checkered history. In early studies, inappropriate samples and failure to control other confounding variables produced inflated or otherwise incorrect conclusions about associations between physical features and criminality. More recent work on this subject has produced strong controversy because of the potential for adversive labeling or intervention that physiological predictors imply.

The specific biological and physical characteristics that have been found to be associated with increased rates of delinquency or criminal behavior include: (1) slow autonomic nervous system (ANS) as measured by galvanic skin response, (2) abnormal EEGs, (3) more frequent presence of minor birth abnormalities, and (4) various neurological deficits (Freier, 1986). It appears that all of these characteristics are associated with impairment in the brain or nervous system, which in turn may impede the normal social learning process.

Familial Experience

It is generally accepted that the family is the primary socializing agent for the child. It is within the family that a child first learns to control his behavior and get along with other family members. This process of early socialization involves a complex interaction between the behavior of the child's parents or guardian and his own unique biological or physical endowments. Studies have consistently identified a number of deficits in family functioning and physical characteristics that are associated with increased risk of delinquency. These familial experiences include: (1) the absence of expressed love and affection by parents toward the child, (2) failure to monitor the behavior of the child, and (3) the failure to impose appropriate punishments for aversive behavior or reward positive behavior in a consistent fashion.

Our understanding of how these parenting variables affect early childhood behavior has been greatly improved by recent studies conducted by Gerald Patterson (1982) and his colleagues at the Oregon Social Learning Center showing how improvements in parenting skills, which can be taught by family therapists, can bring about rapid reductions in some types of aversive behavior and decreases in subsequent delinquency.

Pre-Delinquent Behavioral Flags

Up to this point the predictive factors we have been discussing in Figure 6.1 represent influences on the child—situations he finds himself in or things that are done to him. As we move on in time, and down the diagram, the additional factors that predict future delinquency become things the child does himself. The first of these factors we have labeled

"Pre-Delinquent Behavioral Flags." Among younger children (ages 6–12) behaviors that are predictive of later delinquency include being daring or disobedient, stealing, lying, wandering, excessive aggression, and truancy (Loeber and Dishion, 1983). For older children pre-delinquent behavior includes heavy drinking or smoking, drug use, promiscuous sex, and fighting (Osborn and West, 1978; Robins, 1966). Most studies also find that poor verbal skills and low academic achievement are also associated with later delinquency.

Criminal Acts

The last set of factors involves explicit criminal acts. The earlier a child becomes involved in crime, the more serious and frequent his criminal behavior, the greater the likelihood of his future criminal behavior. All cohort studies have found a strong correlation between juvenile and adult arrests, the number of prior arrests and the probability of future arrests, or the age of first arrest and the number of future arrests. In Wolfgang, Figlio and Sellin's (1972) study of boys born in Philadelphia in 1945, the probability that any one boy would be arrested prior to his eighteenth birthday was 35%. The probability of a subsequent arrest increased with each prior arrest up to about five, where it leveled off at 72%.

In Farrington's (1983) study of 411 boys from working-class families in London, of the 29 individuals who experienced more than three adult convictions, 10 had experienced more than three convictions as juveniles and 6 had experienced two. Only 2% of those with no juvenile convictions experienced more than three convictions as an adult. Most chronic adult offenders had also been frequent offenders when they were juveniles. Most chronic juvenile offenders will go on to commit crimes as adults. The probability that an individual who was never arrested as a juvenile will become a chronic offender as an adult is extremely remote.

Integrating Predictive Factors and Delinquency Theories

Familial experience and physical characteristics can be thought of as interactive because the child's physical and biological makeup determine to some extent the nature of his behavior and temperament and his reactions to his parents' behaviors. Some children may require more love or attention than others. Some may be slower to learn specific social behavior, thereby pushing the limits of their parents' patience and parenting skills. Some may be more hyperactive or easily frustrated, trying their parents' patience in another way. Not all children are equally easy to raise. Not all parents are equally skillful in parenting. Research suggests that the more difficult the child and the more incompetent, distracted or inconsistent the parents, the more likely the child is to engage in continuing aversive behavior and later delinquency.

The connection between family characteristics, familial experience, and physical characteristics should be obvious. Low income families, or those headed by criminal or alcoholic fathers or psychotic mothers, are less likely to provide the necessary socializing familial experience because of parental deficits in skill or preoccupation with their own problems. Large numbers of siblings may detract from the amount of attention that any one child receives, and siblings with criminal records are simply an indication that things have already gone wrong.

To summarize these connections, families headed by criminal or alcoholic fathers and psychotic mothers are more likely to be found among low income families. These families are more likely to pass along biological or physical traits to their offspring, either genetically or through pre- or perinatal influences that hinder normal socialization. Furthermore, these parents are also more likely to lack the necessary skills, temperament or dedication necessary for effective parenting.

Gerald Patterson (1982) sees the development of delinquency as a two-phase process. In the first phase, the failure of parents to monitor and discipline antisocial behavior results in increased occurrence of behavioral problems across home and school settings. The failure of parents to reinforce social behavior is thought to retard the development of social, academic, and possibly work-related skills. The results to children of this first phase are high rates of antisocial behavior, low levels of social and academic skills, and possible rejection by conventional peers.

In the second phase, lack of social and academic skills increases the likelihood that the child will drift into a deviant peer group, leading in turn to increased delinquent behavior. This drift is exacerbated by the parents' failure to monitor their child's behavior or peers.

Using Patterson's two-phase framework, the first phase seems consistent with the control and social learning theories. If we accept the fact that some children may be more difficult to socialize because of their emotional or physiological characteristics, then phase 1 should also include biological and psychological influences.

Phase 2 is much more consistent with strain or criminal personality theories. By this period in life the juvenile's deviant behavior creates influences that beget further deviance, unless there is some decided change in his behavior. The only person who can make that change is the delinquent himself. Given his possible background, not just his environment but the habitual patterns of behavior he has fallen into, those changes would be difficult to make.

The principal point is that the seeds of chronic delinquency are often sown at a very young age. By the time a child's chronic behavior problems become so disruptive that some remedial action must be taken, their pattern is likely to be extremely well set. If behavior is to be changed, there are many behavior patterns to change.

Predicting Chronic Offenders

Most research on criminal careers has been justified in part by the notion that the early prediction of chronic offenders will allow the system to do "something" that it would not be able to do in the absence of this predictive capacity. The "something" that might be done, depending on the philosophy of the researcher and the nature of the predictor variable being used, runs the gamut from early prevention (day care, Headstart, parent training), to heavy investment in treatment programs that focus on specific correlates (drug or alcohol abuse, vocational training), to selective incapacitation during the predicted high-risk years. Many of the negative reactions to the concept of risk prediction are in fact negative reactions to specific forms of intervention which a predictive capability might seem to justify or permit.

Some argue that the ability to predict future criminality is so fraught with error as to make such predictions practically worthless. Others argue that any criminal justice policies based on predictions of future criminality are inherently unfair, regardless of the data on which they are based, and that any attempts at prediction or labeling are bound to become counterproductive, self-fulfilling prophecies.

In this field, any prediction capability is clearly a two-edged sword. On the one hand, it gives us the capacity and rationale for diverting the majority of youth from unnecessarily restrictive placements in the knowledge that their delinquent behavior is unlikely to continue. On the other hand, it also identifies a small group of largely underprivileged or neglected youths who, as a group, pose a high risk of future criminal activity to their communities. Here we focus only on the issue of whether targeting strategies are feasible at all.

The best sources of data for examining patterns of the onset of criminal careers are those longitudinal studies that have obtained accurate information on both juvenile and adult arrests (Farrington, 1979). The best of these studies is the Cambridge study by Farrington and West (1977) for the following reasons:

(1) It tracks a large number of subjects over an extended period of time.
(2) It contains complete juvenile and adult criminal record information.
(3) It includes a significant number of serious chronic offenders.

This study covers 411 boys who were aged 8–9 in 1961–1962 and attending six schools in working-class areas of London. The boys were contacted every two years up to age 21, while their families were contacted every year up to age 15. The study includes all recorded convictions up through age 25. Other longitudinal studies containing data on the relationship between juvenile and adult criminality include: McCord's (1979) study which followed 325 boys up through 1975 who had participated in the Cambridge-Somerville project in the late 1930s; Robins and Wish's

(1977) study of 223 black males born in St. Louis between 1930 and 1934 and followed up to age 18; and Lyle Shannon's (1978) study of 1,352 youths born in 1942 and 2,099 youths born in 1949 in Racine, Wisconsin. The records of both groups were followed up through 1973.

The Farrington and West data provide the most complete and compelling picture of the connection between juvenile and adult crime. In that study, 70% of the sample who were convicted as juveniles (between the ages of 10 and 16) were subsequently convicted as adults (over age 16) by the time they had reached age 24 (Farrington, 1983). The occurrence of convictions of adults who had not sustained any juvenile convictions was only 16%: more than a 4 to 1 difference. Only 13 out of 411 boys sustained more than three convictions. Of these 13, 77% had four or more convictions as an adult. Only 2% of those adults without any juvenile conviction sustained four or more convictions. The small group of boys who were first convicted between ages 10 and 12 averaged six convictions apiece by their 21st birthday (Farrington, 1979).

The sample of 411 subjects contains 23 (5.5%) who experienced six or more convictions prior to their 25th birthday. These "chronics" accounted for half of all the convictions experienced by the sample; and presumably at least half of all the crimes. All 23 were convicted as juveniles. Farrington attempted to predict the chronics at age 13 on the basis of data collected earlier and whether or not they had yet been convicted. The results of these predictions are contained in Table 6.1.[2] The scale predicts accurately in 95% (92 + 3) of the cases. It divides the sample into two groups: one (predicted no) consisting of only 2.6% chronics; the other (predicted yes) consisting of 55% chronics. By focusing on 5.5% of the sample, (the group predicted to be chronic), or about 20% of those with juvenile records, Farrington identified more than half (55%) of the chronics. The predicted "yes" group would then presumably be responsible for at least 25% of all future crimes attributable to that sample. If some of the false positives include offenders who were not chronic, then the percentage of crime attributable to this group is even higher.

TABLE 6.1. Farrington data.

		Actual chronic (6 or more convictions): No	Actual chronic (6 or more convictions): Yes	
Predicted chronic	No	92	2.5	94.5
	Yes	2.5	3	5.5
		94.5	5.5	

The predictive accuracy achieved by Farrington for juvenile offenders at age 13 is consistent with that found in other studies which have attempted to predict high-rate or chronic offenders (Monahan et al., 1981; Chaiken and Chaiken, 1982) and appears to be near the maximum we can expect. Without these early childhood factors that Farrington used in his prediction scale, attempts to predict chronic offenders would be even less accurate or would have to wait until more of a criminal record had been accumulated.

Is the degree of accuracy achieved by Farrington a sufficient basis for treating some juveniles differently from others, even though the number of times they have been convicted may be similar? This is where the concept of bringing just deserts into juvenile court runs headlong into the traditional approach of providing treatment according to needs. If the difference in treatment allows the low-risk juvenile to go free without any punishment or treatment while the high-risk juvenile is placed out of his home or required to participate in an extensive treatment program, then this difference in dispositional severity may be difficult to sustain on the prediction evidence alone. If, on the other hand, both youths were required to participate in some type of programming, the predictive factors might be more easily justified in determining the type of program to which each should be assigned. The low-risk youth might be assigned to perform community service. The high-risk youth might be assigned to a more structured and highly supervised program that would attempt to work on some of his behavioral problems or skill deficits through counseling, skill training or other techniques.

The window of opportunity for dealing with serious delinquent behavior is only about five years in length, extending from the 13th to the 18th birthdate. We cannot afford, nor is it productive in most cases, to make much of a response in the first one or two instances that a juvenile may be arrested. On the other hand, waiting for chronic offenders to build up a record of many arrests and minor dispositions only compounds the problems that must be dealt with later.

In summary, chronic offenders can usually be identified solely on the basis of their juvenile records. However, this evidence normally does not accumulate until after the youth's 16th birthday. If additional factors describing the youth's school performance and home situation are included, the age at which "chronics" can be predicted can be moved up several years to possibly the 13th birthday. This earlier identification might facilitate more productive programming, but it also runs the risk of treating some juveniles who would have resisted on their own. There is little evidence to help us determine the effects of different policies in this area at the current time. The balance we strike must depend on the nature of the interventions imposed and the effects they achieve.

Promising Programs for Preventing or Rehabilitating Chronic Juvenile Offenders

Legal and Practical Limitations on the Intervention Powers of Juvenile Courts

For most of their history, state juvenile courts had almost absolute power to intervene in the lives of juveniles believed to be in need of supervision or services. It was not even necessary for a child to have committed a criminal act to be found "beyond the control of his parents," and the procedural rules for arriving at such findings were informal at best. This awesome power of the state to intervene was justified on the grounds that it was acting primarily in the child's best interests. The years since the mid-1960s have seen a profound change in juvenile law as it affects the rights of those accused of delinquency and in the treatment of less serious delinquents.

The procedural revolution was brought about through a series of Supreme Court decisions granting juveniles all the procedural protections afforded adults, except jury trial and bail. The shift in treatment practices was stimulated by a broad coalition of youth advocacy groups and federal legislation that encouraged local jurisdictions to handle noncriminal truants and runaways through other means than the juvenile court. Because the increase in procedural protection requires the state to prepare juvenile cases just as diligently as if the accused were adult cases, juvenile courts have had to narrow their focus to those delinquents who are charged with fairly serious criminal acts. Although the pattern of changes across states is highly variable, merely troublesome but noncriminal juvenile behavior is increasingly being turned over to community agencies rather than the juvenile courts, or not being dealt with at all. Once a juvenile has been found to have committed a criminal act, the broad dispositional authority of the juvenile courts to act in the child's best interests remains intact. This situation is very unlike that in criminal courts which are increasingly being confined to a narrow range of dispositional alternatives determined by the seriousness of the underlying act.

When one looks beyond the juvenile court to identify community agencies that might deal with troublesome but not yet delinquent youth, public schools are the only game in town. Only they command the authority and the resources to act in more than a marginal way. However, it is not clear exactly what they can do. From the standpoint of public law, targeting special groups of students is a risky business. Thirty years of race sensitivity have generated judicial suspicion of selective programs that will disproportionately single out minority students, which targeted programs of delinquency prevention inevitably would. A combination of a possible negative stigma attached to a specially targeted program and differential racial effect leaves a targeted program vulnerable to the same constitutional challenges that struck down "tracking" policies in public education. In addition, programs containing a negative stigma may implicate due process requirements for pupil assignment (as is the case in public school discipline), infringe on parental or family liberty, or violate a student's constitutional right to privacy.

Dealing With The Perception That Treatment Does Not Work

The ultimate test of any rehabilitation program is not the technique it uses, where it takes place, or how hard it tries—the characteristics that are normally used to describe a model program. The ultimate test is its impact on the criminal behavior of youths after they leave the program: their recidivism rate compared to that of similar youths who were not treated by the program.

One of the most widely accepted and influential conclusions that has been drawn from criminal justice research over the past two decades is the notion that rehabilitation programs do not work. This conclusion is based on several critical reviews of the treatment evaluation literature which found that most experimental programs failed to produce lower recidivism rates and that no intervention method consistently performed better than others, or even that intervention was better than none at all.

The negative conclusion of these reviews has been previously attacked on the grounds that: (1) many of the experimental programs were narrowly based or poorly implemented; and (2) that many of the evaluations were flawed in design or poorly carried out. It can be argued that the "nothing works" conclusion is also based on an inappropriate interpretation of the data.

The problem lies in how one defines a treatment method. The traditional evaluation literature groups programs that employ the same theoretical approach according to some rough taxonomy of intervention strategies. When most of the experimental programs in a given intervention category (say vocational training) do not produce lower recidivism rates, the reviewer concludes that that form of intervention does not work.

This particular method of evaluation turns out to be a test of the hypothesis that one variable, (such as the treatment method), dominates all others (such as type of staff, management, training, etc.) that might be used to define a program. Rejection of this hypothesis simply means that no such dominance exists. Since some individual experimental programs have resulted in lower recidivism rates, even though most of the other programs in the treatment category to which they were assigned did not, variables other than those that are now used to define treatment methods may be important determinants.

In addition to our critique of the negative way in which the evaluation literature has been summarized, there are several other reasons why efforts to develop more effective rehabilitation programs should be encouraged. One is the high recidivism rate experienced by most graduates of traditional state training schools. Another is provided by the evidence suggesting that some particular programs have been effective, at least for a time, in reducing the recidivism rates of particular types of youth. A third is a lack of any more effective alternatives. Although the system can begin resorting to longer incapacitative sentences for the most chronic delinquents, these terms can result in only modest decreases in crime, due to the extremely high rates with which these youths recidivate when they are returned to the street.

The final justification we offer for pursuing more effective intervention techniques has to do with notions of social justice. The youths who are most likely to become chronic offenders have in some sense been failed by their families, their communities, and their schools. It does not seem right that they should be consigned to careers of repeated incarceration without making the maximum effort possible to turn them around. We have identified some programs that are now attempting just that.

Promising Programs for Chronic Juvenile Offenders

In the absence of clear and convincing empirical evidence, let alone any empirical evidence at all, it is necessary to fall back on more subjective references to identify the most promising programs that are operating today. One method of identifying important features that rehabilitation should have is to turn to the most accepted theories of how chronic delinquency begins. Our reviews of these theories produced the following list of seven essential features:

1. Provide opportunities for each youth to overcome adversity and experience success, encouraging a positive self-image.
2. Facilitate bonds of affection and mutual respect between juveniles and their guardians, and involvement in conventional family and community activities.
3. Provide frequent, timely and accurate feedback for both positive and negative behavior.
4. Reduce or eliminate negative role models and peer support for negative attitudes or behavior.
5. Require juveniles to recognize and reflect on inappropriate thought process that rationalizes negative behavior.
6. Create opportunities for juveniles to discuss family matters and early experiences in a relaxed, non-judgmental atmosphere.
7. Vary the sequence and amount of exposure to program components to adapt to the needs and capabilities of each participating youth.

Another source of information is the "effective schools" and "safe schools" literature which attempts to identify and explain the performance of public schools that do much better than expected in improving the achievement levels of poor children or reducing the level of violence within the schools. This body of literature provides another set of important characteristics that focus on management style and attitude rather than program substance. These features include:

1. Continuing instructional leadership and support by school principals.
2. High expectations for student performance and school-wide recognition of success.
3. Frequent monitoring of student progress.
4. Maintenance of an orderly and quiet atmosphere without being oppressive.
5. Collaborative planning and collegial relationships among teachers.
6. Techniques for minimizing turnover among the most competent staff.

A third subjective source of evidence is provided by those judges, researchers, and correctional caseworkers who have taken the time to review and compare a number of alternative programs with those provided by traditional state training schools. Among such individuals there appears to be a developing consensus about what effective programs should look like.

The primary alternatives to traditional training schools that have been developed over the past 15 years include: outdoor education programs that use rugged survival training and other wilderness experience as a means of motivating recalcitrant youths and forcing them to confront their fears; small, secure, intensive treatment units housing no more than 15 violent or acting-out youths who are under continuous supervision and program control; group homes which serve as either entry-level placement or reentry facilities for more secure program components; and tracking programs which monitor and supervise youths who reside in the community on a one-to-one basis. Most of these intervention methods have been developed by programs in the private sector.

VisionQuest and Associated Marine Institutes (AMI) are two programs which embody many of the essential features listed above, and which have attracted enthusiastic supporters among parents and juvenile court personnel. Both programs use an outdoor education approach rather than secure facilities to control and motivate their charges.

VisionQuest and AMI share several common characteristics along with many of the other programs that are starting to be developed by the private sector, and occasionally within a public agency. Each of these programs was founded (and is still run) by dynamic individuals who were discontented with the programs currently being offered by public agencies. The primary focus of the programs is on changing the youth's behavior; not simply custody or academic and vocational training. Line level staff and middle management are held closely accountable for their actions and results. None of these programs will tolerate incompetent or inattentive staff. The morale of the staff appears to be quite high, and there is a shared sense of purpose, allegiance to the program and belief that they are having an impact. Program components are in a constant state of evolution in the search for more effective or efficient approaches.

Whether or not these new wilderness or community program models are anymore effective in reducing recidivism rates than the training schools they were designed to replace remains to be seen. While there are strong differences of opinion about the value of particular techniques or programs, no systematic outcome data has yet been collected that will allow valid comparisons to be made. The principal problem in evaluating new programs is one of identifying appropriate comparison or control groups. Recidivism data for program participants are meaningless unless they can be compared with recidivism rates of other programs dealing with comparable youths.

Promising Programs For All Kids

Although the juvenile court is limited to dealing with juveniles who have exhibited more serious forms of delinquent behavior, the delinquency research literature identifies a much larger pool of younger juveniles who, while they may not yet be seriously delinquent, are clearly at risk. The question is: are there any acceptable intervention strategies that might be used to reach these youths before they become entangled in the juvenile justice system?

The first principle that must be recognized in considering acceptability is that programs should not be narrowly focused on delinquency prevention alone. Rather, they should address the wider range of social problems, such as drug abuse, school dropout, or unemployment, for which likely delinquents are also at risk. We describe four types of programs that satisfy this requirement and show some promise of reducing later criminal conduct: early education, parent training, effective schools, and voluntary youth service programs.

An early education program such as Headstart can help children from high risk families by getting them out of their homes, where they may be neglected or insufficiently stimulated, and bringing them into contact with other children. It helps socialize them to interact with others, prepares them for the discipline of the classroom, and even improves their health by providing them with a good meal. A recent evaluation of one such program showed that Headstart children were less likely to be arrested and more likely to have completed school by the time they were 19 years of age, than similar children who had not participated in the Headstart program.

Parent training as practiced by the Oregon Social Learning Center

(OSLC) involves teaching the parents of acting-out children specific techniques for monitoring and changing aversive behavior. The techniques that are taught are based on behavior modification. Since the techniques themselves are relatively simple, the most difficult task of the OSLC therapists is to overcome the parent's resistance to putting them into practice. Evaluations have shown that OSLC's techniques are effective in reducing aversive behavior and subsequent delinquency but that the outcome is critically dependent on the skill of the therapists and the cooperation of the parents.

The third type of intervention program that we considered are more effective schools. Many inner-cities are plagued by high rates of absenteeism, student dropout, behavior problems, and low student acheivement—symptoms that are also characteristic of chronic delinquency. There is some evidence to suggest that certain school management practices can reduce these problems, and possibly reduce the amount of student delinquency. The evidence is not yet compelling because it is largely subjective and based on comparative case studies.

The fourth type of program considered were voluntary youth service agencies such as the California Conservation Corps. The essential features of such programs are that they provide job skills training, work experience and semi-independent living situations for young men and women in public service programs, who would otherwise probably be unemployed. Although there is no evidence indicating what impact such programs might have on the recidivism rates of former delinquents, they would appear to provide a valuable transition experience for youths who have recently participated in some form of correctional program. There is currently a tendency for the designers of such programs to exclude youth with delinquency records.

Early Intervention Compared to Selective Incapacitation as a Crime Reduction Method

Incapacitation and rehabilitation can be viewed as alternative, or complementary, crime control strategies. Incapacitation reduces the number of crimes that an individual chronic offender commits by periodically removing him from society throughout the length of his career. An effective rehabilitation program would reduce the amount of crime a chronic offender might do by either shortening the length of his career or reducing the frequency of his criminal acts. The relative efficiency of these two approaches depends on individual average career lengths and rates of offending, the accuracy with which high-rate offenders can be predicted, and the effectiveness of the rehabilitation program in reducing subsequent crime rates.

For any specified distribution of career lengths, individual offense rates, and predictive accuracy, it is possible to use existing models of incapacitation effectiveness to determine the minimum level of effectiveness that a rehabilitation program must achieve, and the maximum cost per subject that it can spend, in order to be competitive with incapacitation as a crime control strategy, on a cost effectiveness basis. The analysis requires four basic steps:

1. estimating incarceration rates and costs for current sentencing policies;
2. estimating the increase in offenders incarcerated and expected reduction in crime for particular selective sentencing policies;
3. determining the minimum level of effectiveness (in reduced recidivism) that a rehabilitation program would have to achieve in order to produce the same crime reduction achieved in Step 2;
4. estimating the cost savings in reduced incarceration that would be produced by the reduction in recidivism determined in Step 3, and by dividing this figure by the number of predicted chronic delinquents that would have to be treated, determining how much money could be spent on each one.

An analysis by Peter Rydell (1986) based on average sentencing policies and costs nationwide, suggests that a selective incapacitation policy of doubling prison terms for predicted high-rate offenders would result in a 6% increase in the incarcerated population and a 5% decrease in total crimes. In order to produce this same 5% reduction in crime, a rehabilitation program for young chronic offenders would have to reduce subsequent individual offense rates by 37%. A treatment program that achieved this level of performance would reduce the need for subsequent incarceration by 4%, a cost savings that would produce approximately $29,000 for each juvenile treated.

The Juvenile Court's Role in Establishing Minimum Standards of Care and Maximum Powers of Punishment

The obligation to provide care and authority to punish are two of the essential features of parenting or guardianship. Both are subject to various tests of reasonableness. The obligation to provide care begins with shelter, food, and reasonable protection from harm, and, depending on the setting, extends to educational and recreational programs, health care, and attendance to other special needs. The authority to punish or enforce reasonable disciplinary standards begins with the power to grant or withhold privileges and extends to restricting movement and, in some cases, the imposition of physical pain. Of course, yelling, screaming, and making the child miserable are generally within the accepted rules. What makes the juvenile court's role difficult in policing these obligations and powers is the fact that they are ambiguously defined and vary with the age of the child and the nature of the child's prior conduct.

Let us first consider the case of the parents' obligation to provide reasonable care for their child. If they fail to provide a reasonable level of care the state can step in and take the child from them. The action will be a dependency proceeding in the juvenile court. What are the parent's obligations when the child is very young? In addition to providing food and shelter, the parents are obliged to continuously monitor the child's welfare and safety, or provide for others to do so. They would be derelict if they left an infant unsupervised for long periods of time, neglected to see that the child was adequately clothed against the weather, or if they allowed the child to play in a dangerous situation such as alongside a busy street or a rushing stream. Their negligent care might be reported by a neighbor or might be discovered by an investigation stimulated by the child's need for emergency medical care.

As the child grows older the parents' obligations decrease. No higher quality of food or shelter are required. The older a child becomes the more he can be expected to do for himself—prepare his own meals, be alone without supervision, look out for his own safety. By the time a child is around 14 years of age, he can be expected to be practically self-sufficient. Of course this assumes the developmental pattern of the normal healthy child. The child who is handicapped, retarded, learning-disabled or who has psychological problems will require a higher level of care.

The juvenile court's role in deciding abuse and neglect cases, in addition to looking out for the welfare of the individual child involved, is to establish a minimum standard of care that is sensitive to all of the factors we have been discussing. In fact, those standards will usually not be called into play until the child has already suffered severe physical harm. This is because of a legal principle presuming parents to be competent unless proven otherwise, and the practical consideration that the state (or whatever public entity is supposed to step in to replace the parents) does not have very good alternatives to offer. If we attempt to plot the minimum level of care that parents are obliged to provide, measured against some absolute standard, over the age of the child, it might look something like the curve shown in Figure 6.2.

When we apply the same type of analysis to other potential guardians or custodians of children, we can observe the unique position that parents occupy. Anyone who has ever attempted to adopt a child will know that the level of care and competence required of adoptive or foster parents is considerably higher than that demanded of natural parents, at least as measured by professional standards. The prospective parents social background, behavior, and relationship are examined. The home is inspected. A social worker is assigned to ensure that their obligations are being fulfilled.

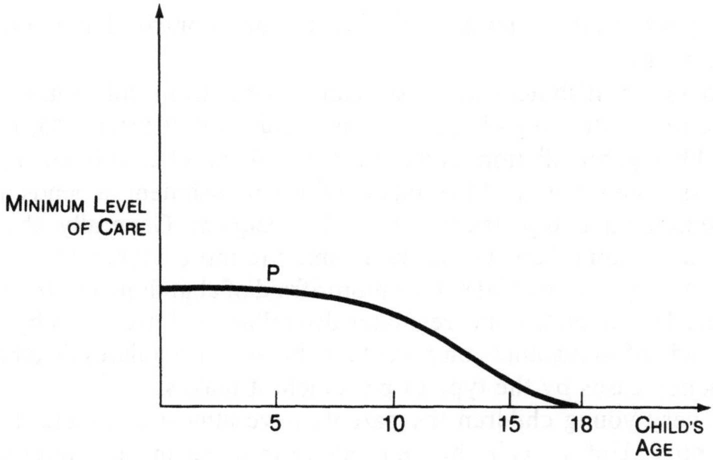

FIGURE 6.2. Minimum level of care for natural parents.

With older children in group living situations the same type of higher professional standards apply. Special health problems and special education needs must be looked after. The qualifications for house supervisors are more likely to include special training or certification. The obligation to look after the children's welfare and safety does not fall off nearly as fast with age for these special guardians as it does for natural parents. Figure 6.3 shows a hypothetical plot of minimum levels of care for foster parents or group home operators as compared to natural parents.

The obligation to care is only one side of the parenting coin that must be regulated by the juvenile court. The other is the power to punish. It is inconceivable to think of attempting to raise or supervise children without some supervisory authority. Without the power to discipline, children

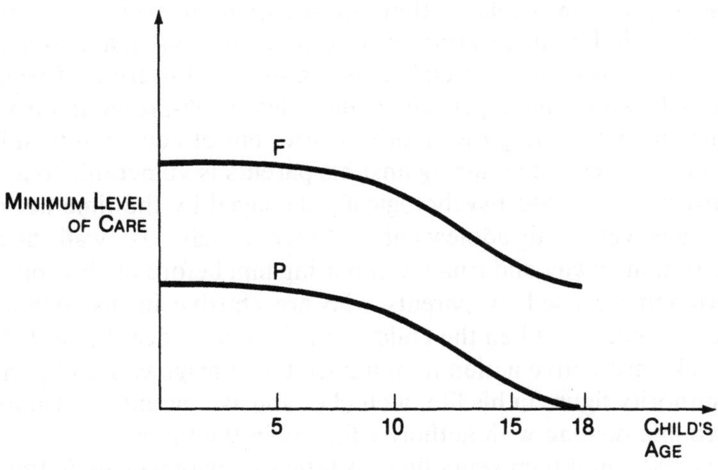

FIGURE 6.3. Minimum level of care for natural and foster parents.

become peers who are no more subject to adult control than contemporaries at work.

Of course, punishment can take many forms, from mild signs of displeasure or withholding of approval to withdrawal of privileges, restrictions of liberty, humiliation, or more extreme forms of emotional or physical duress. The severity of the impact of any punishment depends in part on the emotional and physical state of the recipient. Generally, the more dependent or apprehensive the recipient, the more vulnerable he is to threats. A very young child will be more afraid of abandonment than will a teenager. The juvenile court regulates discipline in abuse cases by establishing and enforcing limits on parental behavior. It regulates discipline in delinquency cases by the type of placement it makes.

With very young children the parents have almost complete disciplinary control. Unless their children require frequent medical attention or the parents are observed and reported for overtly abusive behavior by their neighbors, they can impose just about any disciplinary regime they wish on their young children. That children are virtually helpless to resist is now evidenced by child abuse cases in which preschool children were repeatedly sexually abused by their teachers, but failed to tell their parents because the teachers told them they would be killed if they did.

Parents are generally free to threaten, yell at, and hit their children pretty much as they please. If they are emotionally unstable or immature, the erratic and violent nature of their punishments may have devastating emotional effects on their children, effects which will be largely hidden to outside observers.

As children grow older it is difficult to say whether they become more or less vulnerable to their parents' disciplinary powers. Physically they are clearly less vulnerable. Although they may grow to be less emotionally dependent on their parents, they also become more insecure about themselves. It is possible to think of situations in which a destructive parent could inflict devastating emotional damage on an adolescent child by continually ridiculing or embarrassing the child in front of peers.

Generally we would expect the child to learn self-protection from abusive punishment as he grows more mature, but of course any child who has to take protective action against his parents is vulnerable to a variety of neuroses. If not too psychologically damaged by the time he reaches the teenage years, an adolescent can increasingly just walk away. Of course running away and truancy can bring him before the juvenile court. The problems caused by parents who are abusive in disciplining their children do not end when the child is finally able to flee the nest. Having had to take protective action to minimize the damage caused by the principal authority figure in his life, a child of abusive parents is also likely to have trouble dealing with authority figures in the future.

By a child's mid-teen years there is little that parents can do to enforce discipline. Their relationship becomes consensual, based on the child's desire to continue living in his parents' house or accepting their support. If the situation becomes intolerable the child can leave, assuming he can find someone else to live with or is self-supporting.

Therefore the parental responsibility to care for the child and power to discipline are inextricably bound. Withholding the former is the most severe form of the latter. Only to the extent that the teenager or young adult continues to need their parents' financial or emotional support can the parents exert any coercive disciplinary influence over their child. The hypothetical decline in parental disciplinary authority is plotted in Figure 6.4.

The same is not true of other child rearing institutions. The disciplinary powers of the public school system and the juvenile court increase dramatically with age—in part because of legal and administrative presumptions that with age comes increasing responsibility for one's actions and less allowance for the effects of a disadvantaged childhood. Of course it is also true that antisocial behavior by a sixteen-year-old is relatively more disruptive than the antisocial behavior of a twelve-year-old.

In school settings a disruptive or inattentive ten-year-old will be carefully examined, interviewed, and tested by school authorities. The presumption will be that the child has some type of emotional problem, home situation or learning disability which the school system should deal with. The disciplinary response of the school will be mitigated by rehabilitative concerns. This will absolutely be the case with six-year-olds and unlikely with students who have reached sixteen. By that age, without a record of prior emotional or physical problems, the response to disruptive behavior will be almost exclusively disciplinary. The disruptive child will first be excluded from class, then suspended, and finally expelled from school or transferred to a special disciplinary school. The older the child, the more

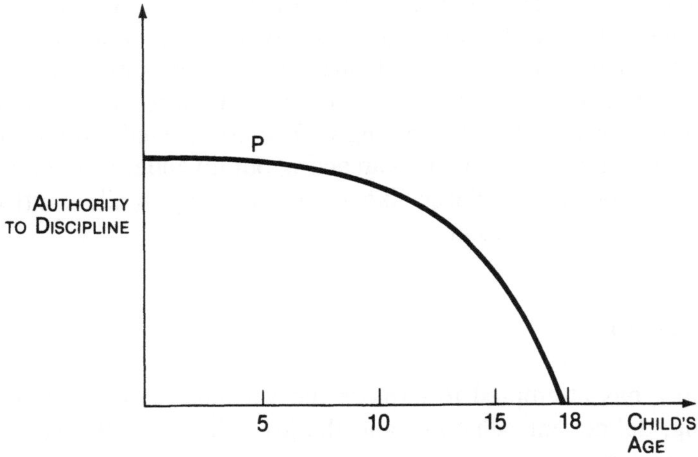

FIGURE 6.4. Parents' authority to discipline.

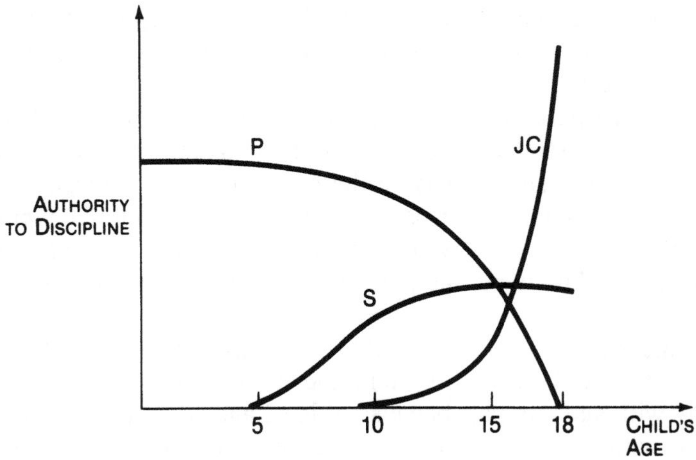

FIGURE 6.5. Parents', schools' and courts' authority to discipline.

likely school officials are to treat antisocial behavior from a purely disciplinary (as opposed to a diagnostic or therapeutic) approach.

The same basic pattern holds true for the juvenile court. Crimes by very young children (say less than 12) will usually be treated as symptoms of underlying problems, and will be responded to through therapeutic-oriented means, no matter how severe their crimes. In fact, the more severe their crimes, the more obvious it becomes that they are deeply disturbed.

Failure to respond to reasonable treatment (recidivism) or increasing age diminish the system's tolerance for delinquent acts. Fourteen-year-old recidivists or serious offenders are likely to find themselves placed in restrictive settings, albeit for short periods of time. Older recidivists or violent offenders will find themselves locked up in mini-prisons or waived to criminal court. Thus, as the plots in Figure 6.5 show, the increasing disciplinary powers of the juvenile court come to supplant the powers of parents during the teenage years. However, in terms of how that power is wielded, the power of the juvenile court is much more formal and costly, and therefore invoked more sparingly. The court itself cannot act anything like a parent in dealing with an acting-out juvenile. If parents can be said to work on their children like sculptors, the juvenile court can be thought of as resorting to an axe.

Conclusion

This paper has attempted to explore the various relationships between parenting, delinquent behavior, and the juvenile court. We have shown that parental characteristics and parenting practices are among the best early predictors of subsequent delinquent behavior. Ineffective parenting and inadequate socialization are at the core of most modern theories of delinquency causation. We have also attempted to demonstrate that although inadequate or improper parenting, in the form of excessive or inconsistent discipline or inadequate care, increases the likelihood of subsequent delinquent behavior or emotional problems considerably, these parental inadequacies are not likely to be discovered nor are they even the concern of social agencies, unless they are so aggravated that the child requires extensive medical care.

It seems that society now accepts inadequate and incompetent parenting as the lesser of two evils; the other evil being excessive intrusion by the state into private family concerns. It may well be that one reason that we accept the lack of adequate parenting is that we fail to attribute all of the negative consequences that result from it to their proper cause. Because it is methodologically simpler and politically expedient, we prefer causal explanations for delinquent behavior that are more contemporaneous with the observed behavior—such as smoking pot or hanging out with delinquent peers—rather than tracing it back farther in the developmental process.

The treatment evaluation literature of the past 20 years suggests that once delinquency has become chronic behavior, it is not easily changed. The recidivism rate for juveniles with five or more arrests, and for graduates of most state training schools, remains extremely high. No matter what advances these juveniles appear to make while in well-structured programs, many appear to revert to earlier behavioral patterns and methods in dealing with problems after they are back in their communities. The end result of this process is the acceptance by society of longer terms of incarceration for those who can't make it, and a burgeoning population of adult prison inmates.

A serious reexamination of parenting policy and its relationship to juvenile delinquency requires additional knowledge in several areas. We need to know more about the quality of parenting now being received by children in high risk families and steps that might be taken to improve it. We need to explore alternative methods of screening for inadequate or marginal care, as well as programatic techniques for raising its level once it has been determined to be insufficient.

Given the consequences of inadequate parenting, it would seem that the state might exert at least as much regulatory power among prospective parents as it does among prospective drivers of motor vehicles. In fact, something like driver's education may very well be the most desirable way to go. But the financial incentives have to be there to make it work. For instance, AFDC payments for young mothers might be made contingent on completing a course in child care, or certain health benefits might be contingent on attending such a course. Without such efforts, it appears that the problems of multi-risk families will be with us for some time to come.

Endnotes

1. The difference in prevalence of criminal acts between boys and girls, as measured by official arrest statistics, is on the order of 4 to 1, (U.S. Dept. of Justice, 1983). Whether or not girls display any of the early behavioral warning signs with the same frequency as boys and, if they do, why their antisocial behavior is curbed, remains a matter of some uncertainty. Participation in serious criminal behavior is predominantly a male behavior. Whether or not the difference in participation rates between the sexes is primarily a reflection of biological temperament, capabilities, or socializing influences is at this point unknown. Some studies show high levels of testosterone associated with higher rates of criminality among boys.
2. Farrington developed a "Burgess Scale" consisting of 7 factors, all equally weighted, in order to see how accurately the chronics could be identified. The seven factors were: (1) rated troublesome by teachers at age 8–10; (2) conduct disorder; (3) acting out; (4) social handicap; (5) criminal parents; (6) poor parental childrearing practices; and (7) low I.Q. Applying this scale to all 411 boys at age 13, 55 boys scored 4 or higher. These 55 included 15 of the 23 chronics, 22 others who were convicted at least once, and 18 who were never convicted. Limiting the prediction sample to only those boys who were convicted as youths and using the following variables in a logistic regression model, Farrington obtained the following results: Of the 17 youths with the highest predicted probability of becoming chronic, 14 were chronics. Lowering the threshold to predict 23 chronics (the same number as there actually were) still only identified 14 true chronics. Of 34 youths first convicted before age 13, 14 became chronics; 13 of these were among the 14 predicted above.

References

Bandura, A. (1968). *Principles of behavior modification*. New York: Holt, Rinehart and Winston.

Bandura, A. (1977). *Social learning theory*. Englewood Cliffs, NJ: Prentice-Hall.

Chaiken, J., and Chaiken, M. R. (1982, August). *Varieties of criminal behavior*. The Rand Corporation, R-2814-NIJ.

Cloward, R. A., and Ohlin, L. (1960). *Delinquency and opportunity: A theory of delinquent gangs*. New York: Free Press.

Cohen, A. K. (1955). *Delinquent boys: The culture of the gang*. New York: Free Press.

Cohen, J. (1983). Incapacitation as a strategy for crime control: Possibilities and pitfalls. In N. Morris and M. Tonry, (Eds.). *Crime and justice: An annual review of literature, 4*. Chicago: University of Chicago Press.

Empey, L. M. T. (1981). Constructing crime: Evolution and implications of sociological theory. In Martin, S. M., L. B. Sechrest, and R. Redner, (Eds.). *New directions in the rehabilitation of criminal offenders*. Washington, D.C.: National Academy Press.

Farrington, D. P. (1979). Longitudinal research on crime and delinquency. In N. Morris and M. Tonry (Eds.). *Crime and justice: An annual review of research, 1*. Chicago: University of Chicago Press.

Farrington, D. P. (1983, June). *Further analyses of a longitudinal survey of crime and delinquency*. Cambridge, England: Institute of Criminology.

Farrington, D. P., and West, D. J. (1977). The Cambridge study in delinquency development. Cambridge, England: Institute of Criminology.
Freier, M. (1985). The biological bases of criminal behavior. In P. W. Greenwood (Ed.). *The Juvenile Rehabilitation Reader: Chap. VI.* The Rand Corporation, N-2236-OJJDP.
Freier, M. (1986). The biological bases of criminal behavior. In P. W. Greenwood (Ed.), *Intervention Strategies For Chronic Juvenile Offenders: Some New Perspectives* (pp. 149–180). Westport, CT: Greenwood Press.
Freud, S. (1963). *An outline of psychoanalysis.* New York: Norton.
Goddard, H. H. (1914). *Feeblemindedness: Its causes and consequences.* New York: Macmillan.
Goring, C. (1913). *The English convict.* London: His Majesty's Stationery Office.
Harmeling, J. D., and Jones, M. B. (1968). Birth weights of high school dropouts. *American Journal of Orthopsychiatry, 38,* 63–66.
Hirschi, T. (1969). *Causes of delinquency.* Berkeley, CA: University of California Press.
Loeber, R., and Dishion, T. (1983). Early predictors of male delinquency: A review. *Psychological Bulletin, 94*(1), 68–99.
Lombroso, C. (1918). *Crime: Its causes and remedies.* Boston: Little Brown.
McCord, J. (1979). Some child-rearing antecedents of criminal behavior in adult men. *Journal of Personality and Social Psychology, 37,* 1477–1486.
Mednick, S. and Volavka, J. (1980). Biology and crime. In N. Morris and M. Tonry, (Eds.). *Crime and justice: An annual review of research, II.*
Miller, W. B. (1958, Summer). Lower class culture as a generating milieu of gang delinquency. *Journal of Social Issues, 14.*
Monahan, J. (1981). *The clinical prediction of violent behavior.* Rockville, Maryland: National Institute of Mental Health.
Osborn, S. G., and West, D. J. (1978). The effectiveness of various predictors of criminal careers. *Journal of Adolescence, 1.*
Patterson, G. R. (1982). *A social learning approach* (Vol. 3), Eugene, OR: Castalia Publishing Company.
Patterson, G. R., Chamberlain, P., and Reid, J. B. (1982). A comparative evaluation of a parent-training program. *Behavior Therapy, 13,* 638–650.
Quinney, R. (1974). *Criminal justice in America.* Boston: Little, Brown.
Robins, L. N. (1966). *Deviant children grow up: A sociological and psychiatric study of a sociopathic personality.* Baltimore: Williams and Williams.
Robins, L. N., and Wish, E. (1977). Childhood deviance as a developmental process. *Social Forces, 56,* 448–473.
Rydell, C. P. (1986). The economics of early intervention versus later incarceration. In P. W. Greenwood (Ed.), *Intervention Strategies for Chronic Juvenile Offenders: Some New Perspectives* (pp. 235–258). Westport, CT: Greenwood Press.
Shannon, L. (1978; 1983, January). *The prediction problem as it applies to delinquency and crime control.* Department of Justice, Juvenile Justice and Delinquency Prevention. *Science, 199,* 563–564.
Shaw, C. R., and McKay, H. D. (1931). Social factors in juvenile delinquency. *Report of the National Commission on Law Observance and Enforcement (Wickersham Commission).* (No. 13, Vol. 2). Washington, D.C.: U.S. Government Printing Office.

Shaw, C. R., and McKay, H. D. (1942). *Juvenile delinquency and urban areas.* Chicago: University of Chicago Press.

Shaw, C. R., and McKay, H. D. (1969). *Juvenile delinquency and urban areas.* (Rev. Ed.). Chicago: University of Chicago Press.

Sutherland, E. H., and Cressey, D. R. (1955). *Principles of criminology,* (5th Ed.). Philadelphia: Lippincott.

U.S. Department of Justice. (1983). *Uniform Crime Report,* 1982. Washington, D.C.: U.S. Government Printing Office.

Wolfgang, M., Figlio, R. M. and Sellin, T. (1972). *Delinquency in a birth cohort.* Chicago: University of Chicago Press.

Yochelson, S., and Samenow, S. E. (1976). *The criminal personality: A profile for change.* (Vol. I). New York: Jason Aronson.

Yochelson, S., and Samenow, S. E. (1977). A new horizon for total change of the criminal. In *The criminal personality: The change process.* (Vol. II). New York: Jason Aronson.

Section III
Socializing Children: Concrete Problems, Now and in the Future

7
Trends in Child Abuse and Juvenile Delinquency

PHILIP J. COOK AND JOHN H. LAUB

Our main purpose is to project the volume of juvenile crime and of child abuse over the next 10 to 15 years. Such projections are necessary as a guide to planning capacity changes in the juvenile court and corrections.

Demographic trends indicate that the current decline in the relevant youth population (aged 13–17) will reverse circa 1990, and this population will be about the same in 1995 as in 1985. Our best guess is that the volume of youth crime will follow the same pattern, although we are inclined to emphasize the uncertainty attached to this prediction. The volume of child abuse is still more difficult to project.

These projections do not have a direct implication for the future capacity "requirements" of the juvenile court. The volume of youth crime and child abuse vastly exceeds the number of cases processed by the court. Implicit policy judgments about which cases should be referred to the court (rather than diverted), and how much of the court's resources should be devoted to each case, are perhaps more important in determining the future capacity needs of the court than is the volume of potential cases. Section 2 includes a statistical characterization of current practices with respect to case processing. These practices differ widely among jurisdictions. We make no effort to project future policy, but rather simply note that future capacity requirements will be influenced by social values as much as by the volume and nature of juvenile crime and child abuse.

The section of this chapter entitled "Recent Trends in Delinquency and Abuse and Neglect" describes recent trends in youth crime and child abuse. The period between 1965–1971 was one of rapidly increasing juvenile arrest rates per capita. During the subsequent years (1971–1983), arrest rates have been more or less constant at the high level reached in 1971. One basis for projecting the future volume of juvenile crime is to assume that this recent plateau in arrest rates per capita will extend for another 10 to 15 years.

It is more difficult to measure recent trends in the prevalence of serious child abuse and neglect. The per capita rate of court referrals for such cases was roughly constant for 30 years but jumped markedly after 1980. There is some evidence that this increase reflects increased public concern about child abuse rather than an increase in its prevalence.

The section of this chapter entitled "Trends in Family Characteristics" presents information on recent trends in the conditions under which children are being raised and educated in the United States. One conclusion from these statistics is that the continuing deterioration in family life is not necessarily predictive of increasing levels of pathology among youths—indeed, some social indicators show improvement since 1980. Given this evidence, we conclude that juvenile crime rates per capita may remain at current levels or even decline over the next 10 to 15 years. Our projections of the volume of youth crime and child abuse follow.

The Funnel Effect

In the juvenile justice system (JJS), as in the criminal justice system, the volume of cases that are within the jurisdiction of the court vastly exceeds the volume of cases actually adjudicated. This case selection process is characterized below for both delinquency cases and abuse and neglect cases. The main lesson from the statistics presented here is that the observed workload of the JJS is the cumulative result of a series of decisions made by JJS authorities. Since the potential workload is far larger than the observed workload at any point in time, it is reasonable to claim that the workload in a jurisdiction is a matter of choice (or de facto policy) rather than being dictated by exogenous circumstances.

Processing Juvenile Delinquency Cases

While national statistics on the processing of juvenile delinquency cases are not routinely available, there have been several recent efforts to piece together the available statistics and estimate the aggregate volume of cases at each step in the process.

There are untold millions of delinquent acts committed each year, ranging from truancy to murder. Only a small fraction of these acts result in any official intervention by the police or the juvenile court. Most cases result in no action at all, or are dealt with by the delinquent's family, neighborhood, or school. Even when the police are called in, they are more likely to "handle" the case in the field rather than make an arrest (Black, 1971). Nevertheless, approximately two million juveniles are arrested each year. It is at this point in the process that we begin to have credible estimates of the nationwide volume of cases.

Black and Smith (1981) estimate that 2.3 million juveniles were arrested in 1977. About half (51%) of these cases were referred to court intake, with most of the others being handled on an informal basis within the police department. The million plus cases that are referred by law enforcement agencies constitute about 80% of all delinquency cases referred to the juvenile court each year.

The national statistics on sources of referral and ultimate disposition of delinquency cases for 1981 are depicted in Figure 7.1, taken from Snyder, Finnegan, and Hutzler (1983). Based on their data we can conclude that for every 1,000 delinquency cases referred to the juvenile court, the distribution of dispositions is approximately this:

507 dismissed
282 probation
64 state or local institution
18 public or private agency
9 waived to adult court
120 other

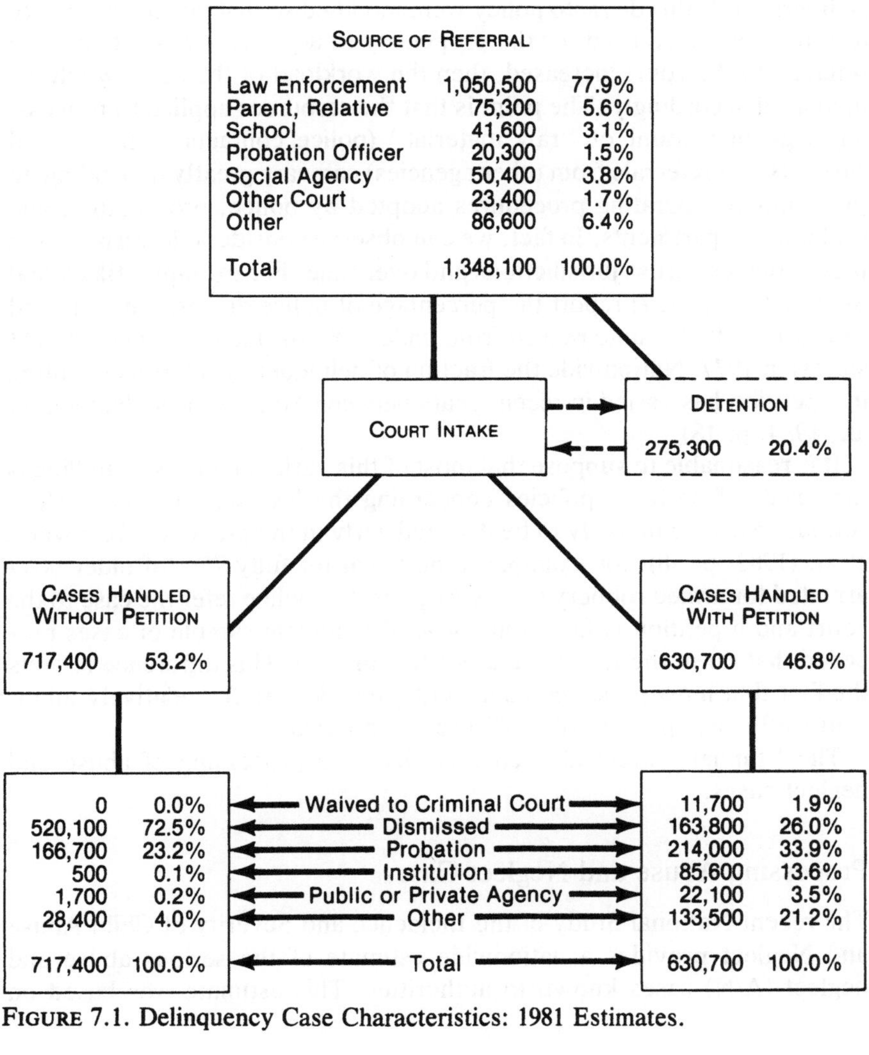

FIGURE 7.1. Delinquency Case Characteristics: 1981 Estimates.

Most of those cases that are ultimately dismissed are handled without petition, which is to say they are dealt with informally by a probation officer or other court official and are not placed on the official court calendar for adjudication.

These statistics on the "funnel" effect can be quickly summarized. First, the police handle an unknown but large number of youthful suspects in the field without an arrest. Of the two million youths who are arrested each year, only half are referred to the juvenile court. Approximately half of these referrals are formally adjudicated. The most common disposition of a case referred to the juvenile court is dismissal, with some sort of formal or informal probation arrangement for most of the remaining cases. A sentence to a state or local institution is a relatively rare event.

Clearly the norm at each of the important decision points in the process is diversion. If this de facto policy were modified so that police propensity to refer cases increased, or the propensity to adjudicate cases that were referred to the court increased, then the workload of the court would be increased accordingly. The point is that the resources applied to processing a given amount of "raw material" (police contacts with youthful suspects and referrals from other agencies) can vary greatly depending on the standard operating procedures adopted by police, prosecutors, and probation departments. In fact, we can observe considerable variations in these policies across jurisdictions and over time. For example, Black and Smith (1981, p. 127) report the percentage of police dispositions referred to court intake by state ranged from under 30% (6 states) to over 70% (11 states) in 1977. Nationwide the fraction of delinquency referrals resulting in a petition has varied in recent years between 41% and 54% (Nimick, et al., 1984, p. 18).

It is reasonable to suppose that most of this variation in case handling is the result of de facto policies concerning the less serious cases. Very serious cases are unlikely to be diverted early in the process. Greenwood et al. (1983, p. 38), for example, report that for fully 75% of older boys arrested for armed robbery in Los Angeles, the police refer the case to the court and a petition is filed; only 38% of a random sample of cases proceded that far in the Los Angeles system in 1980. This difference reflects the fact that most police contacts with juveniles are for relatively minor status offenses, public order offenses, and larceny.

The "funnel" effect also characterizes the processing of abuse and neglect cases.

Processing Abuse and Neglect Cases

The recent National Study of the Incidence and Severity of Child Abuse and Neglect provides a nationwide estimate of the serious abuse and neglect (A/N) cases known to authorities. This estimate was based on data collected from 26 counties in 10 states during the period from May 1979 to April 1980. Based on this sample, the study generated an estimate of 625,000 serious cases nationwide, or 10.5 per 1,000 children under age 18. The study's standard for including a case in their estimate was quite strict: the case had to involve evidence of clear-cut and serious maltreatment causing avoidable injury, illness, or emotional/behavioral impairment, resulting from purposive acts or extreme inattention by a parent or other adult caretaker. Also included were cases of repeated truancy or delinquency if the child's guardian knew about the situation but refused to take any action.

The estimated population of cases were about evenly divided between abuse and neglect, as shown by these rates:

Abuse	5.7/1,000	Neglect	5.3/1,000
Physical	3.4	Physical	1.7
Sexual	.7	Educational	2.9
Emotional	2.2	Emotional	1.0

Of the 625,000 estimated cases, only about one-third were known to child protective services agencies.[1] The remainder were found in the files of other investigating agencies or from records kept by schools, hospitals, and other agencies dealing with children.

During the 12-month period covered by this study, we know from other sources that there were only about 160,000 A/N cases disposed of in juvenile court. Approximately 75% of these cases resulted in a petition for adjudication (Nimick et al., 1984). It is not possible from the available data to estimate how many of the cases referred to the court would have met the standard for inclusion in the National Incidence Study estimate. We can conclude that *no more than* one in four serious A/N cases known to some public agency are referred to the court. And of course there are many serious cases that are not known to any public agency.

The number of A/N cases referred to the court in a jurisdiction will vary as a function of local concern about child abuse and acceptance of formal intervention by the court as an appropriate response.

Recent Trends in Delinquency and Abuse and Neglect

The statistics presented in the previous section document the fact that most delinquency cases and A/N cases are diverted from the JJS early in the process—in the field or the station house or at court intake processing for delinquency cases, and by social service agencies and other public agencies for A/N cases. Thus the court makes little or no investment of its resources in most of the cases that come to the attention of the police or other authorities. The court's resources are concentrated on the relatively few cases—usually the most serious—that are allowed to penetrate the system to the point of formal adjudication and an expensive disposition such as commitment to a training school or removal to a foster home. The resource requirements of the system are thus determined to a large extent by the de facto policies governing screening and diversion of cases at each point in the process. Any prediction of the future resource requirements of the system must be made contingent on a characterization of these policies.

Our concern here is not to predict the evolution of policy governing the processing of juvenile court cases, but rather to predict the trend in the volume of potential cases—crimes committed by juveniles, and instances of child abuse and neglect. The average amount of resources the court should devote to each type of case is ultimately a value judgment, one that has changed markedly over the last two decades and will continue to evolve. The implications of our predictions of future rates of delinquency and child abuse for JJS resource requirements are not direct, but rather conditioned on the evolution of societal values.

The place to begin in predicting the future volume of cases is with a look at recent trends in delinquency and child abuse. This section reports statistics characterizing these trends from 1965 to 1983. Subsequent sections consider several factors that may influence future rates of delinquency, and offer some projections.

Trends in Juvenile Crime and Arrests

The most commonly used indicator of the volume of juvenile criminal activity as it intersects with the JJS is the arrest rate for youths aged 17 or less. An alternative indicator is the rate of juvenile court dispositions for delinquency cases. Table 7.1 displays these indicators for the years since 1965. Both increase by about 50% during the first ten years of this period, with the arrest rate remaining at approximately double the court disposition rate. The two indicators diverge after 1974: the court disposition rate continues to increase rapidly until 1980, whereas the arrest rate declines somewhat after its 1974 peak. Since 1980 the arrest rate for youths aged 10–17 has been about 70 per 1,000, while the court disposition rate has been about 44 per 1,000.

Table 7.2 exhibits trends in arrest rates for the 13–17 age group, the group that is responsible for the great bulk of youth crime. Their overall arrest rate exceeded 100 per 1,000 for most of the years since 1971. About 37% of these arrests have been for the "Index" crimes of violence (criminal homicide, aggravated assault, robbery, rape) and against property (burglary, auto theft, larceny, arson). The most notable thing about these arrest rates is their low variance since 1971.

Interestingly, this stability in arrest rates for youths has been associated with a rather sharp reduction in their relative importance in the overall crime picture. As shown in Table 7.3, violence arrests of youths under 18

TABLE 7.1. Delinquency arrests and juvenile court dispositions per 1,000 youths aged 10–17, 1965–1983.

	Total arrests per 1,000 youths aged 10–17*	Juvenile court dispositions per 1,000 youths aged 10–17
1965	49.3	23.6
1966	50.2	24.7
1967	55.2	26.3
1968	60.1	28.5
1969	62.8	30.7
1970	65.4	31.7
1971	68.9	33.4
1972	66.9	32.8
1973	66.5	33.5
1974	76.8	36.6
1975	72.0	38.8
1976	71.3	42.3
1977	71.6	42.2
1978	75.6	42.1
1979	74.8	43.4
1980	70.1	46.4
1981	70.3	44.0
1982	74.1	43.2
1983	68.4	n.a.

Source: Arrest statistics are from the FBI's *Crime in the United States,* various issues. Juvenile Court dispositions are from the National Center for Juvenile Justice, *Juvenile Court Statistics, 1982* Pittsburgh, 1985.

* Note that the youth age categories in the UCR have changed over time. From 1965 to 1979, the age category included: "10 & under," "11–12," and single years throughout for those arrestees 13 to 17. Since 1980, the age category includes: "Under 10," "10 to 12," and single years for those arrestees aged 13 to 17. Therefore, in the arrest rates for 1965 to 1979, the number of arrests attributable to 11 to 17 year olds was used as the numerator of the rate. Since very few arrestees are 10 or younger, the effect is minimal.

dropped from over 23% of the total in 1975 to 17% in 1983. Property crime arrests for youths dropped from over 50% of the total to 34% in 1983. This decline is a consequence of the large baby boom cohorts aging out of the juvenile court jurisdiction. The result is that the JJS is responsible for a somewhat smaller piece of the crime problem in the mid-1980s than it was in the 1960s and early 1970s.

A final intertemporal pattern of some interest is the relative arrest rate for black and white youths, as shown in Table 7.4. The black arrest rate for Index crimes has been several times as high as the white arrest rate throughout this period. This difference peaked about 1970, with a black/white ratio of about 3.0 for property crimes and over 11.0 for violent

Table 7.2. Arrest rates for youths aged 13–17 per 1,000 population, 1965–1983.

	Total arrests	Total index crime arrests[1,2]	Property index crime arrests[1]	Violent index crime arrests[2]
1965	73.5	26.9	24.8	2.1
1966	74.6	26.8	24.5	2.3
1967	82.3	28.7	26.1	2.6
1968	89.5	30.1	27.3	2.8
1969	93.6	31.8	28.6	3.1
1970	97.4	33.2	29.9	3.3
1971	101.9	34.8	31.1	3.7
1972	98.1	33.5	29.7	3.8
1973	97.5	34.1	30.2	3.9
1974	111.3	42.5	38.0	4.6
1975	103.9	40.0	35.5	4.4
1976	102.0	37.9	33.8	4.0
1977	101.5	37.5	33.6	4.0
1978	106.9	39.7	35.1	4.6
1979	106.8	39.8	35.4	4.4
1980	101.0	38.2	33.7	4.5
1981	102.4	37.3	32.8	4.5
1982	108.0	38.2	33.5	4.7
1983	97.9	35.7	31.3	4.4

Source: Arrest statistics compiled by the FBI, adjusted for population coverage of reporting units.

1. Includes arson, auto theft, burglary, and larceny.

2. Includes aggravated assault, murder and non-negligent homicide, rape, and robbery.

Table 7.3. Arrests for children under 18 (UCR data).

	Percent of all arrests	Percent of index crime arrests*	Percent of violent index crime arrests	Percent of property index crime arrests*
1965	21.4%	48.8	19.7	55.2
1966	22.9	49.5	20.4	56.5
1967	24.3	49.1	21.3	55.7
1968	25.9	48.9	22.0	55.3
1969	25.6	47.8	22.3	54.1
1970	25.3	46.2	22.6	51.8
1971	25.8	45.4	22.8	50.9
1972	25.6	44.6	22.6	50.6
1973	26.4	44.8	22.7	50.9
1974	27.2	45.2	22.6	50.8
1975	25.9	43.2	23.1	48.1
1976	24.9	41.6	22.0	46.2
1977	24.0	41.3	21.0	46.3
1978	23.3	40.5	21.4	45.5
1979	22.5	38.8	20.1	43.5
1980	20.9	35.9	19.3	40.2
1981	19.8	33.5	18.5	37.4
1982	17.9	30.9	17.2	34.5
1983	16.8	30.4	16.8	33.9

* Includes arson.

TABLE 7.4. Ratios of black arrest rates to white arrest rates for youths aged less than 18.

	All index crimes	Property crimes	Violent crimes
1965	2.9	2.7	10.4
1966	2.9	2.7	9.8
1967	3.1	2.8	11.1
1968	3.2	2.9	10.4
1969	3.3	3.0	11.4
1970	3.3	2.9	11.1
1971	3.1	2.7	11.4
1972	3.0	2.6	10.4
1973	2.7	2.4	8.5
1974	2.6	2.3	7.8
1975	2.4	2.1	6.6
1976	2.5	2.2	6.6
1977	2.5	2.2	6.0
1978	2.5	2.2	6.6
1979	2.3	2.1	5.7
1980	2.4	2.1	6.1
1981	2.4	2.1	6.4
1982	2.6	2.3	6.4
1983	2.6	2.2	6.7

Source: FBI
Note: Each entry in the table is the ratio of the black arrest rate per capita to the white arrest rate per capita for youths 17 or younger.

crimes. Since 1975 those ratios have been relatively constant at about 2.2 and 6.5 respectively.

It should be acknowledged that arrest trends are not necessarily reliable indicators of the underlying trends in juvenile crime rates. The likelihood that a crime will result in a recorded arrest depends on a number of factors—the propensity of victims to report crimes to the police and request that the police intervene formally if there is a known suspect, the police department's standard operating procedure for dealing with juvenile suspects, and so forth. If the likelihood that a crime results in arrest changes over time, then to that extent the arrest trend misrepresents the underlying trend in juvenile crime.[2] There are two reasons why this potential problem is not of great concern in the present context. First, the arrest rate is a more direct determinant of the juvenile court's workload than the crime rate, and hence more directly relevant to our inquiry. Second, estimates of the volume of youthful crimes of violence for the period 1973–1982, generated from National Crime Survey data, are quite compatible with the arrest trends reported above (Laub, 1983).

To summarize, the annual statistics on juvenile arrests changed rapidly during the period 1965–1971, and have been relatively static since then. This characterization applies to overall arrest rates and arrest rates for both property and violent Index crimes. If it is reasonable to project that the arrest rate "plateau" will continue for another decade, then predicting the volume of juvenile arrests for 1995 is simply a matter of multiplying the projected juvenile population in that year by the "plateau" value of the arrest rate.

Trends in Abuse and Neglect Rates

Judging by the statistics compiled by Nimick et al. (1985), the volume of A/N cases handled by the court varied remarkably little between 1950 and 1975, remaining throughout this period at a rate of 2.0 ± .3 per 1,000 children under 18. There has been some increase since then, with peak rates of 2.9 in 1981 and 2.7 in 1982. Russell and Trainor (1984) report a much larger increase in the volume of cases reported to child protective services during this period; this reporting rate doubled from 10.1 per 1,000 children in 1976, to 20.1 in 1982. The authors explain this increase by noting the greatly increased public attention and resources devoted to child abuse during this period, resulting in an increased likelihood that suspected abuse or neglect victims would be reported to the relevant authorities.

Given the recent volatility in reporting rates for A/N cases, it is of interest to know whether there has been much change in the prevalence of maltreatment. One indicator of the prevalence of physical abuse is the criminal homicide rate of young children. A majority of homicide victims aged four and under are killed by relatives, suggesting that these cases are the logical extreme outcome of physical abuse in the home. The victimization series depicted in Table 7.5 for the period 1965–1982 suggests that homicide rates trended sharply upward during the period 1965–1973. For children aged 1–4 the victimization rate reached 2.5 per 100,000 in 1973. It has remained close to this level through 1982, the most recent year for which these data are available. A recent study (Jason, Carpenter, and Tyler, 1983) suggests that a number of criminal homicides of infants have been classified as deaths resulting from "Injury undetermined whether accidentally or purposefully inflicted" since that category was introduced in 1968. The addition of this category to the homicide category (in the last column of Table 7.5) does not much affect our conclusion regarding trends for the victim group aged 1–4. This correction is more important for the series on homicides involving victims less than one year, since it helps explain the large drop in the infant homicide rate between 1967 and 1968. Further, what emerges is a pattern quite similar to that of the victimization rates for older children.

If the homicide rate for young children is a valid proxy for the prevalence of serious physical abuse, then we are left wondering about the

TABLE 7.5. Homicide victimization rates per 100,000 for children less than 5.

	Infants		Children aged 1–4	
	Homicide	Homicide and undetermined	Homicide	Homicide and undetermined
1965	5.5	—	1.1	—
1966	5.8	—	1.2	—
1967	6.4	—	1.1	—
1968	4.8	7.7	1.4	2.4
1969	4.3	7.9	1.6	2.8
1970	4.3	7.9	1.9	3.2
1971	5.1	8.2	2.1	3.4
1972	5.2	8.1	1.8	3.1
1973	5.2	8.1	2.5	3.6
1974	5.5	9.1	2.2	3.5
1975	5.8	8.9	2.5	3.6
1976	5.6	9.0	2.5	3.6
1977	5.6	8.9	2.7	3.8
1978	5.0	7.6	2.6	3.5
1979	5.2	7.8	2.5	3.3
1980	5.9	7.8	2.5	3.3
1981	6.1	8.4	2.6	3.2
1982	6.7	8.7	2.7	3.2

Sources: Public Health Service, National Center for Health Statistics, *Vital Statistics of the United States, Vol. II Mortality* Part A, various years. The data for 1980–1982 is currently unpublished, and was communicated by NCHS staff by telephone, 5/1/85.
Definitions: "Homicide and Undetermined" is the sum of the homicide victimization rate and the death rate due to "Injury undetermined whether accidentally or purposefully inflicted."

disparity between the trends in this rate and the court referral statistics—which exhibit little movement between 1965 and 1973, and a sharp increase in 1981.

In conclusion, there is no reliable evidence to suggest that the rate of serious child abuse and neglect has been increasing since, say, 1975. What is clear, however, is that the public and government agencies have become more sensitive to the problem of child abuse in recent years. The volume of reports to child protective agencies and court referrals have increased substantially since the mid-1970s. Whether this trend will continue is difficult to judge.

Trends in Family Characteristics

Juvenile arrest rates per 1,000 have not varied much since the early 1970s. Our best guess for the juvenile arrest rate in 1995 and beyond is that it will remain on the same "plateau" as in recent years, simply because we have no strong reason for thinking it will move either up or down. This section considers and rejects one possible argument for suggesting that juvenile crime and arrest rates will in fact increase during the next decade: the continuing decline in the stability and resources provided children by their parents.

It seems only common sense that children will be less prone to delinquency if they are raised in a stable home environment providing a high level of adult supervision, guidance, and support than otherwise. Indeed, it has long been known that a disproportionate number of delinquents are from single parent and/or low income households. This observation suggests that the increase in the proportion of children raised in households that lack the parenting and economic resources of the "traditional" middle-class nuclear family will lead to a corresponding increase in youthful involvement in crime. As far as we can tell from the available data, this increase has not occurred, at least for the period since 1970

There are various indicators of the decline of the nuclear family. First is the fraction of births that are out-of-wedlock (Table 7.6). This fraction stood at 4.5% for the 1955 cohort, which reached its most active delinquent phase in 1970–71. The 1965–67 cohorts, which reached their most active phase in the early 1980s, included nearly twice this percentage of illegitimate births. (The non-white illegitimacy percentage is much higher than the white percentage, and increased from 20 to 30 percent between 1955 and 1967.)

The period since 1970 has also been characterized by a gradual decline

TABLE 7.6. Trends in out-of-wedlock births and births to young women.

	Out-of-wedlock births as percent of all births				Births to women under 20 as percent of all births
	Total	White	Non-white	Black	
1950	3.9	1.7	16.8	—	12.1
1955	4.5	2.1	19.4	—	12.2
1960	5.3	2.7	21.6	—	14.0
1965	7.7	4.0	26.3	—	15.9
1970	10.7	5.7	34.9	37.6	17.6
1973	13.0	6.4	41.7	45.8	19.7
1974	13.2	6.5	42.7	47.1	19.2
1975	14.2	7.3	44.2	48.8	18.9
1976	14.8	7.7	45.2	50.3	18.0
1977	15.5	8.2	46.5	51.7	17.2
1978	16.3	8.7	47.6	53.2	16.6
1979	17.1	9.4	48.8	54.6	16.0
1980	18.4	11.0	48.4	55.2	
1981	18.9	11.6	48.5	56.0	
1982	19.4	12.1	48.8	56.7	

Source: National Center for Health Statistics, *Vital Statistics of the U.S., Vol. 1 Natality* and unpublished data from NCHS.

TABLE 7.7. Percent of children under 18 living with both parents and percent with mothers in the labor force.

	Percent living with both parents			Percent with mothers in labor force
	Total	White	Black	
1970	85	89	58	39
1971	83	88	54	39
1972	83	88	54	40
1973	82	87	52	41
1974	81	87	51	42
1975	80	85	49	44
1976	80	85	50	46
1977	79	85	47	48
1978	78	84	44	50
1979	77	84	43	52
1980	77	83	42	53
1981	76	82	43	54
1982	75	81	42	55
1983	75	81	41	55
1984	75	81	41	56

Sources: 1. *Statistical Abstract of the U.S., 1982–83*, Table 76.
2. Current Population Report p. 20 No. 389 "Marital Status and Living Arrangements": March 1983.
3. Bureau of Labor Statistics, *Handbook of Labor Statistics*.

in the percentage of children living with two parents (Table 7.7). For all children, this percentage dropped from 85% to 75% between 1970 and 1982; for black children, the percentage dropped from 58% to 42%. During this same period the percentage of children with mothers in the labor force increased from 39% to 55%.

These indicators suggest a substantial decline in the percentage of children raised to adulthood by both natural parents, and an increased percentage of children that were sharing their mother's time and energy with her job. And despite this increase in labor force participation by mothers, the percentage of children living in poor households increased somewhat between 1980 and 1983 (Table 7.8).

In looking ahead to 1995, we know that the youths in the age group of greatest delinquent activity (13–17) will be members of birth cohorts characterized by unprecedented rates of illegitimacy—for black youths the fraction is over half. This and the related trends discussed above are troublesome for a number of reasons, but recent history gives no support for the notion that this continued deterioration in the nuclear family will necessarily lead to an increase in delinquency. Indeed, there is even some slight basis for an optimistic view of the next decade in this respect. One particularly encouraging trend is the reduction in the prevalence of drug use by high school seniors since 1978 (Table 7.9).

TABLE 7.8. Percent of children under 18 living in poverty.

	Total	White	Black
1965	20	14	—
1966	17	12	51
1967	16	11	47
1968	15	11	43
1969	14	10	40
1970	15	11	42
1971	15	11	41
1972	15	10	43
1973	14	10	41
1974	15	11	40
1975	17	13	41
1976	16	11	40
1977	16	11	42
1978	16	11	41
1979	16	11	41
1980	18	13	42
1981	20	15	45
1982	21	17	47
1983	22	17	46

Sources: Current Population Reports Series P60, No. 133, Tables 1, 2; P60, No. 134, Tables 15, 16; P60, No. 145; P60, No. 147.

There is something of a sociological mystery here. We believe that the home is the primary site for "civilizing" children, and that the amount and quality of effort devoted by parents to this task appears to be declining on the average. Since there is no evidence of an increase in "uncivilized" (criminal) behavior by youths in recent years, we are encouraged to search for compensating trends in other institutions that contribute to the civilizing process. But this paper is not the right context in which to

TABLE 7.9. Reported drug use *within last 30 days* by high school seniors, 1975–1984.

Class of	Alcohol	Cigarettes	Marijuana/ Hashish	Cocaine
1975	68.2	36.7	27.1	1.9
1976	68.2	38.8	32.2	2.0
1977	71.2	38.4	35.4	2.9
1978	72.1	36.7	37.1	3.9
1979	71.8	34.4	36.5	5.7
1980	72.0	30.5	33.7	5.2
1981	70.7	29.4	31.6	5.8
1982	69.7	30.0	28.5	5.0
1983	69.4	30.3	27.0	4.9
1984	67.2	29.3	25.2	5.8

Source: *Sourcebook of Criminal Justice Statistics*, 1983, p. 360 (1975–82). 1983 and 1984 provided by Lloyd Johnston, TSR, by phone on 5/3/85.

TABLE 7.10. Trends in the adult-child population ratio.

	Ratio of adults (18–64) to children (10–17)	Ratio of white adults (18–64) to white children (10–17)	Ratio of black adults (18–64) to black children (10–17)
1965	3.57	3.68	2.80
1966	3.55	3.67	2.75
1967	3.52	3.64	2.70
1968	3.51	3.62	2.67
1969	3.50	3.61	2.66
1970	3.49	3.62	2.66
1971	3.51	3.65	2.66
1972	3.55	3.69	2.69
1973	3.60	3.75	2.72
1974	3.66	3.81	2.76
1975	3.76	3.92	2.82
1976	3.89	4.06	2.90
1977	4.03	4.22	3.01
1978	4.19	4.39	3.12
1979	4.38	4.58	3.26
1980	4.50	4.70	3.39
1981	4.64	4.85	3.51
1982	4.83	5.04	3.68
1983	5.01	5.23	3.84
Projections			
1985	5.30	5.53	4.16
1990	5.79	6.03	4.67
1995	5.43	5.68	4.26
2000	5.34	5.57	4.15

Source: Various U.S. Bureau of the Census population reports and U.S. Bureau of the Census, Current Population Reports, Series P-25, No. 952 (1984). Projections of the Population of the United States by Age, Sex, and Race: 1983–2080. Washington, D.C.: Government Printing Office.

launch such a search. For now, we simply note the trend in one indicator that may be relevant—the ratio of adults (aged 18–65) to children (aged 10–17). As shown in Table 7.10, this ratio has increased steadily since 1970, and will continue upward until the 1990s. To the extent that other adults supplement parents' efforts to guide youthful behavior, then this ratio indicates an increase in society's capacity in this respect. The adult-child ratio may also have an indirect influence on youthful behavior through its effect on popular culture, the political process, and in general the tolerance accorded youthful misbehavior. James Q. Wilson (1983, p. 38) gives a related explanation for the crime boom of the 1960s:

> Since the 1960s, an increase in the proportion of young persons in the population has been met by the celebration of the youth culture in the marketplace, in the churches, and among adults . . . This institutionalization in all parts of society of the national desire of youth for greater freedom may well have given legitimacy to all forms of self-expression—including, alas, those forms that involve crime and

violence—and thus helped magnify and sustain what would have been a crime increase in any event.

By symmetry, it is plausible that the more recent *decline* in the proportion of young persons in the population may be causing a drift away from "the youth culture."

Our position, then, is that the long plateau in juvenile arrest rates is the result of opposing trends in powerful etiological factors that have (by chance?) balanced each other for more than a decade. The future course of some of the demographic factors is quite predictable, but we have no reliable way of projecting their net influence on delinquency rates. In the interest of making some concrete projections, we assume the "balance of forces" will continue. But that assumption may prove wrong by a wide margin.

TABLE 7.11. Trends in the population aged 13–17.

	Total (millions)	White (millions)	Black (millions)
1965	17.8	15.4	2.2
1966	18.2	15.7	2.3
1967	18.6	16.0	2.4
1968	19.1	16.5	2.5
1969	19.5	16.8	2.5
1970	20.1	17.2	2.6
1971	20.5	17.5	2.7
1972	20.7	17.6	2.8
1973	20.9	17.8	2.8
1974	21.1	17.9	2.9
1975	21.1	17.8	2.9
1976	21.0	17.7	2.9
1977	20.8	17.5	2.9
1978	20.5	17.2	2.9
1979	19.9	16.6	2.9
1980	19.8	16.4	2.9
1981	19.1	15.8	2.8
1982	18.6	15.3	2.8
1983	18.4	15.1	2.7
Projections			
1985	18.1	14.9	2.7
1990	16.2	13.2	2.4
1995	17.8	14.3	2.8
2000	19.3	15.4	3.2

Source: Various U.S. Bureau of the Census population reports and U.S. Bureau of the Census, Current Population Reports, Series P-25, No. 952 (1984). Projections of the Population of the United States by Age, Sex, and Race: 1983–2080. Washington, D.C.: Government Printing Office.

Projections

Approximately 85% of arrests of youths under 18 involve teenagers age 13–17. This is the group of primary concern in generating our projections. The size of this group peaked in 1974 and has declined steadily since. By 1990 it will be 5 million less than in 1974 (a 23% reduction), but will increase thereafter through the year 2000 (Table 7.11).

Since black youths have an arrest rate more than double that of white youths, it is of some interest to note the trend in the black youth population is highly correlated with that of the white population. Blacks made up 13.7% of the population age 13–17 in 1975: this percentage increased slightly to 14.7% in 1985, and will be about 15.5% in 1995. Because there is so little change in racial population composition over this period, we ignore race in what follows.

As explained in the previous section, we project the future volume of juvenile arrests by assuming the arrest rates in future years will be the same as in recent years. The extraordinary stability of arrest rates in recent years, revealed by the statistics below, justifies this assumption. Note that during the nine year period from 1975–1983, the standard deviation for both the total arrest rate and the Index crime arrest rate was less than 4% of the mean. Extending the series back to include the 13 years from 1971–1983 has little effect on the means but does increase the standard deviations somewhat.

TABLE 7.12. Total arrests per 1,000, for ages 13–17.

	1975–1983	1971–1983
Mean	103.4	103.0
Standard dev.	3.3	4.2
Total index arrests per 1,000, for ages 13–17		
Mean	38.3	37.6
Standard dev.	1.4	2.6

Given the assumption that juvenile arrest rates will remain at the same level through the year 2000 yields the following results, based entirely on census projections of the future population of youths aged 13–17:

TABLE 7.13. Percentage change in number of juvenile arrests.

1985–1990	−10%
1985–1995	− 2%
1985–2000	+ 6%

These projections are meant to apply to total arrests as well as Index arrests. The underlying volume of serious juvenile crime should also follow this pattern.

We believe that the confidence intervals around these projections should be quite broad due to uncertainty about future arrest rates. (Relatively speaking there is very little uncertainty about the size of future populations.) For a historical precedent for the possibility of large changes, note that the Index juvenile arrest rate increased by 30% between 1966 and 1971. The possibility of a swing of this magnitude (in *either* direction) during the next few years cannot be ruled out.

We will not attempt a specific projection of the incidence of serious child abuse and neglect cases. The number of such cases reported to child protective services and/or referred to the court has been increasing rapidly in recent years, apparently as a result of the upsurge of public concern beginning in the late 1970s. The only accurately measured indicator of the trend in the actual incidence of such cases is the homicide victimization rate for young children. This rate is probably correlated with the rate of serious physical abuse (other than sexual), but may not tell us much about trends in other forms of abuse and neglect. We conclude by restating our basic conclusion that the court's workload in dealing with abuse and neglect cases is likely to be more sensitive to trends in public opinion than in the true incidence of such cases.

Endnotes

1. Only one-fifth of the cases reported to child protective service agencies were included in the overall estimate. The other cases lacked substantiation or were not considered serious enough for inclusion.
2. For a general discussion of police arrest statistics, see Sherman and Glick (1984).

References

Black, D. (1971, June). The social organization of arrest. *Stanford Law Review, 23,* 1087–1111.

Black, T. E., and Smith, C. P. (1981). *A preliminary national assessment of the numbers and characteristics of juveniles processed in the juvenile justice system.* Washington, D.C.: Natl. Inst. for Juvenile Justice and Delinquency Prevention.

Felson, M. and Gottfredson, M. (1984, August). Social indicators of adolescent activities near peers and parents. *J. of Marriage and Family,* 709–714.

Greenwood, P. W., Lipson, A. J., Abrahamse, A., and Zimring, F. (1983). *Youth crime and juvenile justice in California.* Santa Monica, CA: Rand Corp.

Jason, J., Carpenter, M. M., and Tyler, Jr., C. W. (1983). Underrecording of infant homicide in the United States. *American J. of Public Health 73*(2), 195–197.

Klepinger, D., and Weis, J. G. (1981). *Projecting arrest trends: An age, period, and cohort model.* Seattle: Center for Law and Justice, Univ. of Washington.

Laub, J. H. (1983). *Trend in juvenile criminal behavior in the United States: 1973–1981.* Albany: Hindelang Criminal Justice Research Center, SUNY.

Nimick, E. H., Dahma, L. L., Snyder, H. N., and Sullivan, D. P. (1984). *Juvenile court statistics, 1981.* Pittsburgh: National Center for Juvenile Justice.

Nimick, E. H., Dahma, L. L., Snyder H. N., and Sullivan, D. P. (1985). Juvenile court statistics, 1982. Pittsburgh: National Center for Juvenile Justice.

Russell, A., and Trainor, C. M. (1984). *Trends in child abuse and neglect: A national perspective.* Denver: The American Humane Assn.

Sherman, L., and Glick, B. (1984). *The quality of police arrest statistics.* Washington, D.C.: Police Foundation.

Smith, C. P., Alexander, P. S., Halatyn, T. V., and Roberts, C. F. (1980). *A national assessment of serious juvenile crime and the juvenile justice system: The need for a rational response. Volume II: Definition, characteristics of incidents and individuals, and relationship to substance abuse.* Washington, D.C.: Government Printing Office.

Snyder, H. N., Finnegan, T. A., and Hutzler, J. L. (1983). *Delinquency, 1981.* Pittsburgh: National Center for Juvenile Justice.

Wilson, J. Q. (1983). Crime and American culture. *The Public Interest 70,* 22–48.

U.S. Dept. of Health and Human Services, Nat'l Center on Child Abuse and Neglect (1982). *Executive summary: National study of the incidence and severity of child abuse and neglect.* Washington, D.C.: Government Printing Office.

Notes Regarding UCR Arrest Data

- The arrest rates were adjusted to take into account the varying population coverage in the Uniform Crime Reports (UCR) over the 1965 to 1983 period. Comparing the population coverage reported in the UCR annual reports with the U.S. Bureau of the Census population counts, the UCR coverage ranges from about 70% to 92% of the U.S. population over the time period in question. In order to use these UCR data, the arrest rates were adjusted each year to correct for under-coverage of the U.S. population. For more information on adjustment factors see Smith et al., (1980: 304–306).
- In 1979, arson was reclassified as an Index Crime. For the sake of comparability, the UCR data reported here *includes* arson in the total index crime category as well as in the property index crime category for each year throughout the 1965 to 1983 series.
- In 1978, the category "manslaughter by negligence" was removed from the UCR reports. For the sake of comparability, the UCR data reported here *excludes* manslaughter by negligence arrests for the years 1965 to 1977.

8
Violent Juvenile Offenders

Donna Hamparian

During the past fifteen years, violent juvenile offenders have been central to debates on the future of a separate juvenile justice system. The juvenile justice system, created at the turn of the century, was given broad discretion to deal with children with problems. It was based on the belief that juveniles are less culpable for their criminal activities than adults and that they are more amenable to treatment than hardened criminals. Thus the juvenile court was less concerned with proving guilt than it was with providing treatment to address the needs of the juvenile. In the process of identifying needs and treatment, the seriousness of the offense was not determinate.

There are several reasons why the issue of violent juvenile offenders came to the forefront in the late sixties and seventies. One is that there were more arrests for violent offenses in the United States during the 1970s than ever before in history. The perception was that juveniles accounted for most of the violent crime during that period. In fact, between 1960 and 1978 arrests of juveniles for violent crimes increased at twice the rate of arrests for adults. The explanations ranged from an increase in 16- to 19-year-olds in the population, to a response to the Vietnam War, to an increase in drug and alcohol use. The cause is open to conjecture. The reality, however, was that persons under the age of 18 accounted for between 20% and 25% of all arrests for violence during those years of high violent crime.

What Does Violent Juvenile Crime Look Like?

Patterns in Violent Juvenile Crime

Between 1960 and 1975 juvenile arrests grew by nearly 300 percent, more than twice the adult rate, with the largest growth occurring in the most violent crimes: robbery, aggravated assault, and homicide. The large increases in juvenile arrests seen in the 1960s and early 1970s began to level off in the late 1970s and then to decline slightly (Strasburg, 1984).

The juvenile population (ages 7 through 17) declined by 11% between 1970 and 1981. While the juvenile arrest rates went up between 1970 and 1975, the pattern between 1975 and 1981 showed both increases and then decreases, finishing in 1981 with a rate 5% lower than in 1975. Arrest rates for violent crime, however, have shown a different pattern. Since 1978, arrest rates for violence have held fairly steady at the relatively high rate they attained in the mid-1970s.

When we turn our attention from arrests to patterns of offending as reported in the National Crime Survey, a different conclusion about the scope of juvenile violence emerges (Strasburg, 1984). In 1981, 9.8% of all cleared violent offenses involved the arrests of persons under 18. This share of violent crimes attributed to juveniles is less than their share of the population (17%), taking the 7 to 17 age group, and only slightly larger than the population share (8.3%) for the 13- to 17-year-olds. This is much different than the juvenile share of arrests for violent crimes (17.2%). The most obvious explanation for this discrepancy is the fact that juveniles tend to commit crimes in groups, and the arrest data double counts the cleared offenses because several arrests result frequently from one violent crime.

Profile of Violent Juvenile Offenders

Only a small percentage of the juveniles who come to the attention of the juvenile justice system are arrested for violent crimes. For example, only 4% of the juveniles arrested in 1980 were arrested for a violent act, and less than 2% of juveniles are ever arrested during their juvenile years for a violent offense. The number of juveniles arrested or adjudicated delinquent for repeat violent offenses is even smaller, so small in fact, that the National Violent Offender Initiative had to change the definition of violent offender from adjudicated delinquent twice for violent offenses, to adjudicated delinquent once for a violent offense and previously adjudicated delinquent for a serious property offense, in order to have enough eligible juveniles for the violent offender programs.

These violent few—the repeat violent offender along with the violent and chronic juvenile offender—are the critical population for the juvenile justice system. The ability to deal fairly and effectively with this population will restore confidence in a separate system of justice for juveniles.

The Violent Few and the Young Criminal Years of the Violent Few

A birth cohort study of juveniles arrested for violent offenses was conducted in 1976 (Hamparian, 1978). A follow-up study tracking the violent delinquents into the adult criminal justice system was conducted in 1984 (Hamparian, 1985). These data added to several other studies conducted during this period provided much needed information about violent juvenile offenders (Strasburg, 1978; Fagan, 1985; Wolfgang, 1972; Youth Policy and Law Center, 1984).

The "violent few" cohort consisted of 1,222 members born between 1956 and 1960, arrested at least once as a juvenile for a violent[1] offense with reported continuous residence in Franklin County during their juvenile years. The two studies (Hamparian, 1978; Hamparian, 1985) describe the juvenile and adult arrests from 1962 to 1983 of the cohort—through their juvenile years to early adulthood (23 to 27 years of age). The studies looked at the relationships of age, race, sex, age of onset, progression, maturation, and termination of criminal behavior. In addition, the studies explored the issues of chronicity and severity and examined the effects of various dispositions upon future behavior over time.

The major conclusions from the two studies are:[2]

There are two groups of juvenile delinquents who are responsible for a disproportionate amount of all juvenile and adult crime by the cohort and a disproportionate amount of violent crime: the repeat violent juvenile offender and the violent and chronic juvenile offender.

The repeat index violent juvenile offender is a rare occurrence. Only 8.1% of the juveniles examined in this study have been arrested more than once for a serious violent crime. However, they accounted for over one-quarter of all such crimes committed by these juveniles. They were also more likely to become adult felony offenders than other cohort members. Over eight in ten made the transition from juvenile delinquency to the adult felony system. Even though this group of offenders recorded a large number of adult arrests, over half (55%) had no adult arrests for index violence.

The second group of juveniles who need special attention are the juveniles arrested at least once for a violent offense and arrested at least four additional times as juveniles, generally for property crimes. This group of juveniles—one-third of the total cohort—accounted for almost two-thirds of all juvenile arrests by the cohort and almost half (forty-five %) of all juvenile arrests for index violence. Not every chronic juvenile offender, even in this cohort of violent offenders, is a serious threat to the community, but this part of the cohort is responsible for far more than its share of the most serious delinquency.

In addition, three-quarters of the violent and chronic juvenile offenders became adult felony offenders. These 293 juveniles were also responsible for over half of all adult arrests by the cohort and 53% of all adult arrests for index violence.

These conclusions were based on the following findings from the "violent few" cohort studies.

1. Juvenile violent offenders were a very small fraction of the total number of age eligible juveniles—not more than 2% were arrested as juveniles for violent offenses.

2. A relatively small number of violent juvenile offenders are responsible for most of the arrests. Nearly one-third of the cohort members had five or more arrests and were responsible for two-thirds of all arrests.

3. Males and blacks are over-represented in the cohort—and males accounted for an even greater proportion of the juvenile arrests.

4. Juveniles do not typically progress from less serious to more serious crimes.

5. Violent juvenile offenders do not specialize in the types of crimes committed. Most of those with an arrest for violence do not have more than one arrest for violence.

6. Relatively few violent juvenile offenders are repeat violent offenders. Only 15.4% of the juveniles examined in this study had been arrested for more than one violent crime as juveniles—and fewer yet (8.1%) for index violence.

7. Less than one-third of the juveniles in the cohort had been sent at least once to a state juvenile correctional facility—but those youths who had been incarcerated generally had a higher arrest rate after release.

The Transition From Juvenile to Adult

The data support the view that not all violent juvenile offenders are equally likely to make the transition to the adult criminal justice system. The 721 cohort members (59.1% of the total cohort of 1,222) who made the transition from juvenile to adult felony offenders were more likely to have been:

- *Male*. Sixty percent of male juvenile offenders became adult offenders, while less than one-third of the female cohort members were arrested as adults.
- *First arrested at age 12 or younger*. The data show that nearly two-thirds of cohort members whose first arrest was at the age of 12 or before were arrested as adults, while 56% of those whose first juvenile arrest came after the age of 12 became adult offenders.
- *Chronic offenders as juveniles*. Not surprisingly, one-time juvenile offenders were less frequently arrested as adults (36.1%), while 77.5% of chronic juvenile offenders make the transition to the adult system.
- *Index violent offenders as juveniles*. Fifty-three percent of juvenile assaulters were arrested as adults, while 63.4% of juvenile index violent offenders made the transition to the adult system. Eight out of ten repeat index violent offenders became adult offenders.
- *Committed to a state juvenile correctional facility*. More than three-quarters of those juveniles who were institutionalized (76%) were arrested as adults, compared to just over half (52%) of those juveniles who had not been committed to a juvenile training school.
- *Re-arrested as juveniles at 16 or 17 years of age*. 70.3% of these individuals were arrested as adults, compared to 38.4% of those cohort members whose last juvenile arrest occurred at 15 years of age or younger. Most cohort members with adult arrests have their last juvenile arrest at

either age 16 or 17 (77%)—and their first adult arrest before age 20 (71.4%).

The Adult Experience

Four out of ten adult offenders were arrested for at least one index violent crime. This is a lower percentage than these same individuals experienced as juveniles (62%). Yet, in contrast to our findings for juvenile offenders, adults were more frequently repeat index violent offenders (15.5%), and among index violent offenders, adults were twice as likely to have three or more arrests for index violent crimes (32.1% as compared to 16.2%).

Almost half of the arrested cohort members were imprisoned as adults—over 80% were released and half were back a second time. For both juveniles and adults, rates of arrest generally increase after each incarceration and the median number of days prior to recommitment—"street time"—decreased.

Continuity of Juvenile and Adult Criminal Careers

Once arrested the likelihood of a subsequent arrest is consistently high. Eighty percent of those who had one arrest went on to a second, and 81% of those with fifteen arrests went on to a sixteenth.

More than 50% of the adult offenders were chronic juvenile offenders (with five or more juvenile arrests).

The 293 chronic juvenile offenders with an adult arrest accounted for over half of all adult arrests for index violence.

Most chronic juvenile offenders were incarcerated—54% were committed at least once to training school, and 63.5% with at least one adult arrest went to prison.

If there had been no chronic offenders (no one with more than four arrests), the number of total arrests would have been reduced by 50%.

The Response of the Justice System to Violent Juvenile Offenders

Juveniles arrested and charged with violent offenses can be handled or treated in several different ways: 1) through the juvenile justice system, 2) through the criminal justice system, 3) through a combination of the juvenile and criminal justice systems, and 4) through specialized components of the juvenile or criminal justice systems.

Most juveniles arrested for violent offenses are handled by the juvenile justice system and are processed by the juvenile justice system with little differentiation in dispositions or services based on the nature of the offense (Fagan et al., 1984; Hamparian, 1985). "Given limited resources, high caseloads and inadequate data, the juvenile justice system has, for the most part, handled violent youth much like nonviolent offenders, using treatment approaches based on theories of delinquency causation and rehabilitation which assume all delinquent acts share common causal factors and etiological roots." (Hartstone and Hansen, 1984, p. 83). In fact, programs targeted toward violent juveniles in the juvenile or adult systems are extremely rare.

There is much variation state to state on the percentage of juveniles arrested for violent crimes handled by the juvenile court/corrections system.[3] Despite the fact that there are no national data to specifically address the issue, two illustrations can be used to suggest these differences. For example, most juveniles (under 18 years of age) arrested for violent offenses in New York State are *initially* handled by the criminal justice system for three specific reasons. First, 16- and 17-year-old youths are handled as adults for any criminal act. Second, 13-year-olds arrested for murder in the second degree and 14- and 15-year-olds arrested for violent offenses, including manslaughter, aggravated assault, rape, sodomy, and robbery are excluded initially from juvenile court jurisdiction. Third, few arrests of juveniles for violent offenses involved juveniles under 14 years of age. (Nationally about 8% of all arrests of juveniles for violent offenses are of juveniles under 13 years of age; over 50% were of juveniles 16 and 17 years of age.)

In contrast, most juveniles arrested for violent crimes in Ohio are handled as juveniles. In 1981, 229 juveniles were judicially waived to criminal court in Ohio (Hamparian, 1983). Ninety of the juveniles (39.3% of those judicially waived) were transferred for a violent offense. In 1981, there were 2,140 arrests of juveniles for violent offenses. Recognizing the methodological problems in trying to relate these two pieces of information, it is still possible to conclude from the data that most juveniles arrested for violent offenses in Ohio in 1981 were handled in the juvenile justice system.

Most juveniles adjudicated delinquent for violent offenses nationally received community dispositions rather than commitment to an institution. Analysis of national juvenile court data by the National Center on Juvenile Justice showed that in 1979 juveniles disposed of for violent offenses received probation and other community sentences over 40% of the time; 18% were committed to state training schools and over one-third (36.5%) were dismissed (Snyder, 1981).

The data from the Columbus cohort study of violent juvenile offenders confirmed that of those juveniles adjudicated delinquent for violent offenses, 18.3% were committed to a state juvenile correctional facility. However, of those juveniles adjudicated delinquent for an aggravated violent offense, 53.8% were committed to a training school; those found delinquent for less serious offenses were committed less frequently—15.5% of the time (Hamparian, et al., 1978). Because violent offenses are committed much less frequently than other serious offenses, it was estimated that fewer than 20% of the youth in state training schools in 1978 had been adjudicated delinquent for violent offenses (Smith et al., 1981).

It is estimated that fewer than 20% of the juveniles arrested for violent crimes in 1978 were handled by the criminal justice system (Hamparian, 1982). There are four basic legal mechanisms by which persons under 18 years of age were treated as adults by courts and corrections in 1981:

- *Judicial waiver*. In all jurisdictions but three, juveniles may enter adult court through a judicial hearing in juvenile court.[4] A judge may waive the juvenile court's jurisdiction over a youth, finding that youth is not "amenable to treatment in the juvenile justice system and/or constitutes a threat to public safety." The juvenile may then be prosecuted in criminal court.
- *Concurrent jurisdiction*. In eight jurisdictions, the juvenile and adult courts share jurisdiction for certain offenses at certain ages.[5] Generally, the prosecutor makes the decision to charge the youth in juvenile court or criminal court.
- *Excluded offenses*. In 1981, 14 states legislatively excluded some serious offenses from juvenile jurisdiction.[6]
- *Age of jurisdiction*. The legislature, by setting the maximum age of initial juvenile court jurisdiction, defines which persons under 18 are adults for criminal prosecution. While most states have established the age of initial criminal court jurisdiction as 18, 12 states have legislated that only youth under 17 or under 16 years of age will be processed within the juvenile court.[7] Generally, when juveniles are tried in criminal court under the above provision, the youth is treated as an adult for detention, adjudication, and corrections. In 1978, over a quarter of a million juveniles were handled as adults because of a lower age of initial criminal court jurisdiction (Hamparian et al., 1982).

During the past 15 years almost every state has considered legislative changes making it easier to try violent juvenile offenders as adults. The most interesting fact, however, is that during that period *no* state has lowered its age of initial criminal court jurisdiction, and six states have increased the age from 16 or 17 to 18. For example, Maine increased the initial age of criminal court jurisdiction from 17 to 18—meaning that 17 year olds charged with any crime are initially handled in juvenile court. Alabama, Oklahoma, Florida, Maryland, and New Hampshire also raised the age of initial criminal court jurisdiction during this period. For many of the twelve states with initial criminal court jurisdiction of 16 or 17 years of age, the current age is the same as it was when the first juvenile court act was passed.

Several states have facilitated the transfer to criminal court of juveniles charged with violent offenses through the addition of excluded offense provisions by which juveniles of specified ages, charged with specific offenses, are initially charged in criminal court. New York, Vermont, Oklahoma, and Idaho have adopted such provisions, and many other states have considered such changes.

Several states have adopted mandatory transfer provisions that require judicial transfer to criminal court of juveniles charged with specific offenses at specified ages if probable cause is established in juvenile court (Connecticut, Minnesota, and Virginia). These provisions do not require amenability hearings (see Minnesota State Ann., section 13:1571.1). Another change in the judicial waiver provision that has been considered by several states is similar to the one adopted by California in 1977 which requires the juvenile to prove fitness to remain in the juvenile justice system instead of requiring the state to prove unfitness prior to transfer to criminal court (California Welfare and Institutions Code, Article 14, Section 707).

And, finally, several states have changed the purpose clause of the juvenile code to make the juvenile accountable for his or her behavior and to provide for the protection of society. These changes facilitate the transfer of first time juvenile offenders charged with violent offenses (see Washington Revised Code, section 1340.010(2)).

While several states have made it easier to transfer violent juvenile offenders to criminal court, there are no data to suggest that this has had a positive effect on violent crime, public safety, or on the youth involved.

Correctional Options for Juveniles Tried as Adults

In most states, a juvenile, if convicted in criminal court and found guilty, can be placed on adult probation, sentenced to the county jail or an adult prison, or receive any other sentence available to convicted adult offenders. In a few states, the youth can be placed in a juvenile facility until reaching the age of majority in that state and then be transferred to adult prison to serve the remainder of his sentence. For example, in New York state, 13- to 15-year-olds convicted as adults and given prison sentences will be initially placed in a juvenile facility. They may be transferred to adult facilities (by court order) at age 16, administratively transferred at age 18 by the state division for youth, and they must be transferred by age 21 to complete time left on their sentence.

Some states have the option of placing youths convicted as adults in juvenile or adult facilities (California and Mississippi). Other state statutes provide that juveniles convicted as adults may be sent back to juvenile court for sentencing (Florida and Colorado).

Pertinent corrections legislation during the past ten years has primarily focused on sentencing guidelines and placement options. These changes generally apply to juveniles tried as adults and young adult offenders. For example, a youthful offender provision established in Florida provides alternative corrections placement. Youthful offenders are persons under age 21 serving their first felony conviction. These youths may be sentenced to a facility for younger offenders with specialized programming or may be given a community sentence. North Carolina has special facilities designated for youthful offenders which provide more vocational and remedial education services than the corrections facilities for older offenders.

In most states, however, the juvenile convicted in adult court and incarcerated will be placed in the prison facility housing the young and less sophisticated adult offenders. In *The Life-Style Violent Juvenile*, Vachss and Bakal comment that, "We can find no evidence whatever that adult prisons offer greater rehabilitative possibilities than their juvenile counterparts, and we feel comfortable in concluding that those juveniles singled out for adult correctional treatment are those juveniles the system considers to be 'beyond rehabilitation' " (Vachss and Bakas 1979, p. 9). They go on to state that juveniles in prison cause serious problems, both as aggressors and victims. It seems safe to conclude that these juveniles seldom leave the adult prison better for the experience.

Determinate Sentencing within the Juvenile Justice System

In the past ten years determinate sentencing has been adopted by several states as an alternative to trying juveniles as adults, particularly for juveniles adjudicated delinquent for violent offenses (the Designated Felony Act 1976). For example, under a 1976 law passed in New York, family court judges are given discretion to impose restrictive placements on juveniles found delinquent for a group of serious offenses (designated felonies). Juveniles found to need such placement must be placed for an initial period of five years if the offense was a Class A designated felony, the first 12 months of which must be in a secure facility and the second 12 months in a residential facility. The remaining period is left to the discretion of the New York Division for Youth. For all other designated felonies, the restrictive placement must be for three years, with six to twelve months in a secure facility. These are minimum sentences, and confinement may be extended beyond the mandated initial confinement.

In 1981, Ohio passed H.B. 440. Among its provisions is the requirement that only juveniles adjudicated delinquent for felony offenses can be sent to a state juvenile correctional facility. Once committed, the juvenile must serve a minimum sentence: until the age of 21 for murder or aggravated murder; one year for felonies 1 and 2; and six months for felonies 3 and 4—unless early release is granted by the juvenile court.

In 1984, Colorado adopted a minimum sentence provision for aggravated juvenile offenders;[8] the court may commit the juvenile offenders to the Department of Corrections. If committed, the juvenile shall remain with the department until the juvenile reaches age 21 unless early release is authorized by the court. The right to a jury trial is provided by the legislation. There are no data available to suggest that long, juvenile correctional sentences increase public safety, reduce violent crime or reduce the likelihood that the violent juvenile offender will continue to be involved in criminal activities.

Specialized Juvenile Justice Programming

Treatment programs specifically geared to violent juvenile offenders have been developed in a few states during the past ten years. In 1981 the Office of Juvenile Justice and Delinquency Prevention implemented its Violent Juvenile Offender initiative by funding five sites in Boston, Memphis, Newark, Phoenix, and Denver to develop specialized programs for violent juvenile offenders. A community reintegration model was used. This model is premised on the belief that "violent delinquency will be reduced and controlled using a social learning approach to strengthen bonds and address psycho-social factors related to violent behavior" (Fagan et al., 1984, p. 210).

The program design contains four structural components: case management, multi-phased program, community reintegration and program autonomy. Some of the ingredients of the program include:

Continuous case management: Periodic review and modification of each youth's service needs and plans is the cornerstone of the program.

A multi-phased program including an intensive diagnostic assessment phase, a secure care phase, a transition phase, and a community living phase. The program begins with intense supervision and gradually tests the ability of the youth to handle less security while insuring the safety of the community.

Community reintegration services: These are essential to sustain treatment gains after supervision control is eliminated. The planning and involvement of community institutions, such as schools, parents, churches, neighbors, and peers, begin when the youth enters the program.

Program autonomy: This is ensured through agreement with the sponsoring agency to guarantee that the theoretical assumptions of the model are fully implemented. This is essential to fully test the delinquency base of the model.

The Juvenile Justice and Delinquency Prevention program is still being evaluated to test its effectiveness. Early results suggest that the program is "making a difference" to the juveniles participating in it.

Summary and Policy Discussion

Where does this review of present knowledge about violent juvenile crime lead us? The amount of information about violent delinquents has increased enormously in the past ten years, but the number of unanswered questions far exceeds the answers. Therefore, the following discussion is presented in the spirit of stimulating creative thought and informed debate about the direction public policy should take in this area in the future.

Trying Juveniles as Adults

The solution to the problem of how to respond to the violent juvenile offender is not likely to lie in the criminal justice system. We have no reason to believe that trying juveniles as adults is likely to prevent them from continuing their criminal careers, or that it increases public safety either in the short or long term.

The data available on outcomes for juveniles tried as adults is almost non-existent. In addition, the data on what happens to violent juvenile offenders is very limited. We know, however, that juvenile court processing time from the filing of the charge to the disposition is much shorter, on average, than the amount of time it takes to process an adult through criminal court. We also know that the number of dismissals and reduced charges through plea bargains is less in the juvenile court than in criminal court. If quick, sure justice is to be desired, the juvenile court is set up to be more responsive to individual cases, and to mete out sentences tailored to the individual.

If juveniles are more amenable to "treatment" than adult offenders, the resources available to the juvenile justice system are much greater, and the likelihood that juveniles will receive medical, mental health, educational, work training and reintegration services is much greater. Also, generally there is a greater range of dispositional options available to the juvenile justice system, thus increasing the likelihood that violent juvenile offenders will receive appropriate services.

The data available suggest that juveniles transferred to criminal court and convicted are more likely to receive community sentences than corrections sentences. Once in criminal court, most juveniles will do less time than they would in the juvenile justice system. However, a significant number will spend a large amount of their young adult years incarcerated. Whether these data apply to violent juvenile offenders awaits further research.

And, finally, there is strong evidence that juveniles singled out for adult correctional treatment are likely to be used and abused both physically and sexually by older inmates and staff, which is hardly likely to increase the probability of success upon return to the community.

Joint Programming for Youthful Offenders

Innovations in treatment for violent juvenile offenders (with a few exceptions) have been limited to very familiar approaches utilizing modifications of organizational structure. Because of the strong evidence of the continuity of juvenile delinquency and criminal careers, it may be appropriate to consider the development of a variety of joint juvenile and adult programs. These initiatives need to ensure continuity and accountability. For example, we need to think about a youthful offender program that would emphasize work readiness, job training, and work experience. The 16-year-old violent juvenile offender, who has few if any high school credits, is functionally illiterate, and has no meaningful work experience is very unlikely to return to a traditional educational program. Hence, we ought to think about "sheltered" employment for many of these youth who have been in trouble with the law from the time they were ten or twelve and in institutions for a large percentage of their adolescent years. These programs would be designed to help youths make it in a noncriminal world. The youth would learn how to apply for a job, balance a home budget, communicate with employers and fellow employees—in summary, how to survive without resorting to criminal activities. For some, a short period of sheltered employment would lead to regular employment; for others, sheltered employment might be necessary for the rest of their lives.

Accountability of the Juvenile Offender

One of the basic tenets of juvenile justice reform holds that whatever is done to any youth in trouble with the law should constitute the least restrictive intervention in that juvenile's life. Given this position, a sequence of sanctions should be designed to ensure some degree of predictable graduated consequences for delinquent acts. These sanctions may range from fines, restitutions, and supervision, to incarceration. Graduated consequences should allow for a response commensurate with the delinquent action, the previous record, and the age of the youth. It is important that intervention come early and that it not be nominal. To quote from *The Violent Few:*

> Experience must not suggest that the system is aleatory. A youth must not conclude that the decision of the court depends on the mood of the judge, a special word from a probation officer, or his own neatly combed hair. He must expect that there will be intervention and that intervention will make requirements of him that he must meet.

However, there is no reason to believe that long, determinate, juvenile correctional sentences are the only disposition that holds the juvenile offender accountable. It is one of the least effective. The data from the Columbus cohort study indicated that the institutional experience did not have a positive effect on subsequent behavior.

The rates of arrests of juveniles who had been incarcerated generally increased after each incarceration, and the median number of days of street time prior to re-arrest generally decreased. Juvenile incarceration, both in terms of number of commitments and duration, also increased the probability of that individual becoming an adult felony offender and subsequently going to prison. While this information supports the conclusion that the most serious juvenile offenders were incarcerated, it also clearly indicates that for most of these juvenile offenders, incarceration is correlated with increased criminality of the offenders.

We need to develop strategies that let violent and chronic juvenile offenders know that there are predictable consequences for their delinquent behavior and increase the probability of breaking this continuous pattern of criminal activity.

There are few treatment programs directed at such juvenile offenders. Programs will be successful with some but not all such offenders. We need to develop new programs, to test them and keep trying.

A Program for Repeat and Chronic Violent Juvenile Offenders

With much caution, I would like to suggest some of the ingredients for programming for this small group of offenders:

Programs for controlling and treating youth must be law-abiding and safe, with strict enforcement of rules for staff as well as for youths. Brutalizing of youths by staff or other inmates cannot be tolerated.

Staff intensive security programming with minimum use of jail hardware is preferable to reliance on fences, barbed wire and bars.

Close ties to the community including family, school, and peers should be encouraged. If the youth is removed from the community, community involvement can be facilitated through community trips, home furloughs, family visits and aftercare worker contact with both the youth and the community.

Contracting for services from private community agencies should be utilized. There is no reason why contracted services cannot be provided even to youth within secure settings.

Juveniles' involvement in choice and decision-making should be maximized. Contracts between the program staff and youth can be a strong motivation and a positive learning experience. A significant reward structure for realistically attainable goals must be included.

Group therapeutic programs seem to be more effective for adolescent offenders than individual counseling.

The helping role for offenders also can increase self-esteem and serve as a positive learning experience.

Age appropriate remedial education that stresses how to "make it" in the real world is important. In addition, preparation for employment and employment experience will increase the possibility of successful transition into the adult world.

The importance of community reintegration services cannot be overemphasized. Whether the juvenile has been in a community program or a secure facility, the need for supportive services does not end with the program completion. Continuity of care between the program/treatment sequence and supportive aftercare program is essential if the positive gains made within the program are to last.

To quote John Conrad, "Until we can give our attention to the creation of means of bringing delinquent youth into society as legitimate participants in its benefits, far too many of them will become adult criminals to scare citizens off the streets. Our inattention to the need of the system for change will produce the crime rates we deserve" (Conrad, 1981, p. 192).

Endnotes

1. Violent offense in these studies included the index violent offenses of murder, rape, aggravated assault and robbery. Assault and battery, molesting, and less serious assaultive offenses are defined as midemeanors and are included as violent offenses.
2. Some of these findings are reprinted from *The Young Criminal Years of the Violent Few,* U.S. Department of Justice, June 1985.
3. The data nationally on the *number* of juveniles processed by juvenile courts and/or criminal courts for violent crimes is inadequate for several reasons, including: 1) almost all data collected is based on cases rather than individuals; 2) the number of juveniles automatically handled in criminal court is not reported in any juvenile justice data; 3) the information on what happens to juveniles judicially transferred to criminal court and tried as adults is not routinely collected; and 4) the dispositions of juveniles handled in juvenile court for violent offenses are not collected nationally.
4. New York, Nebraska, and Arkansas.
5. Concurrent jurisdiction—Arkansas, Colorado, District of Columbia, Florida, Georgia, Nebraska, Vermont, Wyoming. States that have concurrent jurisdiction provisions for traffic and minor misdemeanors only are not included.
6. Excluded Offenses—Delaware, Idaho, Indiana, Kansas, Louisiana, Maryland, Mississippi, Nevada, Oklahoma, New Mexico, New York, Pennsylvania, Rhode Island, and Vermont.
7. Four states have set the initial age of criminal court jurisdiction as 16—Connecticut, New York, Vermont, and North Carolina. Eight states have set 17—Michigan, Louisiana, South Carolina, Texas, Illinois, Missouri, Massachusetts, and Georgia.
8. A child, 12 years of age or older, who is adjudicated delinquent for murder, first or second degree, or whose probation is revoked for first or second degree murder, or a juvenile 16 years of age or older who has been adjudicated delinquent at least twice for felonies one of which is a violent felony; or whose probation is revoked for a crime of violence.

References

Conrad, J., (1981). *Crime and the Child, Youth in adult courts section of readings in public policy, major issues in juvenile justice, information and training.* Columbus, Ohio: Academy for Contemporary Problems.

Fagan, J., and Hartstone, E. (1984). Strategic planning in juvenile justice.—Defining the toughest kids. *Violent Juvenile Offenders: An Anthology*. San Francisco: National Council on Crime and Delinquency.

Fagan, J., Rudman, C., and Hartstone, E. (1984). Intervening with violent juvenile offenders: A community reintegration model. *Violent juvenile offenders: An anthology*. Robert A. Mathias (Ed.). San Francisco: National Council on Crime and Delinquency.

Hamparian, D., Schuster, R., Dinitz, S., and Conrad, J. (1978). *The Violent Few*, Lexington, MA: D.C. Heath and Company.

Hamparian, D., Estep, L., and Muntean, S., Priestino, R., Swisher, R., Wallace, P., and White, J. (1982). *Youth in adult courts: Between two worlds*. Columbus, OH: Academy for Contemporary Problems.

Hamparian, D., Davis, J., and Jacobson, J. (1983). *Juveniles transferred to adult courts: Recent Ohio experience*. Cleveland: The Federation for Community Planning.

Hamparian, D., Davis, J., Jacobson, and McGraw, R. (1985, June). *The young criminal years of the violent few*. U.S. Department of Justice.

Hartstone, E., and Hansen, K. (1984). The violent juvenile offender: An empirical portrait. *Violent juvenile offenders: An anthology*. R. Mathias, (Ed.). San Francisco: National Council on Crime and Delinquency.

Smith, D., Finnegan, T., Snyder, H., Feinberg, N., and McFall, P. (1981). *Delinquency 1978: United States estimate of cases processed by courts with juvenile jurisdiction*. Pittsburgh: National Center for Juvenile Justice.

Snyder, H., and Hutzler, J. L. (1981). *Serious juvenile offenders: The scope of the problem and the response of juvenile court*. Pittsburgh: The National Center on Juvenile Justice.

Strasburg, P. (1978). *Violent delinquents*. Monarch: The Ford Foundation.

Strasburg, P. (1984). *Violent Juvenile Offenders: An Anthology*, San Francisco: National Council on Crime and Delinquency.

U.S. Department of Justice. (1983). *Uniform crime reports, Crime in the United States*.

Vachss, A., and Bakal, Y., (1979). *The life-style violent juvenile*. Lexington, MA: Lexington Books.

Wolfgang, M., Figlio, R., and Sellin, T. (1972). *Delinquency in a birth cohort*. Chicago: The University of Chicago Press.

Youth Policy and Law Center. (1984). *Violent delinquents: A Wisconsin study*.

9
Toward an Effective Policy for Handling Dangerous Juvenile Offenders

JEFFREY L. BLEICH

Over the past two decades statistics from various national crime-reporting services have focused media and public attention upon the problem of serious juvenile crime. The facts, by now, are familiar. American youth under 18 represent less than 14% of the population, but are responsible for one-quarter of all arrests for violent crime (murder, rape, aggravated assault, and robbery) (1982 Uniform Crime Reports). In 1981, the juvenile arrest rates for serious property crimes exceeded the adult rate by nearly 6:1 and the juvenile violent arrest rate doubled the adult rate. (1981 Uniform Crime Reports). Furthermore, the rate at which juveniles are arrested for violent crimes has been growing faster than the rate at which they are arrested for nonviolent crimes, and faster even than the rate at which adults are arrested for violent crimes (Wilson and Boland, 1978).

Public concern over violent juvenile crime rates in the late 1970s prompted the Office of Juvenile Justice and Delinquency Prevention (OJJDP) to consider methods for separating violent offenders from non-violent youths for special treatment. OJJDP hoped to identify the most dangerous juvenile offenders and either isolate them from society or provide specialized care for them suited to their common needs. Between 1982 and 1983 OJJDP commissioned three separate studies to evaluate incidences of violent juvenile crime in the hopes of discerning similar characteristics or patterns in serious delinquents. The research revealed that only a very few juveniles engage repeatedly or exclusively in violent acts *and* that those juveniles who do commit repeat violent offenses also tended to commit many *non-violent offenses* (Rojek and Erickson, 1982; Hartstone, Jang and Fagan, 1983; Fagan, Hansen, and Jang, 1982).

Earlier cohort studies support the conclusion that a relatively small number of offenders are responsible for a disproportionately large amount of all violent and non-violent juvenile crimes (e.g., Wolfgang et al., 1972; Wolfgang, 1977; Hamparian, 1978; Shannon, 1980). Wolfgang's birth cohort study (1972) found that only 6% of the cohort accounted for 71% of homicides committed by delinquents, 73% of the rapes, and 69% of the aggravated assaults. Hamparian's (1978) study suggests that the "violent few" are even more tightly clustered–representing less than 1% of the juvenile population. Like the OJJDP studies, the cohort studies found that the vast majority of violent delinquents are property offenders who commit one violent offense, but that the small core of chronic offenders committed both violent *and* non-violent crimes at astonishingly high rates. Wolfgang, Hamparian, and Shannon each concluded that a history of violence did not reveal a qualitatively different attitude towards offending. But they found that *high rate* violence accurately predicted a unique predisposition to commit subsequent violent and non-violent crimes.

Violence, then, could be viewed not as the specific problem but as an indicator of a more central problem—a serious antisocial orientation which is manifested in continued criminal behavior. Those individuals disposed to commit more than one violent act may be equally inclined to perform a multiplicity of other antisocial and criminal acts. Studies within several juvenile treatment programs have revealed that high-rate offenders exhibit a qualitatively different response to traditional treatment and are uniquely resistant to conventional rehabilitation programs (Agee, 1979; Gadow and McKibbon, 1984; Coates, 1984). Based upon this conclusion, many juvenile justice officials have called for researchers to focus upon this dangerous subset of chronic dangerous juveniles. Conservatives have urged that these youths be identified and incarcerated for the protection of society. Liberal observers recommend identifying these youths for specialized treatment since, quite obviously, they have not responded to traditional treatment. Thus, from a variety of sources, a major movement has developed within the juvenile justice community to separate qualitatively less responsive (and hence more dangerous) juveniles from traditional delinquency programs and assign them to special care facilities.

Dangerous Juvenile Offenders

A policy which focuses upon violent and chronic offenders offers several obvious benefits regardless of which treatment system is ultimately employed. Left unattended, chronically violent offenders pose several distinct and serious threats to society. Most obviously, their extensive criminal activity inflicts personal injury upon their victims and exacts fear and loss from the community (Bureau of Justice Statistics Report, 1983). In addition, because these youths are only arrested for a small fraction of the crimes they commit, serious juvenile offenders drain society at large of both law enforcement resources and public confidence in the effectiveness of those resources (Fagan et al., 1983; President's Task Force on Violent Crime, 1982). Furthermore, dangerous juveniles threaten to undermine our juvenile justice system—either by corrupting other juveniles while they are in treatment and forcing juvenile facilities to adopt harsher treatment technologies and philosophies, or by eroding public support for the notion of rehabilitation (Miller and Ohlin, 1980). Finally, individuals who commit serious crimes at a high rate reveal an attitude which suggests they will continue to engage in criminal activity throughout much of their adult lives, placing a life-long burden upon society's limited criminal justice resources (Farrington and West, 1977).

By identifying these offenders early on and prescribing an effective treatment policy for handling them, the juvenile justice community could achieve at least four important benefits. Theoretically, by removing and/or rehabilitating serious juvenile offenders, officials could reduce total juvenile crime by as much as 50% and violent juvenile crime by up to 70% (Greenwood, 1982; Greenwood and Zimring, 1985). Secondly, by separating these delinquents from their more easily treatable counterparts, the court could protect the effectiveness and integrity of the juvenile system. Thirdly, by making the response of the juvenile court more predictable, a policy for delinquents might actually reduce the onset and perpetuation of juvenile crime (Roysher and Edelman, 1981). And finally, by focusing scarce resources on programs to treat the most intractable offenders early on, this program might ultimately spare society the enormous burden of the offenders' future criminality (Farrington and West, 1977).

Objections

Despite the proposed benefits of selective handling of dangerous juvenile offenders, many critics have argued that such a program could never be put into place, either because it violates the philosophy of the juvenile justice system or because it is incompatible with the existing political and practical realities of our present juvenile court structure. These objections have thus far prevented and undermined most earlier attempts to develop a systematic handling policy for dangerous youths.

Philosophical Objections. Critics have charged that a selective handling policy would be fundamentally inconsistent with the goals and philosophy of juvenile justice (Monahan, 1977). The juvenile justice system, they point out, rests upon the belief that juveniles are qualitatively different from adults in their capacities, their accountability, and their potential for change. Specifically, our society holds that children are incompletely developed beings whose ability to behave correctly depends almost exclusively upon their parents' actions and their surroundings. Therefore, we attribute a child's poor conduct to his parents' negligence in controlling the youth's emotional immaturity and lack of self-knowledge. The notion of parental responsibility has spawned two obvious corollaries: 1) that children are *not* fully responsible for their acts and; 2) that given the proper training a child's behavior may be reformed. Since, according to this philosophy, no sanctions other than time and training are necessary for a child to outgrow mischievous behavior, juvenile delinquents do not require institutional punishments and do not deserve moral condemnation and stigma.

The ideal of specialized treatment for juveniles, they argue, is further reinforced by our conception of justice. American jurisprudence is founded upon the notion that individuals have free will and the ability to choose between different courses of action with full knowledge of their social consequences. Individuals who act in a manner which violates society's codes, therefore, have brought punishment upon themselves.

Under this formulation, an act can only be criminal if the accused individual *intended* to breach social codes, (i.e., to commit a crime). Individuals who act involuntarily, ignorantly, or with no malice have not made a moral choice and thus, neither they nor society would benefit from their suffering punitive sanctions. Therefore, in instances where individuals demonstrate that they are either incapable of rational thought or that they have been coerced into committing an offense, the courts hold that punishment is either inappropriate or unjustifiable on retributive grounds. Consequently, due to these conceptions of childhood and justice, our government has chosen to exclude juveniles as a class from criminal liability on the ground that they lack the requisite will and intent to justify retributive sanctions.

Under this construction of justice, exposing any juvenile—regardless of the crime—to harsh, retributive, or adult-like treatment would seem to violate the spirit of juvenile justice. Some critics have even argued that introducing this specialized category will destroy the juvenile justice system (President's Crime Commission, 1967). The classification—"serious juvenile offender"—they argue, will stigmatize the youth and further restrict his ability to overcome the burden of his youthful errors. The treatment will inevitably require incarceration and adult-like sanctions—violating society's concept of fairness. And finally, they urge, the concentration of dangerous juveniles will inhibit their social development, casting them further apart from society.

However, supporters of a dangerous juvenile offender program argue that treating certain juveniles differently does not necessarily require treating them as adults. They argue that the purpose of a dangerous juvenile program is ultimately to *protect* these youths from the adult system and make available to them the most individualized, intensive (and hence, expensive) resources of the juvenile justice system. They suggest that once these youths have been identified, officials will be better able to apply and develop programs specifically tailored to overcoming their anti-social behavior, developing their self-esteem, and re-integrating them into society. Such a program thus protects more traditional youth from the corrupting influence of chronically violent youth while simultaneously protecting violent youth from the retributory horrors of the adult penal system.

Proponents suggest that a dangerous juvenile offender program could not only function differently than a dangerous offender program, but could express different goals as well. The juvenile justice system, they contend, is functionalist in nature and thus should select its programs on the basis of their ability to reform and rehabilitate youths without causing any undue stigma. The objective of juvenile confinement would not be to mete out the harshest punishments to the most culpable individuals or incapacitate the most dangerous elements of society (although both may result as by-products of this policy), but rather to direct society's most intensive resources and personnel towards those youths who need it most. Thus, the system would remain faithful to its goals of socializing youths and making them more conscious of their connectedness to society. The youths identified by this program are already at risk of being transferred and stigmatized. Therefore the ultimate test of a dangerous juvenile offender program becomes whether or not it can socialize youths better than the programs currently in place.

Criminal justice researchers have also identified several other, more subtle, functionalist justifications for a dangerous juvenile policy. Beyond the reduced crime, fear, and loss promised by such a program, researchers argue that specialized treatment may improve the child's socialization and assist his re-integration into society. Control and strain theorists Weis and Hawkins (1979) concluded that the absence of an effective treatment program for these youths in the juvenile justice system has reinforced their conduct and, consequently, further eroded their social bonds. Similarly, James Q. Wilson (1975) has suggested that a specialized policy might deter youths from future criminality merely by virtue of its being predictable. Finally, many argue, the retention of non-appropriate subjects in traditional juvenile care programs dilutes and undermines the socialization of other juveniles in the treatment community.

Other juvenile justice officials have argued that regardless of the program chosen, selective treatment programs are a logical and not inconsistent extension of current juvenile justice philosophy. These critics point out that the chronic nature of criminality among dangerous juveniles reveals that they are not amenable to traditional forms of juvenile care (Farrington and West, 1977; Agee, 1979; Gadow, 1984). Some have even gone so far as to say that these youths' failure to respond to treatment is a conscious choice reflecting full mental capacity (Silberman, 1978; Van Den Haag, 1975). Thus, they contend, these individuals do not deserve the unique protections of juvenile justice.

Finally, supporters of selective handling contend that retributive origins notwithstanding, our criminal justice is not, nor was it ever intended to be, strictly retributive in practice. Advocates point out that under our present system individuals who do not strictly *deserve* punishment are routinely required to endure social consequences for their actions. The courts impose a variety of punishments which, while ostensibly retributive, are justified on functionalist grounds. Individuals with diminished capacities may be locked up, either to protect society from their future actions, to deter others from committing the same crime or to rehabilitate the individual through training programs. Although these functional justifications for punishment have been constitutionally and scientifically disputed, the courts have employed them with increasing regularity (Packer, 1966). Thus, on a strictly philosophical level, they argue that our system of justice does not preclude some individuals with diminished capacities, including children, from suffering punitive sanctions in order to achieve some other social benefits.

Practical Objections. Several theorists have argued that regardless of whether or not a dangerous juvenile offender program is philosophically viable, such a program is simply unfeasible. In the first place, they contend, selective handling may be based upon the wrong assumptions and, consequently, will not reduce the level of juvenile crime. Blumstein (1983) suggests that chronic offenders are produced by criminogenic environments and thus, removing them from society will only cause other youths to take their place (see also Van Den Haag, 1975). Others claim that because of problems in measuring the extent of criminality, and distortions in self-reported data, the benefits of selective handling have been exaggerated (Moore, Wilson, Gants, 1978; Hamparian et al., 1978; Shannon, 1983). Still others argue that focusing attention on the most dangerous juveniles will further decrease the threat of sanctions to other juvenile offenders, thus causing the majority of delinquents to increase their criminal behavior (Radzinowicz and Hood, 1977).

Some theorists, in fact, have argued that a selective handling policy might produce *more* crime. Jerome Miller, Director of the National Center on Institutions and Alternatives, claims that juveniles who have been singled out as especially problematic may, upon their return to society "resume their previous endeavors with a vengeance" (in Mathias, 1984). If, on top of this effect, the juvenile has become more criminally sophisticated while in prison and other youths have simultaneously taken his place on the street, the net results may be a dramatic increase in total crime. Other researchers have found that the greatest single predictor of later serious delinquency in a juvenile offender is whether or not he was kept in a locked detention center or jail early on in his delinquent career (Coates, 1981).

Supporters of a specialized handling program respond that while these criticisms are theoretically plausible, there is no empirical proof to support them. The so-called replacement effect appears to occur only in gang environments (Cohen, 1955; Erickson, 1971; Klein, 1971; Short, 1968). Yet, studies show that most chronic serious offenders are extremely alienated youths who rarely belong to gangs (Moore et al., 1984). The claim that youths who are locked up early in their careers subsequently become serious delinquents is similarly flawed. Coates himself theorized that serious delinquents receive detention earlier because they commit serious crimes earlier. Finally, the argument that measurement errors and unexpected consequences will mitigate the success of this program is probably true but may be overstated. The actual existence or impact of these factors is impossible to quantify prior to implementing the program. Thus, while these factors present possible explanations for potential failures of such programs, they do not offer any persuasive reasons to *not* attempt a dangerous juvenile program.

Other critics suggest that even if a dangerous juvenile program could work, there are too many irresolvable implementation issues to ever put the program into effect. Specifically, they note that there is no consensus upon which offenses should be targeted, how many offenses constitute dangerousness, what criteria should be used for identifying dangerous offenders, which programs are most effective in treating chronic delinquency, and how these programs could be implemented and evaluated. These questions are considered in the next section.

Implementing a Dangerous Juvenile Program

Defining Dangerous Juvenile Offenders

In order to effect any treatment or control policy, juvenile justice officials must define which offenders and which combinations of offenses they should target for specialized handling. Unfortunately, no consensus exists over how dangerous juvenile offending should be defined and even less over which criteria should be used. Experts disagree over whether the category should include violent offenders, chronically violent offenders, all chronic offenders, or high rate chronic offenders. Similarly, officials disagree over what constitutes a "high rate" pattern, a "serious" crime, or even a "violent" crime (i.e, is burglarizing an occupied dwelling violent?) (Fagan and Hartstone, 1984). Finally, a profound debate continues over what criteria should be used in identifying individuals as dangerous juveniles. Should programs base definitions on social and psychological indicators of future dangerousness, past criminal conduct, or a combination of the two?

Which Offense? From the juvenile court's perspective, the goal of crafting a dangerous juvenile classification is to improve the court's allocation of rehabilitation and/or confinement resources. Thus, the courts would like to focus upon those crimes which cause the most harm, and are most indicative of a chronically criminal or treatment-aversive personality. The first aspect of this—determining which offenses are dangerous—has produced several conflicting definitions. For example, Coates (1981) argued that only violent offenses should be considered. Wolfgang and Sellin (1972) included property losses as well in their definition of seriousness.

And Smith et al. (1980) included drug sales as well as violence and property crime.

However, recent studies of juvenile and adult crime support Coates's argument that violence is the most appropriate measurement for defining dangerous offenses. Fundamentally, violence is the least subjective (though certainly not un-subjective) of all classes of crimes. The effects of violent crime are immediate, tangible, and easy to differentiate from all other violations in terms of fear and injury. More importantly, violent acts reflect a qualitatively more antisocial or unrestrained character, in general, than property offenses—as is evidenced by the fact that all high rate violent offenders are also high rate property offenders although the converse is not true (Wolfgang et al., 1972; Hamparian, 1978; Shannon, 1980). Furthermore, from a practical perspective, the juvenile justice community does not have the resources to provide specialized handling for the overwhelming number of property offenders. Even selecting among chronic property offenders proves virtually impossible. Coates (1981) and Greenwood (1982) found that violent delinquency is the only behavior which can be predicted from analyses of delinquent careers, and that those predictions rest primarily upon past violent criminality.

Which Offender? Just as the evidence suggests that juvenile justice officials should concentrate upon crimes of violence, it also suggests that officials focus upon individuals who commit those crimes repeatedly.* Research indicates that one violent offense is not indicative of a forthcoming career (Wolfgang et al., 1972). Furthermore, subsequent multiple-regression studies have revealed that a history of more than one violent crime is the best predictor of subsequent serious criminality (Wolfgang, 1977).

Finally, regardless of whether the objective is deterrence, isolation, retribution, or rehabilitation, all would agree that chronically violent offenders require more special attention than other youths. Incarceration or specialized treatment are the most intrusive means of court disposition and thus they must be reserved for youths who cannot benefit from less expensive alternatives or who would pose an unacceptable risk in those environments. Juveniles who have committed more than one serious offense, including at least one violent offense, would, by all accounts, satisfy this category.

Criteria

Defining which juveniles are dangerous, however, still does not resolve the question of identifying dangerous juvenile offenders. The literature on

* For our purposes, rate is not an important factor since, given the brevity of delinquent career—3–4 years—virtually any repetition of serious crime may be considered high rate.

this subject presents three general approaches: 1) non-criminal predictors; 2) a combination of past criminality and predictors; or 3) past criminality exclusively. Each of these approaches has a number of benefits and drawbacks.

Non-Criminal Predictors. Several clinicians and researchers have claimed that assessments of youth's psychological, behavioral, and family characteristics, as well as their demographics, are more accurate and predictive in determining future criminality than legal adjudications. They argue that using non-criminal characteristics would allow juvenile justice officials to respond to the needs of potentially chronic violent youths *before* they inflict large-scale harm upon society. These predictors would then provide a triple benefit to society. First, they would protect citizens from being victims of those predicted offenses. Second, they would allow the system to intervene earlier—allowing more time and opportunity to alter the child's behavior. And third, if programs based on them are successful, they offer all of the benefits of reduced crime, fear, loss, and dependence discussed earlier.

A number of studies claim to have identified accurate non-criminal predictors of chronic juvenile violence (Polk and Schaefer, 1972; Wolfgang et al., 1972; Hamparian et al., 1978; Strasburg, 1978; Lefkowitz, 1980; Shannon, 1980). However, when the results of these studies are compared, they reveal the depth of uncertainty about those predictive variables. Polk and Schaefer (1972) found that age at onset of criminal activity predicted future criminality, regardless of the type of offense. However, both Hamparian (1978) and Shannon (1980) concluded that age at onset was *not* a reliable predictor. Similarly, while Wolfgang (1972) suggested that sex, race, socio-economic status, educational achievement, IQ, and residential mobility were all strongly predictive of future violence, subsequent recidivism studies failed to substantiate the predictive power of any of these variables on a case-by-case basis (Schlesinger, 1978).

Attempts to correlate behavior patterns have proved equally dismal. Childhood tantrums, pyromania, cruelty to animals, abuse by parents, and verbal aggressiveness have all been applied as possible predictors of future chronicity (Justice et al., 1974; Glueck and Glueck, 1950; Lefkowitz et al., 1977; Fagan et al., 1981; Kuhl, 1981; Alfaro, 1978). However, despite their theoretical appeal, each of these attempts to predict recidivism generated between 54–99% false positives (Fagan, 1984). Furthermore, even studies which used extensive combinations of these variables predicted between 8–40% false positives (Farrington and West, 1977; Van Dine, Conrad, and Dinitz, 1979; McCord, 1959; Robins and Wish, 1977). The one study (by Farrington and West) which produced an arguably acceptable level of false positives (8%) used such a rigid identification criteria that it also failed to identify future recidivists 30% of the time.

Obviously, the dangers of misclassification are great in terms of undue punishment, stigma, and wasted criminal justice resources. Thus, critics have argued that predictive tests should only be administered if they produce virtually no false positives. Realistically, the Farrington experience indicates that for a predictive criteria to be 100% accurate it would fail to identify most dangerous juveniles as well—making the program essentially worthless (Hamparian et al., 1978; Shannon, 1983).

Combination Criminal History and Predictors. Because of the predictive failures of non-criminal variables as well as strong moral, legal, and constitutional objections to basing confinement on involuntary, demographic factors, several researchers have opted for a combined criminal and non-criminal approach. Advocates of these criteria offer several appealing arguments. First, Greenwood and Zimring (1985) claim that adding social and psychological factors to criminal records yields virtually the same group of chronic offenders as a definition based upon juvenile records alone. Several other studies (Farrington, 1983; Monahan, Brodsky, and Shah, 1981; Chaiken and Chaiken, 1982) had similar success in combining past criminality with predictive correlates of crime—predicting both chronicity and desistance with 97.5% accuracy. Furthermore, by using combination criteria, these researchers were able to identify chronic youth much earlier. Greenwood and Zimring (1985) claimed, on average, to predict chronicity by age 13, as compared to 16, in a record-based identification system. Thus, using this criteria would allow the juvenile justice community to provide rehabilitative services much earlier on in the youth's delinquent career. Furthermore, as Whitaker (1982) notes, these other variables can help the juvenile justice community differentiate between youths whose violence is episodic and those who are routinely, characteristically dangerous.

However, despite these perceived benefits, this combined approach has engendered several critical objections. Most obviously, the inclusion of any subjective or non-criminal criteria in assigning sanctions raises questions about consistency, accuracy, and abuse. Specifically, interpretation and application of behavioral traits may be too difficult to objectify and measure consistently (Fagan and Hartstone, 1984). Secondly, using qualitative criteria heightens the risk of false identification—thus leading to unfair stigmatization, squandering of scarce treatment resources, and distortion of the true results of treatment programs. Finally, discretion in the determination process might encourage programs which seek to improve their record to select the *least* aggressive youth–thus undermining the program's objective. As Fagan and Hartstone (1984) note, the marginal predictive benefits of including socio-demographic and behavioral factors with the youth's criminal record do not justify the potential social and human costs they produce.

Definition Based Upon Prior Criminal Record. Thus, it appears that in the interests of fairness, accuracy and consistency, classifications should be based solely upon past criminal conduct. Wilson and Boland (1978) note that while a broad definition of dangerousness has strong popular appeal, it may not produce the desired results. The OJJDP definition appears to identify all the chronic offenders as well as recidivists who would, on their own, have committed only one or two more crimes. Thus, for each misidentified juvenile, OJJDP expends enormous confinement and treatment resources while preventing only one or two crimes.

Critics of this approach argue that a retrospective definition produces too little too late and may be too restrictive, allowing more opportunities for juvenile crime than necessary. However, researchers have demonstrated that most dangerous juveniles are charged with their second index offense early on in their juvenile careers (Wolfgang et al., 1972; Rojek and Erickson, 1982). In fact, Hartstone and Hansen (1984) found that over half of the chronically violent juveniles identified were charged with a violent offense by their third petition. And, although Polk and Shaefer's (1972) claim that early onset of criminality may be a predictor of chronicity has been challenged, subsequent studies support their conclusion that chronic offenders generally begin their criminal careers earlier than other delinquents (Hartstone and Hansen, 1984).

Some debate still persists, however, over which combination of adjudicated crimes most accurately identifies the target chronic offenders. OJJDP has recently adopted two adjudications for index offenses, including at least one violent offense, as the criteria for judging a youth dangerous (Hartstone and Hansen, 1984). However, results of the OJJDP programs revealed that on average, the truly chronic dangerous offenders had committed more than three violent crimes by the time they were identified. Apparently, these youths commit so many crimes, so early on in their violent career, that other, more conservative criteria could identify these youths just as accurately and without increasing the number of false negatives (Hartstone and Hansen, 1984). Researchers have further suggested that the OJJDP criteria may produce more false positives than a two-violent adjudications criteria, without producing any increase in predictive accuracy. Consequently, this research suggests that classification be restricted to two-time violent offenders or youths who have committed three serious crimes in addition to a violent offense.

Finally, some critics have argued that certain crimes are simply too egregious not to receive some special attention of condemnation. Regardless of society's good intentions and general sympathy towards youths in most instances, its desire for protection or retribution may overwhelm that tolerant attitude in the face of violent bodily assaults such as rape and murder. To many, a first-time rape or murder does not deserve an opportunity for a sequel. Thus, in order to satisfy the competing objectives of justice, it may be worthwhile to classify any convicted rapist or murderer as a dangerous offender. However, the purpose of selecting a restrictive definition in the first place was to insure that resources were not wasted upon episodically violent youth (i.e., ones who murdered a parent after years of physical and sexual abuse) but were concentrated upon chronically violent youths. Therefore, I would suggest establishing a mandatory hearing for all adjudicated juvenile rapists and murderers to determine whether or not the youths pose sufficient danger of repeating their behavior to warrant classification.

Handling Dangerous Juveniles

Having identified dangerous juvenile offenders, the question remains: what can and should be done with these selected youth? At present, it appears that either very little is being done or that the programs presently in place have been ineffective and/or inadequate. The prevalence of violent juvenile crime and the large number of court contacts that violent youths experience are only the most obvious manifestations of the system's failures (Hartstone and Hansen, 1984). A study by Peter Strasburg of the Vera Institute of Justice (1978) revealed that of 191 youths adjudicated guilty of violent offenses, only 17 were singled out for placement in any kind of facility. Even more remarkably, only one-fifth of the chronic offenders identified by Strasburg received any formal placement.

Several factors account for the juvenile court's failure to respond effectively to the needs of dangerous youths. Frequently, these courts do not have good information about the youth's past criminal activities. Courts often fail to identify dangerous youths because previous adjudications have been plea-bargained down or because the court maintains inadequate records (Mann, 1976). Even when they do identify the youths, the court's options are limited. Very few jurisdictions provide any specialized programs for dangerous youths (Miller and Ohlin, 1980; Feld, 1981; Hamparian, 1982). Those courts that do have access to specialized handling programs generally have a shortage of beds available for dangerous youths. Thus, judges are faced with a choice between relying upon treatments which have historically been ineffective with such youths or abdicating all hope by transferring the youth to the adult court. Even if the juvenile court judge decides to take his chances with existing programs, virtually no non-specialized programs will accept or retain custody of these youth (Mann, 1976). Dangerous juveniles threaten to undermine the treatment of other youths, destroy property, jeopardize community relations, tarnish the program's treatment record, and drive away qualified staff. Thus, even if the youth is placed in one of these programs, he is frequently released a few short months after his referral. Based upon these observations, it appears that *any* specialized program would be an improvement over the existing predominant system.

Goals

The specific response which juvenile justice officials ultimately choose will depend largely upon their goals. If the juvenile justice community simply wishes to remove society's most dangerous elements from the community as early as possible, then officials will most likely prescribe incarceration for dangerous juveniles. Youths identified as dangerous could be either imprisoned in juvenile facilities until they are mature enough to fend for themselves as adult felons or could be transferred directly to adult facilities where they would be held until they've grown too old to pose a further threat to society. If, on the other hand, officials believe the goal of a policy for dangerous juveniles is to re-integrate wayward youth into society, then they will support and develop treatment, rehabilitation, and highly-structured community therapy programs to help socialize these youths. Both of these options will be explored.

The juvenile justice system's decision concerning the handling of dangerous juveniles will also depend upon the goals of the larger community. Any change in the treatment or legal status of dangerous youths must ultimately be approved and sanctioned by the state legislature. While legislators may respond to numbers and studies demonstrating the superiority of one system over another, their final decision will most likely hinge upon their sense of how the community will react. Most legislators understand that there is a tension within their constituencies between a paternalistic regard for the frailties and difficulties of youth and a desire for protection from (and punishment of) serious offenders. Thus, legislators will look for a direction which accommodates both of these community interests to some extent. In short, society's response to dangerous juveniles must reflect some common sense.

Finally, the decision over how to handle dangerous juveniles will depend upon what resources the juvenile justice system has available. Proponents of rehabilitation programs frequently dismiss incarceration as unfeasible simply because the U.S. does not have enough prison space to house those youths. On the other hand, advocates of incarceration claim that the abundance of rehabilitation programs now available do not work, and thus are even less of a resource than overcrowded secure confinement facilities. Beyond all the rhetoric, juvenile justice officials will have to determine what they have available, what they can expect to have made available, and what will work.

Incarceration

Advocates of incarceration defend selective incapacitation of dangerous juveniles on both retributive and functionalist grounds. Ernest Van Den Haag (1975), for example, has suggested that by their persistence, dangerous offenders have demonstrated a clear resistance to social norms. Their recidivism, he claims, represents a conscious choice, reflective of a mature and rational will. Thus, these youths do not deserve the special protections afforded juveniles and should receive appropriately retributive sanctions.

Even those less willing to ascribe chronicity to intent or lack of amenability support incarceration on functionalist grounds. Control and strain theorists argue that a punitive component will: 1) provide structure and consistency to the sometimes crazy-quilt process of juvenile justice (Kaufman, 1984); 2) protect society at large from the high number of crimes dangerous youths would commit (Farrington and West, 1977); 3) deter other youths from repeating their criminal conduct because of its certainty and severity (Weis and Hawkins, 1979); and 4) reserve society's scarce treatment resources for those youths whom it might benefit most (Agee, 1979).

Another less enthusiastic group of researchers do not support incarceration for any intrinsic value, but simply because they do not believe anything else works. This sentiment owes largely to work done by Martinson (1974) which concluded that rehabilitative efforts have had no appreciable effect on recidivism. Subsequent studies tended to confirm and expand that conclusion (Lipton, Martinson, Wilkes, 1975; Adams, 1975; Sechrest, White, Brown, 1979). Most recently, Martin, Sechrest, and Redner (1981) concluded that even those programs which appear to lower recidivism were either not replicable or not statistically significant. On the basis of these studies, then, officials have concluded that treatment of juvenile offenders is wasteful and unjustified. They claim that continuing to experiment with chronic youth offenders only exposes society to great danger, squanders scarce criminal justice resources, intrudes into the youths' family and psyche, and most importantly, provides no appreciable benefit. Some researchers have even gone so far as to say that the uncertain nature of rehabilitation programs has actually *increased* delinquency (Weis and Hawkins, 1979). Thus, lacking any evidence to the contrary, these advocates suggest that if nothing else, incapacitation is a superior solution to the existing rehabilitative paradigm.

Nevertheless, the vast majority of juvenile justice officials continue to reject the concept of mandatory incapacitation. First, they contend, it is not at all clear that incarceration works or, conversely, that rehabilitation does not work. Most of the studies which found no significant impact from rehabilitation programs relied upon inadequate research designs for measuring the program's success. Frequently, these studies did not measure the extent to which programs were actually pursued or the intensity of the program's implementation (Mann, 1976). What's more, the researchers frequently made artificial distinctions within programs, failed to measure the adequacy of the program's records, or relied upon faulty follow-up data (Greenwood and Zimring 1985). Even more importantly, these studies applied a wholly unrealistic measure of success. Rather than measuring reductions in the frequency or seriousness of criminality, these studies simply lumped together *any* future adjudication as reflective of a program's failure. Rehabilitation advocates point out that reducing the amount and seriousness of juvenile crime is just as important (from a policy perspective) as eliminating criminality altogether. Thus, they cite more recent studies which suggest that rehabilitation programs may *reduce* individual crime rates by over 70% and cut individual rates of violent crime in half (Lipton, Martinson, Wilks, 1975; Hawkins and Zimring, 1985; Armstrong and Altschuler, 1982).

Critics of selective incapacitation also contest the claim that incapacitation would be more certain and effective than the system presently in place. Our correctional institutions, they point out, are already overcrowded. Not only is there little room for new additions to our prison population, but adding new inmates may only further reduce the effectiveness of incarceration. The system already locks up its worst criminals. Presently, 95 percent of the adults in this country's prisons are violent or recidivist offenders. Unfortunately, there are so many worst criminals that the average time served is only about 16 months (Bureau of Justice Statistics, 1983). Introducing another large set of offenders for processing would simply reduce the average prison term even further and release these youths to the street with absolutely no hope of improvement. Increased incarceration, then, will only produce larger, less manageable prison populations who will return to the streets even more quickly and continue committing crimes. If anything, the time spent in incarceration with stronger, older, more sophisticated criminals may encourage further crime, either by teaching the youth new criminal skills or by increasing his sense of persecution and alienation.

Yet even more than these functional concerns, rehabilitation advocates object to incarceration on philosophical grounds. Incarceration, they contend, is incompatible with the philosophy and mission of juvenile justice. Fundamentally, the juvenile justice system rests on the assumption that antisocial behavior does not stem from an inherently antisocial disposition, but from the community's failure to properly socialize a youth. Under this formulation, recidivistic behavior is not proof that a child is not amenable to treatment, but only that society has failed to apply the appropriate treatment technology. Throughout the development from childhood to adulthood, the burden of socialization gradually shifts until an individual becomes competent and responsible for his own actions in society. Thus, during childhood a youth is entitled to the time and training necessary to complete the maturation process. Therefore, it is inconsistent to hold him morally culpable or to impose any pure punishment, stigma, or retribution upon him during that time.

If the juvenile justice system adopted a punishment and incarceration component, officials would have to adopt a different set of values for treating serious offenders. Acts would then become synonymous with intent, and responsibility would shift squarely onto the fragile shoulders of youth (Greenwood and Abrahamese, 1982). Ultimately, officials would have no reason to pursue experimental strategies for reducing persistent criminality.

In this way, introducing punishment/incarceration for dangerous juveniles into the juvenile justice system might gravely jeopardize all juvenile justice programs. Several key Supreme Court rulings (e.g., *In re Gault, Kent, and Winship*) concluded that juvenile courts which have the discretion to punish and incarcerate youths must subscribe to the same stringent due process principles applied in adult courts. However, the more due process which courts introduce into the system, the less discretion judges will have to resolve cases through informal disposition or referral to a community-based treatment program (Gendon, 1976). Without that discretion, juvenile courts might eventually grow to be more like adult courts (Conger, 1978). Thus, critics argue, the concept of rehabilitation would be undermined, and the special needs and status of children would go largely unattended.

Somewhere between these two sets of inflated claims lies an acceptable program for the handling of dangerous youths. Given our existing conceptions of childhood and justice, incarceration appears to be a repugnant alternative, and an abdication of certain social ideals. Besides, American prisons may be so destructive and inhumane that they will cause more harm than good (Goldstein, Freud, and Solnit, 1975). Yet, with the fear of crime rising and society's resources growing ever more strained, the public is equally repulsed by the prospect that thousands of violent youths will go free and that millions of dollars are being pumped into ineffective rehabilitation programs. Thus, the public is not averse to resorting to incarceration, so long as it is the last resort. Yet, for this position to have meaning other resorts must exist. The question remains–does anything work for dangerous juveniles?

What Works?

As noted earlier, there are two competing definitions for success in a serious offender program. The first measure asserts that the object of treatment is to fully socialize and integrate a delinquent youth into his community. Thus, it measures success or failure on the basis of any subsequent criminal activity. The second measure recognizes that individuals vary in their capacities and incentives to demonstrate socially appropriate behavior. Thus, it measures a program's success by the overall reduction in chronicity and seriousness of a youth's criminal conduct after he has left the program. For the purposes of this paper, that is, identifying policies to reduce the additional burden of serious juvenile criminality, I have relied upon the second measurement wherever that information was available. This measure appears to me to be more consistent with the objectives of a specialized handling policy than one which expects to achieve the same results expected of non-special offenders.

Besides success rate, another key consideration in program evaluation is cost-effectiveness. That is, regardless of how well they work, can they rehabilitate dangerous juveniles at a reasonable cost? Like recidivism, there are two competing methods for calculating cost-effectiveness. The first method simply compares the actual cost of service at each facility against the cost of alternative programs. As a benchmark, they generally compare the cost-per-youth in rehabilitation programs with the total cost-per-youth in an average incarceration program. The second, more long-term calculus, considers both the cost of each program and the reduction of projected social costs from the youth's continued criminality that would have occurred had he not entered the program. This method incorporates a cost-benefit analysis—weighing the cost of a program against its savings in reduced future criminality. Both cost-effectiveness measures are important in determining the relative value of a program, since policy-makers must address both short and long-run cost considerations. However, attempts to actually quantify and compare costs have been uneven at best.

One of the major problems facing analysts are the differences in accounting procedures between programs. For example, some programs include all operating, overhead, and general administration costs in their expense reports while others (arguably for self-serving purposes) report only operating costs-per-youth (Haggart, 1971). Another obvious problem is accurately projecting how much crime an individual would have continued to commit had he received no treatment whatsoever. In order to reduce the extent of these inevitable measurement errors, and in order to ensure consistent comparisons, I have reported financial records only from those programs for which I could ascertain all capital and operating costs, and I calculated all figures in 1979 dollars. In addition, I have only included studies which compare the recidivism rates of dangerous juvenile offenders in rehabilitation with those who are incarcerated.

A final area of concern regards consistency in classification. Although the youths in the programs I reviewed were all identified as dangerous, presumably not all of them qualified under my particular "two-violent-crimes" definition. Thus, recidivism rates in those programs may not actually reflect the exact results we could expect from a dangerous juvenile program.

Methodology

I have reviewed 15 programs representing each of the four most popular treatment models for handling dangerous juveniles: 1) secure confinement with therapy and behavior modification; 2) highly structured community treatment; 3) training, job skills, and remedial education programs; and 4) adventure experiences. Because of the wide variety of factors contributing to delinquency and the virtually infinite potential combinations of these factors among adjudicated youths, none of the programs evaluated was strictly a pure example of these models, but instead, each contained an eclectic assortment of treatment approaches with one dominant thrust. I have not tried to discover if any single treatment program is successful with *all* dangerous juveniles or to unearth some overlooked panacea. Instead, my objective was to determine if *any* approach is consistently successful with *any* subset of dangerous juveniles.

Secure Care with Treatment and Behavior Modification

The form of serious offender program most commonly employed in the juvenile justice system combines psychotherapy and behavior modification in a secure, locked environment. These programs are designed to ferret out the psychological causes of the youth's criminal behavior while training him to function effectively in a community atmosphere. At the same time that the youth benefits from this treatment, society receives the satisfaction of extracting its pound of flesh and feels protected throughout the duration of the youth's treatment. As a result, these programs have received qualified support from both incarceration and rehabilitation advocates (Agee, 1979).

Research, however, has revealed only marginal success rates from psychological therapy in secure care. Berenson and Carkhuff (1967) found that the effectiveness of treatment was independent of the program's specific orientation and technique. Truax and Carkhuff (1964) concluded that psychotherapy itself had virtually no impact on the youth's development, and any perceived gains were due entirely to behavior modification techniques or to the skill and commitment of the staff. Donaldson and Zellman (1977) even went so far as to condemn psychotherapy for provoking greater violence.

Behavior modification fared a little bit better in research studies. Cohen and Filipczak (1971) found that youths in secure care exposed to behavior modification gained more than 1 grade level per year in their Stanford Achievement Tests and experienced lower recidivism rates for 2–3 years after leaving the program. However, they concluded that those comparative advantages faded over time. This, they asserted, was the key flaw in behavior modification programs. Behavioral programs administered in highly structured environments, they claimed, only trained a youth to function well in institutions. Once the child returned to an essentially unstructured environment the system of positive benefits and sanctions collapsed, and gains made in the program began to erode. Ronald Huff (1977) suggested that identical programs which were not administered in artificial settings had substantially lower recidivism rates after the third year.

Generally, the literature concludes that psychotherapy does not have any significant impact on most youths in secure care facilities and that the impact of confined behavior modification is fleeting. However, most of these conclusions were drawn from programs directed at juveniles who had committed serious offenses but were not necessarily "dangerous juveniles." Frequently, these programs did not even accept chronically violent juveniles for fear that they would have a destabilizing influence upon the rest of the treatment population (Mann, 1976). In fact, several studies have condemned evaluations of rehabilitation programs for failing to disaggregate their effects upon the various types of youths in the facilities (Agee, 1979).

Upon closer reflection, it appears that the few programs which included dangerous juveniles had remarkably high success rates with this dangerous population. The Closed Adolescent Treatment Center (CATC), in Denver reported statistically significant reductions in crime rate and seriousness of crime among its graduates. In addition, dangerous juveniles made equally significant strides in educational achievement and securing lasting employment. CATC records indicate a more than 50% increase in these last two categories over control groups (Agee, 1979).

The cost-per-youth at CATC is substantially higher than the average cost for incarceration. CATC reported that it spends $79,870 per youth each year while incarceration programs cost, on average, about $38,000 per individual each year (Bureau of Justice Statistics, 1983). However, Neihoff (1975) compared the cost of CATC treatment to the total reduction in future crime and processing costs achieved by this program (1975). Neihoff's control groups were youths incarcerated for virtually identical crimes as those committed to CATC. He computed the cost of their treatment as the combined cost of their incarceration and the cost of their crimes upon release (in terms of physical financial loss and processing costs). He compared the savings due to incarceration with those due to treatment at CATC (in terms of reduced post-release criminality). Strikingly, he found that while incarceration returns $.70 on each dollar, CATC returned $1.70 on each dollar invested. Thus, he concluded, this rehabilitation program is not only more efficient than incarceration, it actually *saves* social resources.

Obviously, CATC is an exceptional program. However, other secure rehabilitation programs which have fewer resources and experience have still achieved success with certain types of dangerous juveniles. Mackenzie and Roos (1982) discovered three therapy/behavior modification programs which had a lasting impact upon emotionally disturbed offenders. Unfortunately, they point out that the overwhelming majority of secure treatment programs do not welcome disturbed youths and, consequently, are inadequately equipped for violent, emotionally-disturbed youth. Thus, these offenders have historically fallen through the cracks despite the existence of a viable alternative.

Community Treatment Programs. Because early studies on behavior modification concluded that the success of these treatments was partially mitigated by the artificial nature of secure care, a number of *community* treatment centers have sprung up across the country. These programs have generally faced resistance from communities who feared that such programs would let delinquent youths run free in their neighborhoods. Consequently, these programs have received relatively little public support and many have collapsed over the past decade (Mann, 1976). In order to improve their community image, the remaining programs have adopted highly staff-intensive security systems as well as other precautions.

However, there are three major stumbling blocks to the development of more community treatment programs. First, state and local legislatures have historically resisted these programs. Community treatment raises two issues: the problem of locating homes for violent offenders in an unprotected residential community, and the risks of those youths causing a tragedy. Second, because these programs are privately-run, their success depends primarily upon the experience, skill, and enthusiasm of the private vendors. Many observers suggest that the lack of state support has dissuaded several capable vendors from establishing such programs and consequently, very few such programs exist. Finally, because these programs are so rare, reliable data on their overall effectiveness is scarce.

Despite the relative paucity of community treatment programs, researchers have concluded that they do have positive results with some seriously antisocial, or treatment-resistant youth (Zimring, 1975; UDIS, 1976; Kohlberg, 1974). Five year follow-up studies in New Jersey, Michigan, and Missouri revealed that the best programs experienced less than 15% recidivism rates among their wards, or about half the average recidivism rate in secure programs (Huff, 1977; Eggers, 1977). The Missouri study concluded that such programs also cost far less than secure confinement. Weinstein (1979) found that the top programs cost $35,210 per year or almost one-half the cost of secure confinement. Rydell's nationwide study (1985) reported, on average, that community programs cost 15–30% less than secure programs mostly because of savings in guards and overhead.

Schooling and Training

Traditional liberal rehabilitation theory holds that proper training and education are the keys to accelerating a youth's socialization. Advocates of this position claim that learning aids self-awareness and confidence, while it engages the youth with others and gives him future opportunities (Linton, 1971; Barnes, 1974). In fact, even critics of rehabilitation assert that programs focusing on skill development frequently produce positive effects (Martinson, Lipton, Wilks, 1975).

Unfortunately, as with other community treatment programs, political leaders are reticent to take public responsibility for such programs. Consequently, very few exist and of those which do, only a handful have the political backing and stamina to have been able to demonstrate long-term positive results. In addition, some communities have objected to the idea of giving the worst offenders an advantage in gaining employment over other unemployed youth (Cloward and Ohlin, 1960). Yet, regardless of these concerns, educational and vocational training have been effectively proven to rehabilitate serious offenders.

The best examples of skill development programs seem to justify this optimism. One program in St. Louis, the Providence Educational Center, which combined this approach with behavior modification tracked its graduates for four years and found that 70% had not been referred to another court, 22% had been referred but at a lower rate than before, and 8% committed crime at the same or higher rates than before. Furthermore, the program had a 97% effectiveness rate with those dangerous offenders who were initially classified as alienated/learning disabled.

Skill-building programs also offer the highest cost-effectiveness ratio of all rehabilitation models. The St. Louis program, which is not atypical, costs only $8,163 per student served each year. Skill-building then, costs about one-tenth as much as secure confinement or one-fifth as much as incarceration.

Adventure Experiences

Finally, at least five jurisdictions offer so-called Adventure Experiences. These programs may range from karate instruction to outward-bound type experiences but all have the common objective of breaking down the youth's macho illusions and then building a self-image based upon hard-earned successes. The goal is to instill in the youth a sense of pride and self-confidence.

Studies of three programs—Outward-Bound, Vision Quest, and Southwest Martial Arts—have shown dramatic success in reforming violent offenders (Roos and Mackenzie, 1982; Greenwood and Zimring, 1985). Yet, most of these studies also conclude that the results may not be replicable. In each of the programs, the key ingredient of success seemed to be the superman charisma of the program's leaders and the quality of the program's staff. Research of these programs have shown that they are only effective if developed from the bottom-up. Thus, Roos and Mackenzie (1982) found that the kinds of people who can successfully run such programs cannot necessarily be easily recruited. Finally, some community leaders object to providing violent delinquents with karate skills or other survival techniques.

Nevertheless, each of the programs studied boasted recidivism rates of less than 20%. Outward-Bound and Vision Quest cost about $28,000 per student each year, or about the same as community treatment programs.

Although figures could not be obtained for the Southwest Martial Arts program, its director claims that its costs are substantially lower.

Analysis of Programs

It appears, then, that each of these program types, given certain qualifications, may be successful in curbing crime rates among dangerous juvenile offenders. However, before discussing the implications of this finding, we should consider these qualifications in greater detail.

General Concerns. First, the analysis used was frequently deficient in terms of data and survey design. The programs often failed to strictly implement the prescribed treatment either because of resource constraints, a lack of faith in the diagnosis or treatment theory, or because of management considerations within the institution. Even in programs which had been carried out as prescribed, the majority of studies did not allow a broad enough definition of recidivism, or did not track offenders over a long enough period to accurately assess the program's success.

Second, the analysis was limited by the number of programs available which specifically dealt with dangerous juveniles. Because dangerous juveniles constitute such a small portion of the total delinquent population, few jurisdictions believe it justifies establishing a specialized program or a series of such programs. Even those areas which have the resources to support a portfolio of serious offender programs often reject these programs as either throwing good money after bad or for unfairly stigmatizing youth.

Third, no single program or type of program appeared to benefit all serious offenders. Project staffs in the best programs encountered only limited success within each treatment area. Furthermore, the successes within each program varied not only from youth to youth but in the extent, scope, and duration of the change produced.

Yet, for all of these qualifications, it appears that some programs *do* work—and work well beyond a level necessary to justify their risks and costs. Strikingly, the most successful programs shared several common elements.

Elements of Success. First, each of these programs had a high staff-to-youth ratio and a consistent philosophy. The staffs were generally well-trained, committed, and diverse. These programs contained a somewhat eclectic assortment of sub-programs reflecting the various skills and experiences of the staff members. Yet, each had a unifying thrust or mission. In the end, each program provided the youth with a new set of social or vocational skills which, in turn, expanded his opportunities and reduced his frustrations.

Second, each program, with the exception of the adventure-experiences, took a long-term approach to the youths' treatment, including extensive after-care counseling. The average length of stay in the most successful programs was 18 months, with some youths staying on for up to 4 years. The open-ended nature of the commitment (most programs could require annual extensions to a youth's term) gave program directors the opportunity to apply a variety of treatment approaches and, at the same time, diminished the youth's incentive to try and con the staff into granting him an early release.

Third, successful programs are invariably located in areas in which several other treatment alternatives exist. Thus, courts had the flexibility of matching various dangerous juveniles with the programs best suited to them. Furthermore, since trial and error may be necessary before the youth is correctly matched to the appropriate treatment modality, the programs can work together more effectively and are better able to evaluate the youth's particular strengths and weaknesses. Finally, providing a range of treatments encourages experimentation and transfer *between* staffs.

Fourth, these programs were reserved as a last chance opportunity. Youths were informed that failure to reform their behavior while in the programs would result in transfer to adult prison. Over half of the programs included mechanisms to re-refer the youth to the court for sentencing.

Finally, each program contained only a small number of youths and involved them in the management of the institution. All programs included some form of contact with the youth and some form of decision-making process in which youths participated.

Summary

Risk. Rehabilitation programs are risky. By allowing dangerous juveniles to return to the community, society risks being victimized by these youths and wasting scarce resources on youths who will not benefit from these programs. However, society already accepts some degree of risk in its handling of wayward youth. If American society wished to avoid *all* risk of juvenile crime, our government would regulate families' ability to reproduce, and would restrict which parents were fit to raise children. We would probably also have some system of socialist wealth distribution to prevent youths from suffering material deprivation or otherwise feeling alienated and resentful. Yet, we have resisted these policies because, as a society, we feel that delinquency is not an unreasonable price to pay for a free, democratic, individualistic society. The real question we must answer then is: will placing violent juveniles in community-based programs create *too great* a risk?

The programs reviewed seem to have successfully mitigated the major risks of rehabilitation. Of the 15 programs reviewed, only one program averaged more than one runaway per year. More importantly, over the past 10 years, none of the programs have had a youth commit a serious crime in the community while under their care. The most effective secure programs have been able to neutralize youth violence and prevent escapes by carefully manipulating the facilities' internal environments—maintaining a low staff-youth ratio, keeping the youths in small groups, housing them in buildings with open spaces, soft colors and soft furniture all with an eye to reducing the possibility of violence, and if fights do break out, minimizing the harm they can cause. Community programs have used similar management techniques and employed additional staff-members to create a highly staff-intensive security structure.

These programs have also dispelled the notion that rehabilitation programs are ultimately a waste of money. The 15 programs reviewed experienced real recidivism rates of 20% or less. By comparison, straight incarceration programs in those same areas reported between 40–80% recidivism rates among dangerous juveniles. Thus, it appears that properly run programs are considerably more effective than incarceration.

Even more encouragingly, those programs appear to pass the cost-effectiveness test. The average cost of basic confinement in the United States is $38,000 per incarcerated person per year (Bureau of Justice Statistics, 1983). Secure confinement with therapy—such as that offered by CATC—cost an average $79,000 or nearly twice as much as incarceration. However, it reduced recidivism by 70% for those dangerous offenders which, in turn, reduced total physical damage and processing costs by an extra $52,000 per youth. Put more simply, rehabilitation directly recovered its additional cost to society and paid back an extra $14,000 per youth in crime reduction. An even more compelling case can be drawn for community treatment centers and skill-building programs. On average, these programs cost between $20,000 and $35,000 per year. Thus, their average total cost is *less* than incarcerating youth while they *reduce* recidivism among the target population by over 40%.

Rydell (1985) conducted a study comparing the effectiveness of rehabilitation programs for chronic juvenile offenders with selective incapacitation. He concluded that using selective incapacitation, the number of incarcerated offenders would go up by 5.9% and crime rates would fall by 4.8%. Rydell estimated that in order to make the same public safety gains, rehabilitation programs would need to produce a 37% reduction in recidivism—considerably less than these programs already achieve. These programs, he concluded, could reduce the prison population by 4.3% (19,000 inmates) at a savings of approximately $851 million.* Even deducting the cost of treating all the youths in these programs (including those who are subsequently imprisoned) Rydell estimated total savings at $141 million.*

* In 1984 dollars

Strategy

Problems. Despite their proven track record, rehabilitation programs continue to suffer from a variety of practical problems. First, regardless of reassuring numbers and statistics, some communities will still resist being placed at greater risk by unlocked or short-term rehabilitation programs. This, in turn, will make it difficult to generate a political constituency in support of rehabilitation and hence, will deprive these programs of adequate funding. Secondly, successful rehabilitation programs are not easily replicable. Most of the programs reviewed were developed by one or two pioneers with a vision about juvenile care. Their success has depended upon an unpredictable assortment of experimentation, determination, and conviction. Thus, even an enthusiastic legislature or department of youth services may not be able to spontaneously generate a successful program. Third, the delays in court processing, problems in court records, or other statutory delays may prevent the youths which I have targeted from receiving appropriate treatment until they are near majority. Thus, potentially effective programs may end up doing too little, too late. And finally, the most successful programs flourished in areas which supported a comprehensive range of programs for dangerous juveniles. Therefore, communities must be willing to make a multi-program commitment to juvenile care before any single program is likely to succeed.

Recommendation. In order to allay community fears, courts and youth services departments should establish certain minimum security provisions for these programs. Courts may require that community-based programs have a minimum staff-to-youth ratio and, wherever possible, require skill-building programs to be housed outside of residential areas. Finally, the programs should have some mechanism by which they can refer wholly unresponsive youth back to the juvenile court for transfer proceedings. Clearly, there will always be some youths who either are not amenable to treatment or who are so disruptive or so dangerous that they require and deserve maximum security incapacitation. Not only will such weeding improve the programs' operations, it will assure the community that the very worst criminals are indeed being locked up. In order to gain community acceptance, rehabilitation programs for dangerous juveniles must be seen as a serious, highly intensive last resort before imprisonment.

While improving the image of rehabilitation programs may make them more politically viable, it will not automatically create effective programs. As noted, courts need to offer a broad portfolio of treatments. However, at the same time, court-developed programs are unlikely to succeed. To resolve this apparent conundrum, the courts must be willing to make contracts with private vendors or rehabilitation services while taking ultimate responsibility for the mix and effectiveness of the total program.

Massachusetts has employed this type of approach over the past six years with generally positive results. Private vendors ensure a certain enthusiasm and initiative while state control will ensure a fair mix of programs and a security/cost-effectiveness oversight.

Finally, because rehabilitation is an inexact science and because of its demonstrated potential benefits, dangerous juvenile programs should have the option of extending treatment up to age 21. This may include retaining the youth in a specific program until age 21 or continuing aftercare services until that age. Extension of jurisdiction will also prevent potentially treatable youth from being arbitrarily forced into adult programs.

Conclusion

Dangerous juvenile offenders present an exceptional opportunity for the criminal justice system. Only about 5% of delinquent youths commit crimes at a high rate. However, these juvenile offenders are responsible for more than half of all juvenile crimes and about one-seventh of all the crimes committed each year. Thus, they produce a disproportionate amount of criminal and psychological damage in our society. However, unlike their adult counterparts, these youths may still be amenable to treatment. With the proper programs, these youths could be accurately identified and provided with intensive treatment without over-extending the juvenile justice community's resources. Finally, because the prime of their crime-committing years is still ahead of them, successful intervention with juveniles promises to reap even greater rewards than with adult dangerous offenders.

Although there are potentially several ways to identify dangerous juveniles, I have recommended that juvenile justice officials base classification upon the following: adjudication for two-violent offenses, three serious offenses including one violent offense, or adjudication for rape or murder with an accompanying hearing on the youth's capacity for change. Although this classification may appear restrictive, careful analysis reveals that it is the most fair, accurate, and efficient means of identifying the target population.

Youths identified as dangerous juveniles should then be examined to determine the most appropriate form of intensive treatment. Courts should base disposition on which program is likely to make each individual youth respond positively *and* which program can do so at the lowest cost *and* with the fewest restrictions on the youth's liberty. In order to achieve these ends, the court will need to have a variety of programs available and some degree of control over these programs' operation. Proper application of these programs promises to reduce crime, delinquency, and long-run increases in prison populations.

However, in order to make rehabilitation a politically viable option, courts must also include provisions for maintaining security, allowing transfers to adult courts, and extending juvenile treatment terms. These modifications will not only improve program operations but will help gain public support for a dangerous juvenile offender program.

This solution certainly will not satisfy all individuals concerned with juvenile justice. Nor will it offer a panacea to those interested in eradicating juvenile crime. Yet, in the area of criminal justice, any program which can reduce fear and crime at a relatively low cost and without unduly jeopardizing the rights and values of society's members can only be a step in the right direction.

References

Adams, S. (1975). *Evaluative research in corrections: A practical guide,* Law Enforcement Assistance Administration/National Institute of Law Enforcement and Criminal Justice, Washington, D.C.: U.S. Government Printing Office.

Alfaro, J. (1978). *Child abuse and subsequent delinquent behavior.* New York: Select Committee on Child Abuse.

Agee, V. L. (1979). *Treatment of the violent incorrigible adolescent.* Lexington, MA: Lexington Heath Books.

Armstrong, T. L., & Altschuler, D. M. (1982). The serious juvenile offender: Some promising approaches. *New Designs for Youth Development 3*(5), 3–8.

Bandura, A. (1977). *Social learning theory.* Englewood Cliffs, NJ: Prentice-Hall.

Barnes, F. H. (1975, March). A relevant new professional with youth. *American Orthopsychiatric Association.* Washington, D.C.

Berenson, B. G., & Carkhuff, R. R. (1967). *Sources of gain in counseling and psychotherapy.* New York, NY: Holt, Rhinehart, and Winston.

Black, E. T., & Smith, C. P. (1981). *Reports of the national juvenile justice assessment centers,* Office of Juvenile Justice and Delinquency Prevention. Washington, DC: U.S. Government Printing Office.

Blumberg, A. (1967). *Criminal justice.* Chicago, IL: Quadrangle Books.

Blumstein, A., & Cohen, J. (1979). Estimation of individual crime rates from arrest records. *Journal of Criminal Law and Criminology, 70,* 561–585.

Chaiken, J. M., & Chaiken, M. R. (1982). *Varieties of criminal behavior.* Santa Monica, CA: Rand Corporation.

Cloward, R. A., & Ohlin L. E. (1960). *Delinquency and opportunity.* New York, NY: Free Press of Glencoe, MacMillan.

Coates, R. B. (1981). Deinstitutionalization and the serious juvenile offender. *Crime and Delinquency, 24*(4), 477–486.

Coates, R. B. (1984). Appropriate alternatives for the violent juvenile offender. In Robert Mathias et al. (Eds.), *Violent juvenile offenders: An anthology Vol. 1* (pp. 181–185). Santa Monica, CA: National Council on Crime and Delinquency.

Coates, R. B., Miller, A. D., & Ohlin, L. E. (1975). *Exploratory analysis of recidivism and cohort data on the Massachusetts youth correctional system.* Cambridge, MA: Center for Criminal Justice, Harvard Law School.

Coates, R. B., Miller, A. D., & Ohlin, L. E. (1978). *Diversity in a youth correctional system: Handling delinquents in Massachusetts.* Cambridge, MA: Ballinger.

Cocozza, J. J., & Steadman, H. J. (1976). The failure of psychiatric predictions of dangerousness: Clear and convincing evidence. *Rutgers Law Review, 29*(Winter), 1084–1101.

Conger, R. D. (1978). From social learning to criminal behavior. In M. D. Krohn, & R. L. Akers (Eds.), *Crime, law and sanctions: Theoretical perspectives.* Beverly Hills, CA: Sage.

Cohen, A. K. (1955). *Delinquent boys: The culture of the gang.* New York: Free Press.

Cohen, H., & Filipczak, J. (1971). *A new learning environment.* San Francisco, CA: Jossey-Bass.

Donaldson, T. S., & Zellman, G. L. (1976). Programs based on psychology and psychiatry. In D. Mann (Ed.), *Intervening with convicted serious juvenile offenders,* National Institute for Juvenile Justice and Delinquency Prevention. Washington D.C.: Government Printing Office.

Eggers, W. (1975). In *Longitudinal evaluation project of the youth services program, Part II: analysis.* Washington, D.C.: Government Printing Office.

Empey, L. & Erickson, M. (1972). *The provo experiment.* Lexington, MA: Heath Lexington Books.

Erickson, M. L. (1971). The group context of delinquent behavior. *Social Problems, 19,* 114–129.

Fagan, J. A., Jones, S. J., Hartstone, E., Rudman, C. & Emerson, R. (1981). *Background paper for violent juvenile offender research and development program, Part I.* San Francisco, California: URSA Institute.

Fagan, J. A., Hansen, K. V., & Jang, M. (1983). Profiles of violent juveniles: An empirical test of an integrated theory of violent delinquency. In J. Kleugal (Ed.), *Evaluating contemporary juvenile justice.* Beverly Hills, CA: Sage Publications.

Fagan, J. A., & Hartstone, E. (1984). Strategic planning in juvenile justice—defining the toughest kids. In R. A. Mathias, P. DeMuro, & R. S. Allinson (Eds.), *Violent juvenile offenders: An anthology: Vol. 1.* (pp. 31–51). San Francisco, CA: National Council on Crime and Delinquency.

Farrington, D. P. (1978). Family backgrounds of aggressive youths. In L. Hershov *et al.* (Eds.), *Aggressive and anti-social behavior of preschool children.*

Farrington, D. P. (1983). *Further analyses of a longitudinal survey of crime and delinquency.* Cambridge, England: Institute of Criminology.

Farrington, D. P., & West, D. J. (1977). *The delinquent way of life: third report of the cambridge study in delinquent development.* New York: Rossak.

Feld, B. C. (1981). Legislative policies toward the serious juvenile offender: On the virtues of automatic adulthood. *Crime and Delinquency, 27*(4), 497–521.

Feld, B. C. (1983). Delinquent careers and criminal policy: Just deserts and the waiver decision. *Criminology, 21*(2), 195–212.

Gadow, D., & McKibbon, J. (1984). Discipline and the institutionalized violent delinquent. In R. A. Mathias *et al.* (Eds.), *Violent juvenile offenders: An anthology: Vol 1.* (pp. 311–325). San Francisco, CA: National Council on Crime and Delinquency.

Gendon, R. (1976). Separate legal representation for children: protecting the rights and interests of minors?. *Harvard Law Review, 11,* 565.

Glueck, S., & Glueck, E. (1950). *Predicting delinquency and crime*. Cambridge, MA: Harvard University Press.

Goldstein, J., Freud, A., & Solnit, A. J. (1973). *Beyond the best interests of the child*. New York: Free Press.

Greenwood, P. W. (1985). *The juvenile rehabilitation reader: A RAND note*. Santa Monica, CA: RAND.

Greenwood, P., & Abrahamse, A. (1982). *Selective incapacitation*. Santa Monica, CA: Rand Corporation.

Greenwood, P. W., & Zimring, F. (1985). *One more chance: The pursuit of promising intervention strategies for chronic juvenile offenders*. Santa Monica, CA: RAND.

Haggart, R. (1971). Estimating the costs of rehabilitation, cited in D. Mann (Ed.), *Intervening with convicted serious juvenile offenders*. National Institute for Juvenile Justice and Delinquency Prevention. Washington, DC: U.S. Government Printing Office.

Hamparian, D. (1982). *Youth in adult courts: Between two worlds*. Columbus, OH: Academy for Contemporary Problems.

Hamparian, D., Schuster, R., Dinitz, S., & Conrad, J. (1978). *The violent few: A study of the dangerous juvenile offender*. Lexington, MA: Lexington Books.

Hartstone, E., & Hansen, K. V. (1984). The violent juvenile offender: An empirical portrait. In R. A. Mathias *et al.* (Eds.), *Violent juvenile offenders: An anthology*. San Francisco, CA: National National on Crime and Delinquency.

Hartstone, E., Jang, M., & Fagan, J. (1982). *Delinquent careers of the chronically violent juvenile*. Paper presented at 1983 Annual Meeting of Pacific Sociological Association, San Jose, CA.

Hawkins, J. D., & Weis, J. G. (1980). *The social development model: An integrated approach to delinquency prevention*. Seattle, WA: Center for Law and Justice, University of Washington.

Hellman, D., & Blackman, N. (1966). Enuresis, firesetting, and cruelty to animals: A triad predictive of adult crime. *American Journal of Psychiatry, 122,* 1431–35.

Hildelang, M. J., & McDermott, M. J. (1981). *Analysis of national crime victimization survey data to study serious delinquent behavior, Juvenile criminal behavior: An analysis of rates and victim characteristics*. Albany, NY: Criminal Justice Research Center.

Hirschi, T. (1969). *Causes of delinquency*. Berkeley, CA: University of California Press.

Huff, R. (1976). Programs Based on Sociology and Social Work. In D. Mann (Ed.), *Intervening with convicted serious juvenile offenders*. National Institute for Juvenile Justice and Delinquency Prevention, Washington, D.C.: U.S. Government Printing Office.

Justice, B., Justice, R., & Kraft, J. (1974). Early warning signs of violence: Is a triad enough?. *American Journal of Psychiatry, 131,* 457–459.

Kaufman, I. R. (1982). The child in trouble: The long and difficult road to reforming the crazy-quilt juvenile justice system. *Washington University Law Quarterly, 60,* 743–777.

Klein, M. W. (1967). *Juvenile gangs in context.* Englewood Cliffs, NJ: Prentice-Hall.

Klein, M. W. (1971). *Street gangs and street workers.* Englewood Cliffs, NJ: Prentice-Hall.

Kohlberg, L. *et al.* (1974). *The just community approach to corrections.* Cambridge, MA: Moral Education Research Foundation.

Kuhl, A. (1981). An unpublished doctoral dissertation. Cited in R. A. Mathias *et al.* (Eds.), *Violent juvenile offenders: An anthology.* San Francisco, CA: National Council on Crime and Delinquency.

Lefkowitz, M. M., Eron, L. D., Walker, L. O., & Huesman, L. R. (1977). *Growing up to be violent: A longitudinal study of the development of aggression.* New York: Pergamon Press.

Linton, T. E. (1971). The educateur model: A theoretical manuscript. *The Journal of Special Education, 5,* 21–51.

Lipton, D., Martinson, R., & Wilks, J. (1975). *The effectiveness of correctional treatment: A survey of treatment evaluation studies.* New York: NY: Praeger.

Manella, R. L. (1977). *The hard-core juvenile offender.* Nevada: National Council of Juvenile Court Judges.

Mann, D. (Ed.). (1976). *Intervening with convicted serious juvenile offenders.* National Institute for Juvenile Justice and Delinquency Prevention. Washington, DC: U.S. Government Printing Office.

Martin, S. E., Sechrest, L. B., & Redner, R. (Eds.). (1981). *New directions in the rehabilitation of criminal offenders: Final report.* National Research Council. Washington, D.C.: National Academy of Sciences.

Martinson, R. (1974). What works? Questions and answers about prison reform. *Public Interest, 35,* 22–54.

Mathias, R. A., Demuro, P., & Alinson, R. (Eds.). (1984). *Violent juvenile offenders: An anthology.* San Francisco, CA: National Council on Crime and Delinquency.

McCord, W., McCord, J., & Zola, I. K. (1959). *Origins of crime: A new evaluation of the Cambridge-Somerville youth study.* New York, NY: Columbia University Press.

McDermott, J. C. (1982). *The serious juvenile offender: Problems in definition and targetting.* Paper Presented at Annual Meeting of the American Society of Criminology, Toronto, Ontario.

McKenzie, E. & Roos, R. A. (1982). *The kid nobody wants: Treating the seriously delinquent youth.* National Council of Juvenile and Family Court Judges. Reno, Nevada: Delta Institute.

Miller, A. D. & Ohlin, L. E. (1980). *Decision-making about secure care for juveniles.* Cambridge, MA: Harvard University, Center for Criminal Justice.

Monahan, J., Brodsky, S. L., & Shah, S. A. (1981). *Predicting violent behavior: An assessment of clinical techniques.* Beverly Hills, CA: Sage.

Monahan, J. (1977). The prediction of violent behavior in juveniles. In J. Judson & P. Mack (Eds.), *The serious juvenile offender: Proceedings of a symposium.* Washington, DC: Office of Juvenile Justice and Delinquency Prevention.

Moore, M. H., Estrich, S. R., McGillis, D., Spelman, W. (1984). *Dangerous offenders: The elusive target of justice.* Cambridge, MA: Harvard University Press.

Moore, M. H., Wilson, J. Q., & Gants, R. (1978). *Violent attitudes and chronic offenders.* Research Paper for the John F. Kennedy School of Government.

Morris, N. (1951). *The habitual offender*. Cambridge, MA: Harvard University Press.

Murray, C. A., Thomson, D., & Isreal, C. B. (1978). *UDIS: Deinstitutionalizing the chronic juvenile offender*. American Institutes for Research.

Neihof, P. (1975). The economics of secure care. In P. R. Knott & R. Haiduk (Eds.), *Evaluation of the closed adolescent treatment center: Final Report to LEAA*. Unpublished. Cited in V. Agee (1979). *Treatment of the violent incorrigible adolescent,* Lexington, MA: Heath.

Packer, H. L. (1966). The courts, the police and the rest of us. *Journal of Criminal Law, Criminology and Police Science, 57,* 238–43.

Petersilia, J. M., Greenwood, P., & Lavin, M. (1978). *Criminal careers of habitual felons*. National Institute of Law Enforcement and Criminal Justice, Law Enforcement Assistance Administration. Washington, D.C.: U.S. Government Printing Office.

Platt, A. (1969). *The child savers: The invention of delinquency*. Chicago: University of Chicago Press.

Polk, K., & Schaefer, W. E. (Eds.) (1972). *Schools and delinquency*. Englewood Cliffs: Prentice-Hall.

President's Commission on Law Enforcement and the Administration of Justice (1967). *The challenge of crime in a free society*. Washington, D.C.: U.S. Government Printing Office.

President's Task Force on Violent Crime (1982). *Final report*. Washington, DC: U.S. Government Printing Office.

Radzinowicz, L., & Hood, R. (1980). Incapacitating the habitual criminal: The English experience, *Michigan Law Review, 78,* 1305–1389.

Robins, L. N., & Wish, E. (1977). Childhood deviance as a developmental process. *Social Forces, 56,* 448–473.

Rojek, D. G., & Erikson, M. L. (1982). Delinquent careers. *Criminology, 20*(1), 5–28.

Roysher, M., & Edelman, P. (1981). Treating juveniles as adults in New York: What does it mean and how is it working? In J. C. Hall, D. Hamparian, J. Pettibone, & J. White (Eds.), *Major issues in juvenile justice information and training: Readings in public policy*. Washington, D.C.: Office of Juvenile Justice and Delinquency Prevention.

Rydell, C. P. (1985). The economics of early intervention vs. later incarceration. In P. Greenwood (Ed.), *The Juvenile Rehabilitation Reader: A RAND Note*. Santa Monica, CA: RAND.

Schlesinger, S. E. (1978). Prediction of dangerousness in juveniles—a replication. *Crime and Delinquency, 8*(January), 40–48.

Sechrest, L. B., White, S. O., & Brown, E. (Eds.). (1972). *The rehabilitation of criminal offenders: Problems and prospects*. Washington, D.C.: National Academy of Sciences.

Sellin, T., & Wolfgang, M. E. (1964). *The measurement of delinquency*. New York: John Wiley and Sons.

Shannon, L. W. (1980, November). *Assessing the relationship of adult careers to juvenile careers: The transitional years (16–24)*. Paper presented at the Annual Meeting of the American Society of Criminology, San Francisco, CA.

Shannon, L. W. (1983). *The prediction problem as it applies to delinquency and crime control*. Office of Juvenile Justice and Delinquency Prevention. Washington, D.C.: U.S. Government Printing Office.

Short, J. F., Jr., & Strodtbeck, F. L. (1965). *Group process and gang delinquency*. Chicago: University of Chicago Press.

Silberman, C. E. (1978). *Criminal violence, criminal justice*. New York: Random House.

Smith, C. P., Alexander, P. S., Halatyn, T. V., & Roberts, C. (1980). *A national assessment of serious juvenile crime and the juvenile justice system: The need for a rational response: Volume II*. The National Institute for Juvenile Justice and Delinquency Prevention, Office of Juvenile Justice and Delinquency Prevention. Washington, D.C.: U.S. Government Printing Office.

Strasburg, P. A. (1978). *Violent delinquents: A report to the ford foundation for the vera institute of justice*. New York: Monarch Press.

Truax, C. B., & Carkhuff, R. R. (1964). For better or for worse, the process of psychotherapeutic personality change. In B. T. Wigdor (Ed.), *Recent advances in the study of behavior change: Proceeding of the academic assembly on clinical psychology*. Montreal: McGill University Press.

UDIS (Unified Delinquency Intervention Service). (1976). Grant application to Illinois Law Enforcement Commission. In D. Mann (Ed.), *Intervening with convicted serious juvenile offenders*. National Institute for Juvenile Justice and Delinquency Prevention. Washington, D.C.: U.S. Government Printing Office.

U.S. Bureau of the Census. (1982). Preliminary estimates of the population of the United States by age, sex, and race: 1970 to 1983. *Current Population Reports*. Series Washington, DC: U.S. Government Printing Office.

U.S. Department of Justice, Bureau of Justice Statistics. (1983). *Report to the Nation on crime and justice: The data*. Washington, D.C.: U.S. Government Printing Office.

U.S. Department of Justice, Federal Bureau of Investigation. (1970 to 1983). *Uniform crime reports*. Washington, DC: U.S. Government Printing Office.

U.S. Department of Justice. (1981). *Criminal victimization in the United States, 1979*. Washington, DC: U.S. Government Printing Office.

Vachss, A. H., & Bakal, Y. (1979). *Life-style violent juvenile—the secure treatment approach*. Lexington, MA: Heath Lexington Books.

Van den Haag, E. (1975). *Punishing criminals: Concerning a very old and painful question*. New York: Basic Books.

Van Dine, S., Conrad, J., Dinitz, S. (1979). *Restraining the wicked*. Lexington, Mass.: Lexington Books.

Weeks, H. A. (1958). *Youthful offenders at highfields*. Ann Arbor, MI: University of Michigan Press.

Weinstein, N. (1979). *Paying for juvenile treatment programs: The St. Louis experience*. Research Paper for the Washington University School of Law, St. Louis, MO.

Weis, J. G., & Hawkins, J. D. (1979). *Background paper for delinquency prevention research and development program*. Seattle, WA: Center for Law and Justice, University of Washington.

Whitaker, J. K. (1979). *Caring for troubled children*. San Francisco, CA: Jossey Bass.

Whitaker, M. J. (1982). *Overview of the definition of chronic violent offender following seventeen weeks of screening in Shelby County, Tennessee*. A Position Paper. Cited in R. A. Mathias, P. DeMuro & R. S. Allinson, (Eds.), *Violent juvenile offenders: An anthology: Vol. 1.* (pp. 31–51). San Francisco, CA: National Council on Crime and Delinquency.

Wilson, J. Q. (1975). *Thinking about crime,* New York: Basic Books.

Wilson, J. Q., & Boland, B. (1978). Age, crime, and punishment. *The Public Interest, 51,* 22–34.

Wolfgang, M. E. (1977). From boy to man—from delinquency to crime. In J. Hudson & P. Mack (Eds.), *The serious juvenile offender: Proceedings of symposium.* Washington, DC: Office of Juvenile Justice and Delinquency Prevention.

Wolfgang, M. E., Figlio, R. M., & Sellin, T. (1972). *Delinquency in a birth cohort.* Chicago, IL: University of Chicago Press.

Yin, R. K., & Heald, K. (1975). Using the case survey method to analyze policy studies. *Administrative Science Quarterly, 20.*

Zimring, F. E. (1975). *Dealing with youth crime, national needs and federal priorities.* Santa Monica, CA: RAND.

Zimring, F. E. (1978). *Confronting youth crime.* New York: Twentieth Century Foundation.

Zimring, F. E. (1978, April). *The serious juvenile offender: Notes on an unknown quantity.* Testimony for the U.S. Senate Hearing on Serious Youth Crime, Subcommittee to Investigate Juvenile Delinquency, Committee on the Judiciary, 95th Congress, 2nd Session. Washington, DC: U.S. Government Printing Office.

Zimring, F. E. (1979). American youth violence issues and trends. In N. Morris & M. Tonry (Eds.), *Crime and justice: An annual review of research: Vol. 1.* (pp. 67–107). Chicago, IL: University of Chicago Press.

Zimring, F. E. (1981). *The changing legal world of adolescence.* New York, NY: Viking.

Zimring, F. E., & Hawkins, G. (1985). Western European perspectives on the treatment of young offenders. In P. Greenwood (Ed.), *The juvenile justice reader: A RAND note.* Santa Monica, CA: RAND.

10
Status Offenders and the Juvenile Court: Past Practices, Future Prospects

THOMAS R. BEARROWS

Although state-wide juvenile courts in the United States began in 1899, their purpose and practices face increasing opposition from both internal and external forces. In a number of decisions,[1] the United States Supreme Court has imposed due process requirements upon the previously informal juvenile court. Based on these decisions, some commentators suggest that the juvenile court should mirror the adult court.[2] Others have urged the abolition of the entire juvenile court system.[3] Finally, some authors have advocated drastic changes in the court's jurisdiction, such as eliminating status offense jurisdiction[4] or transferring serious offenders to adult courts.[5]

This paper discusses whether the court should continue to exercise jurisdiction over status offenses. To explore the issue, the paper first summarizes the court's history and philosophy, emphasizing recent changes imposed by the Supreme Court. The author finds that a purely historical perspective fails to justify status offense jurisdiction. Accordingly, the writer presents an analytic justification for differential treatment of juveniles in general, then assesses specific arguments for and against status offense jurisdiction.

The author concludes that traditional legal considerations fail to resolve the jurisdiction question, and therefore explores policy arguments. In conclusion, the author argues that the juvenile court should continue to exercise status offense jurisdiction, and provides specific recommendations for the court's response to juvenile status offenders.

History and Philosophy of the Juvenile Court

The juvenile justice system differs from the adult criminal system in many ways, often because of disparate fundamental assumptions. For example, the departures in juvenile law from the tenets in criminal law begin with an uncertainty about whether young persons should be held fully responsible for their conduct. Unfortunately, the particular underlying notions which once created and continue to influence the juvenile court are rarely articulated.

This section briefly examines the history and philosophy of the juvenile court. It summarizes significant events leading to the development of the court, characterizes its early period, and then describes how Supreme Court decisions have affected the juvenile court's ideology and operation since the mid-1960s.

Historical Treatment of Juveniles

One of the oldest status offender laws is found in the Bible and prescribes stoning as the ultimate sanction for a "stubborn and rebellious son."[6] The harsh response to disobedience typifies the indifference with which early societies viewed children's problems. Until the growth of Christianity in Western civilization, laws typically treated children as adults and subjected them to the same punishment.

In the late 1600s, however, a conception of childhood arose as the period during which parents could mold future citizens through strict discipline and training.[7] The 1700s in America witnessed a new emphasis on the nuclear family and its role in administering punishment to children, considered evil by nature. The 1800s brought a growing awareness of external causes of deviant behavior such as family and community corruption. Rationalism taught that people were by nature good, while the environment caused evil tendencies.

America also increased its use of secure institutions, such as asylums and houses of refuge, to maintain social control. The New York House of Refuge, established in 1824, exemplified the impulse for both social control and rehabilitation of wayward children by society's "elite."

Although reformatories and industrial schools began to replace older institutions ("prison warehouses") around 1870, the new institutions resembled the old ones. Reformers concerned about the care, protection, and discipline of children gradually looked to other, more respected institutions, such as the courts, for guidance.[8]

1899: The Early Court and the Doctrine of *Parens Patriae*

A combination of historical factors helped to produce the first juvenile court in Chicago. A natural outgrowth of the 1800s Enlightenment, the court represented the progressives' response to children at risk. The general goal of the court was a benevolent one: save the children. Driven by environmental and psychological explanations of delinquency, the court took aim at poor urban conditions ("immigrant slums") and "depraved" mental states.

The court adopted the doctrine of *parens patriae* to justify its interference with a private institution, the family. *Parens patriae* emerged as a legal doctrine when chancery (equity) courts in medieval England sought to assure the orderly transfer of feudal duties from one generation to another.[9] Beginning in the late 16th century, English courts expanded the doctrine to arrange people, property, and power relative to the monarchy.[10] In short, English courts applied the principle to maintain the structure of feudalism.[11]

An American court first explicitly applied *parens patriae* to justify statutory commitments to a residential institution for juveniles in *Ex Parte Crouse*.[12] Although *Crouse* involved an "unmanageable" (delinquent) child, other courts soon used *parens patriae* to justify state intervention in neglect cases as well. In fact, like 1800s reformers, courts failed to distinguish between neglected, dependent, and delinquent children,[13] and adopted the doctrine as a blanket justification for state intervention in the lives of all children who *might* become a community crime problem. Eventually, states embodied *parens patriae* as a mandate for the court to ensure that "the care, trust, custody and discipline of a child shall approximate as nearly as may be that which should be given by its parents."[14]

The arrival of the juvenile court produced several specific changes. Delinquency petitions, for example, replaced criminal charges. Similarly, the procedure was primarily civil, not criminal. Because state interests naturally coincided with a juvenile's, the hearing itself lacked procedural safeguards found in the adult court, such as a jury of peers, defense counsel, and formal rules of evidence. In fact, the judge frequently sat beside the youth during the hearing.[15]

Finally, the court's emphasis on the child's needs changed its fact-finding focus from a determination of the accused's guilt or innocence to the needs of the child, based upon the child's moral character and lifestyle. As a result, the court enjoyed unfettered power for both pre-sentencing investigations and post-sentencing supervision.

The movement swept the country. By 1920, all but three states had created juvenile courts. Today, all states possess some form of a juvenile court. Despite studies which suggested that the court was not achieving its rehabilitative goal,[16] the court functioned unchanged until the early 1960s, when several Supreme Court decisions signalled a change in attitude toward individual rights and state action.

The Constitutionalized Court

In *Mapp v. Ohio*,[17] the Supreme Court held that the Fourteenth Amendment's due process clause incorporated certain provisions of the Bill of Rights. In a series of subsequent criminal cases, the Court required states to accord criminal defendants certain procedural safeguards, such as protection against unreasonable searches and seizures, the right to counsel, the privilege against self-incrimination, and the right to a jury trial.

In re Gault[18] provided the Court with an opportunity to apply similar due process requirements to juvenile courts. The Court held that in delinquency hearings which threaten institutionalization, juveniles possess the rights of counsel, confrontation, and cross-examination. Additionally, the state must notify the juvenile of specific charges and must recognize the child's privilege against self-incrimination. In reaching its decision, the Court scrutinized the *parens patriae* doctrine:

> The Latin phrase proved to be a great help to those who sought to rationalize the exclusion of juveniles from the constitutional scheme; but its meaning is murky and its historic credentials are of dubious relevance . . . there is no trace of the doctrine in the history of criminal jurisprudence . . . the highest motives and most enlightened impulses led to a peculiar system for juveniles, unknown to our law in any comparable context. The constitutional and theoretical basis for this peculiar system is—to say the least—debatable.[19]

Three years later, the Court further limited the juvenile court's discretion. *In Re Winship*[20] followed the reasoning in *Gault* and applied the "beyond a reasonable doubt" standard to delinquency hearings. In *McKeiver v. Pennsylvania,*[21] however, the Court refused to require jury trials for juveniles.

Many commentators contend that the Court's decisions have stripped the juvenile court of its ideology and effectiveness. They argue that additional procedural safeguards undermine the court's flexible, individualized approach, and transform it into an adult court. As a result, the court is now slow, impersonal, and punitive.

Others respond that the court has never reached the high aspirations of its founders. They cite studies from the 1920s until the present which reveal high recidivism rates for youths "treated" by the court, and observe the abuses which occurred during the court's earlier years; at least now the court must recognize the rights of juveniles.

Principled Justifications for Differential Treatment

Regardless of the ultimate outcome of the historical debate, a review of the early and later juvenile court reveals several differences. First, we are less certain than the progressive reformers that we understand the causes of deviant behavior. Second, we lack complete confidence in the wisdom or effectiveness of rehabilitation as a primary goal. State legislatures have demonstrated our uncertainty by instituting mandatory sentencing and by transforming the insanity defense to guilty-but-mentally-ill.

Finally, although *Gault* and its progeny apply only to delinquency hearings which threaten institutionalization, the *parens patriae* doctrine has lost much of its force as a justification for uncontrolled state (judicial) action in juvenile cases. We view state involvement in private institutions (such as families) with hesitation, not adulation. And, we no longer assume that state and juvenile interests always coincide.

Despite the differences between 1899 and 1984, one idea remains relatively unscathed: treat juveniles differently than adults. The notion persists, for example, that when a juvenile encounters the criminal justice system we should treat him differently. In fact, I suggest that if we can enumerate reasons for differential treatment in general, we may discover a new doctrine, divorced from legal and historical antecedents, with which to endorse and guide the juvenile court of the future.[22] We may find, for example, a rationale for status offense jurisdiction.

What are the reasons, then, which compel us to view juvenile behavior differently? I think there are at least three, all of which remain as valid today as 85 years ago:

1. Diminished Responsibility
2. Extraordinary Capacity for Change
3. Interference with Parental Authority

Of course, not all of the reasons will arise in every case that the court handles. Abuse and neglect cases, for example, usually involve only interference with parental rights. Because the state seeks to protect the child's interests against its parents, the state often terminates the parents' custody. Similarly, status offenses primarily involve diminished responsibility and capacity for change, with less direct interference with parental authority.

It is important to note that the reasons for treating juveniles differently cut across several ideologies that have dominated recent debate. Some would argue, for example, that we should treat juveniles differently because one idea of "justice" (i.e., retribution) requires it. The idea of diminished responsibility corresponds to "justice" notions: we should hold people fully accountable for their conduct only when they are responsible adults.

Similarly, some contend that utilitarian goals (e.g., helping youths develop, or controlling crime) require differential treatment of juveniles. Clearly, youths' extraordinary capacity for change is a utilitarian consideration. Finally, interference with parental authority involves the relationship between the state and private institutions. Different political groups view this relationship—especially its nature and scope—differently.

Note then, that each rationale favors differential treatment. Taken together, they give us good reason to treat juveniles differently. And because the three justifications for differential treatment owe no allegiance to a *single* ideology, the conclusions which they suggest escape pedantic criticism.

The following section briefly examines the three rationales for differential treatment of juveniles. By discussing the justifications separately, we may discern appropriate societal responses for particular cases. When we consider the justifications together, we may discover reasons for the juvenile court to exercise jurisdiction over status offenses.

Diminished Responsibility

The law traditionally has recognized the concept of responsibility by requiring criminal defendants to possess an appropriate *mens rea* (evil mind) to be found guilty of a crime. The requirement contains two elements, both of which must have been present at the time the crime was committed. First, the defendant must have known what he was doing in a literal sense: he must have realized, for example, that he was striking the victim's head and not a cabbage head. I will term this element the epistemological element.

Second, he must have known that what he was doing was wrong: this is a moral element. What do we mean by "wrong"? We do not mean technically illegal, because knowledge of specific criminal statutes is not an element of criminal offenses. Rather, we mean that the defendant recognized the difference between right and wrong *in general* and should have realized that his conduct probably violated accepted standards of conduct. In short, we impose criminal liability only upon those who, despite their conduct, are able to recognize societal values.

Although many juveniles lack both of the *mens rea* elements, most 10-year-olds know the difference between a face and a cabbage. Accordingly, young offenders often lack only the moral element of *mens rea*.

It is important to note here that a desirable outcome of childhood is the attainment of both the epistemological and moral elements of *mens rea*. We want young people to develop physically, psychologically, and morally. Psychologically, we want children to distinguish between themselves and their environment, to understand that people "act" but "things" don't, and ultimately to develop a strong self-identity. Morally, we want children to recognize and adopt certain societal values: to respect the rights of others, and to conform and control their conduct accordingly.

The adoption of societal rules by citizens is, of course, the end of criminal law in general. In a democracy, citizens enact laws by popular consent that forbid certain actions. Unlike civil rules, under which individuals may suffer pecuniary losses when they engage in merely careless conduct, criminal statutes say more: "No, you cannot hit people intentionally. If you do, society will take strong steps to encourage you to adopt its rules, and to insure that you stop acting in this way; we may lock you up." Success in the criminal justice system means an offender who does not repeat, having internalized the common moral code.

Extraordinary Capacity For Change

The "capacity for change" rationale for treating juveniles differently argues that because young people's characters are still developing, they possess an unparalleled potential for reform. Accordingly, they respond better to our character/conduct modification efforts. In fact, their beliefs may be so fickle that rehabilitation is too strong a word; we try instead to habilitate them. Unlike the diminished responsibility rationale, the capacity for change justification is forward-looking: we emphasize the individual's future capacity, not the level of responsibility at the time of the offense.

Why is this rationale important? First, it reminds us of a basic assumption of the juvenile court: juveniles probably are more susceptible to rehabilitative or corrective approaches than many adults. Second, the "change" rationale encourages us to utilize the marvelous opportunity for influencing future citizens. Recall that shared values drive the criminal justice system. It makes little sense to enact criminal statutes yet refuse to instill the same values in our youth. Consider the following argument:

1. We want adults to possess character and exhibit conduct consistent with values expressed by the criminal law.
2. Children's characters are somewhat malleable and therefore more susceptible to outside influence than adults'.
3. Children's extraordinary capacity for change decreases as they age.
4. The juvenile court should actively reaffirm and instill societal values in juveniles.

This approach is not without problems, however. First, we must ask how the court can instill values most effectively. The question raises an old debate about the efficacy of two approaches, nurture and coercion. Commentators have disagreed about the best means to rehabilitate offenders. Typically, courts have favored nurture when offenders are juveniles. The early juvenile court, for example, emphasized the needs of the child and sought to provide beneficial treatment on a case-by-case basis: juvenile offenders needed help, and the court kindly provided it. Others thought that forceful discipline was the proper method to help youths develop.

A second problem arises whenever the state begins to impose a conception of virtue: paternalism. Some undoubtedly will argue that if we allow the juvenile court to impose society's values upon youth, we will produce "cultural imperialism" and the like. In fact, several authors have characterized the early court's actions as forcing middle class values upon immigrant families.

One might respond that this criticism of the juvenile court is mistaken, especially when applied to criminal offenses. The danger of a majority imposing its "will" upon a minority is no greater for young offenders than adult offenders. In both instances, the Supreme Court's interpretation of the Constitution limits the state's power to prohibit conduct. Furthermore, the freedoms of speech and religion shelter expression and beliefs which contain little or no conduct. In the final section, we will see how the existence of status offenses raises similar fundamental concerns.

Interference With Parental Authority

In general, despite the fact that no specific constitutional provision applies and defines parents' legal rights to children, courts have emphasized repeatedly the parents' "fundamental right" to the companionship and care of their children. The Supreme Court, for example, has favored parental decisions based upon religious beliefs over strong state interests. The Court has found that parents can withdraw their children from school after the eighth grade and can withhold non-emergency medical treatment from their children. In fact, the juvenile court's original use of *parens patriae* demonstrates the notion that the state needs significant justification to interfere with the parent-child relationship.

The Court (and society) also has recognized parental responsibilities. Parents possess a legal obligation to provide for the care, custody, and development of their children. In fact, failure to discharge these obligations may lead to termination of parental rights and/or criminal prosecution. As a policy matter, we want to encourage parents to continue to recognize and fulfill their responsibilities.

Although juvenile court cases typically involve different state interests, they all represent situations in which parents have "failed" to discharge an obligation. In abuse and neglect cases, parents have failed to provide a stable and healthy environment. In delinquency cases, parents have failed to shape their children's character to meet society's expectations.

The juvenile court's involvement, therefore, is an instance where a public (state) institution responds to apparent failure by private institutions. Here, families and churches ostensibly have failed to produce good character. This characterization is not intended to place blame, but rather to raise questions regarding the opportunities for, and nature of, state involvement when private institutions need help.

An Application: Status Offenders and the Juvenile Court

To demonstrate the considerations which underlie debate in the juvenile justice area consider a specific issue confronting the juvenile justice system: should juvenile courts handle juvenile status offenders? More specifically, should legislatures enact statutes which grant to the juvenile court jurisdiction over youths who commit status offenses such as chronic truancy, running away, and underage drinking?

Analytically, status offenses represent a classic example of differential treatment for adults and children. By definition, legislatures which create status offenses prohibit certain conduct for *juveniles only*. I will suggest later how the principled justifications—diminished responsibility, capacity for change, and interference with parental authority—support or undermine status offenses.

Historically, juvenile courts have exercised jurisdiction over status offenses and usually treated status offenders and delinquents identically. Influenced by *Gault* and a growing concern for children's rights, lobbyists and children's advocates, such as the Children's Bureau of H.E.W., successfully supported the deinstitutionalization of status offenders. The movement received support by the Juvenile Justice and Delinquency Prevention Act of 1974, which required recipients of federal funds to provide separate, nonrestrictive shelters for status offenders.

Moreover, to avoid the stigma associated with the delinquency label, legislatures have replaced status offenses with a "need for supervision" category known as PINS, CHINS, CINS, or MINS (persons, children, or minors in need of supervision).[23] Accordingly, although nearly every state features explicit or implicit status offense legislation,[24] the vast majority now handle status offenders and delinquents separately. For example, by late 1983 only about eleven states classified status offenders and juvenile delinquents in the same category; six of the eleven had enacted provisions for differential treatment of status offenders.[25]

Arguments For and Against Status Offense Jurisdiction

Traditional arguments about juvenile status offenses generally fall into two categories, constitutional and pragmatic. Because the constitutional considerations have dominated much of the debate, I consider them first.

Constitutional Challenges. Commentators and litigants have raised four different constitutional challenges to status offense legislation: void-for-vagueness, Eighth Amendment, equal protection, and substantive due process.

Some critics argue that status offense laws are impermissibly vague because they fail to provide adequate notice of actions which may violate the law and encourage arbitrary enforcement. The "void-for-vagueness" argument typically has failed when applied to juvenile status offenses. In a recent case, the Supreme Court upheld a New York statute granting juvenile courts jurisdiction over youths who are "incorrigible, ungovernable or habitually disobedient and beyond the lawful control of parent or other lawful authority."[26] Moreover, even when the vagueness challenge succeeds, states need only specify the acts which would create jurisdiction. Massachusetts, for example, has defined a runaway as a youth who "persistently runs away from home," and a truant as a youth who "persistently and willfully fails to attend school."[27]

Some litigants have attacked status offense laws on Eighth Amendment grounds, relying upon *Robinson v. California*,[28] in which the Supreme Court invalidated a criminal law punishing addiction to drugs. Challengers argue that juvenile status offenses similarly punish status and therefore constitute cruel and unusual punishment.[29]

State courts have rejected the argument on the theory that juvenile status offense laws punish specific acts rather than the status of incorrigibility, for example.[30] Adult criminal laws also distinguish between acts and status by prohibiting the sale and purchase of heroin but not the status of addiction.

Some advocates have urged that states deny children equal protection of the law by punishing them for acts which aren't criminal for adults.[31] The Supreme Court has never addressed the equal protection claims of juvenile status offenders. Other courts, however, have rejected this argument, noting that children's immaturity, vulnerability, and need for protection and rehabilitation are factors reasonably related to the need for different treatment.[32]

In a literal sense, children don't receive equal protection of the law. They often receive extra protection. They generally receive more lenient treatment in arrest decisions, adjudications, and dispositions. Society has chosen to treat children differently for a variety of reasons which distinguish juveniles from adults: diminished responsibility, extraordinary capacity for change, and deference to parental authority.[33]

A final constitutional objection relies upon the substantive due process claim that children are deprived of liberty in excess of both the state's police power and its authority to act as *parens patriae*. Since there is little proof that incorrigible children will ultimately commit crimes, the argument continues, the state exceeds its police power by punishing children for noncriminal offenses. In addition, because courts seldom help incorrigible children, its exercise of the *parens patriae* power to aid and rehabilitate minors is inappropriate.[34]

There are several reasons to reject the substantive due process argument. First, the police power point characterizes status offenses as "noncriminal" and therefore begs the question. Legislatures, not legal commentators, determine what conduct is criminal. When legislatures enact criminal statutes, by definition they define and prohibit criminal behavior. One might respond that while status offenses are technically criminal, they aren't serious or harmful. This response raises broad issues about what conduct the state may and should define as criminal and is discussed with the fourth policy argument.

Second, I contend that status offenses are harmful behavior *for children*. Accordingly, the relationship between current behavior (incorrigible children) and future crime is less relevant for children than when we selectively incapacitate adults based on statistical predictions of future criminal conduct. Finally, because the court typically operates as a last resort, its inability to help many children doesn't preclude its involvement.

A third and more general criticism of the substantive due process claim simply emphasizes that the law frequently treats children and adults differently. A substantive due process claim presumably would reject any distinctions, such as requiring children to attend school or obey their parents. This argument parallels an equal protection claim and is discussed above.

It is important to consider constitutional objections to status offense jurisdiction because they represent substantive and procedural limitations imposed by the Supreme Court upon the state. Specifically, constitutional arguments explore whether juvenile status offenses are generally permissible and, therefore, whether legislatures legally *can* enact a particular law. Unlike policy considerations, however, constitutional limits fail to address whether states *should* enact a law. Only policy analysis helps us determine whether particular laws are a wise exercise of state authority and judicial resources.

Policy Issues. The most common policy argument against juvenile status offenses emphasizes historical abuses and failures by the juvenile justice system. Citing incidents such as *Gault,*[35] proponents of this view characterize the juvenile court as a grand experiment which has failed. States uniformly granted courts broad jurisdiction and unbridled discretion over all three kinds of juvenile cases. Courts often abused their power and rendered unfounded decisions, imposed disparate sentences in similar cases, and generally made juveniles worse off than if the court had never acted. To "widen the net" of the court would invite similar tragedies.

Moreover, the court's natural capabilities bear little relation to successful intervention.[36] Traditionally, the court is a forum for fact-finding—deciding questions of liability, or guilt and innocence. When the court exercises jurisdiction over status offenses, it fulfills few of these functions. Instead of determining facts, the court often attempts to monitor family relationships and prescribe social services for children and families.

The countervailing argument is straightforward: we can control discretion, and past abuses should not preclude our seeking a constrained, guided approach to juvenile status offenses. Although the Supreme Court hasn't imposed due process requirements in status offense cases, such requirements might limit a court's ability to institutionalize for chronic truancy without providing some of the rights guaranteed by *Gault.* In addition, the blanket justification for state involvement, *parens patriae,* has been shredded by the Court and no longer shields the courts from constitutional scrutiny. Legislatures can limit aspects of judicial discretion such as dispositional alternatives. In fact, an initial status offense violation could carry only minor sanctions, such as recorded warnings, tickets, or fines.

Dissatisfaction with the juvenile court's performance has led opponents of status offense jurisdiction to suggest that some other organization could and should handle status offenders. These critics predict that social service agencies will arise in communities to help problematic juveniles such as truants. Parents, for example, will form groups to offer educational alternatives to chronic truants.

Although social service agencies clearly can benefit juveniles, to rely exclusively upon them would raise both policy and legal issues. In some communities, private organizations simply will not exist; in others, they will be ineffective. Some private organizations may refuse to handle "difficult" cases. All these possibilities would create inequities for juveniles.

Moreover, to reach uncooperative families, agencies probably would require the state's coercive power.[37] One might question a private agency's ability to determine when and how to intervene coercively. More importantly, parents and children certainly could argue that agencies empowered to balance a family's privacy and a child's liberty against the state's interest in the child's welfare violate due process. Only an impartial tribunal—the court, for example—should balance these interests. Specifically, only a court can intervene in a child's life and force the child to undergo treatment while also preserving the constitutionally guaranteed rights of all affected parties.

If agencies were used, therefore, courts would review organizational decisions routinely, just as they do administrative regulations. Accordingly, in the juvenile justice area, courts should find facts, balance interests, and resolve conflicts in the beginning to avoid repetitive factual determinations and dispositions. Courts then may rely upon public and private organizations for dispositional alternatives.

A second policy argument against juvenile status offenses relies upon a characterization of judicial action. Juvenile courts give orders, and back up their orders by depriving parties of property (e.g., fines) or liberty (e.g., imprisonment). Because these are drastic measures, society should involve the court only when juveniles have committed offenses which are serious enough to warrant deprivations of property or liberty. In short, the argument concludes, judicial responses to status offenders are troublesome in one of two ways: to punish truants with incarceration is too harsh, and to make empty threats dilutes judicial integrity and undermines the court's credibility in other areas, such as serious offenses.

I think this argument misses the mark. We often empower adult courts to exercise jurisdiction over conduct for which we would not automatically impose a jail term or large fines. Many criminal laws which prohibit less serious conduct carry relatively minor sentences. Similarly, we don't always punish offenders, and empower judges to suspend sentences and place first offenders on probation. Moreover, we use the ultimate threat of incarceration or other serious consequences in many situations to "back up" laws and the court's instructions. The threats often work. Finally, we may gain an offender's attention, respect, and obedience through the symbolic and formal legal process.

Our body of traffic offenses is an example of less serious activity that we wish to prohibit and therefore categorize as criminal. Yet, through state agents (e.g., police), we sometimes decide not to impose sanctions upon violators: some people caught speeding don't receive a ticket. Moreover, first and second offenses typically result in supervision or small fines. And, while drivers may insist upon a trial, most do not.

A supporter of the second objection to status offenses might wonder how, under these circumstances, traffic laws work at all. I suggest that traffic laws resemble the requirement to pay federal taxes. In both cases, the laws are effective simply because most people obey the law.[38] Some obey the laws because they agree with them and recognize the importance of compliance. Sporadic enforcement and minor sanctions (tickets and audits) induce others to comply. The mere threat of more severe penalties (license suspension, as well as large fines and imprisonment) motivates others. Finally, demonstrations of severe penalties ("examples") back up the threats. No one would suggest that we should revoke tax or traffic laws, or end the court's enforcement of them, simply because we don't lock up first time offenders!

A third policy argument against status offense jurisdiction is essentially a microeconomic one. When we allocate a significant amount of labor and capital on status offenses we waste scarce resources on a relatively minor problem. Despite the fact that juvenile status offenses produce few victims, we allocate between one-third and one-half of the court's attention to status offenses.[39] Instead, the argument continues, we should focus on juvenile delinquents, who commit "real" crimes such as robbery, rape, and murder. Moreover, the juvenile court also must respond to abused and neglected juveniles, whose cases alone crowd the court's dockets. Until we can handle these cases, we shouldn't worry about less serious ones.[40]

The efficiency argument has incited a heated debate among purveyors of status offense literature. Most studies of juveniles have concluded that status offenders typically resemble criminal offenders in both offense history and personality pattern. One study, for example, found that a significant number of status offenders previously had been—and subsequently became—involved in serious criminal conduct.[41]

Because status offenses often indicate past and future criminal behavior, some experts conclude that courts should respond to status offenders and focus resources on these juveniles. Prevention clearly seems more desirable than rehabilitation. Furthermore, the similarities between delinquents and status offenders suggests that status offenders need as much help as delinquents;[42] to eliminate status offense jurisdiction would leave non-delinquent juveniles without potential aid. Other commentators, of course, contend that the fact that status offenders resemble criminal offenders demonstrates that the court needs jurisdiction over only the latter group.[43]

I suggest that the debate about whether a status offense record will help us "predict" criminal behavior overlooks the state's reasons for, and role in, intervening to help juveniles. The debate focuses entirely upon reducing future crime.[44] I contend, however, that status offenses are significant for two other reasons.

First, conduct prohibited by status offenses is itself undesirable for children. Few people would characterize chronic truancy or disobedience, in most situations, as good behavior. Indeed, most state legislatures agree that children need to attend school and have passed compulsory attendance laws.[45] One response is that truancy and disobedience are merely symptoms of more serious problems and thus should not be "prohibited." Moreover, children skip school for many reasons, some more harmful than others. Accordingly, if we charge absent students with truancy, we will subject some children and families to unnecessary scrutiny.

One way to discover underlying problems, however, is to exercise jurisdiction and seek explanations for misconduct. This suggests a second reason why status offense jurisdiction is important to the court. Regardless of a relationship between status offenses and later criminal conduct, society has a legitimate interest in seeing its children grow into responsible, mature citizens. As a practical matter, lack of schooling and living "on the streets" fail to prepare a children for future employment, a family, or other responsibilities.[46] Status offenses suggest that some institutions, such as schools, churches, or families, are "failing" with some children.[47] The failure may be attributable to the institutions, the child, or both. Regardless of who is most responsible, it is legitimate for society to respond by vesting the juvenile court with jurisdictional authority.

An opponent of status offense jurisdiction might respond that the court's neglect and abuse jurisdiction will detect many, if not all, of the serious parental failures. As a result, status offense jurisdiction is unnecessary. Similarly, schools can handle their discipline and attendance problems. Churches or other institutions simply must work without state help.

Abuse and neglect jurisdiction is inadequate to bring problematic children within the ambit of the court for at least three reasons. First, children need more than just the absence of physical abuse and the presence of food and shelter. As a society, we have recognized additional needs. We emphasize the importance of education and coerce attendance; truancy statutes are a demonstration of this view. We recognize parents' ability to expect their children to obey them, as well as to instill in their children self-discipline, and thus allow parents to discipline their children; chronic disobedience (incorrigibility) laws support parental discretion. We acknowledge the significance of a tolerable environment, and hence want to be able to learn why runaway children have left home.

Second, because neglect and abuse cases are proceedings against parents, the hearing and disposition tend to pit parents against their children. In abuse cases, the state brings criminal charges against parents, and frequently removes children from the home. While neglect cases are civil, the state asserts a failure by parents to provide even basic care for their children. Third, courts have interpreted abuse statutes to require evidence of physical abuse. The mere presence of bruises may fail to meet this burden. Often, children must contradict their parents' testimony denying abuse. Few courts routinely accept the word of a 12-year-old against that of his parents.

A fourth policy argument opposing status offense jurisdiction resembles the substantive due process argument. Specifically, when a state enacts status offense legislation, it 1) intrudes unwisely into family matters, threatening parental autonomy; and 2) exceeds its role generally with respect to the proper relationship between government (the state) and its citizens.

Essentially, the first point is that when we enact status offense statutes and empower the juvenile court to enforce them, we encourage the court to tell parents how to raise their children. Specifically, some fear that the court will tell a truant's parents that they have failed, that they should have done X instead of Y, and then how to get their children to school. Presumably, all parents would be subject to the court's hindsighted scrutiny and judgment. One also might wonder whether legislatures again would enact general laws which direct children to conform to a nineteenth-century conception of the ideal child: studious, serious, subdued, and clean. Moreover, one might suggest that the court will interfere unnecessarily by "hauling in" children who ran away from home for the first time. In such cases, the court would make matters worse by scrutinizing familial relationships.[48]

The meddling state argument provokes several responses. First, critics of the juvenile court must remember that the "proactive" court no longer exists as it may have in 1925. The juvenile court, like an adult court, is, and should be, a last resort.[49] Juvenile courts deal with children and families only after other solutions have failed. The juvenile court rarely solicits cases; dependency and delinquency cases already crowd its dockets. Juvenile courts, in fact, divert to voluntary treatment the majority of children brought before them.[50] Pre-adjudication screening by police and attorneys also eliminates the least serious cases. As a result, juvenile courts rarely intentionally overreach or mistakenly see juveniles who have made one minor mistake.[51] When they do, their investigation will reveal whether the misconduct is isolated. Similarly, statutes may require a specific number of incidents before the court becomes involved.

Second, legislatures haven't regressed—and probably won't—by enacting overly broad or vague laws. In fact, the trend has been the reverse, encouraged primarily by Supreme Court decisions. Many states now require chronic problems (repeated offenses), such as persistent truancy, to confer jurisdiction.[52]

Third, although I have suggested that American society implicitly expects more of parents than simply non-abuse/non-neglect,[53] we sometimes fail to articulate our expectations, or criteria with which to measure discharge of parental obligations. I contend, however, that we are no longer willing to grant parents a right to "screw-up" their kids.[54] Accordingly, when a child's conduct suggests that parents may be failing, or that something is awry, and other private institutions either do not exist or have failed, we at least ought to allow an agency of the state to investigate. I do not suggest that the court and social service agencies will eliminate or drastically reduce adult crime, for example, but I do contend that this strategy is wiser than waiting until a child has developed into an 18-year-old felon.

The more general policy argument, that status offenses represent a departure from the state's proper role in a liberal democracy, raises fundamental questions of political theory. To what extent should the state attempt to influence the "character"[55]—and not just the actions—of its citizens, especially young ones? To what extent, for example, should the state legislate morality?[56] Although chronic truancy and disobedience are unpleasant acts, they are, in a sense, victimless crimes; skipping school differs significantly from assaulting teachers. Accordingly, truancy status may reflect an excessive concern for the child's character.

Historically, political theorists have disagreed about the state's role in shaping the character of its citizens.[57] The debate continues today. A communitarian would support jurisdiction based on a desire to create a community, and would emphasize children's role in a community.[58] A civil libertarian would argue that individual rights/liberties preclude state intrusion except to prevent harm to others. Status offenses infringe upon individual liberties without justification and therefore are an inappropriate exercise of state power.[59]

The status offense issue appears to raise an unresolvable political issue. I argue, however, that advocates of jurisdiction can meet the libertarian challenge. Children are unique. They possess fewer rights (and obligations) than adults. We are less troubled, for example, by limiting a child's choices than an adult's primarily because children are less able to make independent and informed choices. The juvenile court requires status offense jurisdiction to ensure that children have an opportunity to become free-willed individuals.

Accordingly, the next section articulates a position favoring a legislative and judicial response to juvenile status offenders, which relies in part upon reasons for differential treatment of juveniles.

Status Offenders: Recommendations for the Court's Role

Status Offenses Should be Retained and Should Include Habitually Truant, Disobedient and Runaway Children.

For the past 150 years we have acknowledged that children and adults are different. As a legal matter, children possess fewer responsibilities and enjoy fewer rights. Children don't have to face adult criminal sanctions,[60] honor contracts, fight in wars, pay taxes, or provide for their home, food and clothing. Similarly, children can't vote, drink, drive, enter contracts, or marry. From a psychological standpoint, children are generally less autonomous, have not internalized societal values, and often are vulnerable to outside influence.[61] Accordingly, adolescence is a difficult period of development, when children begin evolving into independent and responsible members of society. Finally, children occupy a unique position in a traditional and valued institution, the family. Children reap the benefits of attention, affection, education, and instruction. They also assume obligations—to develop physically, intellectually, and emotionally.

These three frameworks correspond roughly to three justifications for differential treatment—diminished responsibility, extraordinary capacity for change, and deference to parental authority—and demonstrate vividly why status offenses are a legitimate state concern. Status offenses are themselves harmful activities for children and therefore should be discouraged by society. Statutes which prohibit truancy, disobedience, and running away support compulsory education, parental authority, and the importance of a stable and tolerable environment. Finally, society possesses a strong and legitimate interest in helping its children grow into responsible, mature citizens.

The Juvenile Court Should Retain Jurisdiction Over Status Offenders.

Coercive intervention in the lives of children is sometimes necessary and can work. The juvenile court can determine accurately and fairly whether juveniles have committed the alleged misconduct. In addition, the court can direct children to existing services suited to their needs with at least as much uniformity of standards as a non-judicial agency. When private institutions have failed, it also can compel parents or guardians to participate in particular services; compliance may be achieved without frequent or harsh sanctions. Finally, the court can provide more procedural safeguards than a private organization.

Specific Guidelines for the Juvenile Court.

The next three sections provide specific suggestions for the juvenile court's exercise of status offense jurisdiction. Each recommendation stems primarily from a justification for differential treatment or policy consideration.

Jurisdiction

First, because the court interferes with traditionally respected parental authority, it should exercise jurisdiction only when a juvenile exhibits repeated misbehavior. The court should defer to parents' methods, while demanding moderate results. Accordingly, statutes should define behavior specifically, such as describing truancy as a 24-hour absence from home without parental permission. Moreover, laws should confer jurisdiction only after a specific number of incidents. One author suggests, for example, two levels of absenteeism and commensurate responses: 10 to 39 unexcused absences prompts a referral to a community-based hearing system; 40 or more absences justifies judicial intervention.[62]

Second, because the court's goal is to determine the problem and not to lock up children, statutes should subject parents or legal guardians to the court's jurisdiction. The National Advisory Committee for Juvenile Justice and Delinquency Prevention also recommends this action.[63]

Adjudication

Because the Supreme Court hasn't ruled on due process requirements in status offense cases,[64] juvenile courts need not accord status offenders the gamut of adult protections. In general, juveniles possess fewer responsibilities than adults and thus enjoy fewer rights. Juvenile courts also rely upon threats and symbolic power to achieve compliance. Accordingly, I recommend a streamlined procedure in most instances and oppose full-fledged adversarial hearings for status offenses. States may, of course, grant juveniles additional procedural rights.

Justice notions, however, require the court to determine initially whether the juvenile committed the offense. Courts possess fact-finding expertise, and may employ evidentiary rules to protect juveniles and ensure accuracy.

Disposition

Children's diminished responsibility supports milder sanctions than adults receive. In addition, children possess an extraordinary capacity for change, which encourages rehabilitative responses and partially justifies early intervention. Nevertheless, many commentators argue that forceful discipline is more effective than gentle nurture.

I suggest that to embrace either nurture or coercion exclusively would limit the court's legitimacy and effectiveness. Historically, for example, courts have used nurture more—and punishment less—with younger offenders. As a result, the court often has failed to introduce youngsters to the idea of responsibility. In fact, one might argue that the court's actions have suggested to juveniles that they weren't (and may never be) responsible for their actions.[65]

As a result, I recommend a hybrid approach, one which could be called "services providing/responsibility reminding." Clearly, we want to lead children to moral responsibility. Both psychological theorists and common sense suggest that individuals in early stages of moral development respond best to discipline when the "punisher" also does "good things," such as provide for a child's physical and emotional needs. Moreover, I contend that benign punishment *does* exist. Good parents will confirm that, contrary to recent thought, authority and coercion aren't necessarily anti-therapeutic. Finally, courts, in conjunction with psychologists and social workers, also should determine to what extent an individual needs nurture as well, including aid from social service agencies.[66]

The preceding discussion, together with children's capacity for change, confirms the court's need of a wide range of dispositional alternatives. Although a complete listing exceeds the scope of this discussion, courts should be permitted to consider options such as the following:

1. Return the child home subject to conditions or limitations set by the court.
2. Place the child on probation, including judicial conditions or limitations.
3. Require the child to attend counseling or other community services available.
4. Place the child in the temporary or permanent custody of a non-secure home, etc.
5. Commit the child to a secure facility, public or private, under the supervision of the court or state youth authority.[67]

Finally, I hasten to add two qualifications to the last disposition. I would urge states which allow courts to place status offenders in secure facilities to require an independent judicial finding that 1) other dispositional options would fail to meet the child's needs; and 2) the child poses a significant danger to the community. I also would urge states to eliminate secure placement as a disposition for first-time offenders, consistent with the federal policy enunciated in the Juvenile Justice and Delinquency Prevention Act of 1974.[68]

Conclusion

The most important difference between the 1899 juvenile court and the present juvenile court is the difference in attitude toward imposing society's values on people, particularly malleable children. The early juvenile court unashamedly imposed a conception of morality upon juveniles. Importantly, the court as a public institution was created and maintained by a public conception of the ideal child. The legislature defined it (i.e., non-truant, non-lazy, non-promiscuous), and the court applied it.

Today, however, we recoil from the idea of elaborate state-imposed models of good conduct because it conflicts with individual liberty. Similarly, we view the state's dabbling in morality ("legislating morality") as a threat to freedom. For example, the Supreme Court has invalidated most adult status offenses such as drunkenness and vagrancy. Aside from constitutional justifications, the Court's decisions typify our reluctance to impose expectations upon individuals. We clearly have gotten out of the business of imbuing citizens with virtue, especially when the citizens are impressionable.

I suggest that our increasing reluctance to promote virtue and inculcate values in youth is misplaced. As discussed above, the notion of virtuous character and its expression in conduct lies at the heart of the criminal law. Moreover, it would seem that the juvenile court is the very place to begin inculcating virtue when private institutions have failed. To refuse to do so is to spurn a golden opportunity.

Endnotes

1. See text accompanying notes 17–21 *infra*.
2. Some defense attorneys, for example, argue that the court should accord juveniles the same rights as adults, such as the right to jury trials.
3. See, for example, Guggenheim. (1979, January). Abolishing the juvenile justice system. *Trial, 15,* 22–25. McCarthy. (1977). Should juvenile delinquency be abolished? *Crime and Delinquency, 23,* 196–203.
4. Institute of Judicial Administration–American Bar Association Joint Commission on Juvenile Justice Standards, *Standards Relating to Noncriminal Misbehavior* § 1.1 (Tent. Draft 1977). (Later rejected by the ABA House of Delegates). Gough and Grilli. (1972, November). The unruly child and the law. *Juvenile Justice, 23,* 9–12. Kaufman, I. R. (1976). Of juvenile justice and injustice. *A.B.A.J., 62,* 730–734. Ketcham, O. W. (1977). Why jurisdiction over status offenders should be eliminated from juvenile courts. *B.U.L.Rev., 57,* 645–662. National Council on Crime and Delinquency. (1975). Jurisdiction over status offenses should be removed from the juvenile court—A policy statement. *Crime and Delinquency, 21,* 97–99.

   Status offenses are offenses committed by juveniles that would not be crimes if committed by an adult, such as trauncy, disobedience, running away from home, and underage drinking. Status offense laws therefore apply exclusively to juveniles because of their *status as juveniles,* but clearly govern *conduct* deemed inappropriate for juveniles.
5. This process is called "transfer," "waiver," or "binding over."
6. If a man have a stubborn and rebellious son, that will not hearken to the voice of his father, or the voice of his mother, and though they chasten him, will not hearken unto them; then shall his father and his mother lay hold on him, and bring him out unto the elders of the city, and unto the gate of his place . . . And all the men of his city shall stone him with stones, that he die; so shalt thou put away the evil from the midst of thee; and all Israel shall hear, and fear. (Deuteronomy 21:18–21).

7. Empey, L. T. (Ed.). (1979). *Juvenile justice: The progressive legacy and current reforms*. (pp. 10–15).
8. Rinik. (1982). Juvenile status offenders: A comparative analysis. *Harv.J.L. & P.P., 5,* 153, 156–58.
9. Cogan. (1970). Juvenile law before and after the entrance of *Parens Patriae, S.C.L. Rev., 22,* 147.
10. Rendleman. (1971). *Parens Patriae:* From chancery to the juvenile court. *S.C.L. Rev., 23,* 205, 207–09.
11. *Ibid.*
12. 4 Wharton 9 (Pa. 1838).
13. Fox. (1970). Juvenile justice reform: A historical perspective. *Stan.L.Rev., 22,* 1187, 1192.
14. Laws of April 21, 1899, Ill. Laws, sec. 21, at 137.
15. The child who must be brought into court should, of course, be made to know that he is face to face with the power of the state, but he should at the same time, and more emphatically, be made to feel that he is the object of its care and solicitude. The ordinary trappings of the court-room are out of place in such hearings. The judge on a bench, looking down upon the boy standing at the bar, can never evoke a proper sympathetic spirit. Seated at a desk, with the child at his side, where he can on occasion put his arm around his shoulder and draw the lad to him, the judge, while losing none of his judicial dignity, will gain immensely in the effectiveness of his work. (From Mack. (1909). The juvenile court. *Harv.L.Rev., 23,* 104, 120.)
16. Glueck and Glueck. (1934). *One thousand juvenile delinquents.* Healy and Bronner. (1926). *Delinquents and criminals.*
17. 367 U.S. 643 (1961).
18. 387 U.S. 1 (1967).
19. *Id.* at 22.
20. 397 U.S. 358, 364 (1970). The *Winship* holding was made retroactive in *Ivan V. v. City of New York,* 407 U.S. 203, 203–05 (1972) (per curiam).
21. 403 U.S. 528, 545 (1971) (plurality opinion).
22. Few commentators in the juvenile justice field have attempted to enumerate rationales for differential treatment. Instead, most authors recite historical characterizations of the juvenile court's origins and evolution.
23. See, for example, Mass. Gen. Laws Ann. ch. 119 § 39E.
24. Some states grant the court jurisdiction implicitly, such as when "[a] member of a family alleges that some other member of the family is by his conduct imperiling any family relationship . . .". Del.Code Ann. tit. 10, s. 921 (6) (Supp. 1980). The vast majority, however, explicitly empower the juvenile court to handle such cases as habitual truancy, chronic disobedience, running away, and underage drinking. For a complete listing of statutes, see Rosenberg. (1983). Juvenile status offender statutes—New perspectives on an old problem. *U.C.Dav. L.Rev., 16,* 283, 286–91 n. 18.
25. Shichor. (1983, August). Historical and current trends in American juvenile justice. *Juvenile and Family Court Journal, 34,* 61, 64.
26. *In Re Negron,* 409 U.S. 1052 (1972) (mem.) (dismissing for want of a substantial federal question an appeal challenging the New York incorrigibility law, N.Y.Fam.Ct.Act § 712(b) (McKinney Supp. 1982–83), on several grounds including vagueness).
27. Mass. Gen. Laws Ann. ch. 119, § 39E.
28. 370 U.S. 660 (1962).
29. Ketcham, note 4 *supra,* at p. 656.
30. See, for example, *Blondheim v. State,* 84 Wash. 2d 874, 880, 529 P. 2d 1096, 1101 (1975). One author has argued that the Supreme Court's decision in

Powell v. Texas, 392 U.S. 514 (1968) (plurality opinion) indicated that an Eighth Amendment challenge (based on *Robinson*) to incorrigibility statutes would fail automatically. *Powell* upheld the validity of a state law punishing intoxicated persons "found in any place." Rosenberg, note 24 *supra,* at p. 297, n. 50.

31. One of the most deeply rooted principles of American criminal law is the requirement that an overt, prohibited act must occur before a crime is committed . . . Yet the juvenile court is allowed to intervene coercively in a juvenile's life because of . . . antisocial attitudes of nonconformity . . . Thus, status offense jurisdiction prescribes different legal treatment for juveniles than for all other persons. (Ketcham, note 4 *supra,* at p. 656.)
32. For example, *Vann v. Scott,* 467 F. 2d 1235, 1238–39 (7th Cir. 1972). (Neither the Eighth Amendment nor the equal protection clause is violated when a state classifies as delinquents status offenders who have violated a condition of probation.)
33. See text accompanying notes 22–24 *supra.*
34. Rosenberg, note 24 *supra,* at p. 298.
35. In *Gault,* a 15-year-old boy was committed to an Industrial School for a maximum of six years under a delinquency statute by a juvenile court. The maximum penalty for an adult convicted of the same offense was two months. Gerald Francis Gault failed to receive notice of charges, legal representation, the privilege against self-incrimination, or an opportunity to confront and cross-examine witnesses.
36. Martin and Snyder. (1978). Jurisdiction over status offenders should *not* be removed from the juvenile court. *Status Offenders and the Juvenile Justice System: An Anthology,* at p. 6, (R. Allinson, Ed.). Martin and Snyder observe: ". . . [A]s difficult as it may be to define solutions to noncriminal juvenile behavior, the judicial system is certainly not designed, equipped, or able to handle these problems." *Id.*
37. [J]uvenile justice planners have tacitly recognized the integral role played by authority in dealing with the status offender in their somewhat nebulous blueprints for future action by speaking of endowing so-called voluntary agencies with coercive powers. (Gill. (1976, August). The status offender. *Juvenile Justice, 27,* 3, 6–7.)
38. Clearly, if everyone, or even a lot of people, refused to obey traffic laws or to file tax returns, the state would be powerless to compel compliance.
39. Ketcham, note 4 *supra,* at pp. 650–51.
40. Incidentally, the economic argument assumes that the juvenile court and its caseload won't change. It's entirely conceivable that states will change the court's jurisdiction. Serious offenders, for example, may be transferred to adult courts. Similarly, adult courts could prosecute abusive parents and rely upon expert recommendations to place children removed from homes.

    These changes would reduce the juvenile court caseload drastically, and enable it to handle status offense cases more easily. I suggest, however, that to determine whether we would want to change the court, we must recall and evaluate reasons for differential treatment, as well as the arguments presented in the text.
41. Thomas. (1978). Are status offenders really so different? *Status Offenders and the Juvenile Justice System: An Anthology,* at p. 92, (R. Allinson, Ed.).
42. Erlenbach, K. (1981). Status offenders and juvenile court: A proposal for revamping jurisdiction. *Ohio St. L.J., 42,* 1005, 1016 (1981). The author suggests that although the court should retain jurisdiction over both status offenders and delinquents, it should treat them both the same, contrary to most current practices. *Id.* at p. 1021.

43. See, for example, Marra and Sax. (1978). Personality patterns and offense histories of status offenders and delinquents. *Juv. and Fam. Court J., 29,* 27.
44. We could reduce crime by incapacitating and/or rehabilitating juveniles.
45. One might argue that we simply should allow persistent children to skip school. Compulsory attendance laws, however, express society's desire to withhold *that* decision from children (and parents) until children reach an age which suggests that they can exercise good judgment.
46. Rinik, note 8 *supra,* at p. 170.
47. Professor Mark H. Moore of Harvard University characterizes our concern with failures of private institutions such as families as an acknowledgement that children have a "right" to a minimum level of "investments." Desirable investments include physical, intellectual, and emotional stimuli: food, shelter, clothing, education, love, and attention. (See text accompanying notes 47–49.)
48. See text accompanying notes 54–56 *infra.*
49. Rinik, note 8 *supra,* at pp. 167–68.
50. Ohio St. L.J., note 42 *supra,* at p. 1022. Indeed, those who sometimes point out the juvenile court's crowded docket also fear an "activist" court.
51. A personal note: I served as a "hearing officer" for a major state university. My job was to determine the guilt or innocence and recommend sanctions for undergraduates who lived in the university's residence halls.

    Essentially, I was at the fourth level of discipline. Live-in resident advisors typically warned students after initial violations; continued misbehavior was recorded and reported to the Hall Director. Additional problems brought the student before the Area Director. Eventually, I became involved and sometimes referred students to the two levels above me. Only extremely serious cases (e.g., assaulting a staff member) merited immediate high level attention.

    I soon learned that this process successfully screened out "first and only" offenders, victims of circumstance, etc. Generally, when a student came to see me, he had had *at least three* opportunities to modify behavior. I didn't presume guilt, but did gain confidence that in most instances, I wasn't punishing someone arbitrarily for isolated conduct.
52. For example, see text accompanying notes 26–27, *supra.*
53. See text accompanying notes 47–49, *supra.*
54. Traditionally, we have hesitated to interfere with parental discretion, often overlooking evidence of child abuse (until recently). Nevertheless, we care less, within limits, of parents' methods than we do of their results—the adult citizens they produce.
55. I will define "character" to mean an individual's moral values, attitudes, and dispositions.
56. The regulation and prohibition of pornographic material is a classic example. Although the Supreme Court has recognized an individual's right to possess pornography in his home (*Stanley v. Georgia*), it has held that states may regulate (through zoning) or prohibit sale and distribution of pornography. In these cases the Court balances individual liberty and free speech against community/state interests.

    It is critical to note, however, that the Court treats pornographic distributions to children, or pornography involving children, differently. Parental and state interests in the moral values of its future citizens frequently permit regulation of speech. (*F.C.C. v. Pacifica*). Similarly, the Court has valued child pornography little. I suggest that the Court recognizes that children are special.
57. Aristotle, for example, maintained that the state's primary role was to enable citizens to be happy, defined as the activity of the soul in conformity with

virtue. He probably would support status offense jurisdiction. Mill, however, argued that the state could interfere with individuals only to prevent harm to others. Mill probably would oppose jurisdiction, unless he felt children, like "mental incompetents," were unable to make their own decisions.

58. Professor Michael Sandel, Government Department, Harvard University, provided this characterization.
59. One could suggest that when we intervene with juveniles, we decrease later crime and therefore prevent harm to others. The libertarian probably would respond that harm from potential crime is too uncertain to justify this infringement upon individual liberties.
60. Juveniles transferred to adult court, by judicial determination, aren't "children."
61. See generally, Zimring, F. (1982). *The changing legal world of adolescence.*
62. Rinik, note 8 *supra,* at p. 223.
63. National Advisory Committee for Juvenile Justice and Delinquency Prevention. (1980). *Standards for the administration of juvenile justice,* at p. 249.
64. *Gault* requirements apply only to delinquency hearings which threaten institutionalization.
65. I would characterize one goal of the juvenile justice system as creating a "gradient" of increasing autonomy and responsibility.
66. The hybrid approach may be characterized best conversationally: What you did was wrong. Our society will not allow you to act this way. Next time, you will be in big trouble. However, you don't have a father, and this is your first brush with the law. We will look into finding you a better place to live. Meanwhile, we will keep an eye on you, so make sure you go to school. This is a Social Worker, who will tell you what we expect of you and what you can do if you have any questions or problems.
67. Erlenbach, K. (1981). Status offenders and juvenile court: A proposal for revamping jurisdiction. *Ohio St. L.J., 42,* 1005, 1021.
68. 42 USC § 5601 *et seq.* To qualify for funds under the Act, a state had to submit a three-year juvenile justice plan which contained particular provisions, including a prohibition on the use of secure placement for status offenders. See 42 USC § 5633 (12) (A).

References

Arthur, L. G. (1977). Status offenders need a court of last resort. *Boston University Law Review, 57,* 631–644.

Cogan N. H. (1970). Juvenile law before and after the entrance of *parens patriae. South Carolina Law Review, 22,* 147–181.

Empey, L. T. (Ed.). (1979). *Juvenile justice: The progressive legacy and current reforms.* Charlottesville: University Press of Virginia.

Erlenbach, K. (1981). Status offenders and juvenile court: A proposal for revamping jurisdiction. *Ohio State Law Journal, 42,* 1005–1023.

Fox, S. F. (1970). Juvenile justice reform: A historical perspective. *Stanford Law Review, 22,* 1187–1239.

Gill, T. D. (1976). The status offender. *Juvenile Justice, 27,* 3–10.

Glueck, S., & Glueck, E. T. (1934). *One thousand juvenile delinquents: Their treatment by court and clinic.* Cambridge, MA: Harvard University Press.

Gough, A. R., & Grilli, M. A. (1972). The unruly child and the law. *Juvenile Justice, 23,* 9–12.

Guggenheim, M. (1979, January). Abolishing the juvenile justice system. *Trial, 15,* pp. 22–25.
Healy, W., & Bronner, A. F. (1926). *Delinquents and criminals, their making and unmaking: Studies in two American cities.* New York: Macmillan.
Institute of Judicial Administration - American Bar Association Joint Commission on Juvenile Justice Standards. (1977). *Standards relating to noncriminal misbehavior* [Tent. Draft]. Cambridge, MA: Ballinger.
Kaufman, I. R. (1976). Of juvenile justice and injustice. *American Bar Association Journal, 62,* 730–734.
Ketcham, O. W. (1977). Why jurisdiction over status offenders should be eliminated from juvenile courts. *Boston University Law Review, 57,* 645–662.
Mack, J. W. (1909). The juvenile court. *Harvard Law Review, 23,* 104–122.
Marra, H. A., & Sax, R. (1978). Personality patterns and offense histories of status offenders and delinquents. *Juvenile and Family Court Journal, 29,* 27–32.
Martin, L. H., & Snyder, P. R. (1978). Jurisdiction over status offenders should *not* be removed from the juvenile court. In R. Allinson (Ed.), *Status offenders and the juvenile justice system: An anthology* (pp. 6–12). Hackensack, NJ: National Council on Crime and Delinquency.
McCarthy, F. B. (1977). Should juvenile delinquency be abolished? *Crime and Delinquency, 23,* 196–203.
National Advisory Committee for Juvenile Justice and Delinquency Prevention. (1980). *Standards for the administration of juvenile justice.* Washington, DC: United States Government Printing Office.
National Council on Crime and Delinquency. (1975). Jurisdiction over status offenses should be removed from the juvenile court—A policy statement. *Crime and Delinquency, 21,* 97–99.
Platt, A. M. (1969). *The child savers: The invention of delinquency.* Chicago: The University of Chicago Press.
Rendleman, D. R. (1971). *Parens patriae:* From chancery to the juvenile court. *South Carolina Law Review, 23,* 205–259.
Rinik, C. (1982). Juvenile status offenders: A comparative analysis. *Harvard Journal of Law and Public Policy, 5,* 151–228.
Rosenberg, I. M. (1983). Juvenile status offender statutes—New perspectives on an old problem. *University of California - Davis Law Review, 16,* 283–323.
Shichor, D. (1983). Historical and current trends in American juvenile justice. *Juvenile and Family Court Journal, 34,* 61–75.
Thomas, C. W. (1978). Are status offenders really so different? In R. Allinson (Ed.), *Status offenders and the juvenile justice system: An anthology* (pp. 82–99). Hackensack, NJ: National Council on Crime and Delinquency.
Zimring, F. E. (1982). *The changing legal world of adolescence.* New York: Free Press.

Section IV
The Organization of the Juvenile Justice System: In the Shadow of the Juvenile Court

11
Juveniles and Police: The End of the Nightstick

GEORGE L. KELLING

The 1930s represented a watershed for American policing. Heretofore police in the United States lacked a distinctive professional identity or ideology. To the extent they had any ideology, it was derived from the local political party in power. In that respect, American police were distinguishable from their English counterparts. In England, police were created in 1829 only after decades of debate carried on in the highest realms of English politics by the intellectual and political elite of the country. John Stuart Mill, Jeremy Bentham, and Sir Robert Peel were but a few of the advocates devoted to the idea of reconciling bureaucratic police with utilitarian philosophy. When police were finally created, it was by the central government and operated largely under its control. Rowen and Mayne, the first administrators of the Metropolitan Police, initiated practices which established distinctive English police traditions and ideology.

In the United States, circumstances were different. True, some of the problems confronting cities during the early nineteenth century were similar: disorder, migration to cities, industrialization, riots, and crime. But these were generally considered to be local urban problems in a substantially agrarian society. Unlike in England, these problems were not considered to be the responsibility of the national government (states merely allowed cities to create police departments), nor were they buttressed by a carefully delineated philosophical raison d'etre such as that provided by English political and intellectual elites. From its beginning, the American version of policing was intimately linked to local politics. So close were these linkages that scholars such as Jordan (1972) and Fogelson (1977) characterized late nineteenth- and early twentieth-century police as adjuncts to political machines. For the most part, that status merely extended what had always been—police were created locally in American cities to maintain social control in a fashion determined by those in political power.

The struggles for control over police in America have been documented elsewhere (Fogelson, 1977). The first attempt to wrest political authority over police from local politicians and reshape policing took place in the late 1800s and failed—local politicians were too powerful, corruption was too endemic, and links between local police and local politicians were too strongly forged. To the extent that police participated in the debates about their control and reform, however, they did so as political advocates, not from a coherent theory of policing. An intelligible intercity *police* position did not exist. Although the organizational groundwork for a professional identity was laid with the formation of the National Chiefs of Police Union in 1871, it was not until well into the twentieth century that an identifiable unifying police ideology was created (Monkkonen, 1975; Jordan, 1972). Chiefs may have been locally famous or infamous, and they or detectives may have published diaries or anecdotes about their experiences, but no police spokesperson emerged to inspire the confidence and loyalty of other police.

During the 1930s, however, August Vollmer, a police officer who had worked his way up the ranks and became chief of police in Berkeley, California, began to shape a coherent theory of policing. In doing so, he created a profession that would grow to be a formidable institution of social control which would increasingly shape its strategy independent of political control. Although Vollmer's vision of policing was more expansive and eloquent than that of the people who were to carry on his reform tradition—the mantle of leadership of American policing would be assumed by J. Edgar Hoover—his view dominated policing for almost 50 years until the 1970s. Vollmer's views were characterized by deep concern about American character-building institutions: family, church, neighborhoods, and schools which, from his point of view, were failing in their responsibility to properly guide the nation's youth into the twentieth century. Moralistic and puritanical as it was, his vision of policing was developed in direct response to this perspective: it was the job of the police to shore up America's character-building institutions. Armed with this strategy and with Vollmer as its most articulate spokesperson, policing moved to unify and construct itself as a profession. Police would be the thin blue line standing against the moral deterioration of Americans, especially youth, throughout the country. They would do this in three ways: working through the criminal justice system, working through and with community institutions including families, and, working independently.

August Vollmer and the Roaring Twenties

From Vollmer's vantage point in history, the police occupation left much to be desired. The public's view of policing was often derisive and condescending. Keystone Cops, humorous though they may have been to the general public, were a nagging reminder to police of the public's perception of them as inept and venal. And police departments *were* notoriously corrupt. Even the Boston Police Department, which was considered to be an exemplar of good practice (in fact, so much that Scotland Yard studied Boston practices in the early twentieth century), was corrupted by the outcome of the political manipulation of the 1919 police strike and the corrosive effects of prohibition.

Vollmer and his like-minded colleagues looked at post-World War I America and noted the onset of the Great Depression, the "Red Scare," the failure of Prohibition, and what, from a police perspective, was perhaps the most dangerous problem of all—the erosion of manners and morals. The length of women's skirts became shorter and the weight and material of women's clothing became less substantial. Dancing positions changed from distant and decorous to close clutching. Necking and petting were "in." Women were beginning to smoke in public. Cars were providing youth with unprecedented mobility and freedom from oversight by parents and moral guardians. Movies and novels were depicting the new manners and morals in ways that outraged protectors of morality. As Frederick Lewis Allen (1931, pp. 61–62) noted:

> Men and women were still shivering at the Red Menace when they awoke to the no less alarming Problem of the Younger Generation, and realized that if the Constitution was not in danger, the moral code of the country certainly was.

Police were generally among those most indignant about these changes in morals. For them, however, more than manners and morals were at stake. In the minds of police, the nature of crime was changing and it was increasing dramatically. Gangs spawned by prohibition were now organized into cohesive professional crime syndicates. The violence associated with Prohibition seemed to be persisting into the next decade despite its repeal. Police noted an early thirties crime wave. But most disturbing to police was their perception that serious crime was increasingly being committed by a group not disposed to crime in the past. To a certain extent, police could understand crime emanating from poor immigrants and ghettos. What they were baffled by was the growing number of criminals coming from the mainstream American population.

> The key police discovery about the crime wave of the early 1930s was the increasing number of youthful criminals from those areas and groups that had always been considered the strength and stability of America. . . . What could not be explained was the new criminals, the ones that emanated from the "real Americans." This is the symbolic importance of the Dillingers and Nashes, the Barrow and Floyd gangs; they were not foreigners stewing in the ghetto pots of want and despair, but were native Americans, born and bred in the heartlands of America, surrounded by the traditions and institutions that had made America so successful. (Jordan, 1972, pp. 21–22)

For Vollmer and his compatriots, the failure of Prohibition, the Great Depression, changes in morals, the increase in crime, and spread of criminal conduct to new groups were symptoms of the erosion of the authority of character-building institutions. These institutions were failing to instill in youth those character traits which sustained values and made America great. For police reformers, those character traits represented a substantive definition of appropriate youth behavior inherited from nineteenth-century reformers. This definition was quite specific—it was part of the legacy of the "child saving" reform movements. Good children were religious, mannerly, studious, polite, chaste, and respectful of authority. They dressed, danced and courted in particular ways. They avoided smoking, drinking, and hanging around in poolhalls and other places deemed deleterious to their characters.

To the extent primary institutions failed to instill such attitudes and behaviors in children, reform police would arrogate the responsibility of shoring up these institutions. They would be in the vanguard saving America's youth with a program of considerable breadth. First, they would continue their traditional law enforcement role. They would enforce laws about juveniles rigorously and when all else failed, they would arrest and process youths through juvenile and adult courts. Arrest, however, would generally be seen as an undesirable outcome. Special juvenile bureaus would be created to diagnose the problems of children and families, and decide appropriate disposition of cases.

A primary purpose of the juvenile division would be to refer youth to appropriate sources of assistance—police would do case finding for social agencies. They would not be passive in their relations with social agencies; police would exploit their intimate relations with and knowledge of the community and place themselves at the hub of community agencies, chiding and goading them when necessary into appropriate action.

Finally, police would work independently in the community with youth and families. They would do this by providing direct counselling to families and youths in juvenile divisions (often staffed by trained social workers as well as police), and through youth and recreation programs within which police would function as role models.

Police and Youth: the 1930s Beginnings

Police, of course, had dealings with youth long before the 1930s. Street urchins and "Arabs," as they were known, had created problems for police from the inception of American cities. Riots had always involved a significant number of youth—colleges were known for riotous conditions much earlier than they were for scholarship. The capacity of youth for obstreperousness and mayhem had been established for a good share of American history.

Police methods to deal with youth prior to the 1930s were undifferentiated. Foot patrol officers routinely patrolled neighborhoods. Having been politically recruited from the same neighborhoods, they were familiar with its residents. Arrests then were rarer because they were troublesome. After making a "cuff," an officer would either have to walk the arrestee to a station-house or call box and then await a horse-drawn paddy wagon. Whichever he did, the officer often had to handcuff the arrestee to a call box until a relief officer or paddy wagon appeared. As now, arrests of females were even more troublesome. Care had to be taken that neither impropriety nor hints of it occurred. Moreover, arrest of middle class young females was, on occasion, viewed as an attempt to scandalize fathers. Vollmer recounts a tale of an infuriated gentleman who came to a police station with a huge loaded pistol to redeem his family's honor by shooting the officer who arrested his daughter. (Fortunately for everybody, the girl spontaneously confessed her crimes.) (1936, p. 196)

Given the intimate social and political links between police and neighborhoods during the period before the 1930s, many cases of youth crime, disorder, and obstreperousness were settled with the end of a nightstick. More likely than not, the social status of the miscreant or the arresting officer's familiarity with the youth's family would determine whether such an outcome would result, and anecdotal evidence suggests that such outcomes were not rare. As with crimes committed by adults, detective police routinely investigated crimes committed by juveniles.

Special juvenile units were rare. In 1877, the Detroit Police Department created a juvenile delinquency division. By 1920, it was staffed by a captain and 10 officers. In 1917, the New York City Police Department created some 6,000 "junior police" and assigned a welfare police officer to work with difficult youths in each of the city's then forty-seven precincts. In 1925, Vollmer created a community coordinating council to mobilize community resources to deal with delinquency in Berkeley, California (Douthit, 1983). What evidence there is (police statistics of the time did not differentiate between youths and adults) suggests that police handled difficult youths routinely: they arrested a few, released most to their parents, and not occasionally settled matters with curbstone justice.

These traditional police practices came under police scrutiny and were the subject of professional debate during the 1920s and 1930s. Vollmer, however, set the tone with his concern for family, home, and community.

> Family and social integrity are of primary importance as conditions of acceptable social behavior. Where the character of a community is high, there one will find families in which the parents give to their children a sympathetic understanding and an intelligent supervision and direction of their training. From such homes, provided the children are not physically or mentally unsound, come the young people of high ideals, good habits and correct social attitudes, whereas defective homes produced the pampered, spoiled, or antisocial persons who kill, kidnap, rob, and in other ways fail to conform to the established order. (1936, p. 212)

Most local police leaders, impressed by Vollmer's formulations, moved to reshape both the content of police practice and the public's view of police. Learning from the techniques of J. Edgar Hoover, police leaders initiated massive public relations campaigns. They consulted with movie makers and radio show producers, wrote newspaper editorials, appeared on radio, put up displays at county fairs, created speakers' bureaus, and lectured at every opportunity. Moreover, police publicized their formal and informal relief activities (this was the period of the Great Depression) in articles with titles such as "The Santa Claus in Blue," "Penn Troopers Play Santa Claus to Eighty Needy Families," and "Teddy Plays Santa" (Jordan, 1972).

Vollmer led the way in the development of crime prevention activities. When he became Berkeley's town marshall he forbade his police officers to put juveniles in jail. In 1915, he began to keep separate statistics on juveniles. He familiarized himself with writings of well-known social scientists of the day such as William Healy, Clifford Shaw, and the Gluecks. The Berkeley Police Department created the Crime Prevention Division with a psychiatric social worker as its head in 1925. Vollmer initiated research in the Berkeley school system to identify pre-delinquents. Based on this research, Vollmer advocated aggressive police intervention:

> Vollmer suggested that the police department should gather information on the delinquent tendencies of children. With information drawn from the personal observations of police officers and school authorities, the department could plot the residential location of these children on a city map. Then the police would be in a position to "command assistance from parents, teachers, preachers, and recreation supervisors" to eliminate those individual and social factors which would inevitably produce more crime. (Douthit, 1983, p. 106)

Following Vollmer's lead, although not as aggressively or expansively as he would have liked, police throughout the United States developed programs for youth. Enforcement of city ordinances regarding pool and dance halls, movies, and bars intensified. Juvenile divisions, often staffed by policewomen or social workers, were created to diagnose family and children's problems and refer them to court, or preferably, to the appropriate community agencies. Special training for juvenile division staff became routine and was often disseminated to all police officers. Referral of youth to community agencies became a goal of juvenile divisions. Police advocated participation in boys' clubs and YMCAs.

Police recreational programs expanded rapidly. The New York City police department initiated the Police Athletic League (PAL) in 1932, which was emulated throughout the country. Big Brother and Boy Scout programs were routinely sponsored by police departments and police benefit associations. Police became active in schools, both to impress youth with a new image of police, and to educate youth about good citizenship. In some communities participation in police-sponsored programs was made contingent on attending Sunday schools.

Much of this activity was based on assumptions about the dangers of idleness and the importance of supervised recreation by positive role models. These were values typical of the Progressive Era, but it was more than that. Vollmer, as a Progressive, was motivated to maintain a rather narrow vision of public morality by designing policies that effectively reminded socializing institutions of their responsibilities. At the same time, his perception that much of delinquency was symptomatic of other more basic psychological problems amenable to treatment on an individual basis led him to reject coercion and punishment as solutions (see Vollmer, 1936, pp. 189–200). Early twentieth-century policing developed programs which emphasized character building. As we shall see, mid-twentieth-century policing developed programs which emphasized the need for individualized treatment.

Articulation of this ideology and development of these programs were also important to the emerging police profession.

> The main importance of these juvenile activities was the new concept it fostered among the police; not only must they work to save the younger generation, but they also strove to recreate and/or buttress the institutions which once had these responsibilities. (Jordan, 1972, p. 71)

To summarize: during the 1930s police, separating themselves from their history and indignant about immorality and crime, rallied around leaders such as Vollmer and others who saw a unique identity for police as a line of defense against the forces eroding character-building institutions in America. An independent police ethos was taking shape. To be sure, it would be modified over time, but a broad array of delinquency prevention programs which attempted to maintain a particular substantive view of youth morality were among the first police expressions of this ethos.

World War II to the 1980s

This section will review police activities with juveniles during the 1940–1980 era. Information for this section is derived from a content analysis of articles in *Police Chief* magazine for the first three years in each decade. Because *Police Chief* magazine is a vehicle for professional points of view—it is not a refereed journal—there is good reason to believe that it reflects professional practice and aspirations, both meaningful in this discussion.

With juvenile divisions in place, and police taking an active role in youth recreation, the early 1940s were characterized by a solidification of the ideas and proposals of the 1930s. When contrasted with society's concerns about youth today, the problems police addressed during this period seem almost trivial: traffic violations (including bicycle violations); shooting air rifles; Halloween mischief; clinging to autos; and late night revelry by young soldiers and teenage girls. Such mischief and immorality were ascribed to parental failures, poor supervision, and unoccupied time. The most often proposed solution was to provide youth with role models who emphasized good citizenship and wholesome activities. Police could provide this through athletic and recreational activities.

In the 1950s police began to minimize the emphasis on the character-building capacity of families and communities to explain juvenile delinquency and began to rely more on a disease model of delinquency causation. This was a reflection of the second thread of Vollmer's thought: individualized problems and treatment of children. The importance of police in remedying such problems, however, was reduced as pre-delinquent and delinquent children were supposed to receive treatment by the social agency most appropriate for their behavior. Discussions of moral culpability and responsibility diminished.

Police administrators and reformers during the 1960s called for police professionalization and improved bureaucratic functioning. Increased training, recruitment of high calibre and educated personnel, set standards, and rational resource allocation were proposed as administrative methods for improving established programs. The treatment vocabulary persisted in defining a key function of the police officer's job, as did some discussion of recreational programs, but the tone of police discussions of youth began to change. Police grew more stern in their response to the community, calling for a return to law and order. They viewed some juveniles, especially gangs, as malicious, involved in crime and disorder for the sheer amusement of it. The public's belief during the 1930s and 1940s that there were benefits to be obtained from contact between police and youth gave way to the public's fear that youth would be traumatized through police contact. The police responded by designing police-youth interaction in athletic programs to foster improved police-community relations rather than good citizenship.

A concern to mitigate what had become an explosive problem—police-youth relations—dominated police writing during the early 1970s. Communication was seen as the primary means to alleviate problems between police and youth. Rap sessions and school-police liaison programs were developed. Negotiation and arbitration boards were developed as alternatives to traditional police and court practices.

Police were relatively silent about juveniles during the early 1980s. In all of 1983 there was just one indexed entry in *Police Chief* under "juveniles." Some articles on police-youth communications remain. Discussions of abused and neglected children, serious juvenile offenders and alternatives to secure detention appear. Descriptions of police programs designed to deal with juveniles were similar to the description of programs established for adults.

During the 1930s, police had touted a heady new ideology: police were the thin blue line between the maintenance of values and their dissolution. With pride, police held themselves to be the purveyors of society's values and positioned themselves as models for youths through a variety of programs. They envisioned an aggressive police program consisting of law enforcement, referral to and work with community institutions, and independent work with young persons through youth and recreation programs. By the 1960s, the police strategy for handling youths and delinquents had become crystallized. Classic police texts (see Leonard, 1964) recommended that a minimum of five percent of departmental strength be assigned to a juvenile division and should be of equal status with the detective division. Its elementary functions should include discovery of cases and their investigation. But "professional" police departments had a broader point of view.

> In a more professional and enlightened approach, the police juvenile unit assumes responsibility for the disposition of a substantial number of juvenile offenders. . . . The preliminary factual investigation is followed by diagnostic procedures in an attempt to identify those factors in the individual and his environment that have contributed to the end result. The clinical resources of the community . . . may be brought into play on behalf of the youngster. . . . As in medicine, the unit of practice is the patient. . . . Arrest is invoked only as the last resort. (Leonard, 1964, pp. 251–253)

Yet, no sooner had the model become firm, than its erosion began. By the late 1960s, police paid lip service to the idea that they were prepared to develop programs to refer juveniles for individual treatment, however they were not prepared to abandon ideas of moral culpability. At the same time, critics of police saw contacts between police and youth not as character building but as potentially traumatizing. The 1970s saw the police "hanging on" with youth, trying to keep police-youth contacts from exploding into confrontations. The thin blue line was becoming thinner and thinner. By the 1980s, police tactics with juveniles appeared to be edging to a full circle: the handling of juveniles was increasingly seen as indistinguishable from police handling of adults. What began in the 1930s as a venture to maintain youth morality through a program of considerable breadth and intimacy had largely been abandoned.

A variety of forces have given rise to this shift in police handling of juveniles: the changing police organizational strategy; continued liberalization of manners and mores; increased civil liberties of youth; increased police self-consciousness about the validity of the values they represent; antagonism between police and social agencies; and uncertainty about the effect of police on youth.

Despite the breadth of Vollmer's vision, policing has narrowed its focus. Under the tutelage of J. Edgar Hoover, police have moved away from the tasks of order maintenance and the provision of social service towards the control of youth. Police officers have been removed from beats with which they were familiar and put into cars. Intimate relations with neighborhoods and community institutions have largely come to an end.

Youth have continued to enjoy more freedom over the years. Dress, manners, language, and behavior have continued to deviate from Victorian ideals. Self-expression has become valued as an end in itself. Schools have liberalized and tolerated student behavior that was unheard of in the past. Church influence over youth has declined.

Individual rights of citizens have expanded and police behavior have become more constrained. The third degree, a prevalent but condemned practice in the 1930s, has given way to Supreme Court decisions. The Civil Rights movement called attention to discriminatory practices by police and curbstone justice was reined in, signifying the end of the nightstick as a means of social control. Police, at least formally, have turned to criminal law for justification of their activities.

Police, like many others, have become self-conscious about their own values. In a world of liberalized speech and behavior, pornography, strange dress, drugs, and the deinstitutionalization of the mentally ill, the police officer's traditional view of youth appears quaint and Victorian. The perception of the police officer as the final bulwark in defense of those values hardly seems a viable professional option.

Social and diversion agencies, many armed with trivialized versions of labeling theories about the negative consequences of police-youth contact, have tended to become increasingly suspicious of, and hostile to, police. Police, independent to the point of being isolated and already dissatisfied with social service responses to delinquency, have responded in kind. This issue will be discussed in more detail later in this paper.

Police research has also played a role in the change of police functioning relative to youth. The next section of this paper will focus on that research.

Research Into Police Handling of Juveniles

In this section, we will look at what empirical evidence exists regarding the three areas of police activity involving juveniles—in the criminal justice system; referral to diversion and social service agencies; and independent police action.

The Police in the Criminal Justice System

Citizens' decisions to invoke police action provide input to patrol officers; patrol officers' decisions provide input to detective or juvenile officers; and detective or juvenile officers' decisions provide input to juvenile courts, adult courts, and diversionary or welfare programs. At each decision-point one actor's output becomes the next actor's input.

The majority of police contacts with juveniles originate with citizen calls to police. Black and Reiss (1970) found that 72 percent, and Lundman et al. (1979) 66 percent, of police-juvenile contacts resulted from citizen mobilization of the police to deal with some problem. (Contacts for traffic violations are excluded in the Lundman et al. study as a result of a unique policy regarding traffic citations in the city under study.) The balance of police-juvenile contacts resulted from police-initiated actions. Citizen-mobilized police contacts with juveniles represented a small portion of the total calls for police service—generally under 8 percent (Cumming et al., 1965; Galliher, 1979; Karras, 1970; Lilly, 1978; Pate et al., 1976).

Police take seriously calls about juveniles. Cumming et al. (1965) found that although calls regarding youth comprised only 2.6 percent of the total number of citizen calls to police for service, police dispatches to calls regarding youth made up almost 6 percent of the total dispatches. Police were sent to 86 percent of calls regarding youth but, for example, only 51 percent of disputes. Likewise Lilly (1978) found that calls for juvenile problems made up 5.4 percent of calls for service, but 13.2 percent of dispatches. Police were dispatched to 73 percent of calls regarding juveniles—more than for calls regarding theft or family trouble. Similarly, Wilson (1968) found that of the 312 police dispatches he studied, 50 (16 percent) dealt with gang disturbances. Part of the disparity between calls for service and police dispatches might be explained by a recent finding of Pierce (1984): calls regarding juveniles, especially juvenile gangs, tend to originate from relatively small neighborhoods or geographical areas. Thus, although the number of calls for service regarding juveniles represents a relatively small portion of the number of calls for service in a city, new data suggest that juveniles present a more serious problem in particular small geographical areas. Possibly police recognize this and therefore respond more regularly to calls about juveniles.

Generally, the nature of the complaints police respond to regarding juveniles is not serious. Black and Reiss (1970) found that 5 percent of the contacts involved felonies and 60 percent rowdiness. Lundman et al. (1979) found 14 percent of the contacts involved felonies and 45 percent rowdiness. Reflecting this pattern, a small number of police contacts result in arrest—15 percent of Black and Reiss' (1970) sample were arrested and Lundman et al. (1979) found a similar figure of 16 percent. Moreover, Black and Reiss found that approximately three-quarters of juveniles who had committed felonies were arrested, and all of those juveniles in the Lundman et al. sample who had committed felonies were arrested.

Given the size of the samples noted above and the small numbers of felonies committed by youth in those samples, it is not possible to analyze further the types of felonies juveniles committed. Uniform Crime Reports are somewhat useful for this purpose, however. The Federal Bureau of Investigation estimates that there were approximately 1.4 million arrests of juveniles in 1981. A quarter-million of those arrests were for status offenses. Youths under 15 comprised 5 percent of the 460,000 arrests for violent crimes and 14 percent of the 1.8 million arrests for property crimes in the United States. Youth between 15 and 19 made up 25 percent of the arrests for violent crimes and 36 percent of arrests for property offenses. Arrests for property crimes peak at age 16 and for violent crimes at age 16 (Department of Justice, 1983).

The police decision to arrest or take juveniles into custody is determined by a variety of factors. Seriousness of offense is almost universally the most important factor. Extra-legal issues are also a factor, including demeanor, offense history, wishes of the complainant, definition of the event by the dispatcher, and availability of evidence (Black and Reiss, 1970; Lundman et al., 1979; Doob and Chan, 1982; Pepinsky, 1976). Both Black and Reiss (1970) and Lundman et al. (1979) conclude that race is not a factor, although Lundman et al. amend this conclusion: "Instead it would appear that the higher rate of arrests for black juveniles is attributable to black complainants who lobby for formal police action." (1979, p. 84)

Once a juvenile is arrested or taken into custody by the police officer who has initiated a contact, the youth is handled either by the detective or juvenile division/bureau. Four major outcomes generally result: release without referral, referral to juvenile court, referral to adult court, or referral to welfare or secondary police agencies. In 1981, of the approximately 1.4 million arrests of juveniles, 34 percent were released outright with no referral, 58 percent were referred to the juvenile court, 5 percent to the adult court, and 2 percent to welfare or secondary police agencies. Of those referred to juvenile court, it is estimated that 11 percent were for crimes against persons, 49 percent for crimes against property, 6 percent for drug offenses, 15 percent for offenses against public order, and 20 percent were for status offenses.

Less than 20 percent of arrested juveniles are detained. Of those detained in 1979, 28 percent were detained for crimes against persons, 21 percent for public order crimes (weapons, sex, drunkeness, disturbing the peace, etc.), 18 percent for property crimes, 17 percent for drug-related crimes, and 17 percent for status offenses (Department of Justice, 1983).

The basis for deciding the outcome of detective or juvenile division reviews includes many of the same factors shaping patrol officer decisions: seriousness of the offense, previous offenses, demeanor of the youth, and police assessment of the youth's family (Andriessen, 1978; Doob and Chan, 1982; Fisher and Mawby, 1982; Landau, 1981; Landau and Nathan, 1983). In addition, Landau (1981) notes that in England the geographical area in which the offense took place serves to affect police decision-making—when youths commit crimes that are problematic in "bad" areas, police tend both to arrest and refer those youths to court.

Police, Diversion, and Social Agencies

Diversion of juveniles from the justice system is the opposite side of the coin. In its truest sense, diversion is the informal referral to other social agencies, or release of offenders by police or law enforcement officials, both of which avoid any official action (Lemert, 1981). As is apparent from the discussion above, police divert the vast majority of youths with whom they have contact—85 percent of the youths with whom police have contact as a result of citizen complaints or their own initiative are disposed of informally by the patrol officer—although youths committing felonies are almost universally arrested (Black and Reiss, 1970; Lundman et al., 1979). Of those arrested or taken into custody, 34 percent were released outright with no referral and 2 percent were referred to welfare or secondary police agencies (Department of Justice, 1983). To the extent that these studies and data are representative, they suggest that for every 100 youths police have contact with as the result of a complaint by a citizen or pro-active approach by police, 5 are not diverted and penetrate the juvenile justice system beyond the police. For every 1,000 youths police have contact with as the result of a complaint or pro-active approach by police, 3 are referred to welfare or secondary police agencies. These conclusions would generally support the findings of Klein (1976) and Vanagunas (1979) that diversionary and referral programs are not priority operational issues in the vast majority of police departments. Police do not seem to be *net-widening* through diversion; whether they do in any other way is not known.

Independent Police Action

For the most part, independent actions on the part of police to prevent or control delinquency are invisible. We have some descriptive accounts of police social work activities in juvenile bureaus, but little or no statistical information about the volume of such activities nationwide (see, for example, Collingwood, Doud, and Williams, 1979; Johnson, Binder, and Wakamatsu, 1980; LeBlanc, 1978). We know that some police departments still run PAL-like programs, but we do not know how many, or how many youths are served by such activities.

Street handling of youths has been largely unexamined except for analysis of how police exercise discretion in deciding to release or arrest. Black (1980) is one exception, suggesting, on the basis of data collected in 1967, that police respond both more toughly and more leniently to juveniles. For example, police lecture youth, use physical punishment and humiliation, and otherwise degrade youth more than they do adults—an indication of the lower social status of juveniles vis-á-vis adults. Nevertheless, once having gone through such activities, police are more lenient with youths than with adults in their selection of dispositions.

Discussion and Conclusion

The idea that police have a special mission regarding youth is one that gained early currency in the development of police ideology. Despite the rallying power of that ideology, it never became a central part of the organizational strategy of police. Vollmer's vision of police as the bulwark against further erosion of the morals and manners of youth persisted as part of the rhetoric of police, but was largely unimplemented. True, police created juvenile bureaus, which exist in most police departments to this day, but they exist out of the mainstream of police organizations. "Real" policing is done in patrol, detective, and vice bureaus; officers in juvenile bureaus are often considered members of the "empty holster" crowd.

One consequence of the high hopes for the role that police would play as the hub of social services to youth in both referring large numbers of youth to such agencies and reminding agencies of their responsibilities when they failed to serve children properly, never came to fruition. Although data regarding police referrals are not readily available, those that exist suggest that police refer relatively few juveniles to social agencies. Although the data are recent, there is no reason to believe that circumstances were substantially different in the past. Similarly, although police did develop PAL-like programs throughout the country during the 1930s and 1940s, these programs have largely fallen out of favor and are now outside the mainstream of American policing.

This outcome is probably not surprising. The early police vision of youth morality was so specific and so wedded to Victorian ideals that police simply became overwhelmed by the avalanche of social change that swept over American youth. If police were to maintain the level of influence over youth they desired, they would have had to maintain relatively intimate contacts with them. As it turned out, the strategy developed by police went in exactly the opposite direction: police became less and less intimate with citizens, finally withdrawing into professional isolation. Moreover, social agencies developed ideologies and values which were often alien to police, nor would social workers tolerate lectures by police about their responsibilities.

The police strategy which emerged was two-pronged. First, police became gatekeepers for the juvenile justice system, referring "guilty" or intractable youths for appropriate disposition. Once they referred a case to court, police never approved of diversion. Second, police provided independent services to youths they had contact with, both on the street and in juvenile bureaus. Usually, these services consisted of lectures reminding youths of their responsibilities, even though juvenile bureaus did develop some counselling and informal supervision programs.

For the most part, however, these activities and their outcomes are invisible. We know with some certainty both how many youth are diverted by police, and the reasons why police divert them—both on the street and in juvenile bureaus. We know little about the impact of the exercise of police discretion regarding juveniles, however. There are reasons to suspect that such activities are important. Police activities such as returning misbehaving children to their homes and remonstrating both children and parents are not unlikely to have an impact, good or ill, on families and children. When police do get more intimately involved in communities, on foot patrol for example, we know that they often begin regulating youth behavior—sometimes counselling, other times returning to the use of nightsticks. There is reason to suspect that these regulatory activities yield a considerable reduction of fear in communities. Yet we know little or nothing about the shape, substance, or outcome of these regulatory activities on the individual. Arrest itself, and subsequent release of juveniles to parents with all the hassles that this entails for youths and families, may well have substantial impact on them, but we know little about this. The point is that police, working independently in communities and juvenile bureaus, exercise social control over juveniles, and there are reasons to suspect that these activities are important in the lives of children and communities.

References

Allen, F. L. (1931). *Only yesterday: An informal history of the nineteen-twenties*. New York: Harper and Bros.

Andriessen, M. F. (1978). The handling of juvenile cases by the Dutch police. *The Police Journal, 51*(3), 261–265.

Black, D. J., & Reiss, A. J. (1970). Police control of juveniles. *American Sociological Review, 35*, 63–67.

Black, D. (1980). *The manners and customs of the police*. New York: Academic Book Press, Inc.

Collingwood, T. R., Doud, A., & Williams, H. (1979). Juvenile diversion: The Dallas Police Department Youth Services Program. *Federal Probation*, 23–27.

Cumming, E., Cumming, I., & Edell, L. (1965). Policeman as philosopher, guide and friend. *Social Problems, 12*, 276–286.

Doob, A., & Chan, J. B. L. (1982). Factors affecting police decisions to take juveniles to court. *Canadian Journal of Criminology, 24*(1), 25–37.

Douthit, N. (1983). August Vollmer. In C. B. Klockars (Ed.), *Thinking about police: Contemporary readings*. New York: McGraw Hill Book Company.

Fisher, C. J., & Mawby, R. I. (1982). Juvenile delinquency and police discretion in an inner-city area. *British Journal of Criminology, 22*(1), 63–75.

Fogelson, R. M. (1977). Reform at a standstill. In C. B. Klockars (Ed.), *Thinking about police: Contemporary readings*. New York: McGraw Hill Book Company.

Galliher, J. F., Donovan, P. L. & Adams, D. L. (1979). Small-town police: Troubles, tasks and publics. *Journal of Police Science and Administration, 3*, 19–28.

Johnson, R. A., Binder, A., & Wakamatsu, M. (1980). Juvenile diversion by resident counselor in a police department. *Police Chief, 47*(3), 26–27.

Jordan, K. E. (1972). *Ideology and the coming of professionalism: American urban police in the 1920's and 1930's*. Dissertation, Rutgers University.

Karras, John. (1970). Law enforcement in an Iowa town: Kojak it's not. *Des Moines Register,* 6 May.

Klein, M. W. (1976). Issues and realities in police diversion programs. *Crime and Delinquency, 22*(4), 421–427.
Landau, S. F. (1981). Juveniles and the police. *British Journal of Criminology, 21*(1), 27–46.
Landau, S. F., & Nathan, G. (1983). Selecting delinquents for cautioning in the London metropolitan area. *British Journal of Criminology, 23*(2), 128–149.
LeBlanc, M. (1978). Police diversion of juveniles in the 60's and 70's. *Crime And/ ET Justice, 6*(3), 165–168.
Lemert, E. M. (1981). Diversion in juvenile justice: What hath been wrought. *Journal of Research in Crime and Delinquency,* January, 34–45.
Leonard, V. A. (1964). *Police organization and management* (2nd ed.). Brooklyn: The Foundation Press Inc.
Lilly, R. J. (1978). What are the police now doing? *Journal of Police Science and Administration, 6,* 51–60.
Lundman, R. J., Sykes, R. E., & Clark, J. P. (1979). Police control of juveniles: A replication. *Journal of Research in Crime and Delinquency,* January, 74–91.
Monkkonen, E. H. (1975). *The dangerous class: Crime and poverty in Columbus, Ohio, 1860–1885*. Cambridge: Harvard University Press.
Pate, T., Ferrara, A., Bowers, R. A., & Lorence, J. (1976). *Police response time.* Washington D.C.: Police Foundation.
Pepinsky, H. E. (1976). Police patrolmen's offense-reporting behavior. *Journal of Research in Crime and Delinquency, 1,* 33–47.
Pierce, G., Spaar, S., & Briggs, LeBaron. (1987, April). *The character of police work and police technology.* Northeastern University Report, Boston.
U.S. Department of Justice, Bureau of Justice Statistics. (1983). *Criminal victimization in the United States.* Washington, D.C.
Vanagunas, S. (1979). Police diversion of juvenile offenders: An ambiguous state of the art. *Federal Probation, 43,* 48–52.
Vollmer, A. (1936). *The police and modern society.* Berkeley: The University of California.
Wilson, J. Q. (1968). *Varieties of police behavior.* Cambridge: Harvard University Press.

12
Alternatives to the Juvenile Court Process

LLOYD E. OHLIN

The societal interest in child-rearing lies in the support of processes that lead to the development of productive and responsible citizens. In addition, these processes should take place in a context that provides both opportunity and support for the development of individual creative talents. The responsibility for achieving these societal goals is vested in the various institutions for the socialization and control of human conduct. They share in different measure responsibility for the emotional, intellectual, moral, and spiritual development of children and youth. Furthermore, the relative reliance on socialization versus control processes varies along an institutional continuum of primary agencies: the family, church, school, labor market, social service organizations, police, juvenile court, and correctional system. When the first four of these agencies are working well, there is little need to mobilize the resources and authority of the last four. But when the family, church, school, and labor market fail to carry out their socialization and control functions effectively, these agencies, as a final resort, become engaged, since they are invested in various degrees with the power to employ coercion.

Among these agencies, the court has the responsibility to determine how much and what types of coercion are justified to control the conduct of children and youth, and to reach this decision through due process. It would appear that this set of institutional arrangements provides for an appropriate distribution of authority and responsibility with adequate safeguards in the event of failure. Why then be concerned with exploring alternatives to the juvenile court?

Difficult problems arise when misconduct is attributable more to the breakdown of the basic institutions of socialization and control than to willful and stubborn defiance of authority by the children involved. Remedial measures must be taken to control and treat the behavioral problems of the children. But how are the institutional failures to be identified, analyzed and corrected? Where should authority be lodged to monitor operations, assemble data and take corrective action?

One answer might be to enlarge and clarify the responsibility and authority of the juvenile court in this regard. But the court handles problems of children on an individual basis, which makes it difficult to discern systemic defects in the socializing institutions that may be the major contributors to youthful misconduct. However, could not the capacity of the court be strengthened through the provision of funds for the purchase of service and staff to monitor the effectiveness of the socializing institutions? There is apparently a reluctance to do this for several reasons. Juvenile court judges are usually trained in the law and lack special competence in the provision and managing of social services. There is also a hesitancy about excessive intrusion into the domain of executive authority on a regular basis. It is not clear what new authority would be required to allocate such oversight powers to the court, though it is clear it would be strongly resisted by the affected institutions. Consequently, it seems desirable first to explore what alternatives to the court might contribute to fill the gap between the institutional failures in the socialization of youth and intervention by the court. There are really two major problems here that we shall explore separately. What can be done, short of official action by the court, to deal with youth who are as much victims of institutional failure as they are victimizers through their delinquent acts? What can be done to correct defects in institutional operations and organization?

Dealing With the Problems of Failed Youth

Among the approximately 1.4 million juveniles referred to the juvenile court each year, there are a number so beyond the control of the community institutions and service agencies that court-imposed sanctions are the only alternative left. There are many other youth, however, who would be better corrected short of court intervention, if appropriate institutional services were available. There are good reasons to avoid the court process if possible. It is an expensive process with few funds to aid the child directly. Because of limited dispositional options and a greatly overburdened probation staff there is a tendency to rely on short-run isolation and custodial care. Greater stigma attaches to court dispositions, and the court tends to remain involved once engaged.

The effect of court action and correctional dispositions was especially evident in a pilot study of two Boston communities conducted by the Harvard Law School Center for Criminal Justice (Miller and Ohlin, 1985). Samples of correctional processed youth and school students were interviewed with regard to their current circumstances, aspirations, available opportunities, and expectations. It became clear that they were living in quite different career tracks with regard to all four of these areas of our inquiry. The correctional processed youth had more limited aspirations and expectations. They also engaged in more illegitimate activities and perceived that opportunities for such activities and for gang associations were much more readily available. They were more pessimistic about the future and saw fewer prospects in school or work as avenues for getting ahead.

Such differences are perhaps not surprising, but they indicate the difficulty youth perceive in getting out of a deviant or delinquent track once this is confirmed by court and correctional processing. Communities and institutions develop informal expectation systems that become self-fulfilling prophecies for those tracked into them. There is a need then to identify and develop non-stigmatizing re-engagement opportunities that lead from deviant to legitimate channels of development within institutions and the communities of which they are part. The chances are better if this can be done short of court intervention.

Youth Service Bureaus

One proposal to create a new intermediary institution between existing community agencies for youth and the courts was offered in 1967 in the report of the National Crime Commission. It noted that many youth were lost in the referral network for lack of accountability and follow-up by the referring agencies. Some agencies, such as the police for example, were frustrated by the lack of a readily available place where youth could be referred other than the court and, consequently, did nothing or felt forced to use the court option. No one agency had the responsibility for mapping the service network to spot gaps in service that should be remedied. Nor did any agency have the responsibility to conduct studies to monitor the effectiveness of the socialization and control processes for youth, or to identify systemic defects in institutional organization and operation.

The Commission proposed the creation of Youth Service Bureaus within communities to meet these needs (President's Commission on Law Enforcement and Administration of Justice, 1967). It argued that traditional justice system processing should be used as a last resort, and the types of conduct justifying court intervention should be restricted. It sought to reduce the labeling or stigmatizing effect of court intervention by providing other dispositional alternatives and accountability. The Commission recommended: "Communities should establish neighborhood youth serving agencies—Youth Service Bureaus—located if possible in comprehensive neighborhood community centers and receiving juveniles (delinquent and nondelinquent) referred by the police, the juvenile court, parents, schools, and other sources." (President's Commission on Law Enforcement and Administration of Justice, 1967, p. 83).

The Youth Service Bureau was intended to have three major functions. It was to be a referral resource widely available for troubled youth where analysis of the youth's problem and appropriate referral to other agencies could be arranged. Where gaps in available services were identified, the Bureau would help develop such services and then locate them in appropriate agencies providing direct services. Finally, and most importantly, the Bureau would assist the community to mobilize its resources in the prevention of delinquency by developing and monitoring a service plan for troubled and troublesome youth as a group. Thus the bureau was intended to provide a referral source for individual cases, a program development function, and a monitoring and coordination function.

The Commission's proposal was subsequently criticized for not providing sufficiently specific guidelines for the development of Youth Service Bureaus. Since, in my role as an associate director of the Commission, I was responsible for proposing the concept of this Bureau and assisting the Juvenile Delinquency Task Force in its development, I should note that this lack of specificity was to some degree intentional. There was insufficient time to test out this concept with key practitioners providing services for delinquents, and it seemed more practical to allow for experimentation in application of the idea, given the diversity of resources and organization of services in different communities.

The expectation of diversity in the development of Youth Service Bureaus subsequently occurred for better or worse. Several surveys of the emerging Youth Service Bureaus were conducted in the early 1970s. One, conducted by the National Council on Crime and Delinquency, concluded the YSBs should not provide direct services but should concentrate on the delinquency prevention and service brokerage role (Norman, 1972). However, the surveys generally revealed a tendency to concentrate on direct services to youth by the YSBs, often in competition with existing agencies for funds and clients. The results of a national survey of YSBs by the California Youth Authority have been summarized as follows:

> This survey, initiated in fall 1971, documented the increasingly obvious diversity of goals and organizational structures. It found that most Youth Service Bureaus were not independent agencies, but, instead, had definite organizational links to "state or local government." It also found that the vast majority of YSBs focused on individual youths and utilized traditional approaches such as one-to-one counseling. (Bean and Campbell, 1974) It verified the growing impression that most bureaus emphasized direct services, placed much less weight on the referral of clients to other agencies, seldom purchased services which they themselves did not provide, and engaged in relatively few community organization efforts. Finally, the survey found that "only a few programs were effective in achieving coordination with other agencies at a policy making, administrative level." (Youth Development and Delinquency Prevention Administration, 1972) (Source: Palmer and Lewis, 1980, p. 10)

In general, it appears that the popularity of YSBs has declined in most jurisdictions, though many continue to operate, especially in California where their number has been significantly increased in recent years. Most have died from lack of stable funding once federal funds were expended. Others have been too closely tied to the charismatic influence of one individual; though generally the difficulty of attracting and maintaining experienced staff in a low-budget agency has been a greater problem. Many ran into turf or jurisdictional problems with existing agencies either because they provided competing direct services or attempted to play the role of an oversight or umbrella agency.

There appear to be some characteristics in common among those YSBs that have succeeded. Those that tended to be small, with relatively modest resources, seem to endure better. Those with large budgets tended to be seen as threats to existing agencies. Though most of these agencies started with federal funds, those that survived quickly attracted state funds on a stable basis before federal start-up funding expired. The longer time period of operation permitted by the state funding allowed the YSBs to work out turf problems and to find an appropriate role in the local structure of services.

A very important element concerned the issue of community standing or legitimacy. The most successful gained the support and recognition they needed from both the police and the juvenile court, in addition to the relevant social service agencies. There was also genuine community involvement. Not only would representatives of the police and courts be on these YSB boards but also the public and private social service agencies and interested citizens. Such cooperation proved more likely when the agency had developed a clear descriptive account of its goals, guiding principles, modes of operation, and available resources that could be readily communicated, accepted and understood by practitioners in other agencies.

What we now need is more thorough evaluation of the viability of the YSB concept in the structure of community youth services. A good start in this direction has been provided in the evaluation of juvenile diversion by Palmer and Lewis (1980). Current opposition to the YSB idea reflects concerns about the over-reach of public services in bringing greater numbers of young people unnecessarily under some form of official control and intervention. On the other hand, opposition is encountered because of a greater concern about crime rates and a preference for stronger sanctions rather than diversion from the juvenile justice system. The fact that YSBs continue to operate despite these divergent views needs to be explored more fully so that clearer models of successful organization and operation of YSBs can be developed.

Community Boards

A second major innovation to create an intermediary institution between the juvenile court and community agencies for children and youth in trouble has been the development of Community Boards. The growth of such boards has been part of a larger movement to develop dispute resolution forums for a wide variety of civil and minor criminal justice cases (McGillis and Mullen, 1977). They have emerged as a response to the many problems of the courts in handling minor civil and criminal cases, (such as the high costs of processing cases, long delays in scheduling hearings, and complaints about the impersonality of the proceedings and the resulting quality of justice).

These dispute resolution forums employ a variety of techniques depending on the type of cases under consideration. Hearing officers are usually lay citizens who have received some training in the use of conciliation, mediation or more formal hearing procedures. Typically they are representative of the community the forum serves. Cases are referred from various sources such as individual citizens, police, prosecutors, courts, or social service agencies. Some forums are sometimes sponsored by public bodies, (such as court's or prosecutor's offices), others by private groups working with the justice system, and still others with no formal ties to the justice system. For example, the Community Board Program in San Francisco was initiated as an experimental project by a local non-profit social action organization and has since spread throughout the area. Few cases come from the courts and most are referred directly by community residents.

Studies have shown that dispute resolution forums are well regarded by the communities and the participants they serve. Citizens seem to feel that they have a better chance to discuss their problems and to work out acceptable solutions than they would in a traditional court setting. Cases typically are dealt with more promptly to suit the convenience of the disputants. There is no charge for the hearings, and lawyers are not required.

Most of these forums accept referrals of both delinquent and non-delinquent cases of children and youth in trouble along with other types of minor civil and criminal matters. Some of the forums are more specialized in terms of the source of referral, the formality of the hearing, and the type of cases accepted for consideration. A most noteworthy development has been the growth of Community Accountability Boards in the state of Washington. A detailed account is provided in this volume by Mark Sidran. Here it is only important to note that the boards function in their neighborhoods as citizen adjuncts to the juvenile court and prosecutor's office from which they receive referrals of delinquent youth.

These citizen forums for dispute resolution appear to provide a significant, more informal and less stigmatizing alternative to the traditional juvenile court process. The rapidity with which this movement has grown offers testimony to the need which communities have felt for more local control and participation in decisions affecting their daily lives. It represents an important innovation in the development of greater community integration and a sense of responsibility for developing local solutions to the problems of its residents. Through dealing with individual cases, evidence may gradually be acquired of institutional failures in socialization and control that may lead to major reforms. To bring about such reforms, however, requires the collection of more systematic data on institutional deficiencies and the mobilization of a political process focused on reform.

Correcting Institutional Problems of Socialization

Dealing with individual cases through the creation of intermediary institutions, such as Youth Service Bureaus and Community Boards, will help over a period of time to develop awareness and some insights about systemic deficiencies in the organization and operation of institutions for the socialization and control of children and youth. Sometimes this may result in identifying gaps in the structure of services for which no organization has direct responsibility or the resources to respond. The problem then is to secure the needed resources and locate responsibility in an appropriate organization. But how is this to be accomplished? What agency or group will provide leadership that will be recognized by others as appropriate? In some cases, Youth Service Bureaus have been able to play this role. In others, Community Boards have been able to encourage schools or social service agencies to expand their services to fill the gap. In still others, the juvenile court has provided the necessary leadership to bring about remedial action. A community in which all three of these agencies were prepared to collaborate in identifying and remedying the service deficiencies would appear to have the best chance of succeeding.

A solution is less readily arrived at when the problem is perceived to lie somewhere in the organization or operation of an institution, such as the school or the family, and child welfare agency. Who then can command the authority to investigate, collect data, and analyze what the trouble is and determine what the solution would be? Should the juvenile court be empowered to initiate such a procedure, much as a federal court would do in appointing a master to oversee the remediation of constitutionally impermissible practices or conditions in schools or prisons? The unconstitutionality of the practices or conditions provides the basis for intervention by the federal court, but no such grounds are available to the juvenile court.

It would appear that the only solution lies in mobilizing the political process to bring about the needed reform. Collaboration between Youth Service Bureaus, Community Boards and the juvenile court may serve to alert civic and other organizations of the need for change. They in turn are able to mobilize an appropriate constituency to influence political actors to attend to the reform needs. Then, through executive or legislative authority, studies can be conducted and appropriate remedies supplied. Obviously the process is seldom so easy and neat as this chain of events would suggest, but it would take some such process to mobilize the knowledge and the will to make major institutional reforms. (Miller and Ohlin, 1985)

If such a process is to succeed, the existence of a Youth Service Bureau and a Community Board would offer the juvenile court the community-linked support it would need to participate effectively in a reform process. The creation of such intermediary institutions makes sense, therefore, not only as alternatives to court intervention in individual cases but also as sources of insight and support in bringing about reforms in socializing institutions.

References

Bean, A., and Campbell, F. (1974). *Cluster evaluation of five diversion projects, final report*. Sacramento: Office of Criminal Justice Planning.

McGillis, D. and Mullen, J. (1977). *Neighborhood justice centers: An analysis of potential models*. Washington, D.C.: U.S. Department of Justice, Law Enforcement Assistance Administration, National Institute of Law Enforcement and Criminal Justice.

Miller, A. D., and Ohlin, L. E. (1985). *Delinquency and community: creating opportunities and controls*. Beverly Hills, CA.: Sage.

Norman, S. (1972). *The youth service bureau: A key to delinquency prevention*. Paramus, N.J.: National Council on Crime and Delinquency.

Palmer, T., and Lewis, R. V. (1980). *An evaluation of juvenile diversion*. Cambridge, MA.: Oelgeschlager, Gunn and Hahn.

President's Commission on Law Enforcement and Administration of Justice. (1967). *The challenge of crime in a free society*. Washington, D.C.: U.S. Government Printing Office.

Youth Development and Delinquency Prevention Administration (1972). National Study of Youth Service Bureaus. Washington, D.C.: U.S. Department of Health, Education and Welfare.

Section V
The Organization of the Juvenile Justice System: Juvenile Court Jurisdiction and Processing

13
A Short History of Jurisdiction over Juvenile and Family Matters

BARBARA FLICKER[1]

Through a combination of historical accident and design, the power of the state to intervene in matters affecting children and families is distributed among the various courts and agencies of government. The judicial powers of the United States and the several states are vested in the federal and state courts by their respective constitutions, but the allocation of jurisdiction[2] over specific cases derives from British canon, equity, and common law.

Despite the trend to centralize family matters in a single family court, current jurisdiction over the various grounds for litigation is distributed among juvenile, criminal, domestic relations, probate or surrogate, civil, and general trial courts. Both parents and the state have an interest in preserving the traditional family unit by protecting the right of parents to raise their children without excessive state interference. Deference to the fundamental principle of family autonomy nevertheless allows court jurisdiction to resolve issues in ways that may alter the family unit or parental rights in the following categories of judicial action: abuse, adoption, custody, delinquency, dependency, divorce, emancipation, inheritance, neglect and permanent neglect, status offenses, and support.

This article will examine the current organization of the courts in their division of responsibility over family matters and the process by which that organization has evolved. The substantial role of other agencies in exercising power over juveniles and their families will be discussed, but the focus will be on the courts.

The first part reviews court jurisdiction over juvenile crime and status offenses. Child abuse, neglect, and family offenses are then covered. The third part traces matrimonial actions, termination of parental rights, and adoption. The final part summarizes the conclusions drawn and suggests a more coherent organization of court jurisdiction over juvenile and family problems.

Juvenile Crime and Status Offenses

Special Handling for Juvenile Offenders

Until separate juvenile courts were established in Chicago, Illinois on July 1, 1899, children accused of crime generally were handled in the same manner as adults, except that at common law children under seven were presumed to be incapable of committing a crime, and children between seven and fourteen had the benefit of a rebuttable presumption against criminal capacity.

Efforts to relieve the harshness of this practice began in the early nineteenth century. Separate facilities for the detention and confinement of juveniles were initiated in New York in 1825, Boston in 1826, and Pennsylvania in 1828. In 1861 separate hearings for juveniles were introduced in Chicago, with a commissioner to hear petty offenses. Separate trials for juveniles were introduced in Boston in 1870 and in New York in 1892. After 1899 the separate juvenile court was adopted in every state and most other nations, although some countries established administrative tribunals to deal with juvenile offenses (Encyclopaedia Brittanica).

Juvenile laws defining the jurisdiction of the separate courts covered not only criminal acts but also conduct actionable only if performed by juveniles, or status offenses. The Act of May 11, 1901 amended the Illinois Juvenile Court Act to add incorrigibility and "growing up in idleness or crime" to the list of juvenile offenses and the Act of June 4, 1907 added running away, loitering, and using profanity to the court's definition of delinquency (Schultz, 1973).

These legislative declarations of jurisdiction over juvenile misconduct were not unique. From colonial times, the courts have intervened to control noncriminal misbehavior. In 1646 the Massachusetts Bay Colony adopted a "stubborn child law" which made it a capital offense to disobey parents. Similar statutes were enacted in Connecticut, New Hampshire, and Rhode Island (Sutton, 1981).

By the nineteenth century, reform movements led to the construction of separate "houses of refuge" for children convicted of vagrancy or minor criminal offenses in New York, Philadelphia, and Boston. Commitment to these institutions was considered a privilege restricted to children deemed to be amenable to salvation through the infusion of good habits and correct moral principles.

In 1838 the constitutionality of such commitments was challenged in *Ex parte Crouse* (4 Whart. 9 Pa. 1838). The juvenile's father sought her release on the grounds that she had been denied a jury trial. The petition alleging incorrigibility had been filed by her mother. In expounding its reliance on the doctrine of *parens patriae,* the court said that "The object of the charity is reformation . . . To this end, may not the natural parents, when unequal to the task of education, or unworthy of it, be superseded by the *parens patriae,* or common guardian of the community?" (Flicker, 1981; Fox, 1970)

The doctrine had also been relied upon by the English chancery courts to remove children from unfit parents in two cases in the early nineteenth century, but these were custody cases between parents, not state action committing children to reformatories. As destitute juveniles began to attract the attention and concern of social reformers of that era, some minor criminal offenses were seen as symptoms of deficient parental attention, warranting the intervention of the community through removal to houses of refuge, along with other neglected and wayward minors, for purposes of salvation. During this era in the United States, the practice was to mingle children confined for crimes or waywardness with those given shelter as neglected or destitute. In the second half of the century, some reformers began to support the separation of younger children who had not committed crimes for more serious and older offenders.

The inclusion of status offenses with delinquency in the juvenile codes of the early twentieth century and the courts' broad jurisdictional base over neglected and dependent children led to increasingly and deliberately undifferentiated treatment for children brought before the court, regardless of the grounds. In the words of Judge Julian Mack in the Harvard Law Review in 1909, "Why is it not just and proper to treat these juvenile offenders as we deal with the neglected children, as a wise and merciful father handles his own child whose errors are not discovered by the authorities?"

This paternalistic response to juvenile transgressions, while clearly in conflict with the hallowed principles of family autonomy, was viewed by Judge Mack as consistent with the decisions of over two centuries in which "the courts of chancery in England have exercised protection over the unfortunate child." He quotes Justice Caton in *Cowles v. Cowles* (3 Gilman 435, 1846), with respect to the court's power "to interfere with and control not only the estates but the persons of all minors within the limits of its jurisdiction, . . . to enter into the domestic relations of every family in the community . . . to protect the persons and preserve the property of those who are unable to protect and take care of themselves . . ."

Judge Mack (1909) then stated the principle that has prevailed in American courts to this date: that the parents' rights are always subject to the court's control "when the best interests of the child demand it."

Many of the special features distinguishing the juvenile justice system in the first juvenile court act have survived, such as:

1. A separate court for juveniles under 16 "to regulate the treatment and control of dependent, neglected, and delinquent children."
2. Special procedures for the hearing and disposition of juveniles' cases.
3. Separation of children from adults placed in the same institution.

4. No detention of a child under 12 in a jail or police station.
5. Probation officers to investigate cases, represent the child's individual interest, and supervise children on probation.
6. The care, custody, and discipline of a child to "approximate as nearly as may be that which should be given by its parents, and in all cases where it can properly be done the child be placed in an improved family home and become a member of the family by legal adoption or otherwise." (Flicker, 1982)

The lack of differentiation in the treatment of children who had not committed crimes in the early juvenile court statutes eventually caused New York to adopt a new classification in its 1962 Family Court Act, "persons in need of supervision" or PINS. The notion was to avoid the stigma of delinquency for their noncriminal conduct, as the category of delinquent had been created to avoid the stigma of a criminal charge for juvenile offenders. By the early 1970s, at least one-fourth of all juvenile adjudications were for status offenses, and nearly half of all incarcerated juveniles were charged with noncriminal offenses. (Andrews and Cohn, 1974)

Due Process and Deinstitutionalization

The laws governing juvenile courts began to change in the 1960s in many respects, beginning with the New York State Family Court Act of 1962 and the United States Supreme Court decisions in 1966 with *Kent v. United States,* (383 U.S. 541) and *In re Gault,* (387 U.S. 1, 1967). National studies and commissions reported practices that failed to provide adequate protection to juveniles and their families from excessive state intervention. *Kent* and *Gault* emphasized the juvenile's right to due process as a necessary prerequisite to any denial of fundamental freedom by the juvenile courts. In *Gault,* Justice Fortas said of due process of law: "It is the basic and essential term in the social compact which defines the rights of the individual and delimits the powers which the state may exercise."

These decisions marked the trend away from acceptance of the reformation or rehabilitation of the juvenile as the central purpose of contact with the juvenile system. Justice Fortas observed in *Kent* that the juvenile appeared to be getting the worst of both worlds: "[H]e gets neither the protections accorded to adults nor the solicitous care and regenerative treatment postulated for children." In 1974, Congress enacted the Juvenile Justice and Delinquency Prevention Act (JJDP Act) as its response to the following findings:

1. Juveniles account for almost half the arrests for serious crimes in the United States today;
2. Understaffed, overcrowded juvenile courts, probation services, and correctional facilities are not able to provide individualized justice or effective help;

3. Present juvenile courts, foster and protective care programs, and shelter facilities are inadequate to meet the needs of the countless abandoned and dependent children, who, because of this failure to provide effective services, may become delinquents;
4. Existing programs have not adequately responded to the particular problems of the increasing number of young people who are addicted to or who abuse drugs, particularly nonopiate or polydrug abusers;
5. Juvenile delinquency can be prevented through programs designed to keep students in elementary and secondary schools through the prevention of unwarranted and arbitrary suspensions and expulsions;
6. States and local communities which experience directly the devastating failures of the juvenile justice system do not presently have sufficient technical expertise or adequate resources to deal comprehensively with the problems of juvenile delinquency;
7. Existing Federal programs have not provided the direction, coordination, resources, and leadership required to meet the crisis of delinquency.

Funds were appropriated for technical assistance to improve the quality of juvenile justice and "to develop and conduct effective programs to prevent delinquency, to divert juveniles from the traditional juvenile justice system and to provide critically needed alternatives to institutionalization." The purpose clause of the Act also stressed the development and implementation of national standards for the administration of juvenile justice.

The federal initiative of the JJDP Act combined with the Supreme Court decisions to produce many changes in the juvenile justice system. Juvenile court procedures traditionally regarded as non-adversarial, informal, and individualized to serve the best interests of the child became more formal, adversarial, and reliant upon abstract principles of justice. The prominent role of probation in representing the child's interests and advising the court on dispositions shifted to defense and prosecution counsel who performed increasingly important functions in the court. The specific charges alleged in each petition were displacing the needs of the child as the focus of the court's inquiry.

Criminalization of Juvenile Court

While the prospects for rehabilitation of juvenile offenders were fading as a reasonably attainable goal, and procedural protections in delinquency and status offense cases were expanding to resemble those in criminal court proceedings, the "criminalization" of juvenile court produced other consequences. State legislatures amended the purpose clause in their juvenile codes to include the safety and protection of the community in conjunction with the traditional "best interests of the child" objective. Greater emphasis on the offense charged was accompanied by sanctions differentiated by and proportionate to such factors as the prior record and age of the child, the presence of violence, and other factors related to the seriousness of the threat to the community's security, rather than the child's needs.

In the 1980s, a new sensitivity to the importance of habitual offenders and victims' rights occasioned other changes in the juvenile justice system. More states enacted (1) laws to waive juveniles to adult criminal court at earlier ages and for a wider range of offenses; (2) designated felony statutes which required mandatory minimum terms in secure facilities; and (3) fixed sentences related to the offenses committed in determining juvenile court dispositions. Prosecutors performed increasingly significant duties, subsuming much of the discretion previously exercised by the judges and probation officers in filing petitions, selecting the charges, and thereby determining the forum and the range of dispositions available to the court.

Changes in Status Offense Jurisdiction

The pendulum swing of action and reaction also affected the handling of status offenses by the juvenile court. The combined impact of assigned defense counsel, right to treatment decisions, statutes prescribing determinate and proportionate dispositions (relative to the seriousness of the offense), deinstitutionalization movements, and rulings against the commingling of noncriminal and criminal offenders in detention and correctional facilities resulted in many changes in the status offense category, constricting but not eliminating it. These changes included: the removal of most status offenders from secure facilities, unofficial non-enforcement of status offense laws in some jurisdictions, upgraded filings of status offense allegations to delinquency charges in some instances and downgraded filings to neglect petitions in others, fewer overall filings of status offense petitions, and modest expansion of alternative community-based programs, such as family mediation projects. Although constitutional challenges to the status offense jurisdiction as vague and uncertain were unsuccessful, wayward minor laws with penal sanctions were outlawed in *Gesicki v. Oswald* (336 F. Supp. 371, *aff'd mem.* 406 U.S. 913, 1972).

Jurisdiction over status offenses is an unresolved problem. Communities differ in the importance they attach to the enforcement of the various grounds for intervention, with runaways a major problem in locations favored by young people, incorrigibility and sexual activity a priority for suburban and rural communities, and truancy and other school-related misconduct prevalent in urban areas. Deinstitutionalization, or removal from secure facilities, and the construction of community-based facilities were encouraged by the financial incentives and disincentives of the JJDP Act as originally enacted. Most effective was the provision that required every state plan for formula grants under the Omnibus Crime Control and

Safe Streets Act of 1968 to provide for community-based alternatives to juvenile detention and correctional facilities and to "provide within two years after submission of the plan that juveniles who are charged with or who have committed offenses that would not be criminal if committed by an adult, shall not be placed in juvenile detention or correctional facilities, but must be placed in shelter facilities."

Some states responded immediately by enacting legislation barring placement of status offenders in secure facilities. Reaction against these deinstitutionalization laws was vehement and immediate. Judges, police, and probation officers insisted they could not deal effectively with status offenders, especially runaways, if so constrained. Some refused to process petitions, return children to nonsecure placement from which they had absconded, or pick up apparent runaways or truants. Others used delinquency and child neglect petitions in preference to status offense charges. The original JJDP Act deinstitutionalization mandate gradually was eroded in subsequent amendments by postponing the deadline for implementation and adding exceptions to the prohibition against secure placements, such as one for status offenders who had violated court orders.

Even more significantly, effective community-based runaway shelters, alternative schools, drug and alcohol abuse prevention and treatment programs, outreach programs, and other alternative resources did not materialize in sufficient numbers to reassure parents and community leaders that the behavior of troublesome juveniles would be controlled without recourse to lock-ups. Proposals for mandatory diversion of status offense complaints to mediation and counseling programs were defeated by the unwillingness of communities to guarantee the availability of such programs and by the opposition of departments of probation and social services to encroachment on their discretionary referral powers. Parent and school interests objected to the inference that status offense problems were indicative of parental or school inadequacy as well as juvenile intransigence. Therefore, the patently inappropriate remedy of recourse to court in response to resistance to parental or school authority—misconduct that does not rise to the level of the most trivial misdemeanor—continues. The simple reallocation of funds from detention and correctional facilities to community services remains an elusive goal.

Child Abuse and Neglect; Family Offenses

Late Beginning for Child and Spousal Protection in England

Most child protection and child welfare laws did not exist before the nineteenth century. At common law, protection of property was a greater concern than protection of the person, and official intervention in family care, even if that care fell well below prevailing standards, was rare. Although parents had a duty to support and educate their children along with the right to chastise or correct, control custody, and enjoy their children's earnings and services, these were imperfect, or unenforceable, duties (Rosenheim, 1973).

Guardianship originally conferred upon a feudal lord the power to administer a tenant's estate as guardian during the heir's minority, a right designed to benefit the guardian. Gradually it became a trust for the ward's benefit. The Statute of Marlborough in 1267 penalized a guardian for waste but for no other abuse at common law.

As the Court of Chancery expanded, it assumed wardship when the rights of guardianship were abused and gradually acquired jurisdiction over abuse of the power of chastisement. It heard actions for assault by a parent, guardian, teacher, or employer and if punishment of the child resulted in death, the charge was murder or manslaughter (Encyclopaedia Brittanica, 1966).

Destitute children were eligible for grants of relief under the 1601 English Poor Law, but protection against ill-treatment or cruelty came slowly. In 1861, the Offenses Against the Person Act prescribed punishment for the exposure of infants and the neglect or mistreatment of apprentices or servants. The Poor Law Amendment in 1868 made it an offense for parents to neglect to supply necessaries for their children. The National Society for the Prevention of Cruelty to Children (SPCC) was established in 1875 and initiated a series of statutes to protect children from mistreatment.

The child labor movement of the nineteenth century also aimed at achieving shorter hours and more humane conditions of employment for apprentices and chimney sweeps. Education laws could not be enforced against parents at first, so early laws were concerned only with the education of destitute children. The act of 1834 obligated poor law officials to provide an elementary education for children under their care, and the factory acts required instruction periods as part of the regulation of child labor. In 1870 the Elementary Education Act empowered English school boards to compel parents to send their children to school.

The 1601 Poor Law also empowered the churchwardens and overseers to remove children from parents they believed were unable to maintain them. Poor children in England were then apprenticed and employed as servants under the church's compulsion. No hearings or procedures were required.

Initially the English chancery courts invoked the *parens patriae* doctrine to resolve private disputes involving property or guradianships, first to ensure the orderly transfer of feudal duties and later in private custody cases. In *Wellesley v. Wellesley* (4 Eng. Rep. 1078, H.L. 1828) the court appointed a guardian when the father was found to be adulterous and criminal; in *Shelley v. Westbrook* (37 Eng. Rep. 850, Ch. 1817) it withheld custody from a father, the poet Percy Shelley, who deserted his wife and expressed views considered immoral and vicious.

Child Protection in America

As discussed earlier, a Pennsylvania court in 1838 originally applied the doctrine of *parens patriae* to a public custody case in *Ex Parte Crouse,* placing a child in a house of refuge on the mother's petition and over the father's objections, based on a claim of waywardness.

Thus nineteenth-century American courts did not distinguish between public and private custody disputes in applying the *parens patriae* doctrine to justify state intervention in neglect, dependency, and delinquency cases. Child removal statutes were enforced through equitable remedies, the courts arguing that summary proceedings were necessary to serve the child's immediate needs and were not a denial of the parents' rights because the parents could regain custody by proving their fitness at a habeas corpus proceeding (see *Farnham v. Pierce,* 141 Mass. 203, 1886 and *Cincinnati House of Refuge v. Ryan,* 37 Ohio St. 197, 1881, discussed in *Developments in the Law,* 93 Harv. L. Rev. 1156 (1980), footnote 165).

The use of this equitable doctrine to justify intervention in vaguely defined cases of neglect was formalized by the enactment of the Illinois Juvenile Court Act in 1899. Eighteenth-century America had incorporated the English Poor Law, including the church's power to remove children from poor parents who were deemed unfit. In Virginia, local officials could apprentice children of parents who were poor, idle, dissolute, or "incapable." In the nineteenth century, the poor law, child labor laws, compulsory education laws, and wayward children laws began to provide a judicial framework for what had been primarily administrative and only occasionally judicial action. These social reforms culminated in the juvenile court acts to handle neglected, dependent, and delinquent children.

The grounds asserted for the juvenile court's jurisdiction were immaterial because the purpose was the same for all—to achieve the environment for the child which *should* have been provided by the parents. The reluctance to intrude upon family autonomy no longer applied to poor families. The child's contact with the court became the occasion for a social investigation and evaluation by a probation officer to determine whether the parents were providing acceptable care, custody, and discipline.

While welfare and dependency matters were being handled by juvenile courts and child welfare departments, physical assaults on children by parents, guardians, and others in custodial authority were handled in both juvenile courts and criminal courts. In some states, complaints alleging disorderly conduct or assault between spouses or parent and child or between other members of the same household could be brought in either criminal court or family court. Some states permitted transfer of the case between either originating court; others placed exclusive *original* jurisdiction in one and allowed transfer to the other. In family offense cases, an adult would be the defendant or respondent, and the charges usually would be limited to misdemeanors. The outcome in family court could be probation or a protective order enforceable by contempt. A child who was the victim of an assault could be placed with either parent or another relative during the term of an order of protection or removed to foster or institutional care.

The history of child protection laws is largley recent and quite remarkable. Although child mistreatment received some attention before the nineteenth century (abuses of the power of chastisement by a parent, guardian, or teacher were heard in Chancery, and many of the colonies had laws against child mistreatment), the first child protection agency did not appear until the founding of the Society for the Prevention of Cruelty to Children (SPCC) in New York in 1875. In the early twentieth century, juvenile courts and child welfare agencies enforced child maltreatment laws, along with the criminal courts. But charges rarely were brought. Most suspicious injuries went unreported until about twenty years ago, when the first model legislation requiring physicians to report serious physical abuse was issued by the Department of Health, Education and Welfare in 1963. Within four years, all fifty states adopted similar reporting laws. The child protection field is a growth industry increasing from 150,000 reports in 1963 to millions of cases today (Besharov, 1983).

Mandatory Reporting Laws

Before 1963 reports of suspected cases of child abuse or neglect were made to police officers, who referred them to child welfare agencies, to public assistance agencies for families on welfare, or to the court. The first mandatory reporting laws continued the fragmented system of allowing reports to one of several agencies: police, social service, SPCC, etc. Some statutes *required* reports to several social agencies. Although reports were received and investigated, courts and agencies were reluctant to act decisively until sensational press coverage of isolated child fatalities led to congressional hearings and produced the Child Abuse Prevention and Treatment Act of 1974.

As with the JJDP Act, the Child Abuse Act produced results. The infusion of federal funds backed up by technical assistance provided the incentive for which the states were waiting. By 1978, 43 states and territories used special grants to establish comprehensive reporting and investigating systems. Social service resources were supplemented further through Title XX of the Social Security Act. By 1980, federal expenditures for child protective services amounted to over $325 million (Besharov, 1983).

The theoretical process requires suspected cases of child abuse or neglect, as defined by each state's juvenile code, including anonymous tips, to be investigated immediately by the local child welfare department. Based on their investigation, in substantiated cases the agency prescribes appropriate mental health and social services. If the parents refuse to accept treatment or if the child would not be adequately protected during treatment, a petition in juvenile court might be filed. Possible outcomes would be removal and placement of the child or children, and involuntary services ordered. Concurrently, charges might be filed in criminal court.

Many serious problems plague the system: under-reporting and over-reporting, under-removal and over-removal, case backlog, lack of treatment resources, abuse of children placed in foster or institutional care, improvident return to parents, inadequate family reunification efforts, violation of confidential disclosures, and many other deficiencies. But the most alarming problem is the growing caseload, especially the shocking incidence of sexual abuse cases.

These problems seem to be built into the child protection mandatory reporting system. It creates an insurmountable deterrent against seeking voluntary services since the provider would have to file a report of suspected abuse with the child protective agency. The inability to control the constantly rising intake because of vague statutory definitions of neglect and abuse is accompanied by the absorption of agency funds, originally intended for treatment and services, in the inescapable mandatory investigative activities.

Finally, there is the dilemma of the conflict between the therapeutic goals of the service agencies and the punitive goals of the criminal courts, both of which arise from the same report and investigation. Yet, final judgements in child abuse cases concerning the same incident in both juvenile and criminal court are not considered double jeopardy.

It should be noted that there are three categories of children subject to child protection laws: neglected, abused, and dependent children. The category of dependency relates to destitute or abandoned children who are without adequate means of support and care. Neglect and abuse pertain to children whose parents or custodians actively deny proper care or inflict injury. Most statutory definitions of neglect include the caveat that they apply only to parents who have the means to provide the necessary care but fail to do so.

One unexpected consequence of the increased volume of abuse or neglect proceedings in juvenile court has been children left in limbo—abandoned to shuttling between placements in multiple foster homes or institutions. Recent statutes require child-care agencies to demonstrate intensive treatment and reunification efforts to resolve the family's problems in order to return the children to the home. If reunification fails, permanency planning for the child must be initiated, often in the form of termination of the natural parents' rights voluntarily or involuntarily as a precursor to adoption or other permanent placement. The history of jurisdiction to terminate parental rights for permanent neglect is discussed next.

Matrimonial Actions; Termination of Parental Rights; and Adoption

Marriage and Divorce; Legitimacy and Orphans

In England, marriage was considered both a civil contract—a relationship which, at common law, altered the status of a woman for property actions, and a spiritual union consecrated by the church. By the seventh century, matrimonial issues were referred to the bishop. Under canon law, marriage was indissoluble. The wife's legal existence merged into her husband's, and he held her property during coverture (marriage). By the end of the sixteenth century, many of these rules could be avoided under the equitable doctrine of separate use. The Court of Chancery enforced trusts for the wife's sole and separate use. By 1800, the wife's absolute property in equity was postponed until widowhood and could not be anticipated without forfeiture (Baker, 1979).

A wife could not enter into a contract, although as an agent she could bind her husband to contracts made on his behalf. An action for a wife's tort had to be brought against husband and wife jointly. Husband and wife could sue jointly for torts against her, and the damages were the husband's property. He also could sue for loss of consortium.

Under canon law, an illegitimate child (born to a single woman or of an adulterous or void union) was *filius nullius* (no one's child), but a child could be legitimated by subsequent marriage and bastardized by divorce. Inheritance of land was governed by temporal law. However, the bishop's certificate could preclude the common law judges from applying it. The doctrine of legitimation did not become English common law until 1926.

Although the administration of wills and estates was within the jurisdiction of the ecclesiastical courts, land rarely was devised by will. By the middle of the seventeenth century, the courts of Chancery had jurisdiction over the administration of estates.

Under classical canon law, divorce *a vinculo,* leaving the parties free to remarry, could be granted only for lack of capacity (precontract, consanguinity, affinity, or impotence) or absence of consent (duress, insanity, mistake or infancy). Judicial separation, or divorce from board and bed (*a mensa et thoro*) could be granted for a matrimonial wrong: adultery, cruelty, sodomy, and heresy. Although released from their conjugal duties, the couple could not remarry. An innocent wife could be awarded alimony.

Henry VIII manipulated the canonical rules, but did not change them. His divorces bastardized future Queen Mary and Queen Elizabeth, but separate acts of Parliament restored each one's legitimacy. (Baker, 1979; Encyclopaedia Brittanica, 1966)

In 1836 civil marriage was introduced, and in 1857 a Court for Divorce and Matrimonial Causes supplanted the divorce jurisdiction of the church courts. England was slow to separate its divorce laws from Christian doctrine; it did not accept the concept of matrimonial breakdown and divorce by consent until 1969 (Baker, 1979).

In America there were no ecclesiastical courts or, after the early nineteenth century, established state religions. The jurisdiction exercised by the ecclesiastical courts was divided among several colonial institutions: criminal jurisdiction over morals went to the criminal courts, in the courts of quarter sessions, or justices of the peace; probate of wills was handled by officials appointed by the governors. Maryland was the only colony to establish a separate probate court for the administration of estates (Friedman, 1973).

A related concern was the estate of fatherless families and the protection of orphaned minors. The first recorded instance of a borough administering orphans' affairs was in London in 1272. At least nineteen English boroughs ultimately established Orphans' Courts to administer the personal property of freemen who died leaving minor children. The Court of Chancery presided over the system and equitable principles were applied. Chancery was called upon to enforce the decisions of the local Orphans' Courts (Carlton, 1974).

Colonial records also refer to orphans' courts held by the justices of the peace. Funds due to the orphans were paid into the court, and the court could appoint a guardian for the minor. Only Pennsylvania and Delaware *formally* established these courts (Surrency, 1967).

As for marriage and divorce, family law was secular in the United States. Although religious ceremonies were customary and religious principles influenced the laws of marriage and divorce, two secular forms of marriage were authorized: civil ceremonies and common-law marriages. Common-law marriages were verbal contracts, agreements between a man and woman to consider themselves husband and wife, followed by cohabitation without a formal ceremony (Friedman, 1973).

In the south before and after independence, divorce was rare and almost always legislative. The Georgia Constitution in 1798 allowed divorces on a two-thirds vote of each branch of the legislature after a trial and divorce decree in the superior court. The northern states relied on courtroom divorce. New York's 1787 law allowed absolute divorce for adultery only; Vermont's grounds in 1798 extended to impotence, intolerable severity, three years' desertion, and absence with presumption of death.

Private divorce bills became a nuisance and legislative divorce became extinct by 1880. Divorce laws became simpler. It was an adversary proceeding; collusive practices between spouses to circumvent the narrowly defined grounds for divorce did not become commonplace until the end of the nineteenth century. Some states adopted permissive divorce laws from 1850 to 1870, but fear that the family was disintegrating restored stricter laws. Nevertheless, divorces increased. By 1900 more than 55,000 divorces were granted each year. There was and is no national law of divorce. The courts that have jurisdiction over divorce, and the grounds differ from state to state. Final divorce decrees issued in one state, if the parties have established proper jusrisdictional grounds, are entitled to full faith and credit in all states (Friedman, 1973).

Today, lenient divorce laws have evolved into no-fault laws. With the widespread adoption of no-fault divorce laws, migratory divorces and interstate jurisdictional disputes are infrequent.

Divorce is one of the causes of action in which courts may have concurrent jurisdiction. Matrimonial actions usually can be heard in the county's court of general trial jurisdiction and/or in the family court. Matters pertaining to adoption, child custody, and support are even more fragmented, as will be discussed in the following sections.

Termination of Parental Rights

The proceeding for termination of parental rights rarely is the family's first contact with the courts. The progression from a finding of parental neglect to removal from the home and placement in foster or institutional care to permanent termination of parental rights and adoption may lead the family through many courts and agencies. Divorce or separation of the parents, support proceedings, and custody disputes may intervene. In some jurisdictions it is possible that all of these proceedings could be heard in a single family or civil court before a single judge with a single court liaison officer coordinating contacts with the various child care and social service agencies. However, in most states the neglect proceeding would be held in juvenile court, and the placement would be by a local office of children's services referring the child to a private or voluntary child care agency, which then might place the child in a foster home or a residential facility (group home). There might or might not be a requirement of periodic foster care review by the juvenile, family, or trial court of general jurisdiction. If the parents are being separated or divorced, there might be a custody hearing before the judge presiding over the matrimonial action in a family court, probate court, or civil court of general trial jurisdiction. There also might be a separate matrimonial part or division of whichever court has jurisdiction over the matter.

If either parent or a third party has alleged that a parent has neglected or abused the child, there might be a separate proceeding in which the child's custody is an issue in a dependency part of a juvenile or family court, pursuant to a child abuse or neglect petition. The complaint of child abuse or neglect might also be processed pursuant to state child protection laws, as described earlier. A unit of the local department of social services would investigate the charge and if it were substantiated, might remove the child from the home. The department might arrange for a temporary placement in a shelter or foster home, file a petition in juvenile court, and/or refer the complaint to criminal court. Thus, the issue of custody of the same child might be heard by four or five separate courts: juvenile, domestic relations, civil, criminal, and probate.

Formal termination of parental rights is a relatively recent procedure. Its closest analogue in English law would be the removal of children from unfit parents under the poor laws and their placement in almshouses or with another family as apprentices. Both permanent termination and adoption are statutory innovations and, as such, the explicit provisions of the statutes must be observed with exactitude. Because such procedures currently are tied to child protection laws and permanency planning, they are governed by a state's social services laws. Findings that a child is permanently neglected most frequently arise at foster care review hearings in which the agency alleges that the parents have not made sufficient efforts or are unable to resume custody after a statutory placement period has elapsed.

Conflicts between concepts of family autonomy and best interest of the child often arise when the opposing parties are the child's natural parents and long-term foster parents, grandparents, or other custodians. Increasingly complex issues concerning the rights of natural parents are emerging in a new era of unwed (accidental), single (by choice), surrogate, and genetically engineered parents. The concept of "psychological parents," which advocated continuing a placement to achieve continuity of care and stability for the child, rather than return the child to his or her natural parents, gained prominence in *Beyond the Best Interests of the Child* (Freud, Solnit, Goldstein), but it has many critics.

Permanency Planning and Adoption

The relationship between children abandoned to prolonged foster or institutional care and the current emphasis on permanency planning reflects a political response to reports of many children left "in limbo" after voluntary and involuntary placements in foster care and institutions. Not only federal and state funds, but foundation grants (most notably from the Edna McConnel Clark Foundation) have supported a drive for a process of judicial review of reunification efforts for children in placement and an evaluation of prospects for resuming parental responsibilities. This hearing might result in a finding of permanent neglect and, ultimately, termination of the parental rights of the natural parents. In many instances, parents avoid the finding by voluntarily surrendering their rights.

The underlying assumption of the permanency planning process is that by freeing the children for adoption or a permanent placement, the children's circumstances will be improved. The dearth of adoptive parents, the limited pool of children who fulfill the criteria (young, attractive, physically and psychically unimpaired) of prospective parents in the large urban areas most prone to terminate parental rights, and the lack of alternative resources for desirable long-term placements create a dilemma. The limbo from which these children are purported to be rescued may be worsened by eliminating the admittedly inadequate parents who had legal responsibility and, possibly, a residue of emotional commitment prior to permanent termination. Severing parental ties does not help children unless the termination is followed by a satisfactory alternative—adoption or another suitable placement. The results of the permanency planning initiatives remain for future studies to evaluate. Asylums, probation services, and foster care were also heralded as solutions to the problems of troubled children in the past.

Because of the shortage of qualified families willing to adopt older (over six), handicapped, black, or other hard-to-place children, some states offer medical and maintenance subsidies. Most of the parents receiving subsidies have been foster parents. In 1980 Congress enacted the Adoption Assistance and Child Welfare Act (Pub. L. 96–272), but it has not carried a large enough appropriation to have a significant impact on state resources. However, it has contributed impetus to the current emphasis on permanency planning.

Adoption was unknown at common law. Therefore it can be effectuated only by strict compliance with each state's statutory requirements. For example, New York provides for two types of adoption, through a private placement or an authorized agency. Jurisdiction variously has been in Surrogate Court, State Supreme or County Court, and today, in Family Court.

Support and Custody

In deciding custody disputes, judges often refer to the powers of the Chancery Court of England, claiming to act as *parens patriae* to do what is best for the child. For example, the New York Constitution gives the state supreme court original jurisdiction in law and equity. In *Finlay v. Finlay* (240 N.Y. 429, 1925) Justice Cardozo said he interfered for the protection of infants under the crown's prerogative as *parens patriae* (Kram and Frank, 1982). But at early common law, the rights invoked in the parent-child relationship concerning support and custody were considered moral and not legally enforceable obligations (Encyclopaedia Britannica, 1966; Rosenheim, 1973). Because of the legal and economic status of the husband and wife during coverture, the traditional duty of support and custody was the father's, with the mother's duty arising only if the father died or became incapable of support. The father's *prima facie* right to custody was overcome by the Tender Years Doctrine at the end of the nineteenth century, shifting to a presumption that children's welfare would be served by leaving them in their mothers' custody during their tender years. However, these matters were not judicial concerns until the poor laws and the concept of the destitute child began to invoke the court's jurisdiction in public custody actions. Relatives' responsibility first arose in 1597 in an Act for the Relief of the Poor, as follows:

> That the parents or children of every poor, old, blind, lame . . . or other person not able to work . . . shall maintain every such poor person . . . as by the justices at their general quarter session shall be assessed. (Cassetty, 1978, pp. 5,6)

Today there is a Uniform Support of Dependents Law, a Uniform Child Custody Jurisdiction Act, and a federal Parental Kidnapping Prevention Act of 1980. The federal act controls and overrides any inconsistent state law, including the Uniform Child Custody Jurisdiction Act, which has been enacted in 49 states. In what has been called the criminalization of child-snatching between parents, many states have adopted or toughened criminal sanctions against parental child abductions. Therefore, either state or federal courts might have jurisdiction over these acts, depending on the circumstances of the abduction.

Standards for the determination of custody are set forth in several state statutes. Freed and Foster (1984, p. 415) cite the Michigan statute as typical:

> Sec. 3. "Best interests of the child" means the sum total of the following factors to be considered, evaluated, and determined by the court:
> (a) The love, affection, and other emotional ties existing between the . . . parties involved and the child.
> (b) The capacity and disposition of the parties involved to give the child love, affection, and guidance and continuation of the educating and raising of the child in its religion or creed, if any.
> (c) The capacity and disposition of the parties involved to provide the child with food, clothing, medical care or other remedial care recognized and permitted under the laws of this state in place of medical care, and other material needs.
> (d) The length of time the child has lived in a stable, satisfactory environment, and the desirability of maintaining continuity.
> (e) The permanence, as a family unit, of the existing or proposed custodial home or homes.
> (f) The moral fitness of the . . . parties involved.
> (g) The mental and physical health of the . . . parties involved.
> (h) The home, school, and community record of the child.
> (i) The willingness and ability of each of the parents to facilitate and encourage a close and continuing parent-child relationship between the child and the other parent.
> (j) Any other factor considered by the court to be relevant to a particular child custody dispute.

In deciding custody issues, the child's wishes are a factor in about 30 states. Most statutes concerning support of dependents define a "child" to include a stepchild, foster child, child born out of wedlock, or legally adopted child. Today the majority of state statutes impose the obligation of child support on both parents. Custody might go to either parent, with a growing number of states enacting joint custody provisions. For example, in California there is a presumption in favor of joint custody.

Enforcement of support orders also has become increasingly federalized. For example, welfare mothers (AFDC recipients) are authorized to collect overdue support payments from federal tax refunds. More usual methods of enforcement of court-ordered maintenance or child support orders are by payment into court, garnishment of wages, and wage assignment.

Emancipation is the elimination of the parent's legal duty to support a minor child and the surrender of all parental rights. There is no presumption of emancipation. The burden of proving that a child is emancipated must be sustained by the person who asserts or relies upon it. Very few states have clearly defined criteria. Generally, the doctrine is applied to conduct by the parent inconsistent with the performance of parental duties. However, emancipation may not be presumed for the fact that the child is living away from home or earning wages.

The emancipation doctrine was developed at common law to determine an employer's right to pay wages to a child without having to account to the parent for the wages. It arises today in determining the child's right to support from a divorced parent or to sue a parent for tort, in areas in which a parent's consent may be required, as for medical care, or in contract matters in which a parent may be held liable for a child's debts. Therefore the forum in which the issue of emancipation is heard would be the court in which the divorce, personal injury, or breach of contract case is tried.

One final indication of the kind of confusion of jurisdictions that arises in the area of custody and support is the following case note under "Domestic Relations Law" in the New York Consolidated Laws Service (volume 8) at page 320:

> Supreme Court could not consolidate proceedings in Family Court to enforce New Jersey support order with action in Supreme Court for separation where under this section Family Court authority was broader than that of Supreme Court under Domestic Relations Law S 236 to order support for the wife. (*Hanft v. Hanft*, 1965 46 Misc. 2d. 548, 260 N.Y.S. 2d 104)

Conclusions and Recommendations

This article has attempted to trace the historical and social forces that produced the current fragmentation in jurisdiction over family matters. Although it has concentrated on the division of judicial power among civil, criminal, juvenile, and probate courts, that same fragmentation permeates the agency roles in family matters. One troubled family might be involved with officials of the department of public welfare for income maintenance, the department of social services and the police department for child protection, the office of children's services and a voluntary child care agency for foster care, and various health and mental health departments for medical services, aside from other social agencies for specific problems in housing, schools, employment, etc.

Addressing this chaotic situation, many specialists have proposed that all cases involving families be consolidated in one court. For example, the IJA-ABA Standards for Juvenile Justice recommended that a single court—a family court—should have comprehensive jurisdiction over family matters, assigning a single social worker to coordinate services to each family before the court. They provide that the family court should be elevated to the highest court of general trial jurisdiction, of which the family court would be a separate division. Family court judges would be assigned to the court from among the judges of the highest trial court, with a modified rotation of judges among the divisions. The relevant standard is Standard 1.1 of *Standards Relating to Court Organization and Administration* as follows:

1.1 Organizational Structure: general principles.

The traditional juvenile court jurisdiction should be included in a family court division of the highest court of general trial jurisdiction.

A. The exclusive original jurisdiction of this division should encompass: juvenile law violations; cases of abuse and neglect; cases involving the need for emergency medical treatment; voluntary and involuntary termination of parental rights proceedings; adoption proceedings; appointment of legal guardians for juveniles; proceedings under interstate compacts on juveniles and on the placement of juveniles; intrafamily criminal offenses; proceedings in regard to divorce, separation, annulment, alimony, custody, and support of juveniles; proceedings to establish paternity and to enforce support; and proceedings under the Uniform Reciprocal Enforcement of Support Act. Mental illness and retardation commitment proceedings concerning juveniles and adults should be governed by the law of the jurisdiction applicable to such proceedings for nonadjudicated persons.

B. Calendaring methods should follow the general principle that the same judge should consider the different legal issues that relate to all members of the same family. Further, the judge who presides at an adjudicatory hearing should conduct the disposition hearing of the case.

C. General intake procedures to determine the need for formal judicial consideration of juvenile delinquency referrals should be adapted and applied to the different types of cases within the jurisdiction of the family court division.

D. The court should encourage probation and social service agencies working with court clientele to maximize single staff member responsibility of an entire family.

The standard has merit if all of the conditions are met. But as juvenile courts presently are constituted, a wider jurisdiction may not be feasible. The special features of the juvenile court—personnel trained to deal with family matters, judges concerned about children and families, access to social services, more flexible dispositions, and minimal formality—would seem advantageous to unified handling of all cases involving family law. However, the generally inferior status of the court today, its low salaries, poorly trained staff, inadequate resources, entrenched personnel, poor recordkeeping, and lack of public accountability would militate against expanding its jurisdiction. As long as juvenile court deserves the appellation of "kiddie court," it should not be assigned more complex cases.

Therefore, the first recommendation would be that the family court should be part of a unified court system, with judges and other court personnel on the same level as the superior or county (supreme in New York) court. Rotation of judges from the civil and criminal divisions would serve to acquaint the overall judicial system with the needs and principles governing the family division. It also would insure that fundamental juridical values common to all courts would prevail in family court. Finally, it would demonstrate to the community (both local and legal) that family matters are as significant as other cases within the judicial system.

A further recommendation is that in instances where courts now have concurrent jurisdiction over child abuse, family offenses, custody, support, divorce, and adoption, there should be a preemption, eliminating the criminal, probate, surrogate, civil, or other court's concurrent powers in favor of the family court's exclusive authority.

The structure recommended presupposes provision for mandatory training of family court judges and other personnel assigned from other divisions to prepare them for service in the family division, more open proceedings to insure public accountability, and improved records and information systems. At the same time, every effort should be made to preserve the confidentiality of court records and other disclosures, where appropriate. Standards concerning privacy, collection, access to, and destruction of information should be adopted.

The proposed organization of the courts would not solve all the problems affecting the juvenile justice system. Several states have adopted a similar structure without achieving an ideal system. However, since none has attempted to include all of these features and suggestions, the model proposed should be considered for implementation in a pilot program.

Endnotes

1. Special acknowledgment of contributions by research assistants, Michael W. Oshima, Carol Grelecki, and Samuel P. Laufer.
2. Black's Law Dictionary defines jurisdiction as: "The power and authority constitutionally conferred upon (or constitutionally recognized as existing in) a court or judge to pronounce the sentence of the law, or to award the remedies provided by law, upon a state of facts, proved or admitted, referred to the tribunal for decision, and authorized by law to be the subject of investigation or action by that tribunal, and in favor for or against persons (or a *res*) who present themselves, or who are brought, before the court in some manner sanctioned by law as proper and sufficient."

References

Andrews, R. H., and Cohn, A. H. Ungovernability: The unjustifiable jurisdiction. 83 Yale L. J. 1383 (1974).

Areen, J. (1978). *Family law: Cases and materials.* Mineola, NY: Foundation Press.

Baker, J. (1979). *An introduction to English legal history* (2nd edition). London: Butterworths.

Besharov, D. Child protection: Past progress, present problems, and future directions. 17 Fam. L. Q. 151 (1983).

Blake, N. (1962). *The road to Reno: A history of divorce in the United States.* Westport, CT: Greenwood Press.

Carlton, C. Changing jurisdictions in 16th and 17th century England: The relationship between the courts and orphans and Chancery. 18 Am. J. Legal Hist. 124 (1974).

Cassetty, J. (1978). *Child support and public policy: Securing support from absent fathers.* Lexington, MA: Lexington Books.

Clark, H. (1968). *The law of domestic relations in the United States.* St. Paul, MN: West Publishing Co.

Couch, H. The evolution of Parliamentary divorce in England. 52 Tul. L. Rev. 513 (1978).

Custer, L. The origins of the doctrine of *Parens Patriae.* 27 Emory L. J. 195 (1978).

Encyclopedia Britannica. (1966). 5:512 et seq.

Flaherty, D. (1978). Law and the enforcement of morals in early America. In L. Friedman and H. Scheiber (Eds.), *American law and the constitutional order: Historical perspectives* (pp. 53–66). Cambridge, MA: Harvard University Press.

Flicker, B. (1981). Juvenile courts. In F. J. Klein (Ed.), *The Improvement of the Administration of Justice: The Judicial Administration Division Handbook* (pp. 219–233). Chicago: American Bar Association.

Flicker, B. (1981). Prosecuting juveniles as adults: A symptom of a crisis in the juvenile courts. In J. C. Hall, D. M. Hamparian, J. M. Pettibone, and J. L. White (Eds.), *Major issues in juvenile justice information and training: Readings in public policy* (pp. 351–377). Washington, DC: Office of Juvenile Justice and Delinquency Prevention.

Flicker, B. (1982). *Standards for juvenile justice: A summary and analysis* (2nd edition). Cambridge, MA: Ballinger.

Fox, S. Juvenile justice reborn: A historical perspective. 22 Stan. L. Rev. 1187 (1970).

Fox, S. (1972). *Modern juvenile justice: Cases and materials.* St. Paul, MN: West Publishing Co.

Freed, D., and Foster, H. Family law in the fifty states: An overview. 17 Fam. L. Q. 365 (1984).

Friedman, L. (1973). *A history of American law.* New York: Simon and Schuster.

Garlock, P. "Wayward" children and the law, 1820–1900: The genesis of the status offense jurisdiction of the juvenile court. 13 Ga. L. Rev. 341 (1979).

Goldstein, J., Freud, A., and Solnit, A. J. (1973). *Beyond the best interests of the child.* New York: Free Press.

Haertle, E. The history of the probate court. 45 Marq. L. Rev. 546 (1962).
Jordan, E. Specialized courts: A choice? 76 NW. U. L. Rev. 745 (1981).
Juvenile justice and delinquency prevention act of 1974. .18 U.S.C. 5031 et seq.
Kempe, H., et al. The battered child syndrome. 181 J.A.M.A. 17 (1962)
Kram, S., and Frank, N. (1982). *The law of child custody: Development of the substantive law*. Lexington, MA: Lexington Books.
Mack, J. The juvenile court. 23 Harv. L. Rev. 104 (1909).
Mueller, G. Inquiry into the state of a divorceless society: Domestic relations law and morals in England from 1660 to 1857. 18 U. Pitt. L. Rev. 545 (1957).
Note. Developments in the law–the Constitution and the family. 93 Harv. L. Rev. 1156 (1980).
O'Neill, W. Divorce in the progressive era. 17 Am. Q. 203 (1965).
Platt, A. (1977). *The child savers: The invention of delinquency* (2nd edition). Chicago: University of Chicago Press.
Presser, S. The historical background of the American law of adoption. 11 J. Fam. L. 443 (1972).
Rendleman, D. *Parens Patriae:* From Chancery to the juvenile court. 23 S.C.L. Rev. 205 (1971).
Rodman, K. A brief history of marriage and divorce. 23 O. L. Rev. 249 (1944).
Rosenheim, M. The child and the law. 3 Review of Child Development Research 509 (1973).
Rothman, D. (1971). *The discovery of the asylum: Social order and disorder in the new republic*. Boston: Little, Brown and Co.
Ryerson, E. (1978). *The best-laid plans: America's juvenile court experiment*. New York: Hill and Wang.
Schultz, L. The cycle of juvenile court history. 19 Crime & Delinq. 457 (1973).
Surrency, E. The courts in the American colonies (parts 1 and 2). 11 Am. J. Legal Hist. 253, 347 (1967).
Sutton, J. Stubborn children: Law and the socialization of deviance in the Puritan colonies. 15 Fam. L. Q. 31 (1981).
tenBroek, J. California's dual system of family Law: Its origin, development and present status (part 1). 16 Stan. L. Rev. 259 (1964).
Trojanowicz, R. and Morash, M. (1983). *Juvenile delinquency: Concepts and control* (3rd edition). Englewood Cliffs, NJ: Prentice-Hall.
Waite, E. Courts of domestic relations. 5 Minn. L. Rev. 162 (1921).
Wald, M. State intervention on behalf of "neglected" children: Standards for removal of children from their homes, monitoring the status of children in foster care, and termination of parental rights. 28 Stan. L. Rev. 625 (1976).
Zainaldin, J. The emergence of a modern American family law: Child custody, adoption, and the courts, 1796–1851. 73 NW. U. L. Rev. 1038 (1979).

14 Diversion of Juvenile Offenders to the Community in the State of Washington: Back to the Source

MARK H. SIDRAN

The Concept of Diversion: Pushing and Pulling the System

When the home has failed, when the school has failed, when the community at large has failed to produce a normal result in a child, the law undertakes the task; and often it fails.[1]

From its earliest inceptions, the juvenile justice system has struggled to fulfill a role in the socialization of children well beyond the traditional adjudicatory role of a court. Perhaps it was the consciousness of this nonjudicial role in responding to the failed responsibility of other community institutions that led to the very early emergence of diversion to resources outside the court as a method of processing juvenile offenses. In a sense the juvenile court itself originally was a formalized diversion of cases previously heard by adult criminal courts. Yet, as early as 1914, one commentator described the emergence of diversion from juvenile court:

Another phase of juvenile court work which has developed spontaneously and almost universally is the extra-legal handling of children 'out of court' by the probation office. Children are given treatment or placed under supervision by common consent, without trial. Several courts handle as many or more cases in this way than through the regular channels. This is partly to reduce the volume of business, partly to avoid the stigma of trial in the milder cases of delinquency.[2]

More than 70 years later, diversion continues to be a central component of the juvenile justice system, frequently justified on similar grounds of cost and what has come to be called labeling theory. But the impetus for diversion runs deeper and reflects the tension between the concept of the court as a coercive engine of last resort to compel socialization when other institutions have failed, and the concept that socialization must occur in the community and the court can do very little on its own.

This tension between court coercion and community socialization is reflected in the typology of diversion programs depending on the point at which the juvenile justice system intervenes in the case. For example, police diversion programs have been described as a screening process reflecting a decision that the juvenile can be dealt with in the community without intervention by the court. Similarly, more formalized diversion programs follow an intake process by a juvenile court probation officer who assesses the need for court intervention. In short, a juvenile's penetration in the juvenile justice system to the point of court involvement reflects a judgment about the community's capacity to socialize a juvenile without the coercive power of the court. Not surprisingly, the notion that the community itself could and should participate in diversion decision-making has emerged. Perhaps nowhere as clearly as in King County (Seattle), Washington, communities are being turned to as a resource and alternative to juvenile court.

King County Conference Committees: Reinvesting the Community

Patterned after a 1953 New Jersey program, the King County Juvenile Court began a community-based diversion program in one community in 1959 as a response to that community's growing concern over shoplifting and vandalism. The program was stimulated by the local "Mayor's Youth Guidance Committee" and was developed with the active support of the juvenile court. In 1959 the King County Juvenile Court was the judicial preserve of a single judge who had long been permanently assigned to the juvenile court at his request, and the probation staff was under the administrative control of the judge. This concentration of power and decision-making in the juvenile court judge made his support for the diversion project a requisite for success.

The program developed by the King County Juvenile Court was called a conference committee; it was composed of a "team" of three volunteers who met with the juvenile offender and his parents following referral from the juvenile court probation officer, the local police, schools, other social agencies, or voluntary referral by the parents. The program was directed by one part-time juvenile court worker. The growth of the program initially was very slow. A new conference committee was organized every three or four years. By 1972 there were eight committees and 30 volunteers handling a caseload of 841. By 1977, however, the program had expanded to 22 committees and 350 volunteers handling 4,581 cases.[3] In 1984 there were 25 committees with 450 volunteers covering virtually the entire county (with a population of approximately 1.25 million).

This tremendous expansion was accompanied and to an extent promoted by an increase in the staffing of a central program administration from one part-time employee to four full-time positions. Even though probation services in the King County system were removed from court administration and transferred to the executive branch in 1977, the diversion program remained under the administration of the court. Despite the fact that the single permanent juvenile court judge was replaced by a rotational assignment of approximately a dozen superior court judges, the judiciary's support for the conference committees has remained firm.

In an effort to explain the apparent success of this long-term, large-scale community involvement in the juvenile justice system, an evaluation of the conference committee program and several other volunteer programs was conducted in 1978 by Arthur D. Little, Inc. and the National Center for State Courts under a grant from the federal Office of Juvenile Justice and Delinquency Prevention. The study examined 18 projects across the country in which citizens were significantly involved in some phase of the juvenile court process or as decision-makers or advisors to the court. Reflecting desirable conditions from the court's point of view, the study compared the programs using the following weighted evaluation criteria:

1. Reduces workload of court personnel;
2. Increases the court's status in the community;
3. Intensifies services provided by the court;
4. Increases the court's awareness of community attitudes;
5. Provides needed specialized expertise;
6. Improves the quality of justice.

The results of the study showed that the King County conference committee program ranked highest of the programs evaluated.

Of course, there are other criteria by which to gauge community diversion programs, and different weights to be given to the criteria, but those of importance to the court may be the most significant because the court's position is likely to be a decisive factor in the ability of a community to successfully organize a volunteer program. The court is likely to have either control of or substantial influence over the distribution of many referrals, as well as a substantial share of juvenile justice resources. A program which is viewed as threatening to the court and its personnel poses a major political hurdle, while a program supported by the court may reap the benefit of judicial leadership in overcoming obstacles.

Similarly, police confidence in a community diversion project may be important, both as a source of referrals and as reinforcement of the community's perception of its role in crime control. The King County program consciously set out to develop good working relationships with the police by inviting police to observe the committees at work.

Another factor which influences the viability of a community volunteer program is the character of the community itself:

> Communities in the United States vary widely in the quality of their commitment to the public welfare. Some have long traditions of volunteerism and helping neighbors. Scandinavian, Chinese and Jewish communities are frequently cited for a history of concern, for example. On the contrary, some communities have

never galvanized a volunteer tradition and do not have the organizational resources to do so. Beyond the organizational and management skills to establish a court-based program, there must be community leadership and support sufficient to maintain a continuing stream of volunteers and citizen interest.[4]

From the very beginning, the conference committee program required community initiation before the program could be expanded. When concerned citizens complained to the police or court about a delinquency problem in the neighborhood, the matter might be referred to the program's central administration. At this point, paid program coordinators, each of whom represented a different area of the county, were responsible for encouraging the community to form a conference committee. They advised concerned citizens how to assess the nature of delinquency problems in their community and seek or form a community sponsoring group that would be willing to contribute office or meeting space for the conference committee and cover minimal expenses such as postage and supplies. These sponsors typically have been community councils, civic improvement organizations such as the Kiwanis or Rotary Clubs, churches, and youth service organizations. In addition to financial support, sponsors may be expected to help promote the diversion program in the community, recruit volunteers, and develop relevant community resources. In short, the community was required to demonstrate a certain amount of commitment to the ideas of a diversion program before the program would invest in the community.

Once a conference committee is established in a community, the program's central administration provides a high degree of structure and support. Members of the conference committee are selected by local committee chairpeople (themselves volunteers) and by program coordinators. A comprehensive set of volunteer screening criteria has been developed which aids them in interviewing prospective committee members. Prospective candidates are required to observe conference committee sessions and to participate in approximately twelve hours of training and orientation and take part in conference committee sessions. After the training, candidates are evaluated by program coordinators. Candidates chosen to become members of a conference committee are notified and confirmed by a formal written appointment signed by a juvenile court judge.

Each conference committee has a paid consultant, typically a juvenile court probation officer or a counselor or therapist familiar with juvenile issues and resources, who serves as an advisor to the committee, assisting in ongoing training of volunteers and acting as a liaison between the court and the committee. The consultant is present whenever the committee interviews a juvenile and family, but does not actively participate in either the interview or the decision-making process unless asked to by the committee.

Each committee has a designated secretary whose job is to handle correspondence with juveniles and families, schedule and maintain data required by the program, and process required paperwork. The secretary is a citizen who is paid a nominal amount per case.

Finally, the program's central administration provides interagency liaison, program advocacy, monitoring and evaluation, and training for volunteers.

The 1984 budget for the program was $259,000 including salaries for a central staff of four and a half, and fees paid to consultants and secretaries. The 25 committees were composed of approximately 450 volunteers who processed 4,318 cases, 3,062 of which resulted in interviews.[5] (By comparison, the court in the same year formally handled 5,142 cases including cases of failed diversion.) Part of the program's success presumably is due to its significant investment in the structure of support services in the community and the requirement of community initiation.

Another important factor, however, is that the volunteers are given genuine decision-making authority over issues of consequence. The committee typically meets twice a month for three hours in the evening. During this time it hears an average of three cases. Committee members interview the juvenile and his family separately. The nature of his offense is discussed, as well as his family circumstances, attitudes, school situation or other topics deemed relevant. The committee does not decide on the juvenile's guilt or innocence and does not formally require an admission of guilt, but usually it does seek some sort of acknowledgment of responsibility for the offense. The juvenile and family participate in this process voluntarily, although the alternative may be the return of the case to more formal court actions. After the interviews, the committee retires to come up with a resolution of the case, and then its proposal to the juvenile and parents.

For the committee volunteer, this quasi-judicial role of gathering information and making decisions, combined with the role of counselor and concerned neighbor, appears to be rewarding enough so that a four-year stint of service is typical. The satisfaction that some volunteers gain from a sense of identification with and contribution to a community endeavor is enhanced by the geographic division of committees to the neighborhood level.

Some of these same factors help legitimize the conference committees as the community's agent for social control in ways not readily available to the court. Since the conference committee functions at the neighborhood level it may be perceived as more representative of the community than a centralized court, particularly in ethnic and minority neighborhoods. Similarly, the relatively open process of recruitment and appointment of volunteers, and the delegation of decision-making to them, creates a sense of accessibility and community control that a court lacks.

Finally, because the committees are tied to community sponsors of a much broader yet still local constituency (e.g., service clubs, community councils, churches, etc.), frequently tap local resources for services to the juvenile and family, and can impose community service sanctions on juvenile offenders to the benefit of the local community, a broad network of community residents is connected to the committee's work in ways a centralized court cannot duplicate. The involvement of local police further strengthens this network. The court itself may seek to tie into the network by geographic assignment of probation officers according to the juvenile's residence.

The "networking" of the community fulfills one of the goals of diversion in that it returns primary responsibility for the control and socialization of juveniles back to those institutions that *should* be positioned to do so, (e.g., the family, school, and social agency). The community network can promote the accountability of these other institutions more effectively than can the court because it is likely to be more knowledgeable about what, in fact, is going on in the community and who is responsible. Furthermore, the community may lay claim to accountability from some institutions while a similar claim by a court would be suspect. For example, a community may call a school to account in a way that a court may lack the legal or political power to do. In this sense, an activist court might mobilize the community through diversion more effectively than through judicial assaults on allegedly ineffective or unresponsive institutions.

Community-Based Diversion in an Accountability Model

It was the recognition of these strengths of community-based diversion programs that led the State of Washington's legislature to emphasize the development of community diversion as part of a comprehensive reform of the state's juvenile justice system in 1977. Widely recognized as a sweeping and radical reform of the traditional juvenile model, Washington's Juvenile Justice Act of 1977 sought to preserve and expand traditional community diversion while simultaneously integrating diversion into the "just deserts" philosophy of the Act. Diversion became a formal and institutionalized part of the juvenile justice system, even as some of the historical premises for diversion were being eliminated by reforms.

Frequently cited benefits of diversion include cost savings over formal court processing and an elimination of the stigmatization associated with labeling theory. Diversion functions within a treatment model to assess those who require the more intensive "services" available from formal court intervention, despite the labeling, and to allocate limited treatment resources. Diversion in this sense may be "from" the system but not "to" any alternative, particularly if an assessment indicates no significant treatment needs.

In an accountability model, however, diversion serves a different purpose. It is founded on the notion that justice is being adequately achieved by the limited sanctions (and due process) available outside the court. It is not enough to divert a case "from" the court, if the result is no negative consequences for bad behavior. Diversion must be "to" an alternative forum in which appropriate consequences can be addressed. While less expensive than formal court processing, accountability diversion can be substantially more expensive than traditional diversion because it requires that the referral be followed up by a concrete alternative.[6] Moreover, accountability clearly calls forth due process concerns that are less apparent, though perhaps no less real, in traditional diversion; and due process costs money.

Accountability and the treatment model also differ in their approach to labeling. The treatment model historically is structured around a concept of delinquency as a status determined by a court. Although specific criminal acts may be proven to establish the status, the court literally is engaged in labeling the person as a delinquent type. This is so far true that once delinquency "wardship" is established, subsequent criminal acts may be handled as modification proceedings affecting the juvenile's previously established delinquency status.

In contrast, Washington State law abolished delinquency as a status and entirely removed the word from the juvenile code. The focus instead is on the juvenile's alleged criminal acts and his guilt or innocence concerning a specific misdeed, not on his character nor the personality or potential of the juvenile. It's the difference between telling the juvenile, "You are a bad person because of what you have done," and saying to him, "You have done something bad and therefore face consequences." While the juvenile's social background receives major attention as part of the disposition of his case, the implication is that the most negative aspects of labeling are avoided. The juvenile gets a clearer message about the consequences of criminal behavior, he pays his dues, and life goes on.

In order to contain the expected increased costs of accountability diversion, minimize stigma or labeling consequences, maximize the appearance of justice and reinvest the community with greater responsibility for socialization of juveniles, Washington's legislature called for the establishment of community-based diversion programs. RCW 13.40.080(3) provides:

> In assessing periods of community service to be performed and restitution to be paid by a juvenile who has entered into a diversion agreement, the court officer to whom this task is assigned shall to the extent possible involve members of the community. Such members of the community shall meet with the juvenile and advise the court officer as to the terms of the diversion agreement and shall supervise the juvenile in carrying out its terms.

Initially, just under one million dollars was appropriated to the counties to fund diversion programs that were to "be administered and operated separately from the court."[7] Ironically, the conference committee program, a leading example of community based diversion, was created by the court and continues to be administered by the court. Nonetheless, the concept of community-based diversion was statutorily embraced into a formalized accountability model.

With the embrace, however, came other requirements and restrictions that many believed would so hamper the flexibility and informality of community diversion that it would lose its distinguishing characteristics and wither in the bureaucratic tangle of the system. For example, all police referrals had to be screened for legal sufficiency by the prosecutor prior to diversion.[8] Whether a case was diverted or filed was determined primarily by the seriousness of the offense and the prior record according to statutory criteria, not by a social intake process. Comprehensive due process rights, including the right to advice of counsel on the advisability of accepting diversion, were created, and the diversion unit was made responsible for advising the juvenile of these rights. All diversion agreements had to be in writing and signed. Comprehensive record keeping requirements were created, and the juvenile was advised that acceptance of diversion would result in a "criminal history" which, although confidential, would be known to the system and affect both future opportunities for diversion and punishment for future offenses. A diversion referral could be sent back to court by a diversion unit only if accompanied by written reasons. Perhaps most importantly, diversion agreements were limited in their duration and content to a maximum term of community service hours and fines, restitution, and only two hours of counseling or ten hours of education. A violation of a diversion agreement was the only basis for termination; all violations had to be returned to court and the juvenile was entitled to a hearing on the alleged violation. Not only could the juvenile reject diversion and request a court hearing, but in such a case the court's sentence could not exceed that which could have been imposed in a diversion.

While all of this formalization was intended to implement the justice model, it also was intended to hold the community diversion programs and court diversion programs accountable for the responsibilities delegated to them. This seems to have been accomplished without undermining the strength of the established community diversion programs such as the conference committees, while at the same time successfully promoting the creation of community programs around the state.

A comprehensive study of the Washington law reform found that the practice of informally adjusting cases virtually was eliminated.[9] Further:

> Fourteen of the 17 diversion programs examined in detail as part of this study developed programs which included community-based accountability boards or committees with volunteers who actually met with the juveniles and participated

in the development of diversion agreements. Even the programs which were operated by probation officers virtually always included a community-based board and volunteers.[10]

Finding that, depending on how accountability was measured, juveniles were twice or even three times more likely to be held accountable under the post-reform system than previously, the study concluded:

> Regardless of how accountability is measured, most of the increase in accountability is attributable to the fact that the diverted youths of the post system were much more likely to be required to pay restitution or do community service work than were the informally adjusted cases of the past: Twenty-six (26) percent of the diversion cases in King County paid restitution or did community service, 38 percent in Spokane, and 49 percent in Yakima. Less than two percent of the informally adjusted cases involved restitution or service work.[11]

The King County conference committee program accepted the reforms and adopted a statement of goals reflecting an integration of the accountability and treatment models:

1. To provide an avenue for the community to show its concern for youth; to eliminate alienation and hostility on the part of youth, victim, or community; and to establish or restore the youth as a constructive, contributing member of the community.
2. To provide prompt, sure and just discipline/punishment which is the minimum necessary to facilitate accountability, deterrence and restitution.
3. To provide support and information on resources available to assist youth and families in effectively dealing with situations which are problematic to them.
4. To bring to the attention of youth that they will be held accountable to their community for violations of law and unacceptable behavior.
5. To insure the protection of youth's rights as defined by law.
6. To stimulate and maximize citizen participation.

By 1984 The King County program's 450 volunteers were donating 44,000 hours annually. Some 3,062 juveniles were seen by committees and 15,757 hours of community service were assigned. Approximately 30% of those seen were "counseled and released" as provided by law for victimless offenses and minor first offenses. Although the program was concerned that the limitations on counseling requirements would hamper necessary intervention, this does not seem to have been a major issue since only 10% (381) of those seen in 1984 were required to participate in any counseling. Another 12% (484) were required to attend education sessions (e.g., anger management, "skills building," etc.). On the other hand, those requiring more intensive intervention may have been rejected by the diversion program and returned to court. In any event, 87% of some 2,000 diversion agreements handled by the program were successfully completed.[12]

A 1980 study of three largely rural Washington counties showed 148 volunteers serving over 300 hours a month on 27 community accountability boards. "Though no data are available for the exact number of volunteers involved in juvenile justice prior to the Juvenile Justice Act of 1977, most knowledgeable observers agree that volunteer involvement has increased and is more systematic with the advent of Community Accountability Boards (CAB) in the region."[13]

A survey of the 148 volunteers produced a profile of their background and attitudes toward diversion based on 111 respondents. Ranging from ages 16 to 71, the average volunteer was 37 years old and had served for 12.9 months. The majority were not employed by social service agencies, and only one worked specifically with youth. The survey presented the following results:

TABLE 14.1.

Occupation of volunteers Occupation	Percent
Businessperson	25.7%
Professional	22.9%
Homemaker	11.4%
Teacher	10.5%
Student	10.5%
Social Services	8.6%
Retired	5.7%
Laborer	4.8%
	100.1% (105)
Educational level of volunteers **Highest educational level obtained**	**Percent**
Less Than High School	7.5%
High School Degree	14.0%
Some College	26.2%
College Degree	20.6%
Graduate or Professional School	31.8%
	100.0% (107)

The volunteers were asked to agree or disagree with a series of questions, indicating their responses on a ten point scale from "most negative" (1) to "most positive" (10). The results were averaged for each question.

TABLE 14.2.

Survey question	Score
How familiar are you with the new Act?	6.16
How thoroughly have you been trained?	7.66
How fair is diversion for most youths?	8.22
How often are sentencing standards followed?	8.22
Do you feel diversion holds youth accountable for their behavior?	8.15
How satisfied are you with the counsel and release disposition?	6.65

The volunteers were then asked to describe the problems and benefits of community-based diversion. Because they were allowed to list more than one problem or benefit, the total adds up to more than 100%.

TABLE 14.3. Problems of diversion listed by volunteers.

Problem	Percent (N = 111)
No ability to make youths feel accountable	24.3%
No opportunity to counsel youths	17.1%
Lack of resources	17.1%
Problems with other criminal justice agencies	13.5%
Process (i.e. rules are not flexible)	13.5%
No feedback on results	9.0%
Apathy among other CAB members	9.0%
Lack of leadership from coordinator	7.2%
Relationship with community is not good	6.3%
Other	19.1%
	136.1%

These results are strikingly contrary to many predictions made about the consequences of formalizing community diversion in an accountability model. Despite the complications of due process requirements and the bureaucratization engendered in state funding of diversion programs, only 13.5% of survey respondents complained about the inflexibility of the diversion process. Similarly surprising was the finding that more volunteers felt that diversion was not effective in making juveniles feel accountable (24.3%) than felt that diversion afforded inadequate opportunities for counseling (17.1%). This suggests a relatively high degree of acceptance of the philosophical and theoretical premises of the accountability model by volunteers. Such acceptance is similar to that reflected in the previously cited conference committee program goals. It is further evidenced by the survey's report of volunteer perceptions of the benefits of community diversion:

TABLE 14.4. Benefits of diversion listed by CAB members.

Benefit	Percent (N = 111)
Allows community to participate in process	40.5%
Makes youths accountable for offense	38.7%
Serves as alternative to court system	30.6%
Gives youths a "second chance"	22.5%
Enthusiasm of CABs and diversion personnel	5.4%
Saves tax dollars	4.5%
Increases parent involvement	3.6%
Allows adults to better understand youths	2.7%
Other	11.7%
	160.2%

These perceived benefits parallel those sought to be achieved by the law reform. Rather than hampering community diversion, legislative formalization and the investment of public funds in communities as seed money appears to have stimulated volunteer participation. By 1983, statewide statistics reflected that 3,684 volunteers (Washington's population was approximately 4,000,000) contributed 114,463 hours to community-based diversion programs.[14]

Drawing and holding volunteer participation, however, is only one measure of community diversion, albeit an important one. The numbers of volunteers and the length of service presumably reflect perceptions of how the volunteers, and to a degree the community, value the activity. One study sought to measure how the juvenile and family evaluated the community diversion experience.

In 1981 the King County conference committee program surveyed by mail 1,017 randomly chosen juveniles and their parents who had appeared before committees; they received 444 (46%) responses.[15] Four rotated questions measured levels of satisfaction from "very satisfied" (5) to "very dissatisfied" (1) and a fifth question asked what the respondent would like to see changed about the program. The following responses were obtained:

1. Ninety-six percent of the parents and 88% of the juveniles were satisfied or very satisfied that the committee listened to and understood them.
2. Ninety-four percent of the parents and 92% of the juveniles were satisfied or very satisfied with the fairness of the decision by the committee.
3. Ninety percent of the parents and 85% of the juveniles were satisfied or very satisfied that the committee's decision was in some way helpful to the juvenile.
4. Ninety-six percent of the parents and 87% of the juveniles were satisfied or very satisfied with the overall process followed by the committee.

Although 70% of the survey respondents had no recommended changes, the most common comments were:

1. Shorten the length of time between the offense and diversion conference.
2. Insure that dispositions are equitable, especially among youths involved in the same offense.
3. Put more stress on the consequence for future offenses.
4. Follow up to show the youth you care, give positive feedback for successfully completing their diversion agreement, and reemphasize the importance of obeying the law.
5. Do not ask about things unrelated to the offense.

What is striking about the survey results is not simply the high percentage of satisfaction with the diversion experience, but the frequency with which suggested improvements were consistent with an accountability model: prompt, certain, equitable responses to offenses, and an emphasis on deterrence. None of the suggested improvements addressed expansion of treatment opportunities, while one addressed privacy interests which are inconsistent with an expansion of treatment intervention. Although the juvenile survey responses are suspect as being influenced by parents, it is intriguing that the parents, juveniles, and volunteers have a consistent notion of why they are participating in a diversion program and what the program's goals are.

Certainly one theoretical goal of diversion in an accountability or justice model is consistency of sanctions based on the culpability of the offender. Two studies that examined samples of diversion agreements found increasing evidence of consistency in sanctions corresponding to culpability measured by seriousness of offense, extent and seriousness of prior criminal history, and age at the time of offense. In the previously cited 1980 study of three Washington counties which examined volunteer attitudes, less than 4% of the variance in diversion sanctions was explained by culpability-related variables when multiple regression analysis was applied. The analysis covered cases handled in the first year of the law reform. A follow-up study the following year found a seven-fold increase in the consistency of sanctions, with 28% of the variance in sanctions explained by culpability criteria.[16]

Another examination of consistency was a 1982 study of King County diversion programs which sampled 320 cases of first offense misdemeanor shoplifting who were assigned community service by 15 different conference committees to be performed at 8 community service project sites. The study examined the mean hours of community service assigned to each juvenile per project site and found the variance between the projects to range from 16.46 to 22.06 hours of service.[17]

Some of the consistency that has emerged in diversion programs probably comes from the application of sentencing standards for adjudicated offenders published bi-annually by the legislature upon recommendation of a representative sentencing commission. Although not legally binding upon diversion units, many programs have used the sentencing standards as guidelines for diversion sanctions.

Another factor encouraging consistency was the formation of the Washington Association of Juvenile Diversion Units, a coalition representing the majority of community diversion programs. In 1981 the association developed statewide diversion program standards reflecting legal requirements, as well as practices, and policies based on the experience of successful programs. The association has become an information clearing-house for diversion programs and collects and distributes statewide diversion data. It has also represented community diversion interests to the legislature, successfully lobbying an amendment authorizing the imposition of fines in diversion agreements and the convertibility of community service and fines in certain circumstances.

Five years after the law reform, diversion was predominantly community-based. Statewide in 1983, 24,578 cases initially were referred for diversion, of which 4,457 were counseled and released, while 13,629 resulted in diversion agreements. Most of the balance were returned to court. Ninety-two percent of the diversion agreements were successfully completed. The agreements assigned 127,384 hours of community service (108,641 hours completed) and $84,926 restitution ($66,660 collected). There were 23,176 hours of education classes (mostly drug, alcohol, and traffic safety) assigned to 7,346 juveniles and 3,202 hours of counseling assigned to 2,069 juveniles.[18] In short, community-based diversion has become a major component of the juvenile justice system in an accountability model.

The dramatic expansion of community diversion has not been without its problems and drawbacks. It takes time to comply with the formalities when a premium is placed on a speedy response to a delinquent act. It is common for a month to pass between police referral and an appearance before a community board, during which period screening for legal sufficiency and other processing occurs.

The programs cost money. No consistent cost figure can be established, because the program content varies widely. Some programs provide community service site development, high levels of personal contact with the juvenile and family, and other services, while other programs do no more than reach a diversion agreement and leave fulfillment to the juvenile. Costs have ranged from $35 per case to $628 per case, with the great majority of programs falling at the lower end of the spectrum. Finding adequate and appropriate community service sites and supervision is a constant challenge.

No study has found the programs to have a significant impact on recidivism, although this is consistent with the inability to find much impact from *any* type of diversion.[19] On the other hand, police juvenile referrals have steadily declined in number every year since 1980, following the national trend. Of course, an accountability or justice model is not primarily justified on theories of crime reduction in any event.

In many cases there has been a dramatic reduction in informal direct diversion to community boards by police, schools, and other agencies. For example, the conference committees previously had accepted direct referrals from police, schools, social agencies and even self-referral by parents. Following the law reform, the conference committees decided to end services to all except formal diversions that met legal requirements (e.g., screened legally sufficient by the prosecutor). Program administrators were concerned about legal liabilities that might ensue from the continued handling of informal referrals, particularly since the great majority of these referrals had been from the police. It was believed that most other informal referrals did not require a community board hearing process, but rather access to services. In some communities the withdrawal of conference committees from informal referrals led some volunteers to organize replacement services, typically through local youth service bureaus. In effect, there has been a bifurcation of the community investment according to whether the referral involves alleged criminal behavior, or the referral is for services only. Youth service bureaus provide services to both categories of referrals. The same volunteers may be involved in both parts of the system, and conference committees frequently tap youth service bureaus for services, such as requiring counseling at the youth service bureau as part of the diversion agreement.

Police Diversion

Prior to the implementation of the 1977 law reform, direct police diversion in the State of Washington was widespread and took a variety of forms, including in-house programs, referral to local community accountability boards, or referral to a youth service bureau. The formalization of diversion, however, greatly reduced police usage of direct diversion beyond that of a warning and release. For example, in the first full year following implementation of the law reform, police referrals of juvenile offenses to the King County Prosecutor (whose jurisdiction encompasses almost one-third of the state's population) soared over 65% over the last pre-reform year, from 11,578 in 1977 to 17,213 in 1979.

The reduction of police diversion programs that did not involve community participation was consistent with legislative intent and actively encouraged by the King County Prosecutor. The local police historically had a low level of confidence in the formal juvenile justice system. The prosecutor encouraged the police to support the implementation of the law reform by ending their diversion programs in favor of the new formalized diversion, and pointed out its advantages: emphasis on accountability, the opportunity to create comprehensive centralized records of county and ultimately statewide juvenile-police contacts, and the redirection of limited police resources toward basic law enforcement while the community took over primary responsibility for diversion. The withdrawal of the conference committees from direct police diversion programs added impetus to the decline of police diversion.

Although greatly reduced, direct police diversion has not disappeared. In fact, some four years *after* the law reform, the police department in the City of Bellevue, a suburb of Seattle, began a police diversion program. The emergence of the Bellevue police program illustrates some interesting issues in comparing community committees and police diversion, particularly since Bellevue is served by a conference committee which, pursuant to program protocol, does not accept direct referrals from the police.

Bellevue is a suburb of Seattle with a population of approximately 100,000. It is a relatively affluent homogeneous upper-middle-class community with a small minority population. The police chief was a well-regarded innovator and a progressive.

The chief believed that formal court diversion was too slow, cumbersome, and unnecessary, and that most minor offenders were best handled quickly and informally in their own communities. In part, this reflected a belief that the formal juvenile justice system (and the adult system as well) was largely ineffective and was in fact deleterious as a deterrent once offenders saw how the system really operated. In addition, if a juvenile reoffended after informal diversion, there could always be the formal response to the second offense.

The Bellevue police diversion program is designed to handle first time misdemeanants, not involving assaults or weapons. Only Bellevue residents are eligible; nonresidents are referred to court. A detective from the juvenile division reviews all cases to determine eligibility and, as soon as possible after the offense is committed, meets with the juvenile and parents. The detective explains to the juvenile and parents their options: handling the matter through the police or having the case referred to the prosecutor for formal diversion. If after the interview the detective deems informal diversion appropriate and the juvenile wishes to participate, the result might be simply a warning or a written agreement to perform community service, participate in counseling, attend education sessions, pay restitution, write an essay, etc. If appropriate, the detective might refer the juvenile to the local youth service bureau for services. The juvenile is advised that future offenses would result in referral to the prosecutor. The record of the incident is not disclosed to other agencies and there are no consequences if the juvenile fails to follow through on any agreement.

Although technically legal under the 1977 Juvenile Justice Act, the Bellevue police program was opposed by the county prosecutor, the conference committee administration, and the Bellevue conference committee as an unwise policy and inconsistent with the intent of the law reform. Primary objections concerned principles of accountability, theories of justice, and community participation. While police had unquestioned authority and discretion to "street adjust" a case rather than refer it to the system, the Bellevue model called for significantly greater police intrusion, power, and discretion than would result from a formal referral.

A formal referral invoked significant due process safeguards, including prosecutorial screening of legal sufficiency, advisement of rights and the right to counsel, and limitations on the nature and degree of both sanctions and treatment. A formal referral increased the likelihood of uniformity and consistency of treatment since there were 27 police departments but only one prosecutor's office within the county. Further, the 25 conference committees were united in a single program guided by policies and standards. Thus, if a Bellevue juvenile and a central city minority juvenile were arrested together for shoplifting in Bellevue, they would face similar consequences. And to the extent that their consequences differed, it would be the result of a decision by citizens on the conference committees in the juvenile's community, not because of police discretion.

From the perspective of justice theory, the nature of the consequences attached to misbehavior is not primarily a police concern, and citizens as representatives of the community conscience are better positioned to decide just deserts. Due process sets the "rules of the game" and constrains the community, but once an agreement is reached it must be enforceable. Otherwise the appearance of justice in a diversion agreement is a sham, undermining not only the credibility of the community and the law in the juvenile's eyes, but in the eyes of the broader community as well. Under the law reform, formal diversion agreements are enforceable in court, informal diversions are unenforceable.

In sum, police diversion "from" the juvenile justice system is one thing, but the question of "to what?" is quite another. A warning on the street or notifying parents may be an appropriate police response, because whether something needs to be done about an offense is in part a police judgment. In cases in which the judgment of police is that something does need to be done, the issues of what and how are better left to the community or more formalized decision-making.

Conclusion

Community participation in diversion may or may not have any therapeutic benefits for the juvenile, but it is an appealing premise to believe that the message that one's neighbors care about and will react to misbehavior in the community is more clearly conveyed by community boards than by the police or the courts. Similarly, the concepts of reconciliation, forgiveness and a concern for socialization are more likely to be communicated by the community than by more formal authorities.

The belief that justice derives from the participation of the community reaches back beyond the origin of juries. Even if the substantive decisions of the community, police, probation officers, and courts are frequently the same or produce no measurable differences in recidivism or "rehabilitation," justice is largely founded on process as well as result. The process of community involvement in diversion legitimizes the response to a juvenile offense in a fashion not available in the other forums, because it is accessible. Citizens can influence the decisions of police, probation officers, and courts only indirectly, if at all, but as the conference committees demonstrate, they can directly participate in the decision-making of community boards. Further, the process is not dependent upon whether the so-called treatment model or accountability model is the guiding theory. The conference committee program, for example, was created by a treatment model and adapted and institutionalized by an accountability model.

It may be as true today as it was for the Rochester child welfare workers of 1912 that the law "often fails" to succeed where the home, school and community have been unable "to produce a normal result in a child." But if the law does justice and reinvests the community with both the opportunity and responsibility to socialize its children, it will be no small achievement.

Endnotes

1. Handbook of the Rochester Child Welfare Exhibit, 1912 quoted in Eliot, T. D. (1914) *The Juvenile Court and the Community*, New York: MacMillan, p. 143.
2. *Id.* at p. 15
3. Little, Arthur D., Inc. (1978). *Volunteers and the Juvenile Court,* Washington D.C.: Office of Juvenile Justice and Delinquency Prevention.
4. *Id.* at p. 6.
5. King County Conference Committee 1984 data from Bruce Knutson, Program Manager.
6. A study prepared for the Washington Legislature in 1976 found that many cases were informally adjusted, which frequently meant little or nothing was done. In 1974, 45,862 cases were referred to Washington juvenile courts, but only 9,578 petitions were filed. For example, Yakima County informally adjusted 84% of 4,067 referrals and 70% of those adjusted were "released without further action." Similarly, Spokane County informally adjusted 93% of the referrals from police. Naon, B. (1976). *Responding to the youthful offender: An overview and critique of the juvenile justice and correction system.* Olympia, WA: Office of Program Research, House of Representatives.
7. Laws of the State of Washington, 1977 Extraordinary Session, Chapter 291.
8. The statute permitted the prosecutor to delegate screening responsibility to probation officers for misdemeanors, but this has not been done widely. The requirement of screening for legal sufficiency only applies to formal diversion. Police retain traditional "street discretion" about whether to refer a case to the system.
9. Schneider, A. L., and Schram, D. (1983). Executive Summary, Vol. I. From *An assessment of juvenile justice system reform in Washington*. Eugene, OR: Institute of Policy Analysis, p. 17.
10. *Id.* at p. 18.
11. *Id.* at p. 18.
12. King County Conference Committee 1984 data from Bruce Knutson, Program Manager.
13. Guthmann, D. R., and Steiger, J. C. (1982). *An evaluation of the second year of state funded juvenile diversion in Washington State*. Olympia, WA: State of Washington, Department of Social and Health Services, Division of Juvenile Rehabilitation, p. 26.
14. Keith, Polly and Bruce Knutson (1984). *Realities for diverted youth*. Unpublished monograph citing Washington Association of Juvenile Diversion Units 1983 Annual Report.
15. James, Myrtle (1981). *1980-81 Client survey for juvenile court conference*

committees. Seattle, WA: Superior Court of the State of Washington for King County.
16. Guthmann, *op. cit.*
17. Webster, C. (1982). *Diversion projects in Seattle and King County*. Olympia, WA: State of Washington, Department of Social and Health Services, Office of Research and Data Analysis, Juvenile Justice Unit.
18. Washington Association of Diversion Units 1983 Annual Report.
19. Stanford, M. R. (1984). Implementing the multigoal evaluation technique in diversion programs. In Scott H. Decker, (Ed.). *Juvenile justice policy: Analyzing trends and outcomes*. Beverly Hills: Sage Publications, p. 60.

15
Determining the Future Child: Actors on the Juvenile Court Stage

JANET R. FINK

Children in the Eyes of the Law

American jurisprudence, drawing selectively on its common-law antecedents, reflects inconsistencies in perceptions of children—inconsistencies which contribute to the lack of clarity in definitions of the missions of the nation's juvenile and family courts, and, concomitantly, the roles of the various actors in those systems.[1] Juvenile courts were originally founded in the late nineteenth century upon the common-law premise that children were not autonomous individuals with independent rights, capable of willful action or the ability to commit crimes.[2] A child was deemed to have the right not to liberty but to custody, with custodial authority to be exercised by the parent or, if necessary, the State under the doctrine of *parens patriae*.[3]

However, in 1967 in the seminal case of *In Re Gault,* this doctrine, originally invoked at common law solely to protect the person and property interests of the child, was specifically rejected by the Supreme Court as a justification for depriving accused delinquent children who were facing confinement of the same due process rights available to adults.

> The Latin phrase proved to be a great help to those who sought to rationalize the exclusion of juveniles from the constitutional scheme; but its meaning is murky and its historic credentials are of dubious relevance.[4]

A child, under *Gault,* was viewed as an individual with at least a measure of autonomy and a right to liberty which triggered due process protections. The Court held that, "under our Constitution, the condition of being a boy does not justify a Kangaroo court."[5]

The Court in *Gault* thus afforded children charged with delinquent acts with the rights to counsel, confrontation, a privilege against self-incrimination and a transcript for the purposes of appellate review.[6] Subsequent cases recognized children's constitutional rights to proof beyond a reasonable doubt, protection against double jeopardy, freedom of speech, fair school suspension procedures, and qualified rights to privacy and freedom from unreasonable searches and seizures by school officials.[7]

In denying jury trials to juveniles, however, the Supreme Court demonstrated that this due process revolution was not meant to be absolute, but was only intended to inject "fundamental fairness," not full adult rights, into the juvenile court system.[8] Moreover, in its most significant retrenchment from *Gault,* the Supreme Court in *Schall v. Martin* justified preventive detention for juveniles, notwithstanding its general unavailability for adults, by resurrecting the maligned common-law *parens patriae* doctrine.[9] The Court qualified the liberty interest against institutional confinement articulated in *Gault* "by the recognition that juveniles, unlike adults, are always in some form of custody":

> Children, by definition, are not assumed to have the capacity to take care of themselves. They are assumed to be subject to the control of their parents, and if parental control falters, the State must play its part as *parens patriae* . . . In this respect, the juvenile's liberty interest may, in appropriate circumstances, be subordinated to the State's *parens patriae* interest in preserving and promoting the welfare of the child.[10]

Outside of the juvenile court setting as well, the Supreme Court has not followed a consistent trend toward equating juvenile and adult rights. Echoing common law, the Court declined to prohibit corporal punishment, holding that its imposition does not violate the constitutional prohibition against cruel and unusual punishment.[11] Likewise, the premise that "most children, even in adolescence, simply are not able to make sound judgments concerning many decisions, including their need for medical care or treatment," was held to justify the deprivation of due process protections to children when either their parents or the state as guardian seek to commit them to mental institutions.[12] Reflecting the Court's confusion in its perceptions of the judgmental maturity and autonomy of children, this decision was issued simultaneously with a decision that sustained as knowing and voluntary a 16½-year-old child's waiver of his right to counsel and privilege against self-incrimination.[13]

The underlying assumptions of Supreme Court decisions with respect to children have thus followed an erratic pattern, a pattern mirrored in lower court decisions, societal preceptions and legislative enactments. No clear picture has emerged of the child as an individual; no consistent description can be offered of the child's rights and concomitant obligations. Yet a comprehension of the competencies, interests, rights, and responsibilities of the juvenile—the subject, object and, in many cases, participant as either the accused or victim (often both) in juvenile court proceedings—is crucial to an understanding of the ramifications of the juvenile court system in terms of both process and result for the juvenile, his family and society. Achieving an understanding of this present juvenile in the court system is difficult; it is no wonder, then, that the future juvenile, whose best interests the system is ostensibly geared primarily to fulfill, is elusive.

At the same time, recognition of the societal values and interests inherent in decisions and in the decision-making processes in juvenile courts is integral to the attempt to delineate a logical thread in what many have criticized as a chaotic, ineffective system in aimless drift. Identification of these oft-unstated values and interests is not easy; yet their articulation is essential to the development of future policy directions.

In these times of fiscal constraint and heightened community concern over child abuse and youth crime, it is the dearth of resources and creative solutions, rather than lack of clarity of mission and role definition, that may be said to constitute the most compelling problems facing the nation's juvenile courts. Nonetheless, in articulating future resource priorities and strategies for the courts and juvenile justice system at large, it may be useful to explore these issues with regard to the functioning of today's juvenile courts.

To that end, the roles and competencies of the major participants in various juvenile court proceedings will be addressed. Based upon the author's experiences as an attorney for children in New York City, particular attention will be paid to the function of the youth advocate in the court process. One caveat should be noted: while focussing upon the juvenile court and its constituent agencies and participants, this discussion is not intended to diminish the important and often primary role of other institutions of society—families, schools, religious institutions, and community agencies—in addressing the critical problems facing children.

The Juvenile Court: Mission and Method

Observing that "there is a gap between the originally benign conception of the [juvenile court] system and its realities," the Supreme Court in *Breed v. Jones* echoed its admonition a few years earlier in *In Re Gault* that "the juvenile process . . . [must] be candidly appraised."[14] "That the system has fallen short of the high expectations of its sponsors," the Court stated in *Breed,* "in no way detracts from the broad social benefits sought or from those benefits that can survive constitutional scrutiny."[15] This disparity between concept and reality may be attributable to society's overly-high expectations of the juvenile court process itself as distinct from the court's dispositional capacities—expectations that the court process can accomplish the re-socialization of children and resolve the large societal problems that contribute to juvenile delinquency, child maltreatment, and family dysfunction.

The juvenile court's overarching function is as an adjudicative body, not a social agency, and it performs that role relatively well (or at least as well as other courts). In its dispositional phase, the court functions uniquely by utilizing an interdisciplinary approach to identify the needs and marshall the resources necessary to address the manifold problems presented by children and their families. The court's success at disposition furthers the dual aims of the children and the community, and constitutes one of the major reasons for retention of the juvenile court as a discrete body. Its capacity to fulfill its dispositional aims is nonetheless necessarily limited by the quality of the assessments and other information presented, and by the availability of needed resources. As in the fact-finding, the court's primary function at disposition is adjudicative, that is, to render fair and just decisions resolving factual disputes between competing bodies and interests within an adversary framework incorporating due process protections. It is *not* to act as a socializing agency itself, although, as will be explored herein, the infusion of fairness into the court system, through recognition and protection of children's constitutional rights, provides ancillary socializing benefits.

Like school teachers who derive their authority not from parental delegation, but from legislative mandates to educate the population,[16] the juvenile court acts *not* as a substitute parent but as an agent of social control furthering society's aims through its disciplinary and incarcerative powers. It is incumbent upon its participants, therefore, not to substitute personal value judgments or exercise prerogatives or socializing functions still residing in the parental domain.

If the presumption favoring parental custody breaks down because of neglect, abuse, delinquency, or other cause, the State must intervene and, through the juvenile court's adjudicative process, reorder the custodial arrangements surrounding the child. However, as experts have cautioned in urging minimum state intervention into family life:

> As *parens patriae,* the State is too crude an instrument to become an adequate substitute for flesh and blood parents. The legal system has neither the resources nor the sensitivity to respond to a growing child's ever-changing needs and demands.[17]

Over-intrusiveness or over-reaching by the court also fails to take account of child development factors favoring maintenance of parental authority over children, rather than court authority, wherever possible:

> [T]he child lacks the capacity to respond to the rulings of an impersonal court or social service agencies as he responds to the demands of personal parental figures. Parental expectations, implicit and explicit, become the child's own. However, the process by which a child converts external expectations, guidance, commands, and prohibitions into the capacity for self-regulation and self-direction does not function adequately in the absence of emotional ties to his caretakers. . . .
>
> Children . . . react even to temporary infringement of parental autonomy with anxiety, diminishing trust, loosening of emotional ties, or an increasing tendency to be out of control. The younger the child, and the greater his own helplessness and dependence, the stronger is his need to experience his parents as his lawgivers—safe, reliable, all-powerful, and independent.[18]

Overly broad definitions of the juvenile court's jurisdiction have often been the consequence of improper expectations of the court as socializing agency. Child abuse, neglect, and termination of parental rights statutes are frequently imprecise and all-encompassing and invite court intervention based upon subjective value judgments about the quality of parenting rather than objectively identifiable evidence of physical abuse, maltreatment or unfitness.[19] Similarly, the tenaciousness with which state legislatures have retained vaguely defined status offense statutes which authorize sanctions, including institutional confinement for incorrigibility and other non-criminal acts, is indicative of mistaken expectations that the court through its coercive powers can successfully assume a substitute parental role. This assumption flies in the face of widespread recommendations by researchers, clinicians, practitioners, and child advocates nationwide in favor of abolition or, at minimum, a narrowing of status offense jurisdiction with a concomitant refocussing of energy toward community and family-based problem-solving modes.[20] Far from socializing children, use of the court's coercive authority in status offense cases has actually backfired:

> Far from reducing crime, the preoccupation with status offenses has encouraged criminal behavior in several ways. It has produced a heavy overload on the judicial process, leaving judges and probation officers too little time and too few resources to respond in appropriate ways to juveniles who commit criminal acts. And the frequency with which status offenders have been incarcerated—the fact that there has been little relationship between the seriousness of the offenses committed by juveniles and the severity of the punishment meted out to them—has created a caricature of justice that undermines respect for law.[21]

However, when optimally fulfilling the role for which it *is* qualified—fairly adjudicating disputes and fashioning dispositions in situations in which intervention is compelled—the juvenile court necessarily performs an ancillary, beneficial pedagogical function. According to a noted former juvenile court judge, "[d]ue process—fairness—is the best teacher and the best approach to securing client acceptance of our norms."[22] Charles Schinitsky, whose seminal study presaged New York's counsel mandate and was relied upon by the Supreme Court in *Gault,* characterized "establish[ment] of an atmosphere of fairness in its dealings with those persons appearing before it" as an "essential function of the court."[23]

In its *Gault* decision, the Supreme Court rejected the long-held notion that the juvenile benefits from the informality of juvenile court proceedings and pointed to studies which "with surprising unanimity . . . suggest that the appearance as well as the actuality of fairness, impartiality and orderliness—in short, the essentials of due process—may be a more therapeutic attitude so far as the juvenile is concerned:"

> [T]here is increasing evidence that informal procedures, contrary to the original expectation, may themselves constitute a further obstacle to effective treatment

of the delinquent to the extent that they engender in the child a sense of injustice provoked by seemingly all-powerful and challengeless exercise of authority by judges and probation officers.[24]

Utilizing the due process model mandated by *Gault* thus enhances the juvenile court's chances for success in its endeavors by recognizing autonomy of the child at least to the extent of allowing his full participation in the process. Just as children have been found to perform better in school when their self-esteem is bolstered by the ability to make choices, allowing children to have meaningful input and a qualified sense of control over decisions vitally affecting their futures increases their ability to become engaged positively in the dispositions ordered by the court and to develop into responsible adults.[25]

While the adversary system's purported psychological harms to children noted by the Supreme Court in *Parham v. J.R.*[26] have yet to be demonstrated,[27] its benefits are obvious, particularly for older children. Research has established that the more adversary the structure, the more the affected parties have positive perceptions of the control they have exercised and the fairness of the result by virtue of their input into the decisions made.[28] Moreover, the family dysfunction and attendant anxiety evident in juvenile proceedings are not *caused* by the adversary process, but normally *precede* and indeed often precipitate the court's involvement. The finality of the court's judgment and the court's mobilization of needed resources for the child and his family may ease these problems.[29]

Not all matters in juvenile courts are or should be resolved in an adversary manner. Attorneys, in their counsellor-at-law function, are often able and are encouraged to facilitate consensual resolutions. However, when this is *not* possible, the adversary model provides a viable means of determining the necessary facts and developing, implementing and enforcing dispositional plans to resolve seemingly intractable problems. The due process framework provides a system of rules designed to provide fairness, accountability, and a measure of consistency of treatment—a grid within which individualized justice can be meted out—which vitiates some of the disparities between judges and other actors in the system. The oft-quoted maxim that "we are a government of laws, not of men" is thus germane as a functional justification for the constitutionalized juvenile court.

The central benefit of reliance upon an adversary model infused with due process protections in the juvenile court is the enhancement of the court's capacity to make just and appropriate decisions grounded upon the most complete presentation of the competing factors and interests at stake. Not acting simply as truth-seeker through "distillation and evaluation of essential facts,"[30] the juvenile court, like all courts, is charged with the task of distributive justice. The court must appropriately resolve conflicts in interests and values, specifically ordering or re-ordering the public and private custodial and other arrangements surrounding a child once a determination has been made establishing a factually-proven basis for court intervention.

The Supreme Court in *Gault* accurately summarized the superiority of the due process model over the frequent arbitrariness of the pre-constitutionalized juvenile court:

> Failure to observe the fundamental requirements of due process has resulted in instances, which might have been avoided, of unfairness to individuals and inadequate or inaccurate findings of fact and unfortunate prescriptions of remedy. *Due process of law is the primary and indispensable foundation of individual freedom.* It is the basic and essential term in the social compact which defines the rights of the individual and delimits the powers which the state may exercise. As Mr. Justice Frankfurter has said: "The history of American freedom is, in no small measure, the history of procedure." But in addition, *the procedural rules which have been fashioned from the generality of due process are our best instruments for the distillation and evaluation of essential facts* from the conflicting welter of data that life and our adversary methods present. *It is these instruments of due process which enhance the possibility that truth will emerge from the confrontation of opposing versions and conflicting data. "Procedure is to law what 'scientific method' is to science."*[31]

The determination of whether the legal threshold has been met for court intervention is fairly straightforward. It generally requires an adjudication of facts within the context of applicable law as to whether the child or parent, as the case may be, is culpable for commission of the act charged. The dispositional determination, which necessarily involves an element of prediction, is far more difficult. Since a juvenile court disposition takes effect prospectively and may endure until the child reaches the age of majority, the court must consider not merely the interests and circumstances of the present child, family, and community, but also must attempt to envision within the significant limits of the state of the art of prediction the interests and circumstances, as well as the probable effects of particular modes of intervention, upon the *future* child, family, and community. No crystal balls are yet available to answer adequately the key questions, *inter alia,* of whether a child will be abused again, whether a child's development will be fostered or hindered by retention or removal from a particular home, whether a parent will recover from a mental or other condition impeding child-caring capacity, whether a child will commit a future crime or whether a particular treatment modality will help or hinder his progress.

Joseph Goldstein, Anna Freud and Albert Solnit cautioned strongly against courts trying to do the impossible in prognosticating with respect to the child and family and thus have urged courts to limit themselves to imposition of the least drastic intrusion necessary to further the child's paramount interests in affection, continuity, and stimulation:

No one—and psychoanalysis creates no exception—can forecast just what experiences, what events, what changes a child, or for that matter his adult custodian, will actually encounter. Nor can anyone predict in detail how the unfolding development of a child and his family will be reflected in the long run in the child's personality and character formation. . . . In the long run, the child's chances will be better if the law is less pretentious and ambitious in its aim, that is, if it confines itself to the avoidance of harm and acts in accord with a few, even if modest, generally applicable short-term predictions.[32]

The authors cite a lecture by Anna Freud in which she stated:

I name three [factors which] make prediction difficult and hazardous. (1) There is no guarantee that the rate of maturational progress on the side of ego development and drive development will be an even one; and whenever one side of the structure outdistances the other in growth, a variety of unexpected and unpredictable deviations from the norm will follow. (2) There is still no way to approach the quantitative factor in drive development, nor to foresee it; but most of the conflict solutions within the personality will, in the last resort, be determined by quantitative rather than by qualitative factors. (3) The environmental happenings in a child's life will always remain unpredictable since they are not governed by any known laws.[33]

As recognized by the American Psychiatric Association and numerous commentators, it is extremely difficult to accurately predict the dangerousness of an individual, (e.g., the likelihood of future crime commission or child abuse).[34] Justice Marshall, dissenting in *Schall v. Martin,* found the evidence "overwhelming" in support of the District Court's finding in that case that:

no diagnostic tools have as yet been devised which enable even the most highly trained criminologists to predict reliably which juveniles will engage in violent crime.[35]

Nonetheless, in a controversial opinion, the majority in *Schall* legitimized judicial predictions regarding juveniles who, while still presumed innocent and as yet unconvicted, are preventively detained pending trial, but failed to address the substantial distinction between such juveniles and the *convicted* adults in the precedents relied upon.[36] The unavoidable predictive determinations arising out of acceptance of the community's interest in crime prevention as a relevant consideration in delinquency pretrial dispositional decisions underscores the need for full presentation of all pertinent evidence through zealous advocacy by all parties.

Recognizing the appropriate limits of the juvenile court system's mission and competence, as well as its strengths as enhanced by its due process methodology, it becomes clear that the court is necessarily dependent upon the active participation of all who are affected by its decisions. Both in terms of its *process* (the court's treatment of a case from the pre-adjudicatory to the post-dispositional phases) and its *results* (the court's decisions at each stage), the juvenile court must be fair to all concerned. To accomplish this, the court requires competent advocacy by each of the relevant actors so that the court will have the benefit of the maximum amount of information and perspectives. It is to a discussion of the roles and qualifications of these actors that we now turn.

The Child

The child stands at the center of all juvenile court proceedings, even if only in silent shadow. The determination of his current and future interests is the primary focus of the court's attention. The child is subject, object, and often a participant as victim, offender or both, with enormous stakes in the outcome. He may have the most to gain and at the same time the most to lose by the court's decisions. He is subject to the coercive mandates of the court and may face removal from his home, placement or confinement rising to the level of incarceration, extended supervision or court-ordered treatment, restitution or other sanctions.

As noted, American jurisprudence contains varying, often conflicting assumptions regarding the competence and autonomy of the child in decisions determining state intervention into family life. Since the role of the child in proceedings determining his future is critical and is derived from these assumptions, their empirical validity must be re-examined in light of clinical knowledge about child development. Although elucidation of the state of current clinical knowledge is beyond the scope of this discussion, some salient points should be considered.

First, qualified recognition of autonomy and competence on the part of the child to permit his participation in legal proceedings is both ego-reinforcing and healthy for the child *and* helpful for the court in expanding the perspectives and information presented. Ironically, however, only in certain types of proceedings have children been accorded this measure of autonomy and been granted full party status and representation, chiefly proceedings in which they have been accused of wrong-doing, such as delinquency and status offense cases, and proceedings in which they themselves have been abused or maltreated.[37] Children are largely invisible and unrepresented or represented on only a limited discretionary basis in custody, foster care review (parental voluntary placements) and in accordance with *Parham v. J.R.*, mental health commitment cases. This gap in the law, not justified by differences in consequences for the children involved, has understandably become the target of widespread calls for reform.[38]

Second, the general assumption of children's incompetence, which characterized the historical view of children and infuses certain recent legal decisions, does not accord with accepted principles of child development. Justice William O. Douglas, dissenting in part from the Supreme Court's compulsory education decision in *Wisconsin v. Yoder,* objected that children mature enough to express their religious and educational preferences should have the right to be heard. He cited Piaget, Kohlberg and others for the proposition that:

> [T]here is substantial agreement among child psychologists and sociologists that the moral and intellectual maturity of the fourteen-year-old approaches that of an adult.[39]

Some researchers have empirically demonstrated that children at the age of twelve have reached their maximum level of cognitive functioning.[40] While nine-year-olds have been shown to lack full decision-making capacity, they are able nonetheless to articulate reasonable preferences comparable in most cases to those of their elders; the average third-grader has some understanding of the concept of a legal right.[41] Seven-to-nine-year-olds, while not fully developed, "have considerable capacity for self-determination"; pre-school and primary school children "have some capacity for understanding verbal explanations and some ability to communicate their own questions and answers."[42] In short:

> [R]esearch over the past two decades has shown that children can understand the sociolegal and moral bases of social rights at a much earlier age than generally had been assumed.[43]

Third, to the degree that children's capacities are *not* developed sufficiently to assume full competence when confronted with the maze of complex legal decisions inherent in the juvenile justice process, the need becomes ever more critical for effective representation by counsel at an early stage. Empirical research regarding waivers of *Miranda* rights supports this conclusion. Two studies of arrested juveniles revealed an astonishing 90% of juveniles waiving their rights to silence and counsel—perhaps following law enforcement authorities' frequent admonitions to 'cooperate.'[44] Further studies demonstrated that the vast majority of youth ages 14 and younger failed to meet a minimum comprehension level regarding *Miranda* warnings, as compared with approximately one-quarter of the adults. Significantly, prior court experience did *not* bear a direct relationship to understanding of *Miranda* warnings *per se*.[45] One researcher "report[ed] that [juveniles] most clearly understand the explanation of their rights and the court process as given by their lawyer," leading him to recommend "appointment of more diligent legal counsel earlier in the process."[46]

In summary, full participation by children in proceedings in which they are the central foci is compelled, not only by considerations of constitutional law, but also by reference to accepted principles of cognitive and moral development. Recognizing that children, at least those of verbal age, may be able to offer unique perspectives and express preferences contributing significantly to decisions about their futures, it is unjustifiable to allow them to remain invisible, unheard, and unrepresented. At the same time, to the degree that children have not yet developed the competency necessary to make complex legal decisions on their own and require assistance in exercising their right to be heard, the need for counsel assumes pivotal importance.

The Parent

If the child assumes center stage in juvenile court proceedings, surely the parent stands close beside him in prominence. Central to the juvenile court's mission is the determination of when and how the state may intervene in family life to overrule traditional parental prerogatives or reorder custodial relationships. The right to parental autonomy—the "fundamental liberty interest . . . in the care, custody, and management of their child[ren]"—is one of constitutional magnitude, compelling clear and convincing proof of unfitness before parental ties can be involuntarily severed.[47] As one Supreme Court justice has written:

> For centuries it has been a canon of the common law that parents speak for their minor children. So deeply imbedded in our traditions is this principle of law that the Constitution itself may compel a state to respect it.[48]

The recognition of the right to family integrity and autonomy and the concomitant responsibility engendered in parents have a long tradition at common law and in American legal history. In a case according parents discretion to send their children to private schools, the Supreme Court held that parents "have the right, coupled with the high duty, to recognize and prepare [their children] for additional obligations."[49]

Nonetheless, the Court has established limits on parents' rights, (e.g., refusing in one often-criticized decision to constitutionally mandate appointment of counsel in termination of parental rights proceedings on the theory that the parents in those cases do not face the possibility of incarceration, the traditional analytical trigger for the sixth amendment right to representation).[50]

The invocation of at least a rebuttable presumption of parental autonomy is grounded in an equally rebuttable presumption that if they are not unfit or voluntarily relinquish ties, parents will act in their children's interests and indeed share a unity of interest with them. As the Supreme Court stated, with respect to parents' educational prerogatives:

> The history and culture of Western civilization reflect a strong tradition of parental concern for the nurture and upbringing of their children.[51]

More recently, the Court has observed:

> The law's concept of the family rests on a presumption that parents possess what a child lacks in maturity, experience, and capacity for judgment required for making life's difficult decisions. More importantly, historically it has recognized

that natural bonds of affection lead parents to act in the best interests of their children. (1 W. Blackstone, Commentaries 447; 2 J. Kent, Commentaries on American Law 190.)[52]

Dissenting justices in both cases, however, questioned the wisdom, as well as the constitutionality of the court's complete deference to parental judgment to the exclusion of allowing the children the right to be heard. Justice Douglas cautioned:

It is the future of the student, not the future of the parents that is imperiled by today's decision. . . . It is the student's judgment, not his parent's, that is essential if we are to give full meaning to what we have said about the Bill of Rights and of the right of students to be the masters of their own destiny.[53]

Likewise, Justice Brennan noted that:

Numerous studies revealed that parental decisions to institutionalize their children often are the results of dislocation in the family unrelated to the child's mental condition.[54]

Indeed, parental judgment, even in those matters in which juveniles and their parents do not generally occupy adversary positions, such as delinquency proceedings, may not always further the child's interests. At times, this is traceable to the conflict created for the parent when the child is accused of or involved in misbehavior. Stresses on the family, spouse or siblings thus engendered, for example, may cause the parent to seek a remand or placement for the child leading to confinement whose restrictiveness exceeds that which may be legally justifiable or appropriate.[55] Parents too, it must be recognized, are often adolescents themselves, who are thrust prematurely into assuming responsibilities for which they are ill-prepared, untrained and inadequately supported.

At other times, limitations in parental judgment may be due to ignorance or naivete about the legal system. The above-cited studies regarding waiver of *Miranda* rights in interrogations revealed, respectively, that 80% of the parents gave *no advice whatsoever* to their children to assist them in the pre-interrogation process and that "no significant differences [existed] between the legal understanding of parents and their children."[56] A further attitudinal study found that 75% of the parents did not believe that children should possess a right to silence comparable to their own.[57]

This is *not* to say parents shouldn't be present to provide whatever support they can at all stages of the process as is required or at least encouraged in juvenile delinquency statutes and caselaw.[58] However, it *does* underscore the need for *independent* counsel for children; the parent cannot act as a substitute and cannot demand the fealty of the child's lawyer even if the parent pays his fee. Moreover, in cases in which parent and child are potential or genuine adversaries (e.g., child abuse or status offense cases) the need for independent advocates becomes even more apparent.

The Prosecutor

As the representative of the state, the prosecutor acts as guardian of the community's interests, in particular the maintenance of the integrity of the justice system through vigorous enforcement of its laws. These laws include substantive criminal laws and proscriptions against delinquent conduct and laws governing (and, as noted above, *limiting*) the state's interference into family life and the procedural laws and rules controlling the court process. The prosecutor in the juvenile court, therefore, has a triple duty: to ensure community safety through active law enforcement, to maintain the community's and the legal system's commitment to the integrity of the family with the reciprocal parent/child rights and responsibilities which this implies, and to promote the fair and efficient administration of justice through adherence to procedural mandates.

The prosecutor's overarching ethical responsibility is to promote justice in its broadest sense, not simply to convict individuals or win legal battles. This obligation to seek justice is central to the prosecutorial standards embodied in the *Lawyer's Code of Professional Responsibility,* the document currently governing the legal profession, and the recently approved American Bar Association, *Model Rules of Professional Conduct,* the American Bar Association Criminal Justice Standards Project, *Standards Relating to the Prosecution Function,* and the Institute for Judicial Administration-American Bar Association Juvenile Justice Standards Project, *Standards Relating to Prosecution.*[59] As the *Lawyer's Code of Professional Responsibility* explains:

> The responsibility of a public prosecutor differs from that of the usual advocate; his duty is to seek justice, not merely to convict. This special duty exists because: (1) the prosecutor represents the sovereign and therefore should use restraint in the discretionary exercise of governmental powers, such as in the selection of cases to prosecute; (2) during trial the prosecutor is not only an advocate but he also may make decisions normally made by an individual client, and those affecting the public interest should be fair to all; and (3) in our system of criminal justice the accused is to be given the benefit of all reasonable doubts.[60]

Seeking and doing justice for the community as a whole is a grave responsibility. Too often prosecutors in juvenile court take a more parochial approach, viewing their function solely as representation of the complainant. Serving the interests of an individual complainant, *inter alia,* through notification about the progress of the case, expeditious processing, scheduling accomodations, protection against harassing cross-examination or intimidation and applications for restitution, is unquestionably a *part* of the prosecutor's role in promoting the fair administration of justice. However, his role as an officer of the court and representative of the state supersedes and, at times, conflicts with the wishes or interests of particular complainants. For this reason, the establishment of an independent or at least semi-independent agency, such as New York City's Victim Services Agency, whose primary focus is the needs and wishes of victims, is a laudatory development, facilitating an ethically appropriate and pragmatic differentiation of functions.

Specifically in the juvenile delinquency context, the prosecutor's threshold function is to exercise appropriate discretion to refrain from instituting cases unsupported by evidence at least rising to the level of probable cause or cases suitable for diversion from the court process.[61] At the trial preparation stage, he is ethically mandated to disclose exculpatory evidence to the accused or his counsel on a timely basis and otherwise comply with discovery requirements.[62] Advancing to the adjudicatory phase, the prosecutor is obligated to marshal and present evidence to prove the crime charged beyond a reasonable doubt.[63] At disposition, he is charged with the responsibility of arguing the appropriateness of the various dispositional options available to the court.[64] Far from compelling recommendations for the most restrictive sanctions, the community's various interests in protection, in an educated and employable citizenry, and in family autonomy militate in many cases in favor of community-based dispositions specifically tailored to equip the child with essential literacy and vocational skills critical to a responsible, law-abiding adulthood. To the extent that a juvenile offender can be successfully reintegrated into society without returning to or escalating his life of crime, society as well as the offender benefits. While secure confinement is necessary in certain cases, achievement of the maximum sanction should not be, but all too frequently is, the prosecutor's goal.

In status offense cases, the prosecutor must again focus upon vindication of the community's interests in family integrity, development of its citizenry and integrity of the court process. He must *not* view his role narrowly as an attempt to vindicate the desires of a disgruntled parent or teacher, particularly since both the parent and the school often share responsibility for precipitating the problem, and must actively assist in resolving it. Since status offense cases are frequently amenable to resolution in the community and are often inappropriate for court intervention, the prosecutor has an integral role to play in developing and implementing diversion plans.[65] In cases pursued through litigation as well as those terminated prior to disposition, the prosecutor can play a critical part in the often difficult struggle to procure and coordinate the resources required to resolve the problem. These cases generally do not present community safety concerns; they implicate other family and community interests which require social assistance, rather than coercive forms of intervention.

Finally, in child protective cases, the prosecutor must view his role broadly as enforcer both of society's interests in promoting safe and healthy environments for its children and of the parents' or (if necessary) the state's duties to provide those environments. He must not confuse his role with that of a private attorney with a private client; his job is *not* to justify child protective agency decisions if these decisions contravene these larger mandates.

As the *Lawyer's Code of Professional Responsibility* provides:

> . . . A government lawyer in a civil action or administrative proceeding has the responsibility to seek justice and to develop a full and fair record, and he should not use his position or the economic power of the government to harass parties or to bring about unjust settlements or results.[66]

Nor is his job to purport to represent the child's interests as these are often not coextensive with the state's, however benign its intentions. Significantly, federal regulations implementing the mandate contained in the Child Abuse Prevention and Treatment Act of 1974 for representation of children in child protective cases originally permitted utilization of the same attorney who presented the cases (i.e., the prosecutor) as the child's representative. However, the regulations have since been changed to specifically *preclude* prosecutors from performing in that dual capacity.[67]

Thus, the tasks of the prosecutor in juvenile court proceedings may be viewed as more complex than that of the traditional prosecutor. The recognition that a vigorous, professional prosecutorial staff is integral to the juvenile court's success, as evidenced by legislative initiatives in New York[68] and elsewhere, is a much-needed development, but the prosecutor's natural tendency simply to rush to adjudicate and confine must give way to a broader vision of his role.

The Lawyer for the Child

"Wherever coercive action is a possibility," concluded the President's Commission on Law Enforcement and Administration of Justice in 1967, "the presence of counsel is imperative":

> There is no single action that holds more potential for achieving procedural justice for the child in the juvenile court than provision of counsel. The presence of an independent legal representative of the child, or of his parent, is the keystone of the whole structure of guarantees that a minimum system of procedural justice requires. The rights to confront one's accusers, to cross-examine witnesses, to present evidence and testimony of one's own, to be free of prejudicial and unreliable evidence, to participate meaningfully in the dispositional decision, to take an appeal—all have substantial meaning for the overwhelming majority of persons brought before the juvenile court only if they are provided with competent lawyers who can invoke those rights effectively.[69]

Juveniles before the courts in all types of proceedings have distinct perspectives and interests which require the assistance of an independent voice. To place the child on a par with other parties, this advocate must be an attorney, not simply a lay assistant, and must provide energetic, comprehensive legal representation. As the President's Commission stated:

> The most informal and well-intentioned of judicial proceedings are technical; few adults without legal training can influence or even understand them; certainly children cannot. Papers are drawn and charges expressed in legal language. Events follow one another in a manner that appears arbitrary and confusing to the uninitiated. Decisions, unexplained, appear too official to challenge.[70]

The traditional tasks of an attorney—thoroughly investigating facts and legal issues, presenting evidence and legal arguments, examining and cross-examining witnesses, preserving a record and taking appeals or seeking other forms of legal relief, counseling clients to aid them in making decisions and generally utilizing the advocate's persuasive skills—are central to the functions of the child's attorney. However, because the client is a juvenile and because the juvenile court is a "socio-legal" court,[71] a court whose decisions must be grounded upon the expertise and resources of social services and clinical disciplines, these tasks must be performed with an extra measure of sensitivity and specialized interdisciplinary competence. The child's lawyer must be, according to the Administrative Judge of the New York City Family Court, a "lawyer-plus."[72]

It is well settled that the child's attorney performs an essential representational function for children before the courts, a function compelled by constitutional, ethical, and pragmatic considerations. No other participant in the process can effectuate the child's right and need to be heard. Of the numerous officials and parties with whom the child comes into contact on any given case, it is only the child's attorney whose allegiance is solely to the child and in whom the child can place his trust; in an often wholly alienating court environment, it is the attorney who acts as the child's friend and spokesperson. The traditional juvenile court model of the kindly judge and well-intentioned probation officer *cum* prosecutor/counsellor cannot substitute for the child's own attorney in asserting the child's interests. As the Supreme Court held in *Gault:*

> There is no material difference in this respect between adult and juvenile proceedings of the sort here involved. . . . A proceeding where the issue is whether the child will be found to be "delinquent" and subjected to the loss of his liberty for years is comparable in seriousness to a felony prosecution. *The juvenile needs the assistance of counsel to cope with problems of law, to make skilled inquiry into the facts, to insist upon regularity of the proceedings, and to ascertain whether he has a defense and to prepare and submit it. The child "requires the guiding hand of counsel at every step in the proceedings against him."*[73]

Gault and its progeny, as well as its antecedents such as New York's 1962 Family Court Act,[74] long ago laid to rest any doubt as to the applicability of due process to juvenile proceedings since, as in criminal proceedings, the accused may face a significant deprivation of liberty. Although the Supreme Court in *Gault* addressed only trial issues, it strongly implied (and statutes and cases have prescribed) due process ramifications well beyond the issues before it. The Court held:

Recognition of the right to counsel involves no necessary interference with the special purposes of juvenile court procedures; indeed it seems that counsel can play an important role in the process of rehabilitation.[75]

In Re Gault involved a fifteen-year-old juvenile delinquent who was committed to the state training school until his twenty-first birthday solely upon a charge of making an obscene telephone call, a far more severe sanction than the $5 to $50 fine or maximum sentence of two months incarceration that an adult charged with a similar crime in Arizona would have faced. However, its rationale is equally applicable to other categories of cases in which children face an involuntary removal from home, (i.e., status offense and child protective proceedings).

Although the right to mandatory legal counsel has not generally been extended to children facing involuntary foster care or institutional confinement pursuant to their parents' execution of voluntary placement instruments, many courts and legislatures have at least recognized the need for counsel for children facing irrevocable loss of ties with their parents. In granting children the right to appointment of attorneys (known as law guardians) in termination of parental rights cases, New York's Court of Appeals stated:

Our courts have been sensitive to the expanding rights of children, including the right to be heard . . . and, only recently, the importance of having the child represented by a law guardian was emphasized, "[s]ince the child obviously cannot speak for herself."[76]

Advocacy, therefore, lies at the foundation of the child's attorney's role—conveying the child's position to the court, as well as protecting the child's legal rights. As one practitioner stated,

It is the *child's* right to have his or her views heard, not the lawyer's right to have the lawyer's views heard.[77]

In light of the *Gault* decision's analogy to criminal proceedings, there is little dispute about the attorney's advocacy role in delinquency cases and, because of their quasi-criminal consequences, status offense cases. However, the issue of whether the attorney in child protective proceedings should assume a strong advocacy role on behalf of the child's wishes or assert what he perceives to be in the child's best interests has been a hotly debated issue in courts and legislatures nationwide. Section 241 of New York's Family Court Act and a similar statute in New Jersey make it clear that expression of the child's views is an integral aspect of the attorney's function. In all types of juvenile proceedings, attorneys for children are mandated "to help protect their interests and to help express their wishes to the court." Importantly, the statute mentions "interests", *not* "best interests," since the ultimate determination of best interests is left up to the court.

Compelling ethical concerns likewise dictate a strong advocacy approach by counsel for children. Canon 7 of the *Lawyer's Code of Professional Responsibility* states that "[a] lawyer should represent a client zealously and within the bounds of the law." In exercising his integral counsellor-at-law function, an attorney must advise his client as to his range of legal options and may venture a professional opinion as to the likely outcome. However, as an advocate in court, the attorney must "resolve in favor of his client doubts as to the bounds of the law." For a client with sufficient judgmental capacity, the client's wishes must govern the attorney's trial strategy and decisions regarding the exercise of the client's legal rights. The authority to make decisions affecting the merits of the case or the client's rights is thus exclusively that of the client, and if made within the framework of the law such decisions are binding upon his lawyer.[80] Significantly, although authorizing attorneys to make legal arguments, the *Code* specifically *prohibits* attorneys from expressing personal opinions about the merits of a case.[81]

The *Lawyer's Code* recognizes that the attorney's responsibilities necessarily vary according to the age or other disabilities of the client, with the magnitude of those responsibilities increasing for young children. However, regardless of disability, "[i]f the client is capable of understanding . . . or contributing to the advancement of his interests, . . . the lawyer should obtain from him all possible aid." Even where the child is too young to make judgments binding upon the lawyer, the lawyer should look to the child for whatever degree of assistance the child can provide. Where an incompetent has a guardian, the attorney should look to him for decisions otherwise made by a client. But

> if the disability of a client and lack of legal representative compel the lawyer to make decisions for his client, the lawyer should consider all circumstances then prevailing and act with care to safeguard and advance the interests of his client.[82]

From a purely pragmatic vantage point, active participation by the child's attorney enhances the quality of the judicial process and the ultimate decisions made. Effective advocacy facilitates presentation of all relevant information to the court, assists the court in developing adequate plans for the child and may help avoid unnecessary and extremely costly placements. The appearance of fairness enhances the child's ability to accept the decision. Having had his day in court, the child is better able to accept the consequences of his acts or (if he is the victim of maltreatment) the ramifications of his situation, and engage himself in the treatment process.

In juvenile delinquency cases, where the defense posture of counsel is most straightforward, counsel must investigate and present cases for trial or negotiate appropriate pleas, just as in criminal cases—recognizing that a child's altered sense of time magnifies the consequences of pretrial detention, adjudication delays and lengthy placements. Counsel assumes a unique and particularly critical function at the dispositional phase, preparation for which actually must begin at the first contact with the client. Just as the adversary process is beneficial at the adjudicatory stage in providing a method by which culpability can be determined, so, too, in contested cases at disposition, the full testing of the evidence presented by the probation department, the court clinic, as well as the proferring of additional dispositional options by the defense, is crucial to augment the court's capacity to make a fully informed decision.[83] Moreover, many cases are uncontested, due in large measure to the attorney's exercising of his counsellor-at-law function to assist the child in understanding and ultimately accepting the reality of his dispositional options. Post-dispositional monitoring and advocacy is also vital, for the child's need for a legal voice, for example in parole or probation violation proceedings, may well be as critical as in earlier stages.

In status offense cases, the defense attorney, like the prosecutor, must pay particular attention to diversion of cases for which court intervention is not required or appropriate. The factual premise upon which the court's involvement is based—whether the child committed the acts charged—is as important as in delinquency cases and in contested matters must also be proven beyond a reasonable doubt.[84] However, even before this point is reached, it is possible in many instances, particularly with social work assistance, for the attorney to link up the family with services in the community on a voluntary basis, entirely obviating the need for an adjudication. Failing such diversion, adjudicated cases require active dispositional and post-dispositional advocacy. Since status offense dispositions are aimed at furthering the child's needs, the attorney must assist in ensuring that these needs are being met on a continuing basis.

In child protective proceedings, the attorney's role is most complex, particularly when young children who are incapable of expressing themselves are involved. Given the enormous escalation of reported child abuse and neglect nationwide—it doubled nationally from 1976 to 1982[85] and has escalated even more rapidly since then—and given the 50% recidivism rate when assistance is not forthcoming for the child abuse victim and his parent,[86] effective advocacy on behalf of the children to assure needed services and safety assumes ever greater prominence.

Even very young children are capable of expressing preferences, notwithstanding their lack of competence to make decisions. In such cases, it is important for the advocate to master the special skills required to interview young children. The assistance of trained social workers, as well as utilization of techniques such as anatomically correct dolls, doll house models and play therapy may be indicated, particularly to elicit information from relatively non-verbal children.

Representation of a mature client in a child protective proceeding who is capable of understanding the proceedings and articulating a position is virtually indistinguishable from advocacy on behalf of a child in a delinquency case or an adult in a criminal or civil matter (i.e., the client upon being apprised of the options and consequences makes the essential decisions which are binding upon the lawyer although *not,* it should be noted, upon the judge). As discussed above, representation of a client who is not mature or old enough to make these decisions may require the attorney to substitute to a limited degree his professional judgment for the client's—not to inject his own opinion as to best interests, but simply to protect his client's legal interests and rights.

Clearly the child's rights and interests in abuse and neglect cases necessarily include the client's wishes but may extend well beyond them. Since the purposes of child abuse or neglect proceedings are to protect children from physical and emotional injury or mistreatment, a child who is the subject of such a proceeding has a legal right and interest in remaining alive, in being protected from physical injury and psychological damage, in being fed, clothed, and educated. He has an interest in remaining in his own home and with his own parents, and to have every effort made to maintain him at home unless the home situation is shown to present a danger to him. If such efforts fail and he cannot be returned home, he has a right to permanence and stability within a caring, nurturing family, rather than as a ward of an institution or as a foster child in a succession of foster homes.

Protection of each of these rights and interests compels comprehensive investigations and strong advocacy efforts on the part of the child's attorney. In some cases involving children incapable of considered judgment, the lawyer must simply facilitate full presentation of adequate and reliable evidence while essentially remaining neutral as to the outcome; the attorney may fill gaps in the case as portrayed by the parent and the child protective agency so that the court can make a more informed decision. In other cases, the attorney's extensive knowledge of the child, the evidence and the child's statements (if any) compel the lawyer to articulate a more definitive position and to put forward arguments and evidence, as well as to formulate and effectuate plans to advance that position. In those situations where the evidence on the record legally warrants it, he may therefore move, *inter alia,* for discharge of a child to parents or relatives for temporary or long-term placement, or for a finding, suspended judgment or dismissal.[87]

The varied functions of the lawyer for the child can best be carried out when the lawyer has access to sufficient assistance from social workers and/or clinicians well-versed in the resources available and disciplines relevant to the court's decisions. Interdisciplinary representation was pioneered by the Juvenile Rights Division of the New York City Legal Aid Society where, since the early 1970s, attorneys have worked in teams with professional social workers and, in appropriate cases, have utilized clinical and educational consultants as well.

While fiscal constraints limit social work assistance to approximately one-quarter of the cases handled by the Juvenile Rights Division, the presence of a high-quality, professional unit has a natural seeding function, creating a healthy professional interchange and assisting attorneys in their capacities to handle the social work aspects of the cases in which a social worker has not been assigned.[88] When working as a team, although the attorney sets the legal goals and parameters of the cases, the attorney and social worker function jointly in problem-solving and realizing case goals. The infusion of social work assistance in investigation and assessment, comprehension of the language of the clinical disciplines, family and child crisis-intervention, clinical and other referrals, expert testimony and case monitoring enhances the attorney's ability to respond to recommendations of other participants and present reasonable dispositional alternatives of their own to the court. As one attorney stated, "[t]he lawyers provide the 'clout,' . . . while the social workers provide the 'credibility.' "[89]

Additionally, social workers are of enormous benefit in jointly assessing programs and facilities serving the clients, assisting in institutional litigation where necessary, and contributing to the development of public policy positions on behalf of youth. At times, the identification of service gaps has even led to development of direct services programs. The Legal Aid Society, for instance, runs a summer youth employment program, which secures jobs for two to three hundred clients annually.[90] Its staff was also recently honored with a commendation by New York City's Mayor for a vocational program entitled "Partners in Progress" which it helped to establish in conjunction with the City's Parks Department.

In implementing this team representational model, conflicts in the role perceptions and ethical mandates between the professions might have been expected to arise. Yet this has not been the case as professional respect, as well as the client-centered advocacy approach utilized in both disciplines, minimizes possible divergence. Like the *Lawyers Code*, the *Code of Ethics* promulgated by the National Association of Social Workers stresses the primacy of clients, the need to maximize client self-determination, the need for respect for confidentiality and other legal rights of clients and the need for social workers to adhere to commitments made to the host organizations in which they are employed.[91] The meshing and cross-fertilization of ideas thus engendered inures to the benefit of the children represented and ultimately enhances the capacity of the court in its efforts to make informed decisions in juvenile cases.

The type of comprehensive legal representation described above is unfortunately available only in certain metropolitan areas nationally.[92] All too often in many jurisdictions children are discouraged from exercising their right to counsel. Many courts allow the parents to waive the juvenile's rights, even on status offense cases in which they occupy adversary positions. In delinquency cases, waiver of counsel is common. While as of 1977 it was reported that in the largest metropolitan areas children were represented in excess of 80% of the cases, they were represented in only 10% to 25% of the cases in other localities.[93]

A recent study of legal representation of children in New York State (*not* including The Legal Aid Society representation described above) found rampant waivers of counsel by children, a serious lack of specialized expertise and training of attorneys, failures by attorneys to utilize existing statutory mechanisms to obtain clinical and social assistance, failure to engender system accountability through appellate or special litigation, and a glaring lack of preparation, even to the extent of failures to interview clients.[94] Criticising what the authors deemed to be "phantom" representation, the study found seriously inadequate or only marginally adequate representation in 45% of the cases and truly effective representation in only 4%.[95] Significantly, a zealous advocacy approach was rare:

> Even in juvenile delinquency and PINS [status offense] proceedings, under 15% of the law guardians view the representation of youth as analogous to that of a defense lawyer. A still smaller percentage say they could consistently represent their client's wishes in the face of personal disagreement.[96]

These results comport with criticisms frequently encountered with respect to the general quality of legal representation of children nationally, including representation in child protective, as well as delinquency and status offense cases.[97] Indeed, in child protective proceedings, while pursuant to a federal mandate 41 states now require representation for children, only 25 of these require the representatives to be attorneys, and only 2 (New York and New Jersey) explicitly include representation of the child's wishes as part of the definition of the advocates' function.[98]

Comprehensive, active legal representation for children has the potential to provide enormous individual and systemic benefits, a potential which has been realized in only a few jurisdictions with vigorous child advocacy programs. However, the promise of counsel for children, as well as the explicit mandates of the *Gault* decision, remain unfulfilled nationally. Future policy regarding the juvenile justice system *must* address this major gap.

The Probation Officer

Probation officers are among the most neglected, yet are prime actors in the juvenile court. They are directly involved in critical decisions regarding entrance, processing and exit from the system. In most jurisdictions, they are generally responsible for initial screening of cases, investigations, and presentations to judges of information necessary for interim release/detention decisions and selection of dispositional options. If probation is ordered, they are charged with direct provision to youths under their supervision of the tools necessary to prevent recidivism and to enable the youths to participate as law-abiding, productive members of society.

Unfortunately, probation is generally underfunded, underrated, and thus under-professionalized.[99] Significantly, a National Assessment of Juvenile Corrections study revealed that probation officers averaged only 1½ contacts of approximately 30 minutes duration per month with their probationers—hardly enough time to give meaningful assistance or to assert effective control.[100] Economies in the probation area, which have become even more widespread in the last few years, not only seriously short-change youth, but also are short-sighted from the community's point of view in terms of increased recidivism and increased costly and unnecessary placements. Probation, the most frequently ordered dispositional option, requires far more of an investment in order to succeed.

Apart from resource problems, however, the question arises as to the appropriate role of probation officers. In New York, for example, notwithstanding their counselling functions, probation officers are quasi-law enforcement agents with the explicit statutory authorization to obtain orders to search probationers and their property and to bring violators to court.[101] Thus, they are often perceived as adversaries by the juveniles, not as trusted sources of assistance.

Unfortunately, caselaw has not succeeded in resolving this ambiguity. In the Supreme Court case of *Fare v. Michael C.*,[102] a child accused of a crime requested to speak to his probation officer whom he viewed as a surrogate parent or counselor. Assuming a probation officer's primary function is that of peace officer, the Court refused to perceive the probation officer as a parental figure. Again highlighting the probation officer's law enforcement role, the Court recently ruled in the adult context that statements made to a probation officer by a probationer could be used against him in a subsequent criminal proceeding.[103]

Increasing probation's police functions may be made at the expense of its capacity to fulfill its primary assessment, counselling, service provision or referral, and habilitative functions. It significantly impedes probation's ability to prevent recidivism by engaging probationers in useful programs—difficult enough tasks to accomplish in any event, but well nigh impossible unless full trust of the youths can be obtained. It also flies in the face of attempts to strengthen probation's effectiveness through professionalization and implementation of uniform standards.[104]

The Court Mental Health Clinic

Like the probation officer, the court diagnostic clinic, which is a permanent feature of many juvenile courts, has the potential to enhance the quality of judicial decision-making by maximizing the information available to the judge. A full exposition of the clinic's roles, capacities and functioning nationally is beyond the scope of this discussion. However, assuming the New York experience is typical, two pervasive problems should be noted:

1. The court clinic evaluations are routinely perfunctory and inadequate by professional standards. Clinicians are generally underpaid, low status civil servants who must perform too many assessments per day to afford time for professional thoroughness or diagnostic integrity. High quality residential and out-patient diagnostic centers, often run by private non-profit agencies,[105] are unfortunately not available to the majority of juveniles before the courts.

2. Significant doubt exists as to the objectivity of court clinic reports. They are generally used as tools for placement, *not* as the bases for effective community treatment dispositions. In one New York City Legal Aid Society case, for example, a court psychiatrist testified that he recommended placement in a so-called structured setting 95% of the time. Too often the diagnoses follow a predictable pattern, varying far more by the crime and clinician involved, than by individual attributes or the psychological symptoms of the children. All too frequently, professional standards regarding symptoms and diagnosis are ignored in favor of a superficial recitation of the child's misdeeds and the parents' failures.

Despite these major deficiencies in both the quality and objectivity of clinic reports, they are relied upon extensively by the courts and often comprise the most decisive pieces of evidence shaping the judges' determinations. The reports may sway the judges as to whether or not to return a child to parents charged with child abuse, to terminate parental rights, to remand a child to a psychiatric hospital for an emergency evaluation, to change custody or visitation rights of parents or grandparents or to place a child charged with an act of delinquency or a status offense in a secure or residential treatment facility. In New York, for example, diagnostic assessments are ordered by the court pending disposition in a substantial percentage of cases; they are statutorily required in enumerated delinquency felony cases and as a prerequisite to placement.[106]

Particularly in view of the deficiencies noted above, serious questions have been raised as to the ramifications of utilizing court clinic evaluations made in the absence of counsel. Admission of such evaluations at critical stages of court proceedings arguably implicates the parties' rights to confrontation and effective assistance of counsel. While in New York the rights of criminal defendants asserting insanity defenses and parents facing termination of their rights on mental illness grounds to have their attorneys present at mental health examinations have been recognized,[107] no comparable right has been extended to juveniles facing confinement or removal from their homes. Still unresolved in its applicability to juveniles is the Supreme Court's ruling in 1981 that a capital defendant facing a mandatory pre-sentence evaluation for future dangerousness possesses a Fifth Amendment right to be warned that he has a right to remain silent and that any statement made in the examination may be used against him at sentencing.[108]

The difficulties inherent in having clinicians and ultimately judges rendering predictive judgments, and the implication of fundamental interests of children and parents facing the clinic assessment process, underscores the need for clinicians to educate the courts as to the realistic limitations of their respective expertise.[109] Perhaps most important, steps must be taken to enhance the stature and quality of the clinics.

The Juvenile Justice System at Large

The juvenile court would be operating in a meaningless vacuum if it could not draw upon the services of agencies outside the court and relevant institutions in the community—in particular, schools, churches, and both public and private nonprofit sector programs serving children and families—to add content to its decisions and assist it in carrying out its mission. These agencies and institutions play an important role during the juvenile court process itself, as well as during the post-dispositional phase. Representatives are called upon by the various juvenile court participants and the court itself to provide information and bring their expertise to bear on the decision-making process. Ultimately, these agencies and institutions are the keys to success of the results of the court process in those instances in which the court's intervention through invocation of its dispositional authority is determined to be legally justified, as well as in those cases which are diverted to the community for non-coercive, locally-based resolution.

In order to enable the court to fashion interim and final dispositional orders sufficiently tailored to the individual needs of the children, the court must have access to the widest possible variety of options. As has been demonstrated by the experiences of jurisdictions, such as Massachusetts and New York, fiscal incentives are essential to stimulate maximum diversity and creative programing in public agencies or the often more flexible private non-profit sector. Adequate research and evaluation components are likewise crucial so that strategies which are effective for youth in trouble can be well-documented, publicized and replicated.

In the juvenile corrections area, this diversification is needed to rectify a historical imbalance in favor of the traditional restrictive, punitive institutions which failed to equip children with the basic adjustment and vocational and literacy skills needed for successful reintegration into the community. Research has demonstrated that rather than reforming youth, increasing the severity of a juvenile's punishment and depth of penetration into the juvenile correctional system actually increases his risk of future criminal behavior.[110] All too many studies have painted a dismal picture of the high recidivism rates and substantial educational and employment deficits of juveniles after release.[111] Charles Silberman's conclusions, in *Criminal Violence, Criminal Justice,* based upon observation of a wide variety of detention and long-term institutions nationally are still apt:

> The overwhelming majority of detained juveniles receive no help worthy of the name. Those who are kept in adult jails receive no services at all—unless being sodomized is classified as a service. Detention centers do provide schooling, as a rule, but not much else. What data are available indicate that only 1 percent of the youngsters in detention receive psychiatric treatment; 15 percent receive counseling from a social worker, and 9 percent from a probation officer. Yet detention center staff believe that eight youngsters in ten have some emotional disturbance, half of them of a moderate to severe nature. There is no information on *how much* counseling or therapy is provided those youngsters who get any at all; my own observations suggest that it is the rare youngster who sees a psychiatrist, social worker, probation officer, or "counselor" more than an hour a week. "Counseling," especially of a group nature, is more frequent and more extensive in training schools; it usually is aimed at improving inmates' adjustment to the institution, rather than at preparing them to function in the outside world. . . .
>
> After seventy-five years of talk about substituting rehabilitation for punishment, it is difficult to find the rehabilitation, and all too easy to find the punishment. One might be able to justify this imbalance if the punishment were directed against juveniles who commit violent crimes. . . . Most of the punishment meted out by juvenile courts is directed against youngsters who have committed petty crimes, such as vandalism, shoplifting, and other forms of theft, or offenses that would not be criminal if committed by adults.[112]

This is *not* to imply that sources for optimism are entirely lacking in the juvenile corrections arena or that no programs exist that have been demonstrated to be effective. Charles Silberman and James Finkenauer, among other commentators, have pointed out several.[113] But it is clear that the rehabilitative, habilitative or treatment model of the juvenile justice system, so often maligned by the system's critics, has never truly been tested—tested in a manner which strikes an appropriate balance between the juveniles' individual needs and the community's long- and short-range security interests.

Increased diversification and creativity are critically needed in the child protective and child welfare arenas as well. The failures of the foster care system nationwide—the devastating effects of the long-term limbo and frequent dislocation and abuse to which children have long been subjected—have been all too well documented in recent years.[114] These have led to a legislative recognition on a federal level and, at least in New York, on a state level of the need to infuse the system with fiscal incentives toward permanency planning, services to prevent or shorten placements in foster care, and disincentives toward perpetuation of the deleterious practices of the past.[115] As an encouraging preliminary evaluation of the Lower East Side Family Union, one of New York City's community-based comprehensive preventive services agencies, demonstrated persuasively, innovative models exist to intervene constructively in resolving the very problems which all too frequently in the past have led to destruction of families and severance of vital links to community resources and institutions.[116]

Augmentation of the options available to the juvenile courts with a broad spectrum of youth and family agencies in the community enhances the court's capacity to carry out its important missions. The concomitant need for effective monitoring mechanisms through the courts, the legislatures, executive agencies and communities themselves to provide complete accountability by these agencies and social institutions cannot be emphasized sufficiently. The juvenile court must be able to reach out to the community and to enforce the community's responsibility to provide a broad spectrum of services to address the problems of children and families. It is only through such a marshalling of the creative resources of the community that the families of children, and ultimately the interests of the community, will be served.

Conclusion: The Judge as Ultimate Arbiter in the Juvenile Court

Once that zealous advocacy on behalf of all competing interests and extensive multi-disciplinary expertise and breadth of resources have been brought to bear upon the court, it devolves upon the juvenile court judge to make the ultimate determinations as to whether and how the state should intervene in the lives of children and families. The "wide discretion and grave responsibilities" accorded the judges in making these determinations have been explicitly recognized, *inter alia,* in New York's Family Court Act. In addition to requiring legal training and ten years of experience, the Act provides that the judges should be "familiar with areas of learning and practice that often are not supplied by the practice of law" and should be "especially qualified for the court's work by reason of their character, personality, tact, patience and common sense."[117] The statute reflects legislative hopes that "Family Court judges would be individuals of distinction, sensitive to the complexities of community and family life, as well as learned in the law."[118]

The importance of these qualities in facilitating effective performance cannot be overestimated. Juvenile proceedings are often complex multi-party disputes which pit parents against public and private agencies with children caught in the center, and which require a facility for expeditious, often spontaneous rulings. Equally critical, juvenile court judges must be sensitive to the multiplicity of problems arising out of discrimination and poverty that many of the families appearing before them experience. Ideally, the judges should have prior training or background in the social sciences, in family crisis intervention techniques, in psychology and/or social work, and in working and communicating with children. Moreover, the judges should receive extensive and ongoing pre- and in-service training which addresses all of the disciplines relevant to their decisions. In reality, however, most judges are not equipped with all of these tools and must rely upon professionals to supply the needed expertise in these areas.

Additionally, judges must cope patiently and skillfully with extremely volatile situations which sometimes involve understandably distraught or emotionally disturbed individuals; it is their job to assist all parties, regardless of age and background, in comprehending the often confusing and frustrating court process. Judges must be able to listen, to display empathy and to refrain from making class or cultural value judgments in rendering their decisions. At the same time, they must be able to function well under the constant pressure and enormous emotional strain of confronting a myriad of seemingly intractable problems daily.

It goes without saying that *not* all judges meet the standards outlined above, although the trend in recent years away from the use of non-legally trained juvenile judges has measurably improved the quality of the juvenile court bench. As important as these skills are, however, the judges also clearly require sufficient resources, stature and authority to adequately fulfill their complex mandates. If the judges cannot rely upon court-serving agencies to provide them with the information and program options required to adequately tailor dispositions and follow-up orders, the court cannot meet its basic obligations. If the court, as is so often the case, is accorded a low status in the court system and is not provided with enough fiscal and public support to attract qualified personnel to perform its varied functions, the quality of its decision-making necessarily suffers.

In marshalling resources and support, the judges' public advocacy activities are of inestimable importance. In New York, judges are statutorily authorized to participate in religious, charitable, benevolent, or educational organizations, and are mandated to visit juvenile institutions and facilities periodically:

> Family Court judges who are familiar with community and service organizations, particularly those that work with youths or families, are more sensitive to the needs and capabilities of the children, families, and service agencies that come before them. Furthermore, knowledgeable and active Family Court judges can play an important role in the development of services to children and families and in the enhancement of community-life generally.[119]

Additionally, the court requires authority to exercise continuing jurisdiction over agencies and youth in order to ensure enforcement of its orders, thereby assuring agency and offender accountability. In New

York, for instance, the Family Court exercises continuing jurisdiction through a variety of post-dispositional proceedings, some of which may be court-initiated including, *inter alia,* motions for new hearings or modifications, as well as extensions, violations or terminations of placement or probation.[120] A unique *mandamus* provision accords the Family Court wide enforcement powers, enabling elicitation of cooperation from agencies with legal obligations relevant to the court's mission and necessary to the implementation of its orders.[121]

While judicial activism is essential to implement orders necessary to the resolution of cases before the court and to enforce accountability among its constituent agencies, the juvenile court is but a *small* part of the juvenile justice and child-serving systems. Societal conditions contributing to or creating the problems facing the court—poverty, unemployment, illiteracy, discrimination—are in large measure beyond the capacity of the juvenile court to remedy. While able to take steps ameliorating aspects of these problems, (e.g., ensuring safe environments or facilitating developmental opportunities for children), juvenile court judges must possess a thorough understanding of the parameters of their authority and an acute sense of the limitations of their role. In order to restrain the judges in what Charles Silberman has termed their "godlike role,"[122] these tasks must be accomplished with due regard for due process of law.

To summarize, therefore, it is clear that injecting fairness into the process, as required by *Gault* and as set forth in statutes such as New York's, substantially enhances the quality of judicial decision-making because it ensures: (a) maximum advocacy on all sides so that *all* perspectives are fully presented, (b) accountability through the appellate and supplemental litigation processes, (c) maximum information from which to select from the menu of dispositional and post-dispositional options available for troubled or maltreated youth, and (d) continuing jurisdiction to ensure that the child, family, community and victim continue to be well served by the disposition, (e.g., that placement or probation is still necessary and appropriate, that the child or parent is getting education, therapy, or other needed services or that the victim receives appropriate restitution).

Fairness in the *process,* in short, facilitates justice for all parties in the *result*—justice which must be considered the linchpin, the key performance indicator, of the juvenile courts. As Dean Francis Allen so aptly cautioned, "one may rightly wonder as to the value of therapy purchased at the expense of justice."[123]

Endnotes

1. Hereinafter, in the interests of simplicity, the term "juvenile court" will be used to refer to family as well as juvenile courts.
2. Blackstone, W. *Commentaries on the law of England* (1803), p. 21, 23–4, 453–4; Bentham, J., *Theory of legislation.* (Weeks, Jordan, 1840), vol. I, p. 248 [cited in J. Goldstein, A. Freud, and A. Solnit, *Beyond the best interests*

of the child. (Free Press, 1973), p. 135; Goldstein, J., Freud, A., and Solnit, A. *Before the best interests of the child*. (Free Press, 1979), p. 7].
3. Shears. Problems peculiar to children's courts. 48 *A.B.A.J*. 719, 720 (1962); *Ex Parte Crouse*, 4 Whart. 9, 11 (S.Ct. Pa. 1839); *Petition of Ferrier*, 103 Ill. 367, 371–3 (1882) [cited in *In Re Gault*, 387 U.S. 1, 17]. *See also Pierce v. Society of Sisters*, 268 U.S. 510 (1925); *Meyer v. Nebraska*, 262 U.S. 390, 400 (1923).
4. *In Re Gault*, 387 U.S. 1, 16 (1967). *See also Kent v. United States*, 383 U.S. 541, 555 (1966) ("the admonition to function in a parental relationship is not an invitation to procedural arbitrariness").
5. *In Re Gault*, 387 U.S. 1, 28 (1967).
6. *Id*. at 31–58.
7. *In Re Winship*, 397 U.S. 358 (1970); *Breed v. Jones*, 421 U.S. 519 (1975); *Tinker v. Des Moines Independent School District*, 393 U.S. 503 (1969); *Goss v. Lopez*, 419 U.S. 565 (1975); *Carey v. Population Services International*, 431 U.S. 678 (1977); *Planned Parenthood of Cent. Miss. v. Danforth*, 428 U.S. 52 (1976); *Belotti v. Baird*, 428 U.S. 132 (1976), *on re-appeal*, 443 U.S. 622 (1979); *H.L. v. Matheson*, 450 U.S. 398 (1981); *New Jersey v. T.L.O.*, ___ U.S. ___, 105 S. Ct. 733 (1985).
8. *McKeiver v. Pennsylvania*, 403 U.S. 528 (1971).
9. ___ U.S. ___, 104 S. Ct. 2403 (1984).
10. 104 S. Ct. at 2410. Ironically, in New York and most other jurisdictions, children, whose crimes are of such gravity that they may be held criminally responsible and treated as adults, are entitled to bail and may *not* be preventively detained once they enter the adult criminal justice system. *See, e.g.*, New York Criminal Procedure Law §§ 1.20(42), 510.30 (McKinney's 1984).
11. *Ingraham v. Wright*, 430 U.S. 651, 684 (1977). Regarding the common law tradition, see W. Blackstone, *supra*, at 134.
12. *Parham v. J.R.*, 442 U.S. 584, 604 (1979).
13. *Fare v. Michael C.*, 442 U.S. 707 (1979). Clearly seeking the aid of a trusted authority figure, the juvenile naively requested to see his probation officer, instead of a lawyer, saying, "How do I know you guys won't pull no police officer in and tell me he's an attorney?" Additionally, notwithstanding his "prior brushes with the law," the child, according to the dissenting opinion, was crying during the interrogation and appeared to be "immature, emotional and uneducated, and therefore was likely to be vulnerable to the skillful, two-to-one, repetitive style of interrogation to which he was subjected." *Id*. at 734 (Powell, J., dissenting).
14. 421 U.S. at 529–30 [citing 387 U.S. at 21].
15. *Id*. at 530.
16. In *New Jersey v. TLO*, 105 S. Ct. at 741, the Supreme Court held that teachers' public functions in fulfilling state educational interests and mandates precludes them from "claim[ing] immunity from the strictures of the Fourth Amendment."
17. Goldstein, J., Freud, A., and Solnit, A. *Before the best interests of the child*. (Free Press 1979), p. 12.
18. *Id*. at 12, 25.
19. *Id*. at 13–14, 17; Giovannoni, J., and Becerra, R. *Defining child abuse* (Free Press 1979), p. 260; Developments in the law: The Constitution and the family. 93 *Harv.L.Rev*. 1156, 1215 (1980); Chemerinsky. Defining the best interests: Constitutional protections in involuntary adoptions. 18 *J. of Fam.Law* 79, 105, 110 (1979); Note: Constitutional limitations on the scope of state child neglect statutes. 79 *Col.L.Rev*. 719, 727 (1979); Wald, M. State intervention on behalf of neglected children: Standards for removal of chil-

dren from their homes, monitoring the status of children in foster care and termination of parental rights. 28 *Stan.L.Rev.* 625, 649, 688–700 (1976); Note, *Parens Patriae* and statutory vagueness in the juvenile court. 82 *Yale L.J.* 745, 746–7 (1973).

20. *See e.g.*, Goldstein, Freud, and Solnit. *Before the best interests of the child.* (Free Press 1979), p. 28; Silberman, C. *Criminal violence, criminal justice.* (Random House, 1978), p. 347; National Council on Crime and Delinquency, "Jurisdiction over status offenses should be removed from the juvenile court: A policy statement" and Ketchum, O. "Why jurisdiction over status offenders should be removed from the juvenile court," in R. Allinson, (Ed.). *Status offenders and the juvenile justice system: An anthology.* (N.C.C.D., 1978), pages 3–5, 33–50; Nevergold, P., Rosen, M., Block, E. *PINS jurisdiction in New York State today: Critique and recommendations for reform.* (Statewide Youth Advocacy, Inc., Rochester, N.Y. 1983); Rubin, T. The juvenile court's search for identity and responsibility. *Crime and Delinquency, 23, 1* (Jan. 1977), at p. 12; President's Commission on Law Enforcement and Administration of Justice. *The challenge of crime in a free society.* (1967), p. 85.
21. Silberman, *loc.cit.*
22. Rubin, *loc.cit.*
23. Schinitsky, C. The role of the lawyer in children's court. *Record of the Association of the Bar of the City of New York. 17,* p. 24 (1962).
24. 387 U.S. at 25–26 [citing President's Commission on Law Enforcement and the Administration of Justice, *The challenge of crime in a free society* (1967), p. 85]; Wheeler, S. and Cotrell, L. *Juvenile delinquency—Its prevention and control.* (Russell Sage Foundation 1966), p. 33; Allen, F. *The borderland of criminal justice.* (1964), p. 19. *See also* Allen, F. "Criminal justice, legal values and the rehabilitative ideal," in A. and J. Goldstein, (Eds.). *Crime, law and society* (Free Press 1971), p. 280–281. An almost identical observation was made by Andrew Shookhoff, a juvenile court practitioner with long experience representing children in delinquency cases:

    A child who commits a burglary but who feels that he was treated arbitrarily and unfairly by the legal system or that he was sold out by his attorney, is likely to see his predicament as a result of irrational and arbitrary forces of law rather than as the logical and proper consequences of his own illegal actions.

    Shookhoff, A. Providing competent counsel in juvenile delinquency cases: Guidelines for juvenile court practice. *Tennessee Bar Journal* (May, 1983), p. 7. *But see* Stapleton, V., and Teitelbaum, L. *In defense of youth: A study of the role of counsel in American juvenile courts.* (Russell Sage Foundation 1972), p. 171, which criticised the Supreme Court's reliance upon "intelligent guess-work rather than empirical data."
25. Jean Piaget's theory that a democratic, rather than authoritarian, approach to education facilitates positive moral development thus translates directly into milieu of the juvenile court. Piaget, J. *The moral judgment of the child.* (Kegan, Paul, Trench, and Trubner 1932), p. 362–3; Melton, G. "Decision-making by children: Psychological risks and benefits," in Melton, Koocher, and Saks. (Eds.). *Children's competence to consent.* (Plenum 1983), p. 27, 31 [citing, *inter alia,* Selman, "Social cognitive understanding: A guide to education and clinical practice," in Lickona, (Ed.). *Moral development and behavior: Theory, research and social issues* (1976); Brigham, "Some effects of choice on academic performance," in Perlmutter and Monty, (Eds.).

Choice and perceived control (Erlbaum 1979); F. Levine and J. Tapp, "The dialectic of legal socialization in community and school," in J. Tapp and F. Levine, (Eds.). *Law, justice and the individual in society*. (Holt, Rhinehart, and Winston, N.Y., 1977)]. *See also* Parke, R. "Socialization into child abuse," in Tapp and Levine. (Eds.). *ibid*., p. 194; Melton, G. and Lind, E. A., "Procedural justice in family court: Does the adversary model make sense?" in Melton, G. (Ed.). Legal reforms affecting children youth services. *Child and Youth Services Rev., 5,* #1/2 (Haworth 1982), p. 65, 66, 68, 76; Weithorn, "Developmental factors and competence to make informed treatment decisions," in Melton, G. (Ed.). *id.*, p. 98.

26. 442 U.S. 584, 611 (1979).
27. Melton, G. (Ed.). *Legal reforms affecting child and youth services. supra,* note 25, p. 3.
28. Melton, Koocher, and Saks, *op.cit.*, p. 48; Melton and Lind, *op.cit.*, p. 67.
29. Melton and Lind, *op.cit.*, pages 75–79.
30. *In Re Gault,* 387 U.S. 1 (1967).
31. 387 U.S. at pages 20–21.
32. Goldstein, Freud, and Solnit, *supra* note 29, at 51–52.
33. *Ibid.*, at 170, note 36 [citing Anna Freud, Child observation and prediction of development: A memorial lecture in honor of Ernst Kris. (*The Psychoanalytic Study of the Child, 13,* pp. 97–98; New York: International Universities Press, 1958)]
34. *See, e.g.*, American Psychiatric Association. *Clinical aspects of the violent individual.* (1974) pages 27–28; Cocozza, J. and Steadman, H. The failure of psychiatric predictions of dangerousness: Clear and convincing evidence. 29 *Rutgers L.Rev.* 1084, 1094–1101 (1976); Diamond. The psychiatric prediction of dangerousness. 123 *U.Pa.L.Rev.* 439 (1974); Ennis and Litwack. Psychiatry and the presumption of expertise: Flipping coins in the courtroom. 62 *Calif.L.Rev.* 693 (1974); Schlesinger. The prediction of dangerousness in juveniles: A replication. 24 *Crime and Delinquency* 40, 47 (1978); Steadman and Cocozza, Psychiatry. Dangerousness and the repetitively violent offender. 69 *J.Crim.L. and C.* 226, 229–231 (1978); Wenk, Robison, and Smith. Can violence be predicted. 18 *Crime and Delinquency* 393, 401 (1972); Preventive detention: An empirical analysis. 6 *Harv.Civ. Rights–Civ.Lib.L.Rev.* 289 (1971). [All cited in *Schall v. Martin,* ___ U.S. ___, 104 S. Ct. 2403, 2425–6 (Marshall, J., dissenting)].
35. *Schall v. Martin,* 104 S. Ct. at 2425 [citing *United States ex rel Martin v. Strasburg,* 513 F. Supp. 691, 708 (S.D.N.Y. 1981)]. *See also Martin v. Strasburg,* 689 F. 2d 365, 376 (2d Cir., 1982) (Newman, J., concurring) ("The hazards of prediction are well known . . .")
36. *Schall v. Martin,* 104 S. Ct. at 2417–8 [citing, *inter alia, Jurek v. Texas,* 428 U.S. 262, 274–5 (1976) (death penalty case); *Greenholtz v. Nebraska Penal Inmates,* 442 U.S. 1, 9–10 (1979) (parole eligibility case); *Morrissey v. Brewer,* 408 U.S. 471 (1972) (parole revocation case)]. Reacting to criticism of the decision, Senator Arlen Specter (R-Pa.) has spearheaded a call for standards to guide judicial detention decisions and has introduced the Juvenile Preventive Detention Standards Act, now pending in the United States Senate. *See* S. 1188, *Cong.Record,* May 22, 1985; S. 8994, *Cong. Record,* July 23, 1984; *Juvenile Justice Digest,* v. 13, #11, p. 1 (June 3, 1985).
37. Because children accused of status offenses face the potential of confinement, status offense cases have been deemed to be quasi-criminal, triggering the same due process protections mandated by the Supreme Court in *In Re Gault,* 387 U.S.1 (1967). *See, e.g.* N.Y. Fam. Ct. Act., Art. VII; *Matter of Cecilia R.,* 36 N.Y.2d 317 (1975); *Matter of Iris R.,* 33 N.Y.2d 987 (1974).

Chiefly as a result of enactment of the federal Child Abuse Prevention and Treatment Act of 1974, 42 U.S.C. §§ 5101–5115, forty-one states have enacted mandates for representation of children in child protective proceedings. However, of these, only twenty-five require that the representative be an attorney on a par with other parties. Even in these states, the child, with his distinct perspective, is often invisible. Only two states, New York (which has required legal representation since 1962) and New Jersey, specifically include articulation of the children's wishes as part of the attorneys' function. *See* Butz. Lawyering for the abused child: 'You can't go home again.' 29 *U.C.L.A. Law Rev.* 1216, 1222, 1229 (1982).

38. *See e.g.,* N.Y.C. Mayor's Task Force on Foster Care Services, *Redirecting foster care.* (1980).
39. 406 U.S. 205, 246 note 3 (1972) (Douglas, J., dissenting in part). Piaget, in fact, theorized that a child's cognitive structure for formal operational thinking, including incipient abstract thinking, appears at approximately the age of eleven and develops to its highest point, comparable to an adult level, at approximately the age of fourteen. At that point, cognitive development takes place with regard to the formation and differentiation of specific skills, rather than the progression to a higher level of thought capacity. J. Piaget, "Intellectual Evolution from Adolescence to Adulthood," 15 Human Devel. 1–12 (1972); J. Piaget and B. Inhelder, *The psychology of the child* (Basic Books 1969) [Cited in L. Weithorn, "Developmental factors and competence to make informed treatment decisions," in G. Melton (Ed.). *Legal reforms affecting child and youth services, supra* note 39, at pages 93–94] Lois Weithorn adapted this theory to articulate five stages of development along the continuum of a child's progression toward full competency: 1) evidence of choice (expression of preferences); 2) reasonableness of choice with respect to likely outcome; 3) reasonableness of the decision-making process leading to the choice, e.g., abstraction and weighing of alternatives; 4) understanding of the consequences of the choice (the point at which fourteen-year-olds are comparable to adults); and 5) general competence with respect to functioning in society. Weithorn, *id.* at 89–98.
40. Weithorn, *id.* at 94; Weithorn, Involving children in decisions affecting their own welfare. In Melton, Koocher, and Saks (Eds.). *Children's competence to consent. supra* note 39, at page 245.
41. *Ibid;* Melton, G. Children's concepts of their rights. *Journal of Clinical Child Psychology, 9* (1980), pages 186–90 [Cited in J. Tapp and G. Melton, "Preparing children for decision making: Implications for legal socialization research," in Melton, Koocher, and Saks (Eds.). *Children's competence to consent. supra* note 39, at page 225].
42. Ferguson, L. R. The competence and freedom of children to make choices regarding participation in research. *Journal of Social Issues, 34,* #2 (1978) pages 114–121 [Cited in Weithorn, Involving children in decisions affecting their own welfare. *op.cit.,* p. 246]. *See also* Ramsey. Representation of the child in protection proceedings; The determination of decision-making capacity. 17 *Fam.L.Q.* 287, 307 (1983).
43. R. Parke, *supra* note 39, at page 197. Tapp and Levine as well as Tapp and Kohlberg, in cross-cultural studies of children in six countries, found comparable patterns of legal socialization and comprehension. J. Tapp and L. Kohlberg, "Developing senses of law and legal justice," in Tapp and Levine (Eds.). *Law, justice and the individual in society, supra* note 39, at pages 89–105. Tapp and Levine, as well as other researchers in the area, have utilized a model adapting Kohlberg's six identified stages in the development of moral judgment:

1) Punishment/obedience orientation;
2) Instrumental/relativist orientation (the utilitarian values of acts to self and others);
3) Orientation as to interpersonal concordance or desire for approval;
4) Law and order orientation (abstract concepts of moral law and obedience to authority);
5) Social contract/legalist orientation (freedom in the context of constitutional and other laws);
6) Orientation as to universal ethical, or higher guiding principles.

Kohlberg. *Assessing moral judgment stages: A manual* (Humanities Press, N.Y., 1977) [cited in J. C. Westman, *Child advocacy: New professional roles for helping families*. (Free Press 1979), pages 87–88.

44. Grisso, T. and Pomicter, C. Interrogation of juveniles: An empirical study of procedures, safeguards and rights waiver. *Law and Human Behavior, 1,* (1977), pages 321–42 (study of 491 juvenile felony records over three year period) [cited in T. Grisso, "Children's consent in delinquency proceedings," in Melton, Koocher, and Saks (Eds.). *Children's competence to consent, supra* note 39, at page 136]; Grisso, T. *Juvenile's waiver of rights: Legal and psychological competence*. (Plenum 1981), page 191; Seeburger, R. and Wettick, R. *Miranda* in Pittsburgh: A statistical study. 29 *U. Pitt. L. Rev. 1* (1967) [cited in R. Lawrence, "The role of legal counsel in juveniles' understanding of their rights," *Juv. and Fam. Ct. Journal* (Winter 1983–84, p. 49).
45. Grisso. Children's consent in delinquency proceedings. *supra* note 65, at page 140; Grisso. *Juvenile's waiver of rights: Legal and psychological competence. supra* note 65, at page 192, 194; Lawrence, *supra* note 44, at page 52–54.
46. *Id.* at 56.
47. *Santosky v. Kramer,* 455 U.S. 745 (1982). *See also Quilloin v. Walcott,* 434 U.S. 246 (1978) [cited Justice Stewart's statement in his concurrence in *Smith v. O.F.F.E.R.,* 431 U.S. 816 (1977), to the effect that a state cannot constitutionally force the break-up of a natural family unit without a showing of parental unfitness].
48. *Parham v. J.R.,* 442 U.S. 584, 622 (1979) (Stewart, J., concurring).
49. *Pierce v. Society of Sisters,* 268 U.S. 510 (1925). *See also Meyer v. Nebraska,* 262 *U.S. 390 (1923); Wisconsin v. Yoder, 406 U.S. 205, 234 (1977); Parham, v. J.R., 442* U.S. 584, 603 (1979).
50. *Lassiter v. Dept. of Social Services,* 452 U.S. 18 (1981). New York and many states nonetheless provide counsel to parents facing child abuse or neglect charges by statute. *See, e.g.,* N.Y. Family Court Act § 262. However, the rights of parents to attorneys and the roles of those attorneys—indeed the rights to, and roles of attorneys for other long-term caretakers of children as well—is beyond the scope of this discussion.
51. *Wisconsin v. Yoder,* 406 U.S. at 233.
52. *Parham v. J.R.,* 442 U.S. at 603.
53. *Wisconsin v. Yoder,* 406 U.S. at 246.
54. *Parham v. J.R.,* 442 U.S. at 633 [citing Murdock, "Civil Rights of the Mentally Retarded: Some Critical Issues," 48 *Notre Dame L. Rev.* 133, 138 (1972); Vogel and Bell. The emotionally disturbed child as the family scapegoat. In *Modern Introduction to the Family* 412 (1968)].
55. *See generally,* Rodham, H. Children under the law. 43 *Harv.Ed.Rev.* 487–514 (1973). The classic example of this is a problem frequently encountered in New York City–that is, the situation that arises when a parent is faced

with eviction as an "undesirable tenant," because of the child's delinquent conduct.

56. Grisso, T. *Juveniles' waiver of rights. supra* note 65, at 190, 193; Lawrence, *supra* note 44, at page 54.
57. Grisso, T. and Ring, M. Parents' attitudes towards juveniles' rights in interrogation. 6 *Crim.Just and Beh.* 221–226 (1979). In Grisso, Juveniles' consent on delinquency proceedings. *supra* note 65, at page 137.
58. *See e.g., Matter of Gregory W.*, 19 N.Y.2d 55 (1966); *Matter of Michelet P.*, 70 A.D.2d 68 (2d Dept.1979); NY. Fam. Ct. Act §§ 305.2(3), 320.3, 341.2(3) McKinney's 1984).
59. *Lawyer Code of Professional Responsibility,* Ethical Consideration 7–13 (1978); American Bar Association, *Model Rules of Professional Conduct* § 3.8 (1983); American Bar Association Criminal Justice Standards Project, *Standards Relating to the Prosecution Function* § 1.1(a), (b), (c) (Approved Draft 198 __); Institute for Judicial Administration - American Bar Association Juvenile Justice Standards Project, *Standards Relating to Prosecution* § 1.1B (Approved Draft 1979).
60. *Lawyer's Code of Professional Responsibility,* Ethical Consideration 7–13 (1978).
61. *Id.,* Disciplinary Rule 7–103(A). American Bar Association Criminal Justice Standards Project, *op.cit.,* § 3.8(a); Institute for Judicial Administration - American Bar Association Juvenile Justice Standards Project, *op.cit.* § 4.3A (1).
62. *Lawyer's Code of Professional Responsibility, op.cit.,* Disciplinary Rule 7–103(B).
63. *In Re Winship,* 397 U.S. 358 (1970).
64. *See, e.g.* N.Y. Family Court Act § 350.4 (McKinney's 1984).
65. *See* note 20, *supra,* and accompanying text.
66. *Lawyer's Code of Professional Responsibility,* Ethical Consideration § 7–14.
67. 45 C.F.R. § 1340.14(g) (1984).
68. *See, e.g.,* N.Y. Fam. Ct. Act §§ 254, 254–a, 350.3(3) (McKinney's 1984).
69. President's Commission on Law Enforcement and the Administration of Justice, *The challenge of crime in a free society, task force report: Juvenile delinquency and youth crime.* (1967), p. 32.
70. *Ibid.*
71. Schinitsky, C. *op.cit,* page 25.
72. Silberman, C. *op.cit.,* page 365. *See also Report of Joint Legislative Committee on Court Reorganization* (McKinney's Session Laws 1962, p. 3431) ("These proceedings present special considerations, and lawyers must be familiar with social techniques to give truly effective representation.")
73. 387 U.S. at 36 [Emphasis supplied].
74. New York's statutory scheme, which predated and was cited in *Gault,* provided counsel in these types of cases as well, declaring that:

    Counsel is often indispensable to a practical realization of due process of law and may be helpful in making reasoned determinations of fact and proper orders of disposition. [New York Family Court Act § 241].

75. 387 U.S. at 38.
76. *Matter of Orlando F.,* 40 N.Y.2d 103, 112 (1976).
77. Shookhoff, A., *op.cit.,* p. 7.
78. Knitzer, J. and Sobie, M. *Law guardians in New York State: A study of the legal representation of children* (N.Y.S. Bar Assoc., 1984) at 55 [also cited in R. Cohen and M. McCabe, (Eds.). *Child sexual abuse* (Sup. Ct., App. Div., 1st Dept.; N.Y.S. Dept. of Social Services, 1985) at 102].

79. The Legal Aid Society Juvenile Rights Division, *Practice manual for law guardians*. 153–4 (1976); *see also* Cohen and McCabe, *op.cit.* at page 103.
80. *Lawyer's Code of Professional Responsibility,* Ethical Considerations §§ 7–3, 7–7 [emphasis supplied].
81. *Id.* at § 7–24.
82. *Id.* at § 7–11, 7–12. These mandates are reiterated as well in the American Bar Association's various standards applicable to lawyers. The American Bar Association's recently-approved *Model Rules of Professional Conduct* provide that, notwithstanding a client's disabilities, including age, "the lawyer shall, as far as reasonably possible, maintain a normal client-lawyer relationship with the client." Under the rules, the lawyer may seek the appointment of a separate guardian *ad litem* or take other protective action "only when the lawyer reasonably believes the client can not adequately act in the client's own interest." [§ 1.14(a), (b); Approved Draft 1983]. Similarly, the Institute for Judicial Administration-American Bar Association Juvenile Justice Standards Project, *Standards Relating to Counsel for Private Parties,* places emphasis upon advocacy of the client's wishes, where those can be determined. [§ 3.1; Approved Draft 1979]. In the absence of such a determination, the lawyer is advised to seek appointment of a separate guardian *ad litem* to substitute his judgment; where a guardian has not been appointed, the standards provide that:

    [T]he attorney may remain neutral concerning the proceeding, limiting participation to presentation and examination of material evidence or, if necessary, the attorney may adopt the position requiring the least intrusive intervention justified by the juvenile's circumstances. (*Id.*)

83. For elaboration on the defense function at each stage of a juvenile delinquency proceeding, including the requisites of dispositional representation, *see* Fink. *Dispositional and post-dispositional proceedings under the juvenile delinquency procedure code.* (Legal Aid Society, N.Y., 1985); Shookhoff. *loc.cit;* The Legal Aid Society, *op.cit.;* IJA-ABA Juvenile Justice Standards Project. *Standards Related to Counsel for Private Parties* (ABA Approved Draft 1979); Flicker. *Providing Counsel for Accused Juveniles* (Juvenile Justice Standards Implementation Project, June 1983); Knitzer and Sobie. *Law guardians in New York State: A study of the legal representation of children.* (N.Y. State Bar Assoc. 1984).
84. *See, e.g., Matter of Iris R., supra.*
85. Russel, A. and Trainor, C. *Trends in child abuse and neglect: A national perspective.* (American Humane Association, Denver, 1984).
86. Butz, *op.cit.,* page 1216.
87. *See generally, Matter of Apel,* 96 Misc. 2d 839, 844 (Fam. Ct. Ulster Co., N.Y. 1978); Besharov, D. When protecting children means seeking the dismissal of court proceedings. 20 *J.Fam. Law* 217, 235 (1981); Knitzer and Sobie, *op.cit.,* The Legal Aid Society, *op.cit.;* National Legal Resource Center for Child Advocacy and Protection. *Representing Children and Parents in Abuse and Neglect Cases* (American Bar Association 1980); Butz, *op.cit.;* Redeker, J. The right of an abused child to independent counsel and the role of the child advocate in child abuse cases. 23 *Villanova L. Rev.* 521–56 (1977–8).
88. A description of The Legal Aid Society's multi-disciplinary team approach can be found in "Clout and Credibility: A Powerful Combination for Lawyers and Social Workers," *Practice Digest,* vol. 7 #2, pages 13–16 (National Association of Social Workers, Fall, 1984). *See also* Silberman, *op.cit.,* page 365; Prescott, P. *The child savers* (1981). General discussions of the team

approach can be found in: Harris, J. and Bernstein, B. Lawyer and social workers as a team: Preparing for trial in neglect cases. 59 *Child Welfare* 469, (Sept./Oct. 1980); Stein, J. and Golick, T. Public legal programs: A team approach. In Perlmutter, F. *A design for social work practice.* (Columbia 1974); Scherrer, J. How social workers help lawyers. *Social Work* 279, (July 1976).

89. "Clout and Credibility," *id.* at 16.
90. *Ibid.*
91. National Association of Social Workers. *Code of ethics: Professional standards* (adopted 1979, effective July 1, 1980). *See generally,* Reamer, F. Ethical dilemmas in social work practice. *Social Work 31,* (Jan./Feb. 1983); Sloane, H. The juvenile court: An uneasy partnership of law and social work. 35 *Smith College Studies in Social Work 213,* (June 1965); Smith, A. The social worker in the legal aid setting: A study of interprofessional relationships. 44 *Social Services Review 155,* (June 1970).
92. Silberman, *op.cit.,* p. 364; B. Flicker. *Current policy issues: Providing counsel for accused juveniles* (American Bar Association 1983), p. 2.
93. Rubin, T., *op.cit.,* p. 5.
94. Knitzer and Sobie, *op.cit.,* pages 6–11.
95. *Ibid.*
96. *Id.* at 7.
97. *See, e.g.,* Kelly, R. and Ramsey, S. Do attorneys for children in protection proceedings make a difference?—A study of the impact of representation under conditions of high judicial intervention. 21 *J. of Fam. Law, 405* (1982–1983); Rubin, T. *loc.cit.;* Grisso, T. *Juveniles' waiver of rights: Legal and psychological competence, op.cit.,* p. 200–1; Platt, A. *The child savers: The invention of delinquency.* (2d Ed., 1977), pages 163–175; Keniston, K. *All our children: The American family under pressure.* (Carnegie Council on Children, 1977); Melton, G. *Legal reforms affecting children's youth services. supra* note 39, page 38.
98. *See* note 54, *supra.*
99. *See, e.g.,* Citizens Committee for Children of New York. *Lost opportunities: A study of the promise and practices of the department of probation's family court services in New York City.* (1982).
100. Silberman, *op.cit.,* page 334–5.
101. N.Y. Fam.Ct. Act. §§ 360.1(3), 360.2.
102. *Fare v. Michael C.,* 442 U.S. 707 (1979).
103. *Minnesota v. Murphy,* ___ U.S. ___, 104 S. Ct. 1136 (1984). *See also People v. Ronald W.,* 24 N.Y.2d 732 (1969).
104. IJA-A.B.A. Juvenile Justice Standards Project. *Standards relating to the juvenile probation function* (Approved Draft 1979).
105. Outstanding examples in New York City include the Euphrasian Residence and Staten Island Mental Health Service. *See* C. Silberman, *op.cit.,* pages 328–329.
106. N.Y. Family Court Act § 351.1.
107. *Lee v. County Court of Erie,* 27 N.Y.2d 432, *cert. denied* 404 U.S. 823 (1971); *Matter of Alexander L.,* 60 N.Y.2d 329 (1983); *but cf. Matter of Jose D.,* - N.Y.2d - (1985).
108. *Estelle v. Smith,* 451 U.S. 454 (1981).
109. Morse, S. and Whitebread, C. Mental health implications of the juvenile justice standards. In G. Melton (Ed.). *op.cit.* note 39 at pages 17, 25.
110. Strasburg, P. *Violent delinquents.* (1978). *See also* President's Commission on Law Enforcement and the Administration of Justice. *The challenge of crime in a free society.* (1967).

111. *See, e.g.*, Legislative Commission on Expenditure Review. *Impact of youth rehabilitation programs.* (Oct. 1982); New York State Division for Youth, Cohort Study. *A descriptive analysis of the post-release experience of a D.F.Y. discharge cohort: July, 1979-June, 1980.* (Fall 1984).
112. Silberman, C. *op.cit.*, at pages 330, 335. *See also Schall v. Martin,* 104 S. Ct. at 2427 (Marshall, J., dissenting).
113. Silberman, C. *op.cit.;* Finkenauer, J. *Juvenile delinquency and corrections: The gap between theory and practice.*(Academic Press 1984).
114. *See, e.g.*, Mayor's Task Force on Foster Care, Redirecting Foster Care, *op.cit.;* Children's Defense Fund. *Children without homes.* (1978); Fanshel, D. and Shinn, E. *Children in foster care.* (1978).
115. Adoption Assistance and Child Welfare Act of 1980, Public Law 96–272; 42 U.S.C. §§ 670–676; Child Welfare Reform Act of 1979, (New York Social Services Law § 409–a, *et. seq.*)
116. Fanshel, D. *Early findings from a study of families at risk known to the lower east side family union.* (Unpub. monograph, May 16, 1985).
117. N.Y. Family Court Act §§ 124, 141 (McKinney's 1983).
118. *Id.* at § 141. (Practice Commentary).
119. N.Y. Fam.Ct.Act § 144 (McKinney's 1983). *See also* N.Y.Fam.Ct.Act § 142 (McKinney's 1983); *N.Y. Rules of the Judicial Conference,* 22 N.Y.C.R.R. § 20.17 (1982).
120. *See* N.Y.Fam.Ct.Act. §§ 353.2 *et seq,* 355.1 *et seq.*, 360.1 *et seq.*, 756–759, 761 *et seq.;* Fink. *Dispositional and post-dispositional proceedings under the juvenile delinquency procedure code.* (Legal Aid Society 1985).
121. N.Y.Fam.Ct.Act. § 255 (McKinney's 1983). Additionally, in the District of Columbia, the Prevention of Child Abuse and Neglect was construed as a broad mandate for provision of housing to reunify a family. *In Re. D.I.*, Nos. N–269–81, N–339–81, N–340–81 (D.C. Super. Ct., Fam.Div., May 6, 1985); 11 FAM. L. RPTR. 1367–8 (June 4, 1985).
122. Silberman, C. *op.cit.*, page 318.
123. Allen, F. Criminal justice, legal values and the rehabilitative ideal. In A. and J. Goldstein (Eds.), *Crime, law and society.* (Free Press, 1971), page 280.

16
Juvenile Justice in Transition: An Industry Note

MICHAEL W. OSHIMA AND FRANCIS X. HARTMANN

Private-sector managers of large-scale industries often examine companies and their strategic environment in what is called an "industry note." While the content of such notes tends to vary somewhat, depending on the nature of the industry being analyzed, they generally include a description of the basic business of the company, its product lines, the market for its products, and the milieu in which it operates. Among the questions that these notes attempt to address are:

What are the essential characteristics of the business?
What does the company produce, and what functions do these products serve?
Who consumes these products? What other markets are available to the company?
Is the market for the products expanding or contracting? Why?
What are the company's major strengths and weaknesses? What are its distinctive competencies?
Who are the company's major competitors, and what are their respective strengths and weaknesses? What advantages does the company have over its competitors, and how can it best utilize those advantages?
What are the requirements for success in the industry? How do we measure success?
How is the strategic environment likely to change? In light of the social, political, and technological changes that are likely to occur, what strategies are available to the company? How can the company's distinctive competencies best be combined with the opportunities that are likely to emerge?

In this paper, we adopt the strategy of the industry note to examine the viability of the juvenile justice enterprise (the juvenile court and correctional facilities for youths). Like the authors of these notes, we describe the basic business of the enterprise, its product lines, the market for its products, and the milieu in which it operates. And, in our concluding section, we examine the issues that will shape the future of our business and determine the options that are available to it. Among our central concerns throughout is the question of whether we should substantially increase our investment in the enterprise in order to enhance its productive capacity or file for bankruptcy in an attempt to limit our losses.

There are many, no doubt, who will criticize the manner in which we have chosen to depict the courts. While we readily admit that there are problems with the analogy, we have chosen to pursue this course in the hope that such an analysis will provide new insights and provoke discussion. We do not require, then, that our readers accept our characterization of the juvenile court, but merely request that they ask themselves what kinds of questions such an analysis raises about the future of the court. With this in mind, let us turn to our discussion of the juvenile justice enterprise and its strategic environment.

The Basic Business

The problem of what to do with children who are in need of care and protection or whose conduct departs from societal norms is one which all countries share. Different countries have developed a wide range of enterprises to address this problem, each varying greatly in its mixture of public and private initiative, sponsorship, and control.

In the United States, the public enterprise that has had primary responsibility for dealing with youths in need of care, protection, rehabilitation, and control has been the juvenile court, along with the youth correctional facilities. For the past eighty years, this enterprise has been in the business of utilizing the coercive power and financial resources of the state to produce protected children, rehabilitated children, protection for the community, and the fulfillment of a sense of justice. The process by which this occurs (which is described more fully in the following pages) is depicted below in Figure 16.1.

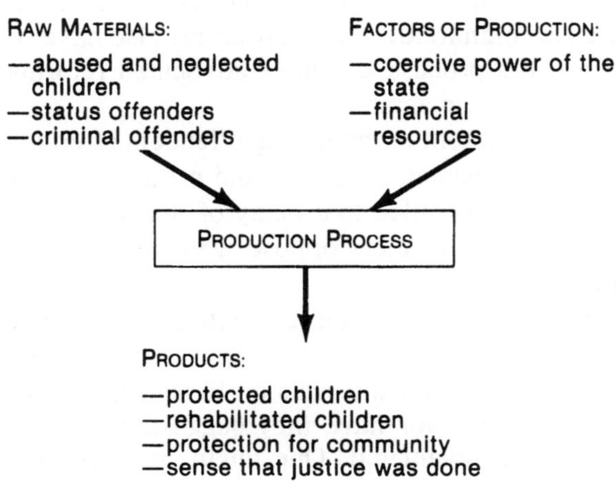

The juvenile justice enterprise, then, has a production process that is not unlike that of many other companies, one which involves the combination of raw materials with the factors of production. Yet, the enterprise is atypical in many respects. Chief among the differences between the juvenile justice enterprise and other businesses is the source of its charter: Whereas most companies come into existence through the matching of opportunities with entrepreneurial initiative, the juvenile justice enterprise has been created through the will of the legislature. Hence, not only is the juvenile justice enterprise regulated by legislation, but it owes its very existence to legislation. Moreover, all of the many forces that move government (e.g., political movements, interest groups, the media) also affect the enterprise, since legislation, reauthorization of funding, and the interpretation of the Constitution are the major means by which the charter is changed.

In recent years, the charter of the juvenile justice enterprise has come under increasingly close scrutiny by scholars, professional groups, government commissions, and the media. While the positions taken by these groups have been quite diverse, individuals within these groups generally can be divided into two major camps. First of all, there are those who believe that the basic business of the juvenile justice enterprise is that of providing "back-up socialization" (i.e., educating youths in their responsibilities as citizens when the primary means of instructing children—families and schools—have failed). The juvenile justice enterprise here stands primarily as a resource which can be used either to buttress families and schools in the process of socializing youths, or to take on primary responsibility for youths whom the families and schools appear to be unable or unwilling to help. As Thomas Bearrows (1984) notes, back-up socialization has been the traditional role of the juvenile court in the United States.

More recently, others have argued that the basic business of the court should be one of "doing justice." The courts, they contend, should be punishing offenders fairly (i.e., in a manner proportional to the seriousness of the offense committed). These observers also have sought to bring victims back into the process and have advocated reforms designed to make these victims whole again.

Yet, those who are intent on punishing offenders often forget the other side of doing justice—namely, the care and protection of those who are defenseless. It may be recalled that many of the substantive and procedural rights that these reformers oppose were granted to youths in the name of doing justice.

How well the juvenile courts and correctional facilities conduct their business is not really clear. It does not appear that the juvenile courts collect information at regular intervals on those aspects of performance that they can measure.[1] Nor have they suggested ways in which their performance might be evaluated. One might, perhaps, be able to gain some idea as to how well the enterprise is doing through such statistics as recidivism rates, proportion of abused children protected by the courts, number of dependency and neglect cases successfully disposed of by the courts, and number of foster home placements.

In recent years, there has been a growing sense that the juvenile justice enterprise has not been entirely successful in dealing with youths in need of care, protection, rehabilitation, and control. And recent legislative proposals (described in the next section) now threaten to put the juvenile court out of business by trimming its mandate and reducing its supply of raw materials. One might argue that these actions may be premature, for whatever the court's eventual fate may be, there will continue to be a need for a company or set of companies to protect children at risk and to deal with youths whose behavior does not conform to societal norms. Before we force the juvenile justice enterprise into bankruptcy, then, we should at least consider what the enterprise currently does and what it realistically can and cannot do.

Capitalization of the Business

The juvenile justice enterprise, like any other company, requires operating capital to carry out its business. For most businesses, this involves obtaining the necessary funds from capital markets—usually from banks. The juvenile justice enterprise differs from ordinary businesses, however, in that its financiers are not bankers *per se,* but state legislatures. And the capital that it requires consists not only of funds, but also of the mandate to exercise the authority of the state in individual cases.

As financiers of the juvenile justice enterprise, state legislators must be convinced that the business is a viable one and that its products are of value, at least to those who comprise the market (the general public). This is, in part, because the financiers are often held responsible for losses incurred by investors when businesses they have funded have failed. More than this, legislators can be voted out of office by the general public and, therefore, have to be somewhat responsive to public opinion. In this sense, the capital of the juvenile justice enterprise can also be seen as being derived from the body of ideas and values accepted as conventional wisdom by the public.

Because funding for the enterprise must be authorized by the legislature each year, opportunities to affect the capitalization of the business arise during each legislative session. During this time legislators may decide to change the level of funding for the enterprise or to stop it altogether. Legislators may also choose to redefine the charter of the business, adjust the flow of raw materials into the business, or change its operating principles. Since the decisions that the legislatures make in this regard are part of the political process, factors which influence political decision-making also affect the operation of the juvenile justice enterprise.

While traditional conceptions of the state often portray laws as reflections—albeit imperfect—of the will of the people, in practice interest groups can have a profound impact on the shape which legislation takes. Groups which have an obvious interest in legislation regarding juvenile justice include the police, juvenile court judges, probation officers, social workers, unions representing workers in the juvenile justice enterprise, "child-savers," and contractors who provide services to the business. Legislators depend very heavily upon these groups, in part because they generally know very little about the juvenile justice enterprise. Even those members serving on juvenile justice subcommittees in state legislatures have only limited access to information about the operation of the system. These groups provide up-to-date impressions of the general condition of the business. They also furnish the statistics that legislators use to make their own evaluation of the performance of the enterprise.

This is not to say that the public has little or no influence in the decision-making process. Many observers in fact regard recent legislation as a response to perceived public dissatisfaction with the juvenile court. A nationwide poll (Gallup 1978:872) has shown that only 6% of those surveyed felt that the juvenile courts were doing an excellent job in dealing with young people who violate the law. Forty-one percent, by contrast, suggested that the court was doing a poor job, and 37% thought that the court was doing only a fair job. While one must be cautious in linking recent legislation to such polls, the issue of when the legislatures will act on expressions of public dissatisfaction is one which will continue to affect planning for the juvenile justice enterprise.

The interest groups identified above, moreover, may vary considerably in their ability to affect legislation and in their viewpoints. The differences in opinion may, in some circumstances, be viewed as an asset, since it gives legislators the ability to take their own stand on issues affecting the business. It also gives those who have the clearest vision of what they wish to accomplish an opportunity to have a significant impact on juvenile justice legislation. At the same time, however, the differences in viewpoint give legislators no clear mandate for any particular course of action. Whether any consensus has developed on what the enterprise should look like and what it should be doing is a second issue which will have an impact on the juvenile justice enterprise's corporate strategy.

The Factors of Production

Productive resources. The juvenile justice enterprise is one of a number of cooperating companies which deal with youths in need of correction, protection, and/or supervision. The revenues that the enterprise receives from the state enable it to purchase a type of long-term care and supervision for youths which the enterprise would not otherwise be able to offer, given its limited resources. The care and supervision that the enterprise is able to provide youths through these other businesses is essential for rehabilitation, the protection of youths, and the protection of the community.

Beyond this, the juvenile justice enterprise also has behind it the coercive power of the state. We tend to see this coercive power most clearly perhaps in the denial of freedom through incarceration, but the enterprise also has used this power to remind youths of their responsibilities as citizens, to compel performance by youths (e.g., community service, enrollment in a counseling program) or by parents (in dependency and neglect cases), and to protect children (in some extreme cases, by removing youths from their natural parents and terminating parental rights).

Although there have been attempts to regulate and limit the use of this power in recent years with extensions of the rules of due process and changes in the enterprise's mandate, the court's mode of operation has always been largely reactive rather than proactive. This means that the business depends very heavily upon others to bring cases to its attention. The court has no real mechanism for acquiring raw materials on its own.

Raw materials. Three classes of children traditionally have comprised the raw materials with which the juvenile justice enterprise has had to work. These are: children at risk because of the behavior of others; children whose behavior, while not criminal, suggests that they might be headed for trouble; and children whose criminal behavior places the community at risk. The distinction among the groups is not always clear.

The first class of raw materials, children at risk because of the behavior of others, contains those who have been neglected or abused, or have received inadequate care from their parents or guardians. The care and protection of such youths fall squarely under the doctrine of *parens patriae,* and thus constitute one of the traditional functions of the juvenile court. In 1980, there were an estimated 152,500 such cases processed by the juvenile courts in the United States (Dahma *et al.* 1982:20).[2]

Status offenders (children at risk because of their own behavior) are those who have committed offenses which come to the attention of the court because of the age status of adolescents in our society. Youths who have committed such offenses technically are not prosecuted in courts as are adults. The state is expected to act in the best interest of the child to prevent further difficulties, and juvenile court judges are granted great latitude and discretion in case dispositions. In 1981, a total of 318,052 arrests were made for such offenses as underage drinking, curfew and loitering law violations, and running away from home (U.S. Department of Justice 1982:165).

The third class of youths, those charged with criminal offenses, is probably of greatest concern to law enforcement officials and the general public. Of special interest here are the violent offenders whose crimes—murder, forcible rape, aggravated assault, and burglary—generally receive the most attention in the mass media. Yet, this third category also includes those accused of serious property crimes (burglary, larceny, motor vehicle theft, and arson), as well as those who allegedly have committed the less serious Part II offenses (which range from disorderly conduct and vagrancy to forgery and counterfeiting and prostitution and commercialized vice). In 1985 there were a total of 72,552 arrests of youths under 18 years of age for violent crimes (17% of all arrests for such crimes), 582,323 arrests for serious property crimes (34% of all arrests for such crimes), and 754,886 arrests for all other offenses excluding underage drinking, curfew and loitering law violations, and running away from home (U.S. Department of Justice 1986:180).

Suppliers of raw materials. In some respects, the juvenile justice system resembles what Paul Hirsch (1972) has called "cultural industry systems." As with the production and distribution of fine art and popular culture, the processing of juveniles entails relationships among a complex network of organizations which both facilitate and regulate the production process. Cases must be "discovered" and brought to public attention by semi-autonomous agents before the raw material can be linked successfully to the production process. And since those agents have a number of alternatives for marketing their discoveries, it is important to gain their confidence and that of any others who can bring raw materials into the production system.

The most reliable supplier of raw materials to the juvenile justice enterprise has been the police. Law enforcement officials currently comprise the first major component of the juvenile justice system to deal with young offenders. The police also handle many noncriminal juvenile matters, like neglect and abuse cases. These agents probably provide most, if not all, of the raw material flowing into the courts. At the same time, the police also possess a great deal of discretionary power in deciding how to market their discoveries. Oxholm (1979:3) identifies no less than seven procedural alternatives available to officers: (1) outright release; (2) release and submission of a field interrogation report; (3) release to parents with official reprimand; (4) referral to another agency; (5) continued supervision; (6) referral to juvenile court without detention; and (7) referral to juvenile court with detention. In almost all cases, the police will contact the parents. The only exception is when the offense is a relatively minor one and a verbal reprimand is deemed sufficient.

Some observers have argued that the police have been losing confidence in the willingness of the courts to punish offenders. Police officers, like many private citizens, apparently feel that the courts let offenders off too easily, and that serious offenders are back on the streets much too quickly. If these observers are correct, then we might expect police officers to make fewer referrals to the juvenile courts than they did ten years ago. This is, in fact, not the case. Uniform Crime Report statistics show that a greater proportion of juvenile offenders taken into custody were referred to the juvenile courts in 1981 than in 1972. At the same time, fewer youths were being handled in the department and released. These changes may be a result of a decision on the part of many police agencies to concentrate on the more serious offenses; arrests for status offenses did drop somewhat during the ten-year period from 1972 to 1981, while the number of youths taken into custody for serious offenses rose. The changes also may reflect a growing realization that traditional police methods for dealing with youths are no longer as effective as they once were. Whatever the case may be, it appears that the police will continue to be reliable suppliers of raw materials to the juvenile courts.

Non-police agencies (e.g., schools, social service agencies, shelters) and individuals, on the other hand, have at least five options for marketing their discoveries. They may choose to: (1) refer to another agency outside the juvenile justice system; (2) refer to the court; (3) handle the case on their own; (4) do nothing; or (5) refer the matter to the police. We know of no national studies on the marketing practices of non-police agencies and individuals, but the literature suggests that referrals by these parties to the juvenile justice enterprise tend to be indirect—through the police.

Trends in the supply of raw materials. The estimated number of dependency and neglect cases showed no consistent trend during the 1970s; a marked increase (from 130,900 cases to 158,000) between 1971 and 1973 was followed by a drop (to 143,200) in 1975, a second sharp increase (to 162,900) in 1979, and another decline (to 152,500) in 1980. The number of cases involving status offenders, by contrast, appears to have dropped slightly during the ten-year period from 1972 to 1981; the number of arrests for underage drinking, curfew and loitering law violations, and running away from home fell at this time from 329,540 to 318,052, a 3.5% decline. Finally, the number of arrests for serious offenses (murder, forcible rape, robbery, aggravated assault, burglary, larceny, motor vehicle theft, and arson) shot up by 23% during the same period, from 521,563 in 1972 to 641,429 in 1981 (U.S. Department of Justice 1982:165; Dahma *et al.* 1982:20). The evidence, then, is somewhat inconsistent, but there does appear to have been an increase in the quantity of raw materials available to the juvenile justice enterprise. And if present trends continue, there probably would be an ample supply of these materials for many years to come.

A number of factors, however, threaten to limit the quantity of raw materials flowing into the enterprise. For one thing, the youth population is projected to decline during the 1980s; the Bureau of the Census now predicts that the number of youths between 10 and 19 years of age will drop by about 14.5 percent, from 39,402,600 in 1980 to 33,671,200 in 1990. What this means is that the rate of offending for this group would have to increase if the business were to be supplied at its current level through the 1980s (U.S. Department of Commerce 1983:12).

More significant, perhaps, are legislative and executive reforms which threaten to divert whole classes of raw materials from the juvenile justice enterprise. The impetus for the initial reforms came in 1967 when the President's Commission on Law Enforcement and Administration of Justice recommended that the "formal sanctioning system and pronouncement of delinquency . . . be used only as a last resort. In place of the formal system, dispositional alternatives to adjudication must be developed for dealing with juveniles . . . " (1968:220). Among the alternatives mentioned by the Commission were the decriminalization of status offenses and the diversion of youths from the juvenile court into public and private treatment programs.

Subsequent government commissions generally concurred with the President's Commission. In 1970, the U.S. Youth Development Delinquency Prevention Administration stated that its primary objective was to "divert youth away from the juvenile justice system" into alternative programs. The National Advisory Commission on Criminal Justice Standards and Goals also supported the President's Commission's findings, although the former took no position on status offenses. And in 1974 the passage of the Juvenile Justice and Delinquency Prevention Act made it clear that it was "the declared policy of Congress . . . to divert juveniles from the traditional juvenile justice system and to provide critically needed alternatives. . . ."

Partly as a result of these pressures for reform, status offenders in many states are no longer referred to as truants, curfew violators, or incorrigibles, but are now called "persons in need of supervision" (PINS), "children in need of supervision" (CHINS), and "minors in need of supervision" (MINS). Barry Krisberg and Ira Schwartz (1983) also suggest that the number of status offenders committed to institutions has declined.

Diversion programs, similarly, were implemented in full force as a result of the availability of new Federal funds for such initiatives. Many of these programs have proved difficult to evaluate (Gibbons and Blake, 1976), however, and the point has often been made that the transfer of cases from the juvenile court to the less-visible diversion programs increases the discretion of decision-makers and the coercive power of the state. We see the latter point most clearly, perhaps, in the net-widening effect: Where formerly the police simply counseled and released a youngster, they are now diverting him, a strategy that has served to expand the population of acted-upon offenders.

A number of other legislative reforms proposed in the 1970s called for harsher sentences for serious juvenile offenders. Among the reforms put forth at this time were proposals to lower the initial age of criminal court jurisdiction, exclude specific offenses from juvenile court jurisdiction (excluded offense provisions), and grant prosecutors more discretion in deciding when a given offender should be tried as an adult.

Some have argued that these recent legislative developments threaten to put the juvenile justice enterprise out of business by reducing its supply of raw materials. Others contend that the enterprise has been overworked through much of the 1960s and 1970s and that the possible reduction in the caseload of the business through diversion, decriminalization, and the drop in the youth population presents new opportunities for changes that might better enable the enterprise to realize its goals of rehabilitation and the protection of children. The issue is undoubtedly complex, yet both sides agree that the future of the enterprise is partly dependent on the type of raw materials with which it has to work. For the way in which the juvenile justice enterprise slices into the market of raw materials will affect both its basic business and its production process, if not the very survival of the enterprise itself.

The Production Process

Direct production. The production process of the juvenile court involves the combination of the coercive power and financial resources of the state with the raw materials. This process is generally comprised of at least three distinct stages: intake and classification, the adjudication hearing, and the disposition hearing.

1. *Intake and classification.* The production process begins when a youth is brought before the court on a petition alleging delinquency, dependency, or neglect. Any responsible adult—school officials, parents, neighbors—may initiate a petition calling for juvenile court action, although in practice most complaints are channeled through the police department. Many of the juveniles brought before the court, then, have already been through a police screening process and may already be in a detention facility or under informal supervision by police or probation officers.

Initial screening of cases brought to the court is usually done by an intake unit which consists of one or more probation officers. At this point, at least five disposition alternatives are available to the intake unit: outright dismissal, admonishment and dismissal, informal supervision by the probation staff, referral to a community agency, and formal action by the court. Many intake units prefer to handle youths in an informal manner so as to avoid the stigmatization and further delinquency that often results from formal contact with the courts. The National Center for Juvenile Justice estimates that approximately 792,400 delinquency cases (55% of the total) and 41,600 dependency cases (27% of the total) were processed informally by the juvenile courts in 1980 (Dahma *et al.* 1982:19, 23).

If the intake unit decides that further action is necessary, a formal petition may be filed with the court and a preliminary court hearing is scheduled. The purpose of the hearing is to decide whether the facts warrant further court action. At this point, the case may be dismissed unconditionally, dismissed with a suggestion for voluntary action, scheduled for an adjudicatory hearing, or transferred to criminal court. If the juvenile court elects to waive jurisdiction, the youth involved must be provided with the legal safeguards required by *Kent v. United States*—a hearing, right to counsel, right to see the court reports, and a written statement by the judge discussing the reasons for the waiver.

2. *Adjudicatory hearing.* At the adjudicatory hearing, the youth and witnesses are questioned about the alleged offense, the circumstances surrounding the case, and the facts that have been presented. The case may be dismissed at this hearing if there is insufficient evidence, or there may be a finding of neglect, dependency, or delinquency. If the latter occurs, it is entered in the record and a disposition hearing is scheduled for the youth.

Between the time of the adjudication hearing and that of the disposition hearing, a probation officer is responsible for preparing a detailed social history on the juvenile. This social history generally includes such information as family relationships, the amount of supervision the youth receives at home, school and community behavior problems, the circumstances regarding his difficulty, and the ability of his parents to provide supervision and guidance at home. Anyone who knows the juvenile can be questioned as part of this investigation. This information is later used by the judge to select the proper dispositional alternative for the youth.

3. *Disposition hearing.* After a judge has examined the social report, he may also question the parents or the probation officer who prepared the report to obtain information that may not have been part of the investigation. After considering all of the relevant facts in the case, the judge may: release the child to his parents; place the child on probation; commit the youth to a training school or other juvenile institution; place the child in a foster home; or make the child a ward of the court so that he can receive needed medical care or other supervision (in cases of neglect).

Officers of the court are responsible for seeing that the decision is carried out, and may be required to see the youth at regular intervals. Any action aside from dismissal results in continued court supervision.

In some states, responsibility for carrying out the court's decision rests with the youth authority, which arranges for services from social service agencies and group homes and which oversees the operation of public training schools and detention centers. These youth authorities, after diagnosis, can and often do alter the court disposition if they believe that a different placement or a shorter period of custody is more appropriate for a given youth. In such cases, then, the youth authority has ultimate authority to determine what is in the best interest of the child.

Technology. The juvenile court had its origins in a doctrine which called for a new kind of court for youths, one with new procedures, new personnel, and a therapeutic orientation. In this new court, early identification and treatment were to be more important than the issue of criminal culpability. Toward these ends, the new procedures were designed to provide individualized treatment and prevent the stigmatization of adjudicated youth.

As delinquency rates started to rise in the 1960s, however, legal scholars and social scientists began to take a closer look at the juvenile court. The informal proceedings were increasingly criticized as promoting procedural arbitrariness and "unbridled official discretion resulting in capricious decisions" (Handler 1965:10). Social scientists also admitted that while the intentions of the juvenile court were probably benign, research and development had not yet progressed to a stage at which the continued denial of basic constitutional rights could be justified. The role of the juvenile court, they argued, had been based on an assumption that the social sciences would provide the knowledge that would enable the judge to prescribe the proper remedy for the delinquent's anti-social tendencies. As Albert Cohen (1968:617) has pointed out, however, the

> failure of the juvenile courts to deliver on their promises goes back to causes that lie deeper than faulty institutional forms, incompetent and unqualified personnel, and meager resources. It goes back to the fact that despite the material progress of our knowledge about juvenile delinquency, we simply do not know enough to diagnose, predict, and prescribe for a very large proportion of offenders.

One result of these criticisms has been the constitutionalization of the juvenile court, through such U.S. Supreme Court decisions as *Kent v. United States,*[3] *In re Gault,* [4] and *In re Winship.*[5] These decisions extended to juveniles the right to counsel, right to confront and cross-examine witnesses, privileges against self-incrimination, right to a transcript of the proceedings, and right to appellate review. The criminal court standard of "proof beyond a reasonable doubt" replaced the civil court standard of "the preponderance of the evidence" in juvenile court hearings. And if the juvenile court wished to waive its jurisdiction over a particular youth, it was required to hold a hearing on the waiver, grant access for the juvenile's counsel to all information considered by the judge in the decision to waive, and state the reasons for the decision. There is as yet no right to trial by jury for juveniles,[6] but fourteen states now allow jury trials.

Along with these changes came a number of conflicting policy recommendations. One set of proposals, embodied in the report of the President's Commission on Law Enforcement and Administration of Justice (1968:223–225), suggested that youths be diverted whenever possible and that correctional programs be based in the community for all but the most dangerous criminals. On the basis of such recommendations, deinstitutionalization, diversion, and decriminalization have been pursued vigorously, with mixed results.

A second set of recommendations favored a return to the classical, punitive concept of justice (van den Haag 1975; Wilson 1975). Sentences here would be based not on social or psychological background, but rather on the seriousness of the offense and prior criminal history. Rehabilitation was not really a concern of these reformers; the goal was instead to incapacitate repeat offenders until they were in their thirties or forties.

While the latter set of recommendations has been applied more to adults than to children, it is beginning to appear with greater frequency in policies developed for youths. The state of Washington, for example, recently passed a determinate sentencing law for delinquents which stipulates that the only factors that authorities are supposed to take into account are age, prior offense history, and current offense, except in cases in which "manifest injustice" would occur.[7] The social histories which traditionally have been used by the juvenile courts now rank very low on the list of factors to be considered in determining sentence.

Disposition technologies also have been changing in recent years. Prior to 1967, treatment methods for youths coming under the jurisdiction of the juvenile justice enterprise were not significantly different from those applied to adult offenders. Juvenile justice legislation did require that children be separated from adults at all stages of the justice system. Yet, the training schools and other correctional facilities established for youths were not different in kind from those used by adults.

In 1967, however, the President's Commission recommended that alternatives to confinement be explored (1968:223–227). Partly as a result of this recommendation, as well as the availability of Federal funds, the number of group homes grew rapidly during the early 1970s. In mid-1975, there were a total of 1,046 such facilities in operation. This represented a 150% increase over the number in operation in 1971, and made group homes nearly three times more numerous than any single type of juvenile institution in 1975 (U.S. Department of Justice 1979).

The more traditional training schools, however, also grew between 1971 and 1975, though not quite so rapidly. The number of public training schools rose by 2% in 1975, after declining 3% from 1971 to 1974; and private training schools increased by 7% between 1974 and 1975 (U.S. Department of Justice 1979).

As of mid-1975, group homes and halfway houses comprised about 22% of the 874 non-Federal public facilities in the United States and 67% of the 1,277 private facilities. Training schools, by contrast, made up 21 percent of the public facilities and only 5% of the private institutions. Other significant juvenile institutions were detention centers, shelters, reception centers, and diagnosis centers (which accounted for 45% of the public facilities and 5% of those in the private sector), and ranches, farming camps, and farms (which comprised 12% of the public facilities and 23% of the private ones). The facilities together housed a total of 76,576 individuals (3% of whom were not juveniles) and spent nearly $868 million in 1975—two-thirds by public institutions and one-third by private facilities (U.S. Department of Justice 1979).

Organization and Management

Up to now, we have been focusing on the juvenile courts and on correctional facilities designed specifically for youths. The juvenile justice system, however, is also said to include the police, social workers, and private group homes and halfway houses for youths. Other agencies like the schools and related social service agencies can be considered part of the system as well, although these function mostly as sources of referral to the police or the juvenile court.

There is a tendency sometimes to think of these various agencies as comprising a monolithic organization which we have developed for youths in need of care and supervision. Yet, the juvenile justice system in the United States is really only a loosely articulated set of sub-systems. This is, in part, because the various agencies belong to different branches of government. The probation officers and juvenile courts, for example, belong to the judicial branch, while the police and correctional facilities (as well as the youth authority, which in some states, administers the latter) generally belong to the executive branch. Their placement in different branches of government means that they belong to different chains of command and answer to different governmental imperatives.

The juvenile justice system, moreover, has no chief executive. Nor, for that matter, are the sub-systems arranged in a hierarchical order. What this means is that decisions in one sub-system cannot be directly and effectively enforced in others by administrative or other organizational sentences. The law itself, rather than organizational hierarchy, generally governs such relationships (Reiss and Black 1967).

All of this is not to say, of course, that there is no cooperation among sub-systems in the juvenile justice system. Each sub-system is, in fact, dependent upon the others, since the sub-systems are so organized that the outputs of one become the inputs of another. Professional ideologies formed around the principle of helping youths in need of care and supervision also serve to hold the system together in the absence of organizational hierarchy. Yet, the lack of organizational hierarchy and the differences in administrative responsibility do inhibit cooperation and present a challenge to those who would like to reform the system.

The Competition

There are at least two major competitors for the business of the juvenile justice enterprise. The first of these, social service agencies and community-based treatment facilities, presently receive youths who have been diverted from the formal adjudicatory process, as well as those who have been referred by the juvenile court for the purpose of rehabilitation. Adult courts, on the other hand, are processing increasing numbers of young criminal offenders who have been transferred from juvenile court jurisdiction.

We know of no national studies or statistical reports which provide estimates of the number of youths diverted each year from the juvenile courts, though the Uniform Crime Report for 1985 (U.S. Department of Justice 1986:240) does indicate that 22,694 (or 1.9%) of the youths taken into custody by the police during that year were referred to welfare agencies. National statistics on judicial waivers are also difficult to obtain. In 1978, the most recent year for which we have statistics, over 12,300 youths were bound over to adult court as a result of waiver provisions, and an additional 250,000 sixteen- and seventeen-year-olds in twelve states were tried as adults because of lower ages in criminal court jurisdiction (Hamparian *et al.* 1982).

While some observers claim that present trends in diversion and waivers to adult courts threaten to put the juvenile court out of business, it is not altogether clear that the competitors of the juvenile justice enterprise have captured the confidence of the general public. Although social service agencies are probably better equipped than are the juvenile courts to implement the technology gained from the social sciences, the public appears to be somewhat leery of the promises of rehabilitation that the social service agencies offer. Surveys have indicated that the public also harbors doubts about criminal courts' willingness to give offenders the punishment they deserve. Gallup Poll surveys in 1965, 1968, and 1969, for example, show increasing dissatisfaction with the leniency of the courts; 60% of those surveyed in 1965 and 75% in 1969 felt that the courts were not dealing harshly enough with criminals (Gallup 1972:1962, 2108, 2182).

Many of these observers fail to note, moreover, that adult courts are already overwhelmed with their present caseload, and prisons already filled beyond capacity. And while it is true that the adult courts have the authority to hand out much longer sentences than the juvenile courts, it is by no means clear that the former will in fact exercise this authority. In a comprehensive, nationwide study, Donna Hamparian and her associates (1982:228) found that roughly three-fourths of the juveniles tried in adult courts in 1978 received sanctions which juvenile courts could have handed out. Approximately one-half of the youths tried in adult courts that year were ordered to pay fines and were put on probation, while an additional one-fourth received maximum sentences of one year or less.

The adult courts, then, on the average, were not punishing young offenders more severely than were the juvenile courts; criminal court dispositions differed from those of the juvenile courts primarily in the fact that the former became part of a record which was not subject to the same provisions of confidentiality as those of the juvenile court.

Lastly, although criminal courts, juvenile courts, and social service agencies all have the power to coerce, the juvenile courts are able to use this power more advantageously than their competitors. The juvenile courts, for one thing, have fewer due process requirements than do the adult courts and can process a greater percentage of their cases informally, thereby avoiding the stigmatization of the offender which usually attends the process of adjudication. And while social service agencies do have the power to withhold resources—the provision of which can, in principle, be tied to good conduct—they do not have as broad a mandate to compel performance or to change a child's living situation.

Given the public's lukewarm support for the competition, as well as the apparent weaknesses of this competition, it does not appear that the demise of the juvenile court is as imminent as some observers might suggest. This is not to say, of course, that involuntary bankruptcy is completely out of the question for the juvenile court; legislators may choose to ignore the weaknesses of the competition or may seek to remedy these by passing new laws to limit judicial discretion in criminal court sentencing and by increasing the level of funding to the adult correctional system. The above discussion does suggest, however, that one cannot simply assume that present trends will in fact continue or that the demise of the juvenile court is indeed a foregone conclusion.

Conclusion: Strategic Issues and Scenarios

As one surveys the literature on the juvenile justice enterprise, there appears to be mounting evidence that the business is in great danger of sliding into bankruptcy, and that the 1980s may witness the demise of the juvenile court as we know it. The enterprise, it is said, has lost the confidence of consumers (the general public) who see it as unable or unwilling to deal adequately with serious offenders. And the erosion of the enterprise's mandate threatens to restrict seriously the quantity of raw materials flowing into the court. Under these circumstances, it is difficult to imagine how the business can continue to function.

Yet, as we mentioned above, it does not appear that the competition has captured the confidence of the consumers. Given demographic trends, moreover, one might argue that we may be abandoning the juvenile justice enterprise at a time when we need it most. Census statistics show that the percentage of American children under 18 years of age living in single-parent households increased from 11.8 to 17.1 between

1970 and 1976. And in 1984, more than half (51.8%) of all black families, and 16.5% of all white families, were headed by a single female parent. As normal household and support activities (including holding down a job) increasingly become the responsibility of a single parent, one may find growing numbers of mothers or fathers with less free time to devote to the care and supervision of children.

On the basis of such developments, one can construct a number of scenarios, ranging from foreclosure of the enterprise and declaration of bankruptcy to the resurgence and expansion of the business. One might imagine a situation, for example, in which there is no juvenile court: youths charged with criminal offenses are handled by adult courts, status offenders (or youths headed for trouble) are sent to social service agencies and community-based treatment facilities, and dependent children are referred to welfare agencies. Alternatively, one might picture a strong court which not only makes determinations of delinquency and suggests proper treatment, but also seeks to impart moral values and takes a leading role in coordinating the juvenile justice system. The reader can probably construct several intermediate scenarios.

How the enterprise will look in the future is often said to depend on how legislators and other decision-makers choose to address a number of issues. These issues include: training of personnel; staffing levels; adequacy of funding; the need for better record-keeping; fear of crime; the needs of single-parent families; and youth employment.

Beyond these, one might argue that the choice of an appropriate strategy for the juvenile justice enterprise will depend very heavily on how we answer the following questions:

1. What is the distinctive competence of the juvenile justice enterprise? What does the business do now that sets it apart from its competitors, and what will it know how to do in the near future?

2. Which idea or combinations of ideas could command widespread support? Where can the enterprise draw its legitimacy and authority? One must be careful here to distinguish between transient fads and durable ideas. As Lloyd Ohlin (1983) cautions, "The process of change has a rhythmic character." Although the enterprise is presently being shaped by "those who believe that the traditional system of punishment can be fine-tuned to control offenders by increasing the predictability and certainty of punishment," the public may be unwilling to tolerate the level of repression that would be necessary to attain the type of crime control that the public presently desires.

3. What attractive public purpose could the juvenile court serve?

After examining these questions, we may still decide to declare the business bankrupt and liquidate our remaining assets. Alternatively, we may decide to work with different combinations of raw materials. Whatever the case may be, it is important that our decision be an informed one.

It is our hope that this discussion will produce such an informed basis for plotting future strategies for the juvenile court and for youth correctional facilities.

Endnotes

1. Only a few states such as Utah, Pennsylvania, and Florida have detailed information systems reporting on the flow of youths from arrest to juvenile court disposition, and even these data bases are relatively new and not easily adapted for research purposes.
2. It should be noted that a dependency and neglect case may require periodic reviews by the court over a number of years but is only counted once in the yearly totals—during the year of the court's first disposition of the case (Dahma *et al.* 1982:9).
3. 383 U.S. 541 (1966).
4. 387 U.S. 1 (1967).
5. 397 U.S. 358 (1970).
6. In *McKeiver v. Pennsylvania,* 403 U.S. 528 (1971), the Supreme Court held that the due process clause of the Fourteenth Amendment as applied to juvenile court proceedings did not require the right to trial by jury.
7. "Title 13, Juvenile Court and Juvenile Delinquents." *Revised Code of Washington,* 1975.

References

Bearrows, T. R. (1984). The juvenile court: Philosophy and jurisprudence. Paper prepared for Executive Session on the Juvenile Justice System, Harvard University, 26–28 January.

Cohen, A. K. (1968). An evaluation of *Gault* by a sociologist. *Indiana Law Journal, 43* (Spring) pp. 614–618.

Dahma, L. L., Snyder, H. N. and Sullivan, D. P. (1982). *Juvenile court statistics—1980.* Pittsburgh: National Center for Juvenile Justice.

Danzinger, S., and Gottschalk, P. (1985). *How have families with children been faring?* Prepared for the Joint Economic Committee of Congress.

Flanagan, T. J., van Alstyne, D. J. and Gottfredson, M. R. (Eds.). (1982). *Sourcebook of criminal justice statistics—1981.* Washington, D.C.: U.S. Department of Justice, Bureau of Justice Statistics.

Gallup, G. H. (1978). *The Gallup poll: Public opinion 1972–1977.* Wilmington, Del.: Scholarly Resources, Inc.

Gallup, G. H. (1972). *The Gallup poll: Public opinion 1935–1971.* New York: Random House.

Gibbons, D. C., and Blake, G. F. (1976). Evaluating the impact of juvenile diversion programs. *Crime and Delinquency, 22* (October) pp. 411–420.

Hamparian, D. M., Estep, L. K., Muntean, S. M., Priestino, R. R., Swisher, R. G., Wallace, P. L. and White, J. L. (1982). *Major issues in juvenile justice information and training. Youths in adult courts: Between two worlds.* Washington, D.C.: U.S. Department of Justice, Office of Juvenile Justice and Delinquency Prevention, National Institute for Juvenile Justice and Delinquency Prevention.

Handler, J. F. (1965). The juvenile court and the adversary system: Problems of function and form. *Wisconsin Law Review* (Winter) pp. 7–51.

Hirsch, P. M. (1972). Processing fads and fashions: An organization-set analysis of cultural industry systems. *American Journal of Sociology, 77* (January) pp. 639–659.

Krisberg, B., and Schwartz, I. (1983). Rethinking juvenile justice. *Crime and Delinquency, 28* (July) pp. 333–364.

Ohlin, L. E. (1983). Rethinking juvenile justice policy and research. *Crime and Delinquency, 29* (July) pp. 463–472.

Oxholm, C., III. (1979). The juvenile court: Dysfunctional justice for dysfunctional behavior. Paper submitted to the Workshop II Committee, John F. Kennedy School of Government, Harvard University, 18 April.

President's Commission on Law Enforcement and Administration of Justice. (1968). *The challenge of crime in a free society*. New York: E. P. Dutton & Co.

Reiss, A., Jr. and Black, D. J. (1967). Interrogation and the criminal process. *Annals of the American Academy of Political and Social Science, 374* (November) pp. 47–57.

Trojanowicz, R. C. (1978). *Juvenile delinquency: Concepts and control.* (2nd ed.). Englewood Cliffs, N. J.: Prentice-Hall, Inc.

U.S. Department of Commerce, Bureau of the Census. (1983). *Provisional projections of the population of states, by age and sex: 1980 to 2000.* Current Population Reports, Series P-25, No. 937. Washington, D.C.: U.S. Government Printing Office.

U.S. Department of Commerce, Bureau of the Census. (1978). *Characteristics of american children and youth: 1976.* Current Population Reports, No. 66, Series P-23. Washington, D.C.: U.S. Government Printing Office.

U.S. Department of Justice, Federal Bureau of Investigation. (1982). *Crime in the United States—1981*. Washington, D.C.: U.S. Government Printing Office.

U.S. Department of Justice, Federal Bureau of Investigation. (1986). *Crime in the United States—1985*. Washington, D.C.: U.S. Government Printing Office.

U.S. Department of Justice, Law Enforcement Assistance Administration. National Criminal Justice Information and Statistics Service (1979). *Children in custody: A report on the juvenile detention and correctional facility census of 1975*. No. SD-JD-4F. Washington, D.C.: U.S. Government Printing Office.

van den Haag, E. (1975). *Punishing criminals*. New York: Basic Books.

Wilson, J. Q. (1975). *Thinking about crime*. New York: Basic Books.

Section VI
The Organization of the Juvenile Justice System: Assuming Responsibility for Children in Trouble

17 Classifying Juvenile Dispositions

SAUL N. WEINGART

Introduction

As a child makes his way through the juvenile justice system, he encounters a number of points at which his case may be resolved. If the child misbehaves on a public street, a police officer may warn him and send him off. School officials may refer a truant to a social service agency or a private practitioner for counseling. As the child penetrates further into the system, he may come into contact with a police diversion program or a youth service bureau. Designed to spare the child from the trauma or stigma of justice system contact, voluntary participation in one of these programs terminates prosecution. Even at juvenile court intake, intake or probation officials may recommend diversion or informal adjustment rather than full juvenile court proceedings.

Full court proceedings have two stages. The first is the adjudicatory hearing, in which a juvenile court judge decides if a child is a delinquent, a person or child in need of supervision (PINS/CHINS), or a victim of abuse or neglect. If a youth is so adjudicated, the juvenile court judge next holds a dispositional hearing. In most states, judges conduct dispositional hearings informally, under relaxed rules of evidence. To dispose of the case, the court chooses among a set of placement alternatives, or *dispositions*.

To describe a diamond (and thereby to distinguish it from other diamonds) one assesses its weight, clarity, and shape—its relevant dimensions. Similarly, one both describes a disposition and distinguishes it from other dispositions by evaluating how the disposition ranks along the relevant dimensions. For diamonds, the relevant dimensions are few and unambiguous. Dispositions, learning and residential programs with complicated and confusing human interactions, possess an enormous number of potentially relevant dimensions.

Practitioners and policymakers usually describe juvenile dispositions in terms of only one or two dimensions. The most common dimension describes its degree of secure care. For example, New York State's Division for Youth describes its system of disposition alternatives as a range extending through seven levels of care from secure, limited secure, non-community-based, community-based homes and centers, and foster care/alternative programs. Programs at the secure end of the scale have locks and razor ribbon. Limited secure programs are institutions like training schools. Noncommunity-based programs are camps and rural youth centers. Community-based facilities include foster and urban group homes. Level of secure care corresponds so closely with type of facility that one may use them interchangeably.

Security corresponds with clientele as well as facility. Secure programs hold tough delinquents who have committed serious and repeat offenses and are experienced in the juvenile justice system. A juvenile's offense record and his propensity to violence decline with the security rating of the facility. At the other end of the spectrum, noncommunity-based or community-based programs hold clients with limited or no criminal experience. They contain a large percentage of PINS or neglected youths.

Is "level of secure care" an adequate description to characterize and distinguish among dispositions? Does it capture the important aspects of dispositions, reflecting their mode of operation and effect? The conclusion of this chapter is that it is not sufficient. Selective attention implies selective inattention. In juvenile dispositions, attention to level of security or to its analogs, facilities and clientele, cause one to miss important pieces of the picture. The task of the following pages is to lay out all the dimensions that may be relevant to describing dispositions and to show how a broader scheme provides additional insights into dispositions, a better language to describe them, and implications for improving their design.

Dimensions of Dispositions

Characteristics of the Facility

The first important dimension of a disposition is the set of characteristics which describe the program's facility—its physical plant.

One attends readily to characteristics of facilities. They include the size, age, and character of the buildings, how well they are maintained, whether they have locks and bars, where they are located, and if they have adequate facilities for academic or vocational education, athletics, or other activities.

Perhaps because buildings and grounds are easy to see and describe, or because administrators must account for them in executive budgets, corrections reports devote considerable space to describing characteristics of facilities under their control. This is misleading. Observing the façade of a building permits one to infer only so much about what goes on inside. Similarly, an inventory of a program's capital plant tells one relatively little about how the program actually operates.

Character of the Client Population

The character of a disposition is also determined in part by the composition of the resident population (McEwen, 1976). This occurs because the youth subculture affects the operation of a program. And the composition of the resident population in part determines the youth subculture.

Some community-based programs manage the inmate subculture by granting residents responsibility for program operation, equalizing the status of youth and staff, and strengthening staff supervision of youths' activities. This strategy helps to create an inmate culture consonant with the honest, open, and therapeutic aspirations of these programs. Observers of institutional programs, on the other hand, find the inmate subculture characteristic of traditional penal institutions. Inmate solidarity confounds staff efforts toward rehabilitation or therapy, and street values like toughness, violence, and machismo predominate.

Among all programs, inmate cultures derive in part from the program itself, and in part from the attributes of the juveniles comprising the resident population. Older youths, youths with extensive (especially serious or violent) prior records, and youths committed under the auspices of the youth authority as delinquent contribute to the traditional, negative inmate subculture more than do younger, first-time, and voluntarily-admitted youths.

Since the attributes of youths who are already in a program are important determinants of the youth subculture there, and the youth subculture, in turn, affects the ability of program administrators and staff to create and manage a peaceful, humane, and therapeutic environment, judges and program managers can have a profound impact on the nature of these programs by the way they assign youths to them. No doubt judges already take into account the kinds of youths currently enrolled in a program when making disposition decisions (as in "We can't put him there; he'll get eaten alive."). A strategy of targeting certain kinds of youths to certain programs can, over time, change the character of the programs. An interesting implication is that dispositions stratify according to the badness of their residents. The judge's dilemma is this: sending good kids to bad places makes the bad places more therapeutic, but takes a toll on the good kid pioneers. But as programs accept more delinquents and less status offenders, there are fewer and fewer well-behaved youths available to leaven the mix. Does this mean that client populations will get meaner and meaner and that judges will become even more reluctant to place milder cases?

Attributes of the Program

Programs vary along many more dimensions than do facilities or populations. Unlike facilities or populations, they also have dimensions which are particularly hard to describe, much less measure, because they are a series of activities, performed in some organized fashion, having some meaning or substantive content. For example, an alternative education program for delinquents imparts substantive information about history, mathematics, English and so forth to its students. It does so in an organized manner: administrators manage personnel, scheduling, budgetary, and support needs; teachers plan lessons in accord with scheduled responsibilities; counselors attend classes and provide therapy in a regular, orderly way. Absent either substantive content (education) or organization (schedules, administration) and the program could not endure (Katz and Kahn, 1966).

It is useful to think of programs as consisting of two types of dimensions. The first type are dimensions that constrain a youth's freedom to do as he pleases. They build a box around the child that limits his autonomy. The second type helps the youth to make sense of, to understand, or to rationalize the constraints imposed by the first type. The more convincing the rationale, the less onerous the constraints. Legitimacy is usually measured from the point of view of the child. It is also meaningful from the perspective of society which worries about whether the grounds for restriction of liberty are fair and just.

There are three dimensions or ways that programs constrain youths' autonomy. First, programs constrain children by regulating the amount of time they must maintain *program contact*. The programs demanding highest contact are secure residential programs in which virtually all a youth's time is encompassed within the confines of the program. A group home, since it allows greater community contact, is less constraining. At the far end of the range are programs like probation which require youths to maintain only minimal contact with the program.

The second way that programs constrain youths is by their level of *supervision*. Programs high in supervision have high staff-resident ratios, employ qualified and experienced staff, allow little unscheduled time, and provide individualized attention. They are "all over" their charges, in terms of both time and intensity of supervision. The third way programs constrain youths is by imposing *obligations* on them. Obligations include the duty to participate in group activities, not to fight, to follow the rules, to take advantage of treatment opportunities, to keep one's room clean, and so forth. Demanding obligations, especially combined with high levels of both supervision and program contact, confine a youth's sphere of autonomy to a matchbox.

A youth's discomfort in a program is attenuated by his ability to rationalize the harshness and constrictiveness of the program (Barnum, 1984). Like weight and counter-weight, an otherwise close or suffocating program is more tolerable if its demands make sense to the youth. Demands which make sense are those which the youth perceives as legitimate or believable. Presumably, a legitimate program commands a youth's attention and understanding, and modifies behavior more readily than a program which is perceived as phony or artificial.

There are four dimensions or ways that programs gain legitimacy. First, programs providing a high level of *investments and amenities* have a claim to legitimacy. Investments include academic and vocational education, counseling, and therapy—all of which serve to increase a youth's human capital in order for him to develop the skills necessary to succeed. Amenities, like the food, shelter, and medical care a youth receives while in a program, help to provide a comfortable enough environment so that youths will take advantage of the available investment opportunities. A youth may feel that a restrictive program is less onerous if he believes that the investments and services he receives are important and worthwhile.

A program's *philosophy* is a second way to enhance its legitimacy. The philosophy of a program—its attitude toward community contact, its sanction of residents' participation in management of the program, its equalization of relationships among staff, and between staff and residents, and whether it feels comfortable and family-like or austere and hospital-like—is important for creating a culture which engages and motivates youths to assume responsibility for themselves and for the program (McEwen, 1978).

Third, the *conditions of participation* under which a youth enters a program help him to legitimate the burdens of program participation. Did a judge commit him? Was his case informally adjusted? Did he voluntarily participate? A voluntary admit is probably better able to rationalize his loss of autonomy than someone committed involuntarily.

Legitimacy is, of course, subjective. In general, a program seems legitimate if it fits a participant's expectations of fairness or balance. The concept of legitimacy introduces the idea that programs are more than what they "are"; they are also what they "mean." Balancing constraints on autonomy with legitimacy illustrates that programs are more than the physical sum of the pieces that make them up. Since programs not only exist, but mean something as well, one must consider who they have meaning for besides their youthful charges. The audience who is interested in youth dispositions includes legislatures, victims, communities, the person a troubled youth will become ten years hence, as well as the youth today. All these actors care about youth programs. They care about all the dimensions listed above as do the youths, but they also care about the *auspices* under which a program operates: is it public, private for-profit, private not-for-profit, or "spontaneously" community-based (like the firehouse that adopts a youth)? The auspices under which a program operates, while it may be irrelevant or invisible to a youth immersed in the program, has important implications for the interested program overseers.

TABLE 17.1 Dimensions of Dispositions

1. Facility
2. Client population
3. Program
   a. Program contact
   b. Supervision
   c. Obligations
   d. Investments and amenities
   e. Philosophy
   f. Conditions of participation
   g. Auspices

TABLE 17.2

			Constraint		
	Facility	Client population	Program contact	Supervision	Obligations
Juvenile Institution					
Training school	large, isolated	older, serious	high	low	low
Secure facility	size varies, isolated	older, serious	high	high	very low
Medical/psychiatric hospital	large, isolated	psychologically or physically ill or addicted	high	high	low
Other Traditional Programs					
Probation	own home in community	not applicable	low	low	low
Foster home	comfortable home in community	younger, less priors, less JDs	medium	very high	high
Ranch	fewer facilities, rural, isolated	medium age and experience	high	medium	high
Community-based Programs					
Group home	comfortable home in community	wide range	medium	high	high
Social services	own home, social service facilities	wide range, more voluntary	low	low	medium
New Alternatives					
Restitution	own home in community	not applicable	low	low	medium
Wilderness experience	wilderness	generally younger, less experienced	high	very high	very high

Taking Inventory

There are several ways that practitioners group dispositions in order to discuss them conveniently. A somewhat arbitrary but conventional breakdown is given below. Dispositions are classified into five sets: juvenile institutions, medical/psychiatric hospitals, other traditional placements, community-based programs, and new alternatives. For each set, the program is described in conventional terms, and then analyzed using the dimensions described in the previous section. Program dimensions are emphasized, especially the balance of constraining and legitimating program features, in order to illustrate the added insight of program dimensions over more conventional characteristics like facility or client population. The chart below will serve as a guide.

Legitimacy			
Investments and amenities	Philosophy	Conditions of participation	Auspices
medium-low	closed, unequal	court	public
high	closed, unequal	court	public
high	closed	court, informally adjusted, voluntary	private
low	open	court	public
high	open, participatory, equal	court informally adjusted, voluntary	publicly sponsored, privately run
medium	closed, some equal and participatory	court	public
high	open, participatory, equal	court informally adjusted, voluntary	public and private
medium-high	open, participatory	court, informally adjusted, voluntary	public and private
low	open	court, informally adjusted, voluntary	public
low	open, participatory equal	court, informally adjusted, voluntary	private

Juvenile Institutions

The term juvenile institution brings to mind the horrors of youth prisons: abusive, custodial, prolonged, inhumane treatment of children, many of whom committed only minor or status offenses. Though youth prisons have become largely a bad memory, institutions live on.

The defining characteristics of an institution are few. Institutions—including adult prisons, universities, hospitals, as well as institutions of juvenile justice—are large, residential, bureaucratically organized, and isolated (Goffman, 1961; Coates, Miller, Ohlin, 1978). Institutions are also easy to identify because they consist of an extensive physical plant. A large, isolated residential organization, bureaucratically organized and administered, requires facilities for residence, management, and services.

Despite these common characteristics of institutions, one finds much variation with respect to purpose, scale, and effect. Indeed, there is enormous variety among the subset of institutions which exist only within the juvenile justice system. Training schools and secure facilities are the most common examples, together representing 13 percent of all dispositions made in 1977 (Black and Smith, 1981).

Almost every state has at least one *training school*. Training schools hold youths who have a variety of personal and behavioral problems, including aggressiveness, neuroses, and drug dependency. Many of these youths have had substantial contact with the juvenile justice system and have been found guilty of criminal offenses. Training schools hold about one hundred residents. The youths are often housed in dormitory-like cottages with a dozen or so residents in each. Residents enroll in an academic or vocational program. Though some training schools provide counseling, many are custodial rather than rehabilitative. The relationship between custodial and treatment staff is often tense, and strong negative inmate cultures frequently subvert treatment efforts. Training schools have changed over the past fifteen years. There are less of them, and they house fewer youths. Few training schools contain youths who have committed no serious offense. In fact, some training schools look suspiciously like the community-based programs to be discussed later (Trojanowicz and Morash, 1983, ch. 7; McEwen, 1978; Edelman, 1976).

Not so in the case of *secure facilities*. Secure facilities holding juveniles represent the end of the line: lock-up. Secure facility residents are severely violent, self-destructive, incorrigible, and unmanageable youths, often transferred from training schools, who could not function without threat to themselves or others. Since the residents are so very difficult to handle, the programs are intense, individualized, but often fruitless. Remedial education and recreation often accompany intensive treatment regimes and token economies.

One secure facility, the South East Secure Treatment Unit (SETSU) in West Chester, Pennsylvania, is a state-run, 20-bed facility on the grounds of a state mental hospital. The program holds functionally retarded 14- to 18-year-old males, with an average of nine previous arrests each and at least two prior placements in less restrictive settings. Teachers, psychologists, family members, and the youths themselves cooperate to work out individualized treatment plans. A program description states that the SETSU program does not use isolation, mechanical restraints, or medication as a means of managing juvenile misbehavior. When a youth acts out, three or more staff people immobilize the youth until he is under control and willing to talk about what is bothering him (Woods, 1982, p. 94).

Applying the classification scheme sketched out above confirms that secure facilities and training schools, often classified together as institutional programs, are indeed quite similar. They differ a bit in facility; secure programs have more locks and tend to be smaller than training schools. Their client populations are similar in that they both contain older, more serious offenders, though secure facilities have more violent or deeply disturbed youths. Training schools and secure facilities are also a fairly close match in program characteristics. Differences in program characteristics, therefore, should illuminate the finer distinctions between the two.

The programmatic differences between training schools and secure facilities are in supervision, obligations, and investments and amenities. Supervision is high in secure facilities since behavior is carefully monitored and evaluated, while training school residents are relatively free from minute-to-minute scrutiny (probably because training schools are relatively large and because their inhabitants are relatively more autonomous). Few obligations are expected of residents of either program, though especially few obligations are required of securely confined clients. Again, the higher degree of autonomy of training school residents makes them better able to handle more obligations. Training schools provide fewer investments and amenities like food, clothes, education, and recreational programs, compared with the special programs and treatment investments that secure residents receive. As a youth's autonomy increases (that is, his capacity to care for himself and to coexist with others), his placement supplies fewer investments, provides less supervision, but requires more obligations.

If this observation is correct, it poses interesting policy questions. Should society continue to provide more amenities (at higher cost in resources expended) to the juveniles worst-off, or would the final payoff be higher by helping most those closest to succeeding? If so, then how should one structure the balance between legitimacy and constraints? In other words, when does freedom from constraints (like obligations) outweigh increases in legitimacy (like amenities)? Do serious juvenile offenders balance constraints and legitimacy differently than do policy makers?

Medical/Psychiatric Hospitals

The juvenile court sends very few juveniles (about 1% of disposition decisions) to hospitals (Black and Smith, 1981). Those sent usually require either mental health care or treatment for chemical abuse or dependency. Mental health care for youths usually is appropriate for severe emotional or psychiatric problems. Some programs deal specifically with retarded children. Chemical abuse and dependency programs in hospitals typically provide short-term, intensive care for alcohol or drug problems. As with psychiatric care, medical and mental health professionals supervise the residents. These programs usualy serve both adults and youths.

Medical facilities for troubled youths closely resemble juvenile institutions. Like other institutions, hospitals are large, residential, bureaucratic, and isolated. In terms of program dimensions, medical facilities are very close to secure placements. Like secure facilities, medical programs are high in program contact and supervision (medical staff monitor closely their patients) and high in investments and amenities (drugs and medical equipment, trained caretakers). Both secure facilities and medical programs require little in the way of obligations from their clients because the clients are incapable of so providing. And both operate under philosophies which give residents little say in the operation of the facility.

The major differences between secure facilities and medical programs exist because residents of medical facilities are psychologically or physically ill or addicted—their criminal record is therefore shadowed by health concerns. Consequently, medical programs admit youths voluntarily or through informal adjustment, besides under court order (they have broader conditions of participation). And finally, the auspices under which medical facilities operate is often private, while juvenile institutions are normally public.

The differences between medical facilities and secure facilities suggest that a youth should prefer a hospital to a secure facility because the hospital is as constraining as the secure facility but more legitimate. Medical programs are more legitimate than training schools or secure facilities because they provide high levels of investments, relaxed conditions of participation, and private auspices. Like the criminal residents of secure facilities, we do not hold the sick residents of medical programs responsible for their behavior. Treatment model aside, hospitals are more comfortable places to live than are many institutions.

Other Traditional Placements

This category is an assortment of programs that belong together only because one finds them almost universally on the menu of court dispositions. They also make up a large percentage of the dispositions decisions that judges make. The category includes probation (49 percent), foster care (3 percent), and ranches and camps (6 percent) (Black and Smith, 1981).

Probation serves new offenders as an alternative to more secure or supervised care. Under probation, a child lives at home in his community, working or studying like any other child. He is, however, under the supervision of a probation officer with whom he must meet and to whom he is accountable. These officers provide surveillance, counseling, and referral to appropriate service providers. Probation officers have disciplinary responsibilities also. They assure that youths abide by the terms of their probation (including, for example, avoiding criminal activity or delinquent associates, attending school, or obeying parents). Probation officers often have caseloads that are too large for them to handle effectively, though some programs have experimented with small caseloads or increased supervision by employing the services of volunteer officers.

Courts have long used *foster homes* as temporary placement for troubled youths, particularly when removal from the natural home appeared necessary. Foster homes are typically small (6–8 children), and are supposed to supply a supportive and congenial family atmosphere. Critics have attacked the foster home system for being more permanent than temporary: one study found that children stay an average of five years in foster care (Mnookin, 1974, p. 170). Furthermore, foster care disorients children who move repeatedly from one home to another. A variation on the foster home theme is intensive foster care, where no more than two young status offenders live with two specially-trained foster parents. One foster parent is present at all times. Youths attend school and receive special social services like counseling, 24-hour emergency consultation, and referral.

A *camp or ranch* holds about sixty youths for several months of structured activities in a non-secure, rural, outdoor environment. Often run by state youth authorities, these programs are distinct from wilderness experiences, in which small groups of youths practice survival skills in rugged, remote areas. Camps and ranches are larger, more organized, and have more facilities. California has a particularly extensive ranch program. Activities at camps include both outdoor projects such as stream conservation, construction of recreational areas, brush cutting, and painting, as well as more traditional activities like remedial education, recreation, and group counseling (Edelman, 1976).

These three programs bear little resemblance to one another. Probation is practically a non-disposition. It is low in all program dimensions, there is no client population to affect the character of the program, and the facility is often a youth's own home. Making few demands and providing little rationale for its existence, probation may be no more than an accounting scheme.

Foster care, on the other hand, ranks at the high end of almost every program dimension. It is high both in constraints like supervision (foster parents keep close tabs on few youths) and obligations (youths in foster homes are often responsible for chores around the house, good behavior at school, etc.). Foster care also ranks high in perceived legitimacy since it provides many amenities and investments (a comfortable home with lots of parental care); a family-like, open, and cooperative philosophy; often-voluntary conditions for participation; and private operation subject to public funding and certification.

Ranches resemble institutional programs. They do, however, retain several significant differences. Since youths hold many responsibilities for making the ranch operate, the level of required obligations at camps is higher than at other institutions. In order to handle those obligations, youths at camps and ranches are of only medium age and criminal experience, and accordingly, are relatively manageable and cooperative. Camps also offer fewer comforts, conveniences, or specialized treatments. This is in accord with our earlier observation that youths more able to handle responsibility receive more obligations. They are subject to more types of constraints and receive fewer legitimizing amenities.

It is no accident that probation, foster care, and camps are widely found in state juvenile justice systems. Since probation is low in both constraints and legitimacy, foster care is high in both, and camps are fairly high in constraints and somewhat low in legitimacy, they represent three very different types of program. Preserving different kinds of programs is useful and beneficial for it enables a judge to tailor dispositions to particular youths.

Community-Based Programs

Since the early 1970s, youth authorities have moved toward a community-based system of juvenile corrections: a network of small, often contracted on a fee-for-service basis, treatment-oriented placements located in or near the communities where youths have their homes. The rationale for community-based placements is that they offer more humane and better treatment opportunities than traditional institutional programs. Reformers in the early 1970s hoped that community-based programs would reduce the stigma of the label delinquent, offer more effective rehabilitation, and make communities assume responsibility for their children.

Community-based programs are more diverse than institutional programs. Some community-based programs like group homes are residential, while others allow youths to live at home with their families or in their own apartments. Most nonresidential programs offer a variety of social services. Though some programs offer little formal supervision and demand minimal participation, others bring together youths for many hours of recreational or educational activity each week.

Group homes comprise a wide range of residential placements. The emphasis of these programs is on individualized treatment within a supportive group setting. Typically, between eight and thirty residents live in a group home. The residents include delinquent or dependent youths in addition to voluntary adult admits. Staff is often comprised of program graduates.

Many group homes follow a particular treatment philosophy or serve a particular target population. For example, some exclusively treat youths with drug-related problems. Others emphasize to varying degrees methods of group therapy. One Massachusetts program, for example, began each day with a

> meeting in which the house concept was recited, announcements were made, and residents described their "learning experiences" (punishments such as wearing a sign around one's neck). From then until lunch youths acting as crew heads and "ramrods" closely supervised a variety of housekeeping chores, including, at the extreme, picking the lint out of a rug by hand. After lunch, a two-hour seminar was scheduled that ranged in content from a discussion and recitation of nicknames to angry confrontations. An hour of free time preceded and followed the evening meal and the day was closed with a two-to three-hour group confrontation session, at which people let out their hostilities toward one another at varying decibel levels.

At another program,

> [a] small second-floor room contained the elaborate organizational chart that classified residents by function . . . part of every resident's day was devoted to carrying out these responsibilities under close supervision, a large portion of it was taken up by encounter groups, "primals" (primal scream therapy groups), and verbal "haircuts" (short sessions in which a youth was dressed down for a failure to carry out responsibilities), which went on almost nonstop. The record for "haircuts" was 75 in one day (McEwen, 1978, pp. 223–225).

Other programs are more casually organized, simulating a big family. Youths freely come and go, pursuing work and school activities in the community (McEwen, 1978; Trojanowicz and Morash, 1983, ch. 7).

Many nonresidential, community-based *social service programs* have grown over the past two decades. They serve a wide range of youths, from neglect cases or first-time status offenders all the way to training school alumni. The range of services they provide is also wide. Some organizations provide numerous services under one roof. For example, open programs and alternative schools for troubled youths typically offer a package of recreation, education, job skills, and counseling. Other programs provide only a single service, though they may create individualized treatments by coordinating their program's offerings with those of other community organizations.

Counseling youths or their families by qualified welfare or mental health professionals is among the most common of social service dispositions. It is appropriate in cases in which state custody of the child would be inappropriate as, for example, when a child's misbehavior is a symptom of family problems largely beyond the child's control. The range of counseling placements varies widely. Some private practitioners or clinics conduct programs, as do public social service agencies and private non-profit groups associated with religious or other philanthropic groups. Some counseling programs are intense, short-term crisis interventions; others are for chronic, long-range adjustment problems. Many programs focus primarily on the individual child while others treat parents or the whole family (see Woods, 1982, for examples).

Attending to the dimensions of dispositions provides insights into both group homes and social service programs. Turning first to group homes, one observes that the dimensions describing group homes match those of foster care very closely. As usual, the differences are instructive. Group homes are larger than foster homes and function under a philosophy which emphasizes therapy to a greater extent than does foster care. Perhaps the size and therapeutic thrust of group homes has encouraged judges and youth authorities to send older youths and youths with more criminal experience to group homes and gentler youths to foster care. This may be an error. Foster care imposes more constraints on youths than do group homes. Supervision, contact, and obligations in foster care are probably more exacting than in group homes since foster parents monitor and enforce the behavior of relatively fewer youths than do group home parents. Again we observe that the juvenile justice system imposes more obligations on youths who are responsible compared with their more deviant peers. Might we not prefer to impose constraints in a different fashion?

Social services also comprise an interesting case. Social services have many legitimating features. They provide a series of investments like counseling, health services, special educational services, and job training. They may be under public or private auspices, are open philosophically, and use relaxed conditions of participation. Their constraints, on the other hand, are usually weak. Social service programs are usually not residential, provide mild supervision outside the program, and generally limit obligations to attendance plus a demonstration of effort or involvement. Social services are interesting because they provide few constraints and much legitimacy. In contrast, group homes are high in both constraints and legitimacy, while institutions are high in constraints and low in legitimacy.

New Alternatives

Grouped here for convenience and to reflect common parlance, "new alternatives" like restitution and wilderness programs seem to represent new directions for juvenile dispositions. Analyzing their content may provide more insight into how these programs function.

Restitution has two facets: reimbursement of victims and reimbursement of society. Restitution requires that a youth repay his victim, usually indirectly through the court and over a period of time, for the damages or injury he imposed on the victim. When the victim is society (as in cases of subway vandalism or public disorderliness), the court may also order restitution. Alternately, the court may order the youth to serve a specified number of hours of community service. This may include maintenance work at a public facility, clean-up of a local park, or supervision of nursery school children. Disciplinary measures like temporary incarceration or extension of sentences may enforce the payment schedule or ensure good work.

The concept and practice of restitution finds strong support from advocates of the just deserts model of corrections. Washington State's juvenile code, for example, stresses heavily the importance of restitution as a means of compensating victims and society for losses due to young offenders, and for penalizing offenders in proportion to the damage they inflict. Some advocates of restitution believe it builds citizenship by teaching youths about the value of hard work and about the consequences of irresponsible behavior (Schneider and Schram, 1983).

Wilderness programs, like restitution, make demands of youths. Wilderness programs are strenuous, highly-supervised, outdoor experiences for youths. Designed to increase their self-confidence, independence, and teamwork skills, these programs of varying duration serve as alternatives to institutionalization of delinquents or status offenders. Colorado Outward Bound School's Corrections Project, for example,

> is a series of programmed physical and social problem solving tasks conducted in a high-stress environment. The physical challenges are created through . . . backpacking, rock climbing, canoeing, sailing, route-finding, etc. The social challenge comes from the organization of participants into small groups (7 to 15 youths) that demand cooperation and leadership (Woods, 1982, pp. 31–32).

Evaluating restitution along its program dimensions presents a program which looks remarkably like social services. Both social services and restitution programs combine relatively few constraints (little contact or supervision) with medium to high levels of legitimacy (open and informal philosophy; sometimes administered under private auspices like a youth court). The nature of the obligations in the two programs is different. Social service programs require attendance and some level of effort towards self-improvement. With restitution, the requirement is much more narrowly defined—to work and to repay. A narrow obligation is both easier to discharge and to understand. Restitution's primary result is for a youth to compensate his victim. Character development is a subsidiary, but secondary benefit. In social service programs, on the other hand. personal development is the primary consideration. But since it is also an abstract objective, both society and the youth may find it more difficult to discharge or to determine if it has been discharged. The victim's role in restitution guarantees that the job gets done, even if the same youth might not be motivated to take advantage of the social service investments available to him. In short, restitution offers a high probability of a youth fulfilling a modest obligation, while social services offer a lower probability of completing a more demanding task. Restitution, then, is appropriate for youths unable to help themselves, or in cases where the victim's interest in compensation and just deserts predominates.

The wilderness experience catches the eye and appears innovative in large part because of our bias toward facilities; we are a bit awed by a program without a place. But if program dimensions describe what is most important about a disposition, then perhaps we can convert wilderness programs into terms that sound familiar.

Wilderness programs are high in both constraints and legitimacy. In fact, they rank at the very highest level in all seven program dimensions. Nature enhances the level of obligations and program contact. Program contact is high since youths cannot escape from the outdoors or from full-time supervision by counselors. Youths must fulfill many obligations in order to simply eat and sleep (pitch tents, build a fire, cook, etc.). The program is low in amenities like swimming pools, electric lights, and plumbing, though youths live under a philosophy granting them much participation, responsibility, and equality with staff. The conditions of participation may be voluntary, and wilderness programs are often run under the auspices of private organizations. In effect, the wilderness experience is a program which resembles the balance of constraints and legitimacy of group homes and foster homes—without the homes. It may be our best example of a program which tightly squeezes youths but at the same time provides a convincing rationale to make sense of their discomfort.

Implications

Conventional categories for classifying juvenile dispositions by describing buildings or client populations focus one's attention on only a few of the salient features of dispositions. Sometimes the classification works fine: for example, one institutional program looks very much like another. Subtle and not-so-subtle *differences between programs* may be teased apart by rating programs along program dimensions which indicate how confining (program contact, supervision, and obligations), or how legitimate (investments and amenities, philosophy, conditions of participation, and auspices) they are. The balance between constraint and legitimacy seems to suggest these important implications:

- Juvenile institutions like training schools, secure facilities, and even medical/psychiatric programs, look alike according to conventional wisdom and along program dimensions as well. However, it seems as if programs impose more obligations on youths able to handle more autonomy. Does this make sense? If so, it suggests that the most troublesome youths do not receive the most severe constraints, or at least it suggests that different types of constraints might be appropriate for different kinds of youths. Heavy constraints, if balanced by legitimating features, may be good for marginal youths. Since greater investments are made in youths with more problems, it also raises the question of whether programs ought to target resources at youths in the very worst shape, or at those who are closest to becoming autonomous citizens.

- Traditional placements like probation, foster care, and camps constitute a broad spectrum. Probation ranks as a non-disposition. Camps resemble institutions without walls. Foster care ranks highest in both constraints and legitimacy, perhaps making it appropriate for youths who require enhanced supervision.

- Though group homes and social service programs are products of the same era of community-based programming, they little resemble one another. Group homes, contrary to popular wisdom, are less confining than foster homes. Social service programs, high in legitimacy but low in constraints, are the converse of institutions (at least in program dimension terms).

- Restitution is a program with much the same structure as social service programs, without the social service investments and with different obligations. It is therefore appropriate for different youths. A wilderness program is like a foster home without the home because it ranks high in both constraints and legitimacy. It uses environmental rather than social contingencies to give it coercive power and legitimacy.

Besides distinguishing between programs, thoroughly elaborating the dimensions of dispositions permits one to *refine existing programs*. By separating a program's mode of action into those pieces which constrain and those pieces which legitimate, we make available a broader portfolio of tools to bring to bear on a youth or within a program. There are many ways to constrain a youth: contact, supervision, and obligations. But enhanced constraints are hard to bear without a concomitant enhancement in the investments, philosophy, conditions of participation, or auspices which legitimate a program. Manipulating a program's dimensions provides an additional way to structure its environment.

The dimensions of dispositions also provide a basis for one to *create new programs*. By taking permutations of the dimensions, corrections administrators should be able to create unique and useful options. For example, picture a child who requires a program with dimensions XYZ. Institution A offers XYQ and community program B offers JKZ. What to do? If a sufficient number of children require XYZ and it can be provided at low cost, authorities should create a new placement with XYZ.

Not only might this scheme help one to develop new dispositions, it might suggest also how to better *design systems of dispositions*. Since youths move through a set of dispositions in their careers within the juvenile justice system, they confront not only the disposition which the court selects, but a series of consequences and contingent dispositions which result from their behavior. By understanding the systematic variation of dispositions along their many dimensions, and by understanding how youths move from one disposition to another, a better system may be designed for juvenile corrections.

For example, the career path for serious delinquents within the juvenile justice system begins with probation or foster care and gradually moves to institutional programs. Psychological theory suggests that a short, severe, burst of punishment is more effective for modifying behavior than a sanction which gradually increases in intensity. Consequently a brief but more severely constraining (i.e., high contact, high supervision, demanding obligations, few investments, etc.) disposition for first offenders may be an appropriate element in a system of dispositions. Besides considering "sequential linkage" as the transition of youths from youth authority supervision back to community life, one ought also to think about sequential linkage within juvenile corrections, using these dimensions as a guide. A simple two-by-two array which maps programs that are high or low in constraints and in legitimacy is a first step to charting youths' progress within the juvenile justice system (Moore, 1976; 1978; 1973).

Finally, and perhaps most compellingly, dimensions of dispositions provide *a language* for discussing more accurately and profoundly the character and quality of juvenile dispositions.

References

Barnum, R. (1984, June). Treatment, punishment and coercion in the juvenile justice system. Paper prepared for the Harvard-Office of Juvenile Justice and Delinquency Prevention (U.S. Department of Justice). Third executive session on the juvenile justice system. Oakland, Calif.

Black, T., Smith, E., and Smith, C. P. (1981). *Reports of the national juvenile justice assessment centers: A preliminary national assessment of the numbers and characteristics of juveniles processed in the juvenile justice system*. Washington, D.C.: U.S. Government Printing Office.

Coates, R. B., Miller, A. D., and Ohlin, L. E. (1978). *Diversity in a youth correctional system: Handling delinquents in Massachusetts*. Cambridge, Mass.: Ballinger.

Edelman, P. B. (1976, September). Progress report on placement diversification in the division for youth. Presented to The Association of Judges of the Family Court of the State of New York, Inc.

Goffman, E. (1961). *Asylums: Essays on the social situation of mental patients and other inmates*. Garden City, N.J.: Anchor.

Katz, D. and Kahn, R. L. (1966). *The social psychology of organizations*. New York: John Wiley.

McEwen, C. A. (1978). *Designing correctional organizations: Dilemmas of subcultural development*. Cambridge, Mass.: Ballinger.

Mnookin, R. H. (1974). Foster care—in whose best interest? In *The rights of children,* pp. 158–197. Reprint Series No. 9. Cambridge, Mass.: Harvard Educational Review.

Moore, M. H. (1976, Fall). Anatomy of the heroin problem: An exercise in problem definition. In *Policy analysis, 2,* 4. pp. 639–662.

Moore, M. H. (1973). A 'feasibility estimate' of a policy decision to expand methadone maintenance. In *Public policy, 26,* 2. pp. 285–304.

Moore, M. H. (1973). Policy towards heroin use in New York City. Unpublished Ph.D. dissertation. Harvard University, Cambridge, Mass.

Schneider, A. L. and Schram, D. D. (1983). A comparison of intake and sentencing decision-making under rehabilitation and justice models of the juvenile system. Vol. V, and Executive summary: An assessment of Washington's juvenile justice reform. Vol. X, from *An assessment of juvenile justice reform in Washington State*.

Trojanowicz, R. C. and Morash, M. (1983). *Juvenile delinquency: Concepts and control.* (3rd ed.). Englewood Cliffs, N.J.: Prentice-Hall.

Woods, M. L. (1982). *Alternatives to imprisoning young offenders: Noteworthy programs*. Fort Lee, N.J.: National Council on Crime and Delinquency.

18
Principles for Juvenile Detention

ELLEN SCHALL

Detention is both temporary and transitional. These two facts have served too long as an excuse for not making the most of the time children spend in detention. We have allowed detention, even for children, to be little more than dead time, a time set apart between arrest and action. This paper explores some of what detention is around the country, but more importantly, challenges our notion of what it can be. These children who are locked up after arrest are in trouble with the law, but are also just in trouble. Detention can and should be used as an opportunity to intervene, to reclaim these children for productive lives.

Purpose of Juvenile Detention

In 1984, 1,804,688 children under the age of eighteen were arrested and charged with committing crimes or delinquent acts. Thirty-five percent were detained.

Detention is the temporary care and maintenance away from home of children held for the court, or at the direction of the court, pending adjudication of their cases. Children are also held in detention pending transfer to state institutions after placement or sentence.

On any given day, 14,376 such children are in custody. These children, aged 7–19, are charged with crimes ranging from misdemeanors to murder, and in some states violations of traffic or game laws. Their cases are prosecuted both in the juvenile and the adult court systems. Some are in custody for a day, but some stay in pretrial status for over a year. Some are remanded to institutions specifically designed for pretrial detention of juveniles, others are kept in adult jails, often not segregated by sight or sound from adult offenders.

Like most of the justice system in the country, juvenile detention is largely a matter of state and local concern. The federal government prosecutes violations of federal law and detains and imprisons federal offenders, but deals with very few juveniles under the age of eighteen. There is no federal juvenile facility. The variety in state laws concerning detention of juveniles is substantial and cuts across lots of areas: the minimum and maximum age for jurisdiction; the sentencing structure and authority; who serves what time where; and who runs local detention. In California the Youth Authority's responsibility is for 16- to 21-year-olds, while in New York children under 16 at the time of arrest are managed in the juvenile justice system, and those over 16 are the responsibility of the adult court and correctional system.

Who are these children being detained across the country? In large measure, they are the same children who make up the caseload of the other side of the Family or Juvenile Court: the children in need of supervision (status offenders); the children whose parents are accused of abuse and neglect; and the children who swell the ranks of the foster care system.

Just as this at-risk population is over-represented in the detention system, so are low-income children and children of color. In New York City, for example, 60% of the admissions to detention are black and 33% Hispanic. In Philadelphia, 78% are black, while across the state of Pennsylvania 60% of the children in detention are black.[1] In New York City more than 40% come from families on welfare.

What else do we know about the children who are detained? In the New York City detention system, 80% were born to mothers who first gave birth before they were 20 years old themselves.

A high percentage of delinquents have been abused. Dr. Dorothy Lewis and her colleagues at the New York University School of Medicine have done some very interesting studies in this area.[2] They compared more violent and less violent incarcerated juveniles. Seventy-five percent of the more violent group had suffered serious abuse by a family member, while "only" 33% of the less violent group had been abused. Seventy-eight percent of the violent group had been witnesses to extreme violence, while 20% of the less violent group had been witnesses. Forty-six percent of the more violent group had one or more major neurological abnormalities, while only 6% of the less violent group fell into that category. And finally, just to tie these two points together, the more violent children were 4.4 years below grade level while the less violent were 2.3 below level.

In general, this is a population with significant educational deficits. In the New York detention population, while the average age of children tested was 15, 38% read below the fourth grade level and 37% read between the fourth and sixth grade level. The children's math abilities were even weaker: 23% performed below the fourth grade level, while 54% scored between the fourth and sixth grade levels. Forty-eight percent of children admitted to detention in New York had been previously certified by the public school systems as requiring Special Education. Of these, 68% were thus classified because of some emotional handicap. These findings should be coupled with the generally unsatisfactory school experiences and negative orientation toward school common to most of these children. When asked to report their grade levels, many youngsters indicated that they had not been attending school for some time prior to detention, and many of those registered said they attended only sporadically. The high school dropout rate of minority students in New York City is 68%. (The overall dropout rate is 42%.)

Not every juvenile arrested is sent to detention, and more children are arrested every year than are detained. Children are held in detention for a variety of reasons: the nature of the charge, their previous record, a history of not appearing in court, lack of an adult to whom they can be released, a judge unavailable on nights or weekends, or even for an extralegal reason—to teach the kid a lesson. The Supreme Court in a landmark case, *Schall v. Martin,*[3] recently approved a New York State Family Court statute allowing preventive detention of juveniles if there is finding that there is a "serious risk" that if released, the juvenile may commit an act which, if committed by an adult, would constitute a crime before the return date.[4] The court upheld the New York statute even in the absence of any statutory definition of serious risk or requirement that the rationale of the conclusion be stated on the record.

Supreme Court Justice William Rehnquist, writing for the majority, emphasized both the need to protect children from their own acts and the fact that children are in custody all the time anyway—because they're in the custody of their parents. "Children by definition, are not assumed to have the capacity to take care of themselves. They are assumed to be subject to the control of their parents, and if parental control falters, the state must play its part as *parens patriae*."[5] The Court went on to note that "[S]ociety has a legitimate interest in protecting a juvenile from the consequences of his criminal activity—both from potential physical injury which may be suffered when a victim fights back or a policeman attempts to make an arrest, and from the downward spiral of criminal activity into which peer pressure may lead the child."[6]

The actual data about who is in detention is interesting, given the statutes and case law. A cross-sectional study of children in detention in six counties in Pennsylvania in 1981[7] revealed the following:

The kinds and seriousness of the charges holding juveniles within each of the counties varied notably. Nearly one in five were held on misdemeanor-related charges only. Moreover, one-eighth of all detainees appeared to be held only as a result of noncriminal offenses. Although more than seven-tenths of the juveniles detained in Philadelphia, Lancaster, and Delaware counties were held on charges equivalent to felonies, in Allegheny County only half and in Montgomery County only about one-third were held on felony-level charges.

The proportions of juveniles held on charges involving serious crimes against the person[8] varied widely from county to county: only 18% of the Montgomery juveniles, for example, were so charged, compared with 51% of the Philadelphia and 65% of the Delaware County juvenile populations.

In all the counties, charges involving serious injury or death to a victim were exceedingly rare (no more than 10%). Moreover, approximately *70% of the confined juveniles were not held on charges involving actual injury or even threats of injury to a victim.* The variation across counties was slight in this regard.

Approximately 30% of all the juveniles studied had no prior record of adjudicated offenses. Only 31% of all juveniles had been adjudicated delinquent previously on the basis of charges involving crimes against the person. Prior adjudicators for robbery specifically were less in evidence—in only about 22% of the cases.

No reasons were given by judges or intake officials (at least as could be detected in the juvenile files) explaining the reasons for the confinement of the juveniles in a majority of the cases, although this varied by county. When reasons were noted, they were highly varied, although statements relating the likelihood of absconding, or posing a threat to the community, or danger to person, property or the juvenile were a minor theme.

Fourteen percent (roughly one in seven) of all the detained juveniles had their cases totally dismissed. (In Philadelphia, as many as 23% later had their cases dismissed.) In addition, 17% were placed later on probationary status, not involving confinement after adjudication. Roughly 37% were assigned to nonsecure residential programs. In short, in the aggregate, roughly 70% of the juveniles confined in the detention facilities of the six counties (a maximum security approach) were granted dispositions in later processing that can be classified as not involving confinement or involving only nonsecure residential placements.

The author of the study argues that examples of the least appropriate cases of juvenile detention can be found among the following category of juveniles:

1. Those confined only on the basis of noncriminal matters (13%).
2. Those held on offenses ranked no higher than misdemeanors (within this category least appropriate might be juveniles with no prior records of arrests or adjudications) 17% had no prior arrests and more than 40% of whom had no prior adjudications.
3. Those whose subsequent dispositions (or case outcomes generally) suggest that detention was unnecessary.

Structure of Juvenile Detention Facility System

The institutions and spaces in which children are detained—pretrial and preadjudication—vary tremendously across the country. Although the Federal Juvenile Justice and Delinquency Prevention Act was amended in

1980 to require the removal of all juveniles from adult jails where they may have sight or sound contact with adult inmates by 1987, estimates of the number of juveniles still being held in adult jails go as high as one-half million annually, three-quarters of them charged with delinquency.[9] Some state statutes expressly prohibit juveniles from being placed in adult jails.[10] The unconstitutionality of this practice has been successfully challenged in litigation in some parts of the country, but the problem remains even if its extent is debated.

Clearly, if children are to be detained, the preference is to detain them in facilities designed and operated for that purpose. These facilities across the country vary in size, extent of secure hardware, and program offerings. They are operated by different government agencies (probation, sheriff, court, detention agency) and by private for-profit and non-profit organizations. Conditions in these juvenile detention facilities vary also. Some of the issues regarding the conditions of confinement in juvenile facilities are the same as those raised in challenges to adult prisons—overcrowding, arbitrary punishment and use of excessive physical force. Other challenges are peculiar to juvenile institutions in their attack on the adequacy of the programs offered.

A child in detention, then, can be detained in the 600-plus bed Central Juvenile Hall in Los Angeles or in one of two double-bunked cells set aside for juveniles in the Androscoggin, Maine jail constructed in 1857 and now holding thirty to forty adults. In New York a detained child could be in Spofford, the 196-bed secure juvenile facility with razor ribbon and barred windows, or in a bed in a private home with a foster family.

Detention is by definition a transitional community. Some children leave to return home, others are placed in or sentenced to institutions either run by the state or under contract to the state (the old training schools, now often spoken of as treatment or rehabilitation facilities). Each child's length of stay and disposition is unpredictable and not at all within the control of the detention facility. Some other actor in the juvenile system, often but not always a judge, decides who gets detained, for how long, and where the child goes from detention.

Juvenile detention presents difficult issues because it has no clear goal or model. Should it be like adult detention? No, because we are dealing with children. Should it be like juvenile treatment institutions? It can't because these residents haven't been adjudicated or convicted. In addition, a child's length of stay is unpredictable since it depends on the court case and judge.

Because of this unpredictability, detention in both the adult and the juvenile systems has most often been regarded as dead time, as time suspended in these children's lives while decisions are being made. When detention was a matter of days or weeks at the most, the need to define its nature and make some use of the time was less pressing. We can no longer afford this. Now more children are tried in adult systems with longer case processing times. More states back up sentenced or adjudicated children (and adults) in local detention facilities awaiting transfer to state institutions. Simply put, some large number of children are now staying in detention for many months–a time long enough to make a difference in these children's lives.

In New York City the average length of stay in detention was sixteen days in fiscal year 1985. But the average is misleading. While 61% of the children admitted to secure detention left within ten days (and 45% left within three days), on any given day more than half the children have been there more than thirty days, and almost a quarter of them have been there more than 100 days. During fiscal year 1985, fifty children remained in secure detention for nine months or more, with one child spending 545 days in detention before being sent upstate.

In 1973, the U.S. Senate Subcommittee to Investigate Juvenile Delinquency determined that juveniles were detained an average of two weeks.[11] The GAO found in a sample of 876 juveniles that children were held in secure detention for periods varying from a few hours to 612 days with 181 or 21% lasting over thirty days.[12] Another report, based on U.S. Census data, found that in 1979 the average length of stay in juvenile detention ranged from three days in Arkansas to thirty-three days in South Carolina.[13]

How Should Detention Centers Work

The warehouse model from the adult detention world (three hots and a cot), whether appropriate for adults or not, is clearly insufficient here because children's lives and needs cannot be put on hold. Adolescence is a critical time in a person's life development, and these children in detention are among the neediest in our society today.

What then should we expect from a juvenile detention system? In trying to answer that question, one turns first to the two sets of existing professional standards. These two sets of standards fail in some very significant ways.

For the first set of standards, we look to the work of the Institute of Judicial Administration and the American Bar Association. They established a Joint Commission on Juvenile Justice Standards that issued twenty-three volumes of standards addressing what they refer to as the "entire field of juvenile justice administration." Only eight standards address the area of juvenile detention facilities. Of those eight, the first five discuss which kind of juveniles should be in which types of institutions. The sixth standard calls for the need for children in detention to have access to their regular school or equivalent programs "adequate to their needs." The seventh lays out the rights of a juvenile in detention, including the right to privacy, visiting, telephones, mail, and restrictions on the use of force. The last standard calls for an annual statewide inventory of detention facilities.

Under these standards a facility with a school that paid attention to certain rights of children would pass muster. That is not enough, not for these at-risk children at this point in their lives.

The second set of standards, promulgated by the American Correctional Association (ACA), are more extensive but still fail in specificity. The ACA standards for secure juvenile detention facilities are intended to provide administrators of juvenile programs with the "opportunity to develop a plan for upgrading facilities and procedures in accordance with nationally reorganized and respected benchmarks"[14] and "the means by which to ensure that their programs are humane, protect the individual rights of children and operate efficiently and effectively."[15] The standards cover twenty areas, from administration, organization, and management (2.8001: "the agency operating a detention facility is a legal entity or part of a legal entity") to citizen and volunteer involvement (2.8417: "written policy and procedure provide that the administrator curtails, postpones or discontinues the services of a volunteer or volunteer organization when there are substantial reasons for doing so"). Of the 417 standards, the statement prefacing the program section is worth particular note. "Juveniles have the right to a program of supervision, care, counseling and/or placement that complies with the dispositional order of the court and that will best meet the juveniles' personal growth and development needs."[16]

Standard 2.8354 calls for the facility to provide or make available the following minimum services to programs:

an educational program;
visiting with parents and guardians;
private communication with visitors and staff;
counseling;
continuous supervision of living units;
medical services;
food services;
recreation and exercise; and
reading material.

The problems with these standards are their vagueness, (what is an adequate medical program?) It is thus difficult to hold a juvenile detention system accountable, and emphasize affirmatively what can be done in detention, even in the short term.

On what terms then can—and should—juvenile detention facilities be held accountable? For custody clearly, as any secure institution. For care, particularly because the residents are children. For connection, because detention facilities are transitional organizations and most children leave them to return to their families and communities.

Custody

Traditionally, detention facilities, whether for adults or children, have had two basic objectives: to keep detainees in and to get them to court for their court appearances.

Keeping detainees in without escapes—while allowing a program to go on—is basic. Failure to achieve this goal is one of the clearest ways to fail. Escapes capture public attention easily and threaten administrators' job security.

Producing detainees in court for their appearances is fairly straightforward but in larger systems may present some problems. In New York City, for instance, in 1981, children were delivered on time in only 55% of the cases. The rate is 90% now, but the earlier sloppy performance led to unnecessary adjournments of cases and unnecessary interference with the efficient operation of other parts of the system. The detention facility must acknowledge its responsibility to function as part of a whole, a responsibility it owes not only to the other agencies in the system but also to the children. The failure in coordination which leads to unnecessary delays in processing of children's cases interferes with what I submit should be a third custody objective of the detention system: to keep detention stays as short as possible.

One obvious measure of this third goal is to study the average length of stay. Detention systems are often characterized by heavy turnover in the first few days which brings the average down, so it is important also to look at the number of children who stay more than six months and the length of time from final disposition to transfer to a placement facility. This is critical. The detention facility must also have some role in seeing that this legnth-of-stay problem is addressed. Often detention administrators argue that they have no role in reducing delay or keeping stays short. This is true on an individual level: an administrator takes the children that judges send for as long as the judge decides. But administrators can act on a system level. Often they are the only ones watching lengths of stay in the aggregate, and whether out of concern for overcrowding or out of a belief that children are better off elsewhere, detention administrators are in a position to be the most powerful advocates in reducing detention stays. Possible interventions include: compiling and distributing a list of children in detention for more than six months (in New York City, we give out such a list monthly to judges, district attorneys, and defense lawyers); quickly producing birth certificates so court determination of jurisdiction based on age can proceed expeditiously; producing children for interviews by probation, defense attorneys, or voluntary agencies; questioning long adjournments; getting judges to order the placement authority to pick up children on set dates; pushing for state regulations establishing time frames for transfer from the detention to the placement facility; suing the state for failure to comply with already established guidelines.

In New York the average number of children awaiting transfer to placement facilities has gone from 40 in 1981 to 22 in fiscal year 1985 after two lawsuits brought by Legal Aid established time frames for transfer. In Los Angeles' Juvenile Hall, more than 20% of the population is waiting transfer to CYA, and many have been in that status for months. Circulating a list of children in detention for more than six months is a strategy adapted from efforts at population management in the adult jail system. The evidence across the country is clear that disseminated data can generate action. Our New York City experience confirms this.

Care

The first objective of providing care in detention is do no harm. Children—as adults—are entitled to come out of a detention system at least no worse than when they entered. This is not an easy task, given both the nature of institutions and the influences of peer culture. Attention should be paid to the number of assaults and allegations of abuse (child on child, staff on child, child on staff) and to the number of suicides or attempts. Institutions should also guarantee that each child's health status is maintained or improved rather than diminished. A National Institute of Justice publication, *Measuring Prison Results*, suggests looking both at days lost from a program attributable to Occupational Safety & Health Administration (OSHA) reportable injuries and rates of hospitalizations, sick days, and death as percentages of average daily populations.[17]

Institutions must also seek to maintain or improve a child's educational level, as demonstrated by improvement in test scores or completion of educational milestones (e.g., completion of GED).

The second care objective is to learn what we can about the child in detention so as to increase the chances of appropriate intervention. For example, what can we learn during detention so that a child's placement is effective and targeted? Or, what can we learn so that a child will return to an appropriate school or get follow-up medical attention if he or she is released home? Success would involve the ability to assess basic needs (educational, social services, medical and mental health at a minimum). It is also critical that a detention facility know about its population in terms of its aggregate:

average length of stay
groupings within lengths of stay
reading levels
grade levels
percentage attending schools
percentage in special education
reasons why children were classified as handicapped
"related services" children received in their home schools

A third and related objective is to provide access to the kinds of services children would have had access to if they had not been arrested and detained. Children in detention are generally very needy, and neither a stay in detention nor the fact of an arrest should keep them from getting services available to other children. The goal is to provide services appropriate to the specific needs of each child. Service delivery is particularly complicated in a detention setting because of the varying and unpredictable lengths of a stay of residents. A facility has to be prepared to provide services appropriate to children—some of whose stays are measured in days, some months, and some even a year. This has to be done even without the benefit, of knowing in advance how long children will stay.

An education program in a detention system should be measured in terms of the basics. Children who stay more than x months should show a proportionate increase in reading scores. Curricula and teaching should be geared to a transitional population. Where possible, children who are long-term detainees should have the opportunity to earn credit. Referral mechanisms should be in place for children with special needs. Efforts should be made to improve communication between the sending school, the institution, and the receiving school. Finally, the school should provide the required number of hours of instruction and days of school operation.

Social service systems in a detention setting are often more intensive than those available in the community. Still, one needs to ask about the frequency of access to the programs and the level of training of the caseworkers. Sophisticated systems also will have some mechanism to integrate the work of the social service unit with the rest of the program.

The quality and extent of medical and mental health systems vary widely in detention settings, from an on-call nurse to a staffed 24-hour infirmary. There should be, at a minimum, provision for a daily sick call and a system for response to emergencies.

Detention institutions also can be judged on their success in providing access for kids to family services and to employment opportunities. Many communities offer "preventive services" to families. The goal of these services is to try to help families and avoid having to place children outside the home. These preventive services should be made available to families whose children have been arrested and detained. If a child in detention is in foster care, provisions should be in place for both the natural parent and the foster parent to visit. If a detained child is also a parent, the detainee's children should be given the right to visit.

Job skills are key to living a responsible adult life. Many communities fund summer youth employment programs or allocate some JTPA funds specifically to youth. Are children who have been detained or who may be in detention eligible for such programs?

A fourth objective is to run the institution and the programs in a way that promotes the values we think children should have learned on the outside and didn't: how to settle disputes without violence, how to choose, how to make decisions, how to take responsibility for one's own actions. This involves staff modelling appropriate behavior and giving children opportunities to learn new behaviors.

Is there a fair and consistently applied discipline system? Are the rules known to children? Is there some opportunity for children to make choices? Is there a grievance or ombudsman system? In a responsive detention system, the answer for all these questions should be "yes."

A fifth objective is to see that other government entities pay attention to the juvenile detainee population and that kids who have been detained get what they need from the other parts of the system. Drop-out prevention funds, for example, may include in their target population children who have been arrested and detained. Detained children may be allowed to re-enroll in their community schools. The priorities of other government youth-funding agencies should reflect the importance of this population.

A final objective in this care series is to see that each child in detention has an opportunity to experience a positive success. In New York we trained children and staff in CPR and emergency life-saving techniques. Children in detention for the first time learn to paint, or beat some athletic record, or learn to read.

Connection

Because detention is a transitional community, it is not sufficient to operate it based only on notions of custody and care if those notions are limited to the time spent in detention. Children in detention are on their way to somewhere else and for most of them[18] that somewhere else is back home, to the family and neighborhood from which they came. Given the at-risk status of these children, and the history of deprivation and abuse that accompanies many of them, it is crucial to use the time in detention to try to connect the child in a positive way to his or her community. Detention should be viewed as an opportunity to intervene, to make a difference, to increase the likelihood of each child reaching his or her potential and becoming a productive member of society. And most importantly, detention should promote each child's relationship with his or her family.

Detention is a moment of crisis for child and family alike. We can let the crisis weaken further the bonds that hold a family together, or we can work hard to use it to reposition the child, his family and their relationship. With the latter goal in mind, visiting regulations should encourage family involvement, and family members should participate in planning the child's program. Detention systems might also re-examine their definition of family itself. In New York City, when we convened a group of staff to think about how to broaden our involvement with the children's families, the children made the important point that they were both children of parents as well as parents of children themselves.

Assuming some responsiblity to connect the child to his or her family and community is a new concept for detention. The legal mandate of detention does not extend this far; therefore the source of this third goal of detention—connection—is a utilitarian or moral concern not mandated by the court.

In New York City, we have chosen to take on this goal of connection through the development of an Aftercare program. Aftercare is a voluntary program that attempts to connect children released from detention with services in their own community. Its primary objective is to return children to school and to provide them and their families with the support they need to remain there. In addition, Aftercare attempts to develop an individualized service plan and to connect each child and family with services in the community they need. Currently, 85% of the children in Aftercare are re-enrolled in school after release. Next year, our goal is 90%.

The Aftercare program is the community-based piece of a developing case management system. Case management is a service delivery system that provides unified and comprehensive needs assessment and service planning and coordination. It is currently being applied in many fields and is quite accepted. But to apply those concepts to a detention setting is new.

While still a work in progress, New York City's case management system currently has four components, which are in various stages of development and implementation. When a child enters the detention system, we first perform a *needs assessment* and make a systematic effort to learn as much as we can about a child's health, educational, and family background. With this knowledge, an interdepartmental team next develops an individualized *service plan* for comprehensive services that matches the child's specific needs. *Service delivery,* the third step, includes health, mental health, and dental care; education; casework; and recreational activities—all of which are provided in detention or in the community if the child has been released from detention and is participating in Aftercare. The last component, *service monitoring,* will assure, when fully implemented, that the services we plan are provided and that new services are developed where needed.

It is clear from the "nothing works" literature that follow-up with these difficult kids is crucial. We do this with our Aftercare program, which attempts to follow a child back into the community and continue the work begun in detention. By establishing this continuum of care from admission through release, we hope to identify what works with the juvenile detention population.

Conclusion

The work of the future for juvenile detention lies in pushing the boundaries of the system as we know it, in learning more about what works with whom and in using every opportunity to attempt to return some of these children to productive lives. Their lives, and ours, are too important to do any less.

Endnotes

1. Goldkamp, J. S. (1984). Characteristics of detention populations in selected Pennsylvania counties. Unpublished report. Juvenile Law Center of Philadelphia.
2. Lewis, D. O., Shanok, S. S., Pincus, J. H., et al. (1979). Violent juvenile delinquents: Psychiatric, neurological, psychological and abuse factors. *Journal of American Academy of Child Psychiatry, 18,* 307–319.
3. *Schall v. Martin* 104 S. Ct. 2403 (1984).
4. 320.5(3) (b) of the New York Family Court Act.
5. 104 S. Ct. 2403, 2410 (3,4), (1984).
6. 104 S. Ct. 2403, 2410 (3,4), (1984).
7. Goldkamp. *op cit.,* pp. 10–12.
8. Serious crimes against the person were defined as those causing harm or injury to the victim, including murder, voluntary manslaughter, involuntary deviate sexual intercourse, rape, statutory rape, robbery, kidnapping, and aggravated assault.
9. The data is conflicting. The National Coalition for Jail Reform estimates that 500,000 juveniles under 18 are held in the nation's 3,943 local jails each year, 25% of whom are held on status offenses. Community Research Forum at the University of Illinois counted 479,000 children held in adult jails or lockups in 1979. The OJJDP estimate is much lower. It recorded 62,238 children, excluding those juveniles held less than six hours as well as those held for criminal charges in the adult court.
10. Maryland, Rhode Island, Connecticut, and Arizona. See also California Senate Bill 1637.
11. The detention and jailing of juveniles: Hearings before the subcommittee to investigate juvenile delinquency of the committee on the judiciary, 93rd Congress, 1st Session 299 (1973).
12. GAO report at hearings before the subcommittee to investigate juvenile delinquency of the committee on the judiciary. 93rd Congress, lst Session 299 (1973).
13. Krisberg, B., Litsky, P., Schwartz, I. (1982). *Youth in confinement: Justice by geography, 18.* Hubert H. Humphrey Institute of Public Affairs, University of Minnesota.
14. *ACA 1983 Standards,* p. vii.
15. Introduction. *ACA 1983 Standards,* p. xvi.
16. *ACA 1983 Standards,* p. 97.
17. Burt, M. (1981, June). *Measuring prison results: Ways to monitor & evaluate corrections performance.* U.S. Department of Justice, National Institute of Justice.
18. In New York City 42% of children released from detention are released home, although some of these are eventually placed.

19
Notes on an Accounting Scheme for a Juvenile Correctional System

PHILIP J. COOK

In general, the public's impression of the performance of the juvenile correctional system or Youth Authority (YA) is based on a collection of unrepresentative incidents that are deemed newsworthy by the media: spectacular crimes committed by inmates of the YA, or evidence of corruption within the agency, or reports of violence or abuse against inmates of YA institutions. The attempts of juvenile corrections managers to minimize adverse publicity may result in excessive caution or other distortions in programmatic decisions. A partial antidote to this problem would be a good systematic account of YA performance which could serve as a basis for educating the public about the overall context in which the isolated headline stories arise.

What is needed therefore, for juvenile corrections is a valid statistical basis by which everyone concerned—internal management, the governor, legislature, and the public—can evaluate its overall performance. The ultimate purpose of such an accounting scheme would be to improve YA programmatic decision-making both directly, by giving management the information necessary to evaluate its programs, and indirectly, by modifying the political context in which the YA operates.

Objectives

Each year, about 60,000 adjudicated delinquents are committed to long-term residential facilities. They are held for an average of six months, but some are held for as long as two years or more. By law, and increasingly in practice, commitment to training schools and other residential facilities is the solution of last resort, reserved for those juveniles who have been cycled through the juvenile court a number of times and/or have been convicted of serious crimes. It is an unfortunate fact that most of these youths will continue their criminal activity following release.

Clearly the public has a considerable stake in the activities of the Youth Authority. First and foremost is the public's concern with crime: the YA is responsible for preventing its inmates from committing crimes (especially crimes against the outside community) and for working toward their reform and rehabilitation. Second, the YA is expected to assume the responsibility of providing their inmates with the services that more fortunate youths receive from family, community, and school—nurturance, education, work experience, a network of useful contacts, and protection against physical abuse. Finally, the YA is required to exercise restraint in its use of authority, respecting the rights of inmates to be free from excessively harsh punishments or unreasonable restrictions on their day-to-day activities. These three general concerns constitute a normative framework for a useful accounting system. They are developed in greater detail below.

Crime

From one perspective, delinquents are a problem primarily because they are at much greater risk of graduating to adult crime than their nondelinquent peers. The youths who constitute the bulk of the training school population are at very high risk of making this transition.* The primary efforts of the training school should therefore be directed toward reforming its inmates, training them to assume noncriminal adult roles in the community and diverting them from their incipient (or perhaps well-established) criminal careers.

This future-oriented focus has been weakened during the last fifteen years by the accumulating evidence that correctional programming has little discernible influence on the duration or intensity of criminal careers, except insofar as those careers are interrupted by spells of incarceration. Most delinquents eventually reform, but the technology for hastening reform is unknown.

Recognition of this ignorance should foster in corrections managers an experimental approach to rehabilitation-oriented programming, experimental both in the sense of trying a variety of approaches, and in the sense of subjecting these approaches to systematic evaluation. But the recognition that most rehabilitation efforts are likely to be failures in this respect opens the door to a quite different perspective on the delinquency problem.

From this second perspective, delinquents are a problem because they are active criminals right now. Youths under 18 make up about 40% of the felony arrests. Among these are a relatively small group who commit serious crimes at a high rate—a group that is well represented in the training school population. A worthwhile (and feasible) objective for the juvenile correction system from this perspective is to incapacitate these youths from criminal activity while they are in YA custody. Effective

* See Hamparian, *Violent Juvenile Offenders,* printed in this volume.

incapacitation is a very important and widely recognized objective for delinquents sentenced to residential programs. The public is much quicker to hold the YA accountable for crimes committed by a youth who has escaped from a training school than one who has in the normal course of events been released from YA custody. A more ambitious objective is to send a message to juvenile offenders that crime has unpleasant consequences, in the hope of enhancing the general deterrent effect of the juvenile justice system.

Promoting Healthy Development

More fortunate adolescents benefit from a nurturing family, an effective school, and a community that provides opportunites for wholesome recreation, an introduction to the legitimate job market, and proper adult role models. Most youths in custody have not grown up in this kind of environment. Nevertheless, there is an expectation that training schools and other residential facilities will create an environment that approximates this ideal insofar as possible.

The demand for providing youths in custody with a relatively high standard of living and opportunites for development derives primarily from a sense of the special obligations that are properly implied by the exercise of the state's authority. When the state incarcerates a youth and thereby deprives him of whatever opportunities for normal growth are available to him on the "outside," then the state must create acceptable substitutes for these opportunities. The standard by which these substitutes are evaluated is derived from some sense of the decent minimum—perhaps what middle-class people judge to be appropriate for their children. The fact that delinquent youths are not protected by such standards while free is not relevant, since the state's responsibility for fostering the development of free youths is far less direct than its responsibility for youths who are held in the state's custody.

To some extent, the obligation of the youth authority to provide minimum standards for food, shelter, protection from abuse, and education, is imposed by the courts, acting at the behest of child advocates. It is possible that a majority of voters would not endorse the large budgets implied by these minimum standards—more than $20,000 annually per inmate. But the courts, using civil rights arguments, limit the discretion allowed the legislatures.

It is possible but unlikely that providing inmates with a decent standard of living and opportunities for self-improvement will reduce their recidivism rate following release. Whether or not it does, the provision of decent opportunities for youths in training schools is considered an end itself. We value good health, educational achievement, and freedom from fear of abuse for these youths, just as we do for all youths. To be specific, a correctional program that is effective in teaching its students to read is preferable to one that fails in this task, even if the programs are similar in other respects (including recidivism rates).

Limiting Use of Authority

Just as the decision to incarcerate a delinquent entails an obligation to take responsibility for fostering his personal development, it also entails an obligation to exercise reasonable restraint in the exercise of authority over him. Obviously, youths sentenced to residential programs will, to a considerable extent, be deprived of autonomy, isolated from the outside community, and subjected to the internal rules governing behavior of inmates. These limits on personal freedom require justification. One possible justification—that serious delinquents deserve punishment—has little or no standing in the jurisprudence of juvenile justice. What remains are a collection of utilitarian justifications, beginning with protection of the community and creating an orderly environment for delivery of services. But child rights advocates insist that these utilitarian concerns must be balanced by the fundamental value our society places on personal freedom. It is desirable, then, to place the youth in the least restrictive of the available programs that have the capacity for protecting the community. The right to orderly contacts with family and other outsiders should be protected. Punishments for violations of internal rules should not be excessively harsh, and these rules should allow for a reasonable degree of autonomy.

Two rather vague but nonetheless important principles can be stated in this context: 1) The less restrictive and coercive the program the better, other things (such as protecting the community and fostering individual development) being equal; and 2) There are absolute limits to the use of coercion in a residential program, regardless of other concerns.

The three objectives discussed earlier provide a general framework for thinking about the value of Youth Authority programs. It should be noted in passing that this evaluation framework omits mention of a number of concerns about the day-to-day process of effective public management: the administrator is responsible for keeping the agency free of corruption, maintaining good personnel management practices, and developing a productive working relationship with other government agencies and the press. Relatedly, it is commonplace to evaluate the performance of public managers by their ability to preserve the autonomy of the agency from "meddling" by the courts or the legislature, their ability to maintain a good public image for the agency, and their success in budget battles. But these matters are secondary to a discussion of the "bottom line"—the value of YA programs for youths in custody and for society at large. The next section attempts to translate these objectives into operational measures that can be used to monitor the performance of the YA as a whole, or of specific programs or residential units within the YA.

Operational Measures of Performance

The owners of a publicly held corporation are primarily concerned with a single dimension of the corporation's performance—the contribution of the corporation's activities to the owner's wealth. The relative performance of any one corporation can be judged by comparing its profitability with an average profitability measure for other corporations. Shareholder reports focus on these matters.

Evaluating the activities of public human service agencies, including a Youth Authority, is more difficult for at least three reasons: 1) "Performance" is a multidimensional construct; 2) There is no consensus concerning the relative importance of the various dimensions; and 3) Measuring performance along these dimensions is often difficult, as is finding an operationally useful standard of comparison.

Partly as a result of these difficulties, the annual reports of social service agencies often have little or no information on performance. They focus instead on budget and process measures. This information is of some interest, but it is a long way from the "bottom line." For the purposes of our discussion, we can think of the bottom line for the Youth Authority as having a number of columns, grouped in the three categories we discussed above: crime reduction, promotion of healthy development, and maintenance of personal freedoms. These are the dimensions of ultimate concern to the public, and a performance-oriented accounting system should include information on each of them.

Crime Reduction

a. The YA is expected to prevent inmates from committing crimes against other inmates, staff, or the outside community. The YA's annual accounting statement should report crimes committed by its youths, distinguishing between "on campus" and "off campus" incidents.
b. The YA is expected to strive for the reform of the delinquent youths in its custody. The public's principal concern is post-release criminal activity, but the public is also interested in other aspects of a juvenile's post-release behavior—job holding, family relationships, alcohol and drug abuse, and so forth. However, there are a number of problems that arise when the YA takes interest in generating relevant follow-up measures. Most significantly, collecting information on inmates' post-release behavior requires an effort that is beyond the normal purview of the YA. One recidivism measure that might be possible and useful to generate within the YA is the percentage of youths who are resentenced to the YA within a year or two of their initial release. But this measure is incomplete, since it omits arrests and convictions that do not result in a new sentence to the YA. A more complete measure of recidivism could be developed by com-

puting recidivism rates on a routine basis in jurisdictions that have an offender-based data system that includes juveniles. In jurisdictions which lack such a data base, follow-up studies of released delinquents would have to be limited to occasional special studies.

If it were possible to determine any "leading indicators" based on an inmate's behavior that suggested a potential for rehabilitation, then they could be routinely measured for current inmates, and might serve as a practical alternative to follow-up measures. Unfortunately, there are no such reliable leading indicators. The observable variables that are useful in predicting post-release behavior are already known when the youth begins his sentence—age, prior record of arrests and convictions, drug and alcohol use. Hence this approach does not appear promising.

In sum, it is difficult to see how the YA can routinely measure its success in rehabilitating its inmates for the purposes of an annual report. Measuring success in preventing criminal activity by current inmates is much more straightforward.

Promotion of Healthy Development

The Youth Authority is responsible for fostering the development of its inmates. It assumes the role of the public schools in providing youths with opportunities to develop basic education and vocational skills. It assumes the role of the family, school, and community in fostering physical fitness, health maintenance, social skills, and nurturance. The YA's performance in these respects may be measured by a combination of testing and coding of day-to-day records.

Standardized tests are probably the most appropriate tool for measuring educational achievement and personality development. Physical exams could be administered once or twice a year to monitor physical fitness, although these exams should be supplemented with data from the inmate's medical history. Other dimensions of the youth's development and general well-being for which it may be possible to develop statistical proxies based on day-to-day records is the daily quality of life. The list of possibilities is long, and could touch on everything from the quality of food and recreation opportunities to the relationships between inmates and between inmates and staff.

Maintenance of Personal Freedom

The YA mandate to seek the "least restrictive alternative" type of institution for each of its inmates reflects the value the public places on maintaining the autonomy of the inmate and his opportunity to interact with the world outside the institution. They YA's performance in this area can be indicated by the percentage of inmates being held in each of several levels of security, from low security group homes with open door policies to maximum security units. This traditional approach to measuring the restrictiveness of the terms of confinement is useful insofar as there is a clear definition of degree of security for each category of institution.

In regard to the extent to which the inmate is able to maintain contact with people on the "outside"—family, probation officer, former therapist, and potential employers—the frequency of such contacts should be measured as a rough indicator of isolation.

Standards of Comparison

The statistical indicators discussed above are measures of performance. By what standards are the YA scores on these indicators to be "graded"? There are three standards that may be applicable, depending on the objective of the evaluation.

The first standard is a comparison of how well the YA inmates would have done if they had been given a probationary sentence rather than incarcerated. Some child advocates believe that the training school environment is detrimental to the youths' development, and may even increase their commitment to a criminal career. To make this "what if" standard operational, we would need to estimate how each cohort of youths in YA custody would have scored on the indicator measures (crime rate, educational achievement, health and so forth) if the judge had not sentenced them to the YA. Unfortunately there is no practical method for generating an accurate estimate of this sort on a continuing year-to-year basis, as is required for an accounting system. It may be possible to implement special one-shot experimental studies in which delinquents with serious criminal records are randomly assigned to either training schools or probation in the community, and then monitored for a number of months. Such experiments are potentially very useful in addressing basic issues about correctional treatment, but not for tracking YA performance.

The second standard is how well the YA inmates are doing in comparison to some absolute reference. For example, the YA could be awarded an "A+" for the year if inmates committed no serious crimes against the outside community, gained on average of 15 points on a standardized reading test scores, kept up with their age group in terms of physical growth and fitness—and so forth. Such comparisons require considerable effort and care, but ultimately it may be possible to apply them to a number of performance indicators.

A third standard, useful for internal management purposes, is a comparison of different programs and units within the YA. To be valid, such comparisons must take into account the baseline differences in the youths assigned to the different programs.

Finally, complete evaluation of the YA must take into account the cost. An "A-" program may be preferrable to an "A+" if the former can be operated at half the cost per inmate.

Notes on Input and Process Measures

My main concern has been to characterize a system of accounts that would provide the public and YA management with a basis for monitoring performance. The focus has been on the human service agency's equivalent of the corporation's bottom line.

Statistics on performance are useful in signalling successes and failures, but not for seeking explanations for success or failure. Additional data are needed to develop understanding of the essential ingredients of a high performance program, or of a total flop. At the most primitive level, performance is produced by "inputs"—facilities, program staff, community volunteers, medical professionals, materials, and the inmates themselves. Each of these "inputs" can be described on a number of dimensions. They are brought together in a process that is defined by formal and informal rules and procedures—the "technology" of producing the outcomes that are of direct concern to the community of interests surrounding the YA.

There are many ways of describing the process in a YA program. One type of description focuses on the written policies that nominally govern activities in the program. This is almost exclusively the method adopted by the American Correctional Association's Commission on Accreditation for Corrections (*viz., Standards for Juvenile Training Schools,* Second Edition, 1983), and by the courts. This concern with written policy is understandable, since written policy is less expensive to monitor than actual practice. But it seems likely that written policy has a rather weak relationship to ultimate performance.

Developing an understanding of what makes for a successful program may require an intense effort to describe what actually transpires on a day-to-day basis in a program. How do the staff relate to the youths? Whom do the youths respect? To what extent are the youths held accountable for their behavior? What are the de facto rewards for making progress in developing skills? Our current level of ignorance dictates a wide ranging quest for those particular elements that make a YA program a success.

It is not appropriate, however, for the YA's annual report to include much data on process, any more than it is for General Motors' annual report to include a detailed description of how a Chevette is produced. For the public, the main concern is what has the YA been able to accomplish with the delinquents assigned to its custody. Has it prevented them from engaging in criminal activity while in custody? What fraction of the delinquents will return to crime following release? Have they developed new skills? Are they healthy? Have they been allowed to maintain a reasonable degree of autonomy? What sort of contacts do they have with the community? A systematic report on issues such as these may encourage accountability in the juvenile corrections system and an orientation towards improving performance.

20
An Alternative Approach to Managing Juvenile Corrections

EDWARD M. MURPHY

Alexis de Tocqueville, an admiring but normally discerning observer of American mores, toured our penal institutions in 1831. Reflecting on the condition of the children he saw, de Tocqueville subscribed to the view that "the children were not victims of persecution, but merely deprived of fatal liberty." His opinion represents one side of an argument that has persisted for more than 150 years. The dispute concerns what to do with children who break the law, and whether or not the state should confine them for their own protection against "fatal liberty." It remains the central question in juvenile justice today.

This paper concerns itself with juvenile correctional policy and is limited to discussing that group of offenders who have committed serious acts of delinquency. Although status offenders and minor delinquents present important policy issues, those groups are presumed to lie outside the realm of juvenile corrections. In addition, the observations here are presented from a management perspective. The intended audience consists of those who are responsible for, or who seek to influence, the management of juvenile correctional organizations. This perspective, frankly, implies greater concern with the overall operation of a correctional system than with the handling of individual delinquents.

In the pages that follow, I intend to advance the following line of argument:

1. That the success or failure of the juvenile justice system depends primarily on the efficacy of the dispositional alternatives available in that system.

2. That juvenile correctional organizations, as the main dispositional arm of the system, must be permitted to organize themselves to take advantage of the best available professional knowledge.

3. That the best available knowledge suggests that, while there is no one formula for success with all offenders, many different types of programs have succeeded with different types of offenders.

4. That it is, therefore, the responsibility of juvenile-correctional orga-

nizations to create and sustain a broad range of programs from which to select in making placement decisions about individual offenders.

5. That the best way to create and sustain program diversity is through a system of purchasing services from private service providers, thereby taking advantage of market forces, competition, creativity, and the flexibility available to organizations unbound by the restraints placed on government bureaucracies.

This line of argument departs from the traditional approach to juvenile corrections, in which dispositional alternatives are usually limited to a yes or no decision regarding institutional placement. More importantly, the idea that a broad range of programs should be delivered by people and organizations who are not part of government officialdom implies a fundamental rethinking of the role of juvenile correctional agencies. Although several jurisdictions have moved at least tentatively away from a strict reliance on institutions and towards increased participation of private service providers, the field has yet to develop a systematic conceptual framework for the investment of public resources in an alternative approach to juvenile corrections. The existing institutional framework was created more than a century ago and continues to dominate juvenile corrections policy.

Policy debates on how best to array juvenile correctional resources are now generally pervaded by two related themes. One is the argument over the value of institutions, and the other concerns the toughness of official response to juvenile crime. It is widely assumed that arguments in favor of continued use of institutions are also arguments in favor of stern dispositions. Conversely, proponents of alternatives to institutions are usually seen as soft when it comes to crime control. Because crime control is an issue of much greater salience for the public than institutionalization, the "tough" versus "soft" question takes on the character of a litmus test by which all related matters are judged. Discussions of deinstitutionalization thus acquire an ideological bias that has little to do with the effectiveness of institutions, and everything to do with public concern about crime. A century of experience with institutions as the *only* response to juvenile crime has made it difficult to see the problem differently. Any new framework must avoid the toughness trap and accommodate an array of political and philosophical opinions about crime control. That is to say, there are ways to be tough on crime without relying on institutions.

In addition to arguing for development of a new conceptual framework for the investment of public resources in juvenile corrections, this paper will examine the impediments to such a development. The association between institutions and crime control is one such barrier. Others lie in the tangled web of executive–judicial relationships that intrude upon dispositional decision-making. The traditional case-by-case way of thinking about juvenile justice and the normally hierarchical organizational structure of public agencies charged with administering the system present additional roadblocks to constructive change. Finally, and perhaps most crippling, is the absence of an appropriate vocabulary to describe what should exist in an ideal juvenile correctional system. These impediments to change are subtle and difficult to overcome. An analysis of each of them is offered in the hope that implicit assumptions, once recognized, are easier to change. The final sections of this paper will explore how a diverse array of juvenile correctional programs might be described and administered if existing impediments were eliminated or reduced.

The Management Context

Few public managers confront a more difficult set of circumstances than the officials who run juvenile corrections organizations. They face a complex set of executive-judicial relationships in which powerful judges are likely to be organizational adversaries. They confront public opinion that insists on a stern response to young offenders but will not tolerate poor institutional conditions. They work under statutory arrangements that envision successful rehabilitation programs, but they read in professional literature that nothing works. They have custody of large numbers of sullen adolescents who are supposed to receive treatment but whose most fervent wish is to be elsewhere. All the while, there is the risk that a young person will become involved in a single notorious crime, the public consequences of which will overwhelm any perception of effectiveness on the part of the juvenile justice system. It is hard enough to maintain the status quo under these conditions. The administrator who actually plans to make progress must have a clear sense of purpose, a firm grasp of operational details, and must overcome four major problems.

The Problem of Judicial Ethnocentrism

When juvenile courts were created during the first decades of the twentieth century, they quickly became the focus of attention in the juvenile justice field even though they were predated in many states by juvenile correctional institutions. Born in a burst of optimism, the court was to be the moral and legal center of *parens patriae*. Excessive claims and expectations for success obscured the fact that the true measures of success or failure with offenders are only found in what happens after they leave the courtroom. That exaggerated sense of the court's capacity explains the profound disappointment and harsh criticism to which the court is subject even today.

It is nonsensical for the court to be credited or blamed with the success or failure of the system. Particularly with respect to those most serious offenders who catch the public eye, the court's involvement is usually limited to the time it takes to try, adjudicate, and commit the offender to a state-run juvenile correction agency or one of its institutions. Accountability should lie with the people who have control of the offender around-the-clock for months or years, rather than with the judge who handles the case while it is on the court's docket. The black-robed judge on the elevated bench is an image of such potency, however, that it is tempting to believe that the court can control the disposition. The fact that this belief is held by some judges further skews the perception of how the juvenile justice system works and how it should work.

To the degree that debate about the efficacy of the juvenile justice system focuses only on the court, that debate fails to enlighten the public or policymakers. Implicit in the debate is the assumption that improvements in the broad measures of the system's success can be brought about by affecting how the court works. Certainly the operations of the court determine the efficiency with which cases are processed, the fairness of fact-finding, the protection of individual rights, and the wisdom of dispositional choices from among the available alternatives. All of these are essential aspects of the system, but the final judgment of the court's value hinges on how well its dispositional decisions are executed. If the correctional system is well run, effectively rehabilitative, and able to keep its failures below the threshold of public intolerance, the court is esteemed and controversy is minimal. If, however, the correctional system is inept, the court is held to blame. The irony is that individual judges have little or no capacity to affect the day-to-day competence of correctional programs, even in jurisdictions in which those programs are an element of the judicial branch. In the more routine cases, in which correctional programs are a function of the executive branch, judicial impact is even less. Thus, the degree to which the juvenile court is valued as an institution for dealing with delinquency depends more on the effectiveness of correctional programs outside of the court's control than on anything the court can do for itself.

Organizational Barriers to Diversity

Correctional managers must try to operate programs that address the problems presented by the delinquents in their care. One of the clearest lessons of professional experience in this regard, and one of the most difficult to apply, is that juvenile correctional organizations function more effectively when they provide a wide range of programs in which delinquents can be placed. Research has shown that while no one program formula works for all offenders, many different types of programs have had measurable success with some participants. The task is to match the profile of the individual offender with the type of program best calculated to address his or her needs. With increasingly sophisticated diagnostic tools available, it is possible to make carefully gauged placement recommendations. Those recommendations are rendered meaningless, however, if the program type called for is not available to the organization making the placement decision. Virtually all caseworkers in the juvenile field have had the experience of knowing exactly what a youngster needed to succeed but did not have the capacity to deliver it.

The primary operational challenge to the management of a juvenile correctional organization, therefore, is to create and sustain a diverse programmatic network. Unfortunately, the impediments to accomplishing this goal are formidable. First, the traditional response to serious or persistent delinquency has been to send the offender to a reform school. These institutions do some things well, but their attraction lies in a comfortable consistency; they do not provide a framework for program diversity. If a jurisdiction has more than one institutional option, the disposition is most commonly made on the basis of geography, gender, or age rather than the offender's needs.

Second, bureaucracies have a tendency to continue to do what they have always done. The flexibility and openness to innovation that are required to create and sustain diversity are not characteristic of most public organizations. Third, the way that public budgets are usually structured contributes to the bureaucracy's inertia because it is difficult to move money from one place to another, and to do many different things with money from the same source. Beyond whatever vested interests will resist reallocation of funds, it is possible that government accounting and control systems will simply be unable to accommodate the financial flexibility required to pay for diversity. Fourth, several other features of government organizations, most notably personnel practices and collective bargaining with employee unions, reduce the capacity of those organizations to act swiftly in effecting the need for programmatic change even if they are otherwise inclined and able to do so. Finally, public organizations lack political incentive to encourage diversity because diversity necessarily entails taking risks. The routine assignment of delinquent youngsters to reform schools does not entail much risk for the decision-makers, and it offers an apparent accountability in that everyone knows where the kids are. The result is more likely to be disparity than diversity.

The Reductionist Perspective

The obstacles facing the juvenile corrections administrator intent on creating program diversity within his or her jurisdiction are multiplied by the particular philosophical and clinical orientation of juvenile justice professionals. There is a subtle habit of mind that characterizes the way practitioners think about their field. This habit is best described by the concept of the synecdoche. A synecdoche is a figure of speech in which a part is used to represent a whole, (i.e., saying "50 sails" when referring to 50 ships). This is the standard mode of description in the juvenile justice field.

Practitioners think synecdochically about their work because they routinely speak as if the characteristics of one individual case can be generalized to the entire system. As agents of *parens patriae*, juvenile corrections managers are oriented by training and tradition to focus on the specific needs of individual children. For many of them, each case is a separate window on the juvenile justice world. The strengths and defects of that world are measured by its ability to respond to *this* case. Dissatisfaction is expressed in terms of an individual child whose case was badly handled. The criticism is usually valid enough, but it is not expressed in a way designed to promote systemic change. Unsystematic and invalid generalizations occur on the assumption that what can be said about a part can also be said of the whole. Since it is usually the system's failures that attract most of the public attention or comment, the correctional organization tends to react piecemeal to its failures in individual cases when it could be establishing a diverse system capable of responding to a range of needs.

This kind of management by inversion is not well suited to the systematic development of diversity, but it is an almost inevitable by-product of the way in which key parts of the juvenile justice system are organized and staffed. The most important actors in the juvenile justice system—lawyers and social workers—are trained to think in terms of cases rather than systems. It is a kind of thinking that is common in a political world in which, according to one critic, "the plural of anecdote is data." Because of the way a court approaches its workload, cases and problems can be dealt with in serial fashion and even the busiest courts are relieved, at least momentarily, from the need to confront many cases simultaneously. Even though this approach is not conducive to the development of an overall systemic view of programmatic needs, judges are nevertheless likely to have the major say in how juvenile correctional services are organized, either through advocacy for policy change or through the cumulative weight of their decisions in individual cases. Judges are thus frequently in a position to make decisions affecting program management even though the formality and procedural ritual of the courtroom make it almost impossible for judges to manage anything that must occur oustide a courtroom.

The Language Problem

Even when they are talking to each other, juvenile justice professionals have a terrible time describing what it is they do and how their system works. This is not because these individuals are dull or because they do not understand their work. It is because the language used to describe the system is inadequate to the task. The absence of clear and powerful words with commonly understood meanings handicaps the construction of a conceptual framework for juvenile justice and inhibits careful analysis of the existing system.

The key terms used in the field tend to be metaphors, words transferred from other disciplines because of their figurative insight, but which have lost their power. This is especially true of the words used to describe the dispositional aspects of the system. The policy debate concerning how to handle juvenile offenders centers around a conflict over which of two analogies is more appropriate: the *treatment/rehabilitation* language of the medical profession, or the *just deserts* language of the adult criminal justice system. The experience of history shows that these models have lost their meaning in discussing juvenile justice. Rather than promoting insights and fruitful discussion, the images have fostered rigidity and bitterness between well-meaning persons.

The system uses other words and phrases that avoid the perils of hidden metaphors, but at the expense of meaning. Much of the literature depends on the use of double negatives to define things by what they are not. For example, a major policy thrust of juvenile justice in the past decade concerned the transfer of children guilty of "noncriminal misbehavior" to the "least restrictive alternative." These terms at least have a superficial precision that "deinstitutionalization" does not.

Simply put, the current images used in the juvenile justice field are too narrow; the words and symbols do not adequately encompass the subtlety, complexity and range of what is real and what is possible in the field. Part of what is needed to bring diversity to juvenile corrections is a new metaphor, or perhaps several. Fresh transfers of figurative insight, new analogies, and unusual perspectives might make it possible for professionals to see things differently, and to talk about their field in ways that lead to constructive change. This might be done, as other disciplines do it, by borrowing symbols from outside their normal context. Some resonant images can come from combinations that seem strikingly inappropriate. For example, nuclear physicists pressed to describe the attraction among certain subatomic particles call it "charm." Computer scientists, judging the efficiency of software, refer to the "elegance" of a program. These images are a far cry from the lifeless and limited medical metaphor that characterizes much of the discourse about juvenile delinquency. So long as the new metaphor avoids the flat and easy sports metaphors, the trite military analogies, and the popular pseudo-scientific operant conditioning jargon, the field will benefit by having new tools for analyzing and thinking about juvenile justice.

Out of Context

The juvenile justice system as it exists today is the result of a long series of decisions, choices, accidents, and changes that occurred over a period of more than a century. It is the accumulation of years of actions and reactions that were sensible and explicable in the context in which they took place, but the product now seems awkward, ill-fitting and somehow less than the sum of its parts. There is widespread dissatisfaction among the public at large, and defensiveness in the profession. In this state of affairs, it is instructive to ask what a juvenile justice system would look like if it were created today from the ground up.

New language, including a set of terms that would promote rather than inhibit different ways of thinking about the problem, would be the first priority. A systematic perspective, in which policy and program decisions are made on the basis of a clear view of the problem as a whole would avoid the distortions of the past. Flexible organizational structures could be devised to develop rather than to discourage a diverse range of programmatic options. The new framework would, in short, provide a sound and systematic method for the response to serious juvenile delinquency.

The best way to break away from the old forms of response is to understand that the resources committed to juvenile corrections are an investment. When viewed as an investment, the key question for juvenile corrections becomes: What is the most productive way to invest the resources available to the system? In most jurisdictions this is a meaningless question because to ask it implies that there is a choice. If the resources of the system are routinely invested only in the maintenance of institutions and if periodic public budget decisions are largely preordained, there are no choices to make.

Such is the case in many jurisdictions as, for example, in Massachusetts. The Lyman School, founded in 1846, was the first state-supported reform school in the United States. Within a generation it became the focus of criticism because of its remoteness, large size, and ineffectiveness in rehabilitating its residents. Because the existing bureaucratic framework did not allow for doing anything else, the state continued to support that institution for another century. It was not until 1972 that the Lyman School was closed, and the funds used to support it became available for other investments. Massachusetts threw good money after bad for 126 years, an error remarkable for its longevity, but otherwise not much different than the experience in many jurisdictions. The power of inertia, combined with the political, economic, and professional constituencies served by such institutions, make change difficult. The failure to see correctional programs and institutions as investments, to be continued if successful, and to be cashed in if not, results in waste of resources and energy.

Investment decisions involve making choices and necessarily include the possibility of error. That possibility is defined as risk, a concept quite familiar to juvenile corrections practitioners. The juvenile system rests on the assumption that young offenders are more amenable to rehabilitation than adults and that their return to unsupervised life in the community will be relatively swift. Practice and research show that the gradual reduction of correctional control is the most effective way to return offenders to the community. Those released from environments with minimal controls do better than those discharged directly from high security institutions. Professionals thus confront a situation in which they should, in a fairly short time frame, make a series of decisions about how much control should be applied to an individual offender. The trick is to apply sufficient control to ensure that the juvenile does not seriously offend public safety, while at the same time keeping the level of control low enough so as not to impede the offender's progress towards full freedom. The risks associated with making these decisions are obvious. Criticism of the juvenile justice system occurs when decision-makers err on one side or the other. Excessive control and an exaggerated fear of crime lead to the abuse of state power and the abuse of delinquent children. Insufficient control leads to those all-too-familiar notorious acts of crime by recidivist juvenile offenders.

Given the salience of crime control as a political issue, it is not surprising that most jurisdictions have chosen to take the risks associated with excessive control rather than those associated with insufficient control. Because institutions are the predominant technology for exercising a high degree of short-term control, public resources are routinely invested in training schools, and juvenile offenders are routinely sent to them. In this way, judges and correctional administrators, who are paid to make decisions and take risks, ensure that they do not have to do so. From a crime control perspective, institutions represent the low-risk option, but the elimination of risk entails the elimination of diversity. Concomitant with a lack of diversity is a lack of opportunity to make choices and, at least in the short run, the agents of government are protected against making the wrong choice.

Contrast this low-risk, low-diversity state of affairs with a system in which resource decisions about juvenile correctional programs are seen as true investments. The management of these investments would call for the same degree of prudence and thoughtfulness that would characterize any other large investment. What investor would operate with the restrictions that apply to investments in juvenile corrections: risks are not permitted; everyone must invest in the same company; there is little recognition that investment objectives may vary from case to case; there is no opportunity to terminate poor investments or to make informed choices from many gradations of investment risk. With these limitations, it is not surprising that the return on public capital invested in juvenile corrections is unsatisfactory.

The purpose of a juvenile correctional organization should be to create and sustain a diverse range of programmatic vehicles through which to manage responsibly the risks associated with public investment in the field. In this context, the role of the correctional organization thus becomes similar to that of an investment bank and brokerage house for the system. The brokèrage house substitutes its judgment for that of investors who could not possibly know as much about the market and could not manage their investments with equal diligence. The correctional organization would be a repository of expert advice about the market which is applied to the investment needs and goals of its clients. The brokerage firm specializes in its field.

It has combined the methods of research with the capacity of data processing to amass vast knowledge about the vehicles it chooses for investment. The qualities that a broker looks for in a company are many of the same ones that distinguish between good and bad juvenile justice programs: past track record; special expertise; market niche; organizational strategy for the future; quality of management. A broker constructs a portfolio that takes advantage of some higher risk opportunities for growth but balances them with conservative investments to protect against serious loss. The result is a sound asset mix.

Brokers have a clear sense of their own role in the overall system of investment. They recognize the need for venture capital to start promising enterprises with no guarantees of success. They establish minimum qualifications for investment programs so that there is a threshold below which one cannot be listed. Their fiduciary responsibility leads to a dispassionate but powerful mandate to abandon investments that are obvious losers.

The brokerage analogy for juvenile corrections suggests that decisions about correctional investments should flow from different principles than those adhered to now. It envisions a system in which diversity, competition, innovation and change are given a higher priority than predictability and the elimination of risk. It implies an approach to dispositions that is neither a medical model nor just deserts, but more like a free market model in which a knowledgeable professional chooses from among many options the one best calculated to satisfy the combination of factors that exist in individual cases. Correctional administrators are disposition brokers whose responsibility is to understand acceptable levels of risk, to diversify the program portfolio, to distinguish between situations calling for fast growth or steady dividends, and to ensure that orderly and stable markets are available to the investing community.

The disposition broker also proposes the radical idea that none of these programs has claim on an indefinite flow of resources. Investment will end when, in the judgment of the disposition broker, a program offers no further promise of satisfactory return. Thus, the portfolio of programs and facilities maintained by a juvenile correctional organization could change continuously in response to shifting client characteristics, fresh knowledge of adolescent behavior, and newly developed program ideas.

The brokerage analogy contemplates an arrangement according to which the juvenile court has the power to authorize an investment on behalf of an individual child and to establish the broad goals for the return on its investment. It is the responsibility of the correctional agency to structure the specific aspects of the investment by selecting from among the placement options available to it. The agency continues to manage the investment for the duration of its stewardship of the child and is accountable for the outcome. While the distribution of power between courts and correctional agencies varies dramatically across jurisdictions, the relationship described here is not far removed from the traditional youth authority model. The brokerage analogy does not require statutory change in jurisdictions where courts make commitment decisions and correctional agencies make placement decisions. It does require correctional organizations to be much more imaginative, flexible, and responsive in the use of their power. From the courts it requires restraint, appropriate trust in the judgment of corrections professionals, and the recognition that success is not measured in individual cases but in the aggregate performance of the portfolio as a whole.

A Path to Diversification

The most profound change in the juvenile justice system suggested by the brokerage analogy occurs in the structure of juvenile correctional agencies. The typical correctional organization consists of a central office, one or more institutions, and perhaps an aftercare component. The relationships among these parts establish the organization's priorities and define its typical patterns of action. Normally, institutional needs have first claim on agency attention because that is where most of the money and staff are assigned. The leadership of the organization generally does not have the option to withdraw investment from a component part of the agency. Guided by tradition, by structural budget considerations, and by comradeship stemming from the fact of a common employer, all levels of the organization tend to act within the framework of the status quo and take it for granted that things will stay more or less the same. It is unrealistic to expect that such an organization would easily engage in a continuous process of program change and reinvestment.

The disposition broker must act within a different organizational structure. The broker must have no vested interest in the vehicle chosen for investment other than a professional judgment as to its high quality. If any such interest does exist, it must be recognized as a conflict and disclosed. The disposition broker must be able to add and delete elements of the portfolio in order to obtain the most productive return on investment.

A strategy that accommodates the needs of the disposition broker is the purchase of services from private providers. One advantage of this approach is its lack of permanent commitment. A contract between a correctional agency and a service provider has a time limit. It has a mutually agreed upon renewal point at which time the correctional agency can decide not to renew its investment in the contracted program. This is an opportunity that the agency rarely has with institutions operated by its own employees, even when those facilities no longer perform a service that the agency needs. A purchase of service system provides valuable protection against the loss of investment that can accompany government-run programs which cannot be terminated.

This kind of contracting system with private service providers brings other benefits that a correctional agency cannot otherwise acquire. In addition to the flexibility to start and stop programs more readily, contracting allows for the swift implementation of policy decisions. Private organizations can act with a speed that is difficult to match in government bureaucracies. The management prerogatives of private industry, such as more adaptable personnel systems, less cumbersome fiscal management and purchasing procedures, work to the benefit of public organizations as well. An open bidding process encourages competition among providers. Public organizations have no other way to avail themselves of the price efficiency and program creativity engendered by competition.

The main potential disadvantage of a purchase of service approach to juvenile corrections is one that can come with any market system in which consumers are neither smart enough to know what they want, nor strong enough to insist on getting it. Governments must resist the temptation to buy what is available instead of what is needed. Discussions of private participation in the juvenile correction system frequently include optimistic talk of public-private partnerships, but the relationship is a partnership only to the extent that each side benefits. The investment decisions of correctional administrators must be characterized by a ruthless determination not to continue any program that has lost its usefulness as a productive part of the portfolio.

If juvenile correctional organizations move to purchase services from private providers, they will be able to give themselves a systematic way of creating and sustaining program diversity. Program diversity is an element that is crucial to a successful juvenile correctional organization but is often missing. This competitive framework for the investment of public money can invigorate the correctional network and give it channels through which to change and grow. Contracting promotes trial and error on a broad scale without committing government to the continuing support of its mistakes. It offers a method for weeding out weak investments and for redirecting capital to more productive ends. Instead of attempting to adapt an outmoded framework to current conditions, contracting provides a process for the constructive management of inevitable change.

Conclusion

Correctional administrators are heirs to a nineteenth-century framework governing the response to juvenile crime. In order to capture the full benefit of public appropriations, administrators must see themselves as disposition brokers who can offer a wide range of investment alternatives. They must break the hidebound monopoly of institutions and institutional thinking and let market forces work to create diversity. Diversity can be readily created and sustained in a purchase of service system. Competition adds an incentive for the development of better methods of solving specific problems, and the forces of the market encourage providers to identify needs that are not being adequately serviced and design programs to meet those needs. This approach to managing juvenile corrections could give administrators the tool they need to overcome the institution vs. no institution stalemate paralyzing juvenile corrections policy, and become a major force for change in the field.

21 Conclusion

Francis X. Hartmann

A "Conclusion" can take different forms. It can be a summarizing statement of what has preceded, or it may be the final statement totally built on what has gone before. This conclusion is neither. Nor is it a statement of consensus drawn from the Executive Session itself. In this volume it means a concluding statement, informed by other members of the Executive Session on the Future of Juvenile Justice, but the sole responsibility of this author. While some members of the Executive Session may be uncomfortable with the positions taken, taking no position or taking one which permits multiple interpretations would not contribute to the dialogue. I trust that members of the Session who disagree with my position will feel that I listened to them.

The convening and unifying theme of the Executive Session and its members was that the current system is deeply troubled. One could probably convene in any society a group of persons concerned about the issues of children, but the many examples of the erosion of the current system confirm that this is a particularly difficult issue for contemporary society. By current system, we mean both the narrower system of justice—police, courts and youth authorities—and the much broader system which includes the family, schools and other institutions. That these institutions and the working arrangement among them are troubled is not to be equated with total failure. Members of the Executive Session spoke of the great successes of the current system. After all, the overwhelming majority of children are never seen by the formal juvenile justice system, and the majority of children which it does see once or twice never appear in the system again. But what we call the traditional system, dating back to the turn of the century, has been greatly changed by Supreme Court decisions beginning in the late 1960s. The transition is much more than systemic. It involves a conflict of values.

Peter Greenwood says that ". . . society now accepts inadequate and incompetent parenting as the lesser of two evils; the other evil being excessive intrusion into private family concerns. It may well be that . . .

we accept the lack of adequate parenting (because) we fail to attribute all of the negative consequences that result . . . to their proper cause."

The price for incompetent parenting, for failed socialization, is multifold. It includes neglected children, abused children, and juveniles who commit crime. These three groups (and it is not unusual to have one child belonging to all three) frequently become the adults who commit crime. And the same cohort is the major contributor to the various adult dependencies, ranging from welfare status to institutionalization for emotional disorders. The cost of such failed socialization is not immediately apparent except in the case of those physically abused and neglected. Further, payment for the failure is deferred and at the same time remote from many people in society, especially those with power. Nonetheless, few would disagree that the price is enormous.

The price for intervention other than under the strictest set of legal criteria governed by due process is also considerable. The rights of parents are attacked and eroded. Children, parents, and families can be unjustly stigmatized. Excessive moralism concerning what is appropriate narrows the range of legitimate possibilities and variations of behavior and attacks the family as an integral unit which can have confidence in itself and its own particular values. All of this leads to a homogeneity within society which may be comforting at any particular moment, but is both contrary and debilitating to the American vision.

One might take a worthy stand on either of the above points of view, but society is left in a dilemma. Its actions regarding children seem to generate blessings which are mixed at best. Weariness and paralysis have ensued. The weariness is the result of well-intentioned people locked in different positions which are based on principle, the paralysis the result of any action seeming to create harm.

To some extent, the paralysis results from the quandry about what a good juvenile justice system should look like and what its purpose is. This is not unrelated to society's indecision about what today's good child should look like and what good parenting consists of. Certainly, good children and good parenting differ in important ways from those of the turn of the century.

One way to approach the gordian knot of unyielding positions might be the development of a substantive statement about what constitutes the contemporary good child and good parenting. Now the creation of such a statement is an exceptionally dangerous enterprise in a liberal democratic society. There are few easier ways in which to have one's head handed back on a platter of indignation, vituperation, and newsprint. Accusations will fly: racism, ethnocentrism, and being wed to middle-class values. Let me hasten to say that I am not courageous enough to draft such a statement, nor do I have the standing to be attended to. But saying that I cannot and am not empowered to develop and make such a statement is quite different from saying that such a statement is unnecessary to the effectiveness of the broad juvenile justice enterprise. After all, how can that enterprise be effective if it does not know what its goals are and what it is about?

For every society must socialize its children. While one hopes that it will be around a noble vision of citizenship, it will finally be around some vision, perhaps substantially less noble. If the manner in which society addresses that socialization process is tentative for a period of time, that hesitance is temporary. The society is unlikely to tolerate ongoing ambiguity concerning socialization. There is current evidence of a movement away from tentativeness and towards a definitive position as seen in the clamor for the transfer of numbers of children from the juvenile court to the adult criminal court.

The status of the current juvenile court is an example of the societal dilemma. In transition from its traditional status, post-*Gault* and other Supreme Court opinions, it would not seem to know what it can do, or what it wants to do. It reminds one of a prizefighter well past the end of his career attempting to eke out yet another bout, and appearing cautious, inept, and self-protective in an arena in which one is most effective by being aggressive. Its sense of mission is diminished, it is derided as the "kiddy court," and the derision carries with it low priority regarding allocation of resources. Its reaction to real world events and needs is untimely and slow. It is being bullied to construe justice primarily as punishment meted out to juvenile offenders. No wonder that it is on the defensive; it is being circled for the kill.

If the juvenile court is gradually beaten and its jurisdiction narrowed or finally abolished, we shall be left with two alternatives for children posing risk and at risk: the adult criminal court and social welfare agencies. The former has sufficient difficulty addressing non-conforming adults without adding the complexity of handling children whose non-conformity is very different. There is also no evidence that the adult court treats young offenders referred to it any differently than the juvenile court. Social welfare agencies addressing non-conforming children and families are likely to be more coercive regarding what is acceptable behavior and in exacting a price for unacceptable behavior—perhaps as defined by the case worker. And this will be done privately and out of the public view. The public will not even realize that coercive powers are being exercised in its name.

The alternative to developing a substantive statement about children and parenting and revitalizing the society's vision for its children is to leave the shaping of that vision to the shifting pressures which happen to be present at a particular time and in a particular place. Unfortunately, the forces which generate many of the pressures for change are in reaction to crisis and, more often than not, are hasty, over-reactive, and distorting of a balanced approach to the society's children. Given the troublesome nature of the problems posed by children who are at risk or who cause risk to the larger community, a juvenile system which is built upon public reaction to occasional outrageous acts is bound to be episodic, shallow, unevenly coercive, probably unfair, and unresponsive to the overall needs of society for its children.

One wants to base the vision of citizenship and the process whereby children become citizens not on pressures of the moment, but on the lasting values of the community. These are expressed in various ways: through the Constitution, legal statutes (which may change), religion, tradition, mores, and through an ongoing discussion about which values are most important in the long run.

The first task of those concerned with juvenile justice and the making of children into citizens is to place responsibility for the development of the substantive statement about good children and the good parenting which forms such children. Who, or what institution, will have the courage and standing to assume such responsibility?

One hears considerable discussion of leadership, sometimes utilizing the concept of "champion," as public policy issues are addressed. The champion must visibly, vocally and persistently espouse a certain cause if that cause is to receive its fair share of the public's attention and resources. The concept is not new to the field of juvenile justice. Whether it be the child-savers or advocates for children, many have championed the cause of children.

I believe that the juvenile justice champion must address the issues of the child not only as an individual with rights but as a member of the community. While the former is undeniably true, implicit in the individual rights position seems to be an assumption that the child's necessary and desired individuality and independence separate him or her from the community. The child as individual with rights becomes confused with the child as unformed by his or her community and therefore alone. For if the exercise of individual rights seriously blocks the process whereby a child becomes an adult member of the community, that person will be out of step with his or her society in significant ways, not just marching to a different drummer. Franklin Zimring asks the key question of a democracy:

> But how do we train young people to be free? If the exercise of independent choice is an essential element of maturity, part of the process of becoming mature is learning to make independent decisions. [This] is a risky process for the pupil and the larger society. . . . We want adolescents to make mistakes, but we hope they make the right kind of mistakes. . . . An important part of cutting our losses during the period of development is minimizing the harm young persons do to themselves . . .[1]

Is the child then a pawn of the society, without rights? Not at all. Rather, the rights of the individual child at that moment are balanced against the rights of the future individual as an adult. Is Catherine Ryan not correct when she states that the child has an obligation to prepare to hold a job as an adult? There are obligations, other than attending school until one is 16 years of age, which the child, as nascent adult, must meet. The community, speaking through the court, makes judgments about the balance among rights when imposing duties and obligations.

"Socialization" has become a loaded term. One thinks twice about using it when speaking about children because it apparently smacks of authoritarian lock-step conformity, lack of choice, and, perhaps, even racism. I believe that this is the overextension of a reasonable fear—reasonable because we are uncomfortably aware of recent societies which demanded too much by way of conformity and of those persons and movements in our own society who wish to do the same. But the fear is overextended because, in the name of that fear, the society is effectively backing away from making demands on some of those who will be full citizens in several years.

Somewhere in our society at this moment are presidents-to-be, the future Supreme Court and Congress, along with other leaders of the society. More important are the future parents. All of these people with future responsibilities are currently children. Among the character traits being given to them as they move toward their responsibilities as citizens are a sense of importance and value, some intellectual challenge, opportunities to recognize their own strengths, ambition, and a sense of civility and self-discipline. As Peter Greenwood says, "It is inconceivable to think of attempting to raise . . . children without some supervising authority. Without the power to discipline, children become peers, no more subject to adult control over the long-run than contemporaries at work." Would they achieve their goals without supervision and discipline? While not every child is raised to think of himself or herself as a potential president, is it fair to the child and the society if each child is not given sufficient measure of all that is necessary to achieve citizenship? And who will champion that child, those children and their needs? Who will address, with authority, not just the individual child, but more importantly, the institutions surrounding that child? For children themselves are not at the center of the problem; the institutions surrounding children are. While the statement is simple, its ramifications are not. If institutions serving children are the problem, the society needs a way to hold accountable, help or change those institutions. The complex of institutions affecting children, ranging from the family to the Youth Authority, must be addressed.

The discussion above is fore-shadowing the suggestion of an expanded role for the court. Why ought it be expanded when it has failed in so many ways in the past? Because it is the best of the alternatives which might carry the burden of leadership around the issue of the society's investment in children, especially children posing risk and at risk.

Before attempting to re-frame a new position, let me echo the thoughts of those who are uncomfortable with any but the narrowest role for the court. Recent discussions with a concerned and thoughtful critic revealed two underlying themes. First, government is most to be feared when it says that it is reaching out to help; and second, no deliberative body should ever be allowed to make decisions unattended. I agree with those positions, but not to the point of leaving a vacuum of need within the society. Further, the two themes seem intertwined, and by addressing the latter, the former is made possible within the bounds of a democratic society.

In a broad sense, every government is meant to be of help to its citizens. Abuses arise when the helping and intervening take place in a nonpublic manner, in a way which leaves the government unaccountable to the community. If the issue of public accountability can be resolved, placing responsibility for intervention within a branch of government may become more acceptable.

It is clear that society's interest in children extends beyond children who are currently committing crimes. In the opinion of this writer, the juvenile court should play a role among the many institutions responsible for this broader societal interest. That judgement about the role of the juvenile court runs counter to the direction in which popular sentiment has been moving. And if we are talking about the stereotypical court, one finds it difficult to disagree. The court that evolved from its original conception in Illinois in 1899 into something less noble and far more whimsical has few defenders, and rightly so. The court became self-righteous and secretive. It over-extended its authority and did not hold itself accountable to the community, a combination of traits which is inherently destructive within a democratic society.

Alternative candidates for the leadership role are the police, the schools, and, at one time, youth service bureaus. Despite the amazing breadth and depth of police involvement with the community and its children, and despite the understanding and compassion with which they often operate, the police certainly would neither seek out nor welcome the additional responsibility of speaking publically in the name of children at risk. The schools find themselves in a position of being overwhelmed by the responsibilities they are already carrying. While the schools often seek a wider responsibility regarding children, their history is generally one of backing away from troublesome individuals and situations as being too distracting from their main enterprise, education for the majority. The children most in need are most troublesome, and despite claims to the contrary, schools and school systems are less than eager to address these needs. There was a time in the 1970s when Youth Service Bureaus seemed to answer problems of the system. With a few exceptions, they have disappeared largely because they had no real power.

Who remains with the courage to step into the vacuum and the standing to demand a hearing? Public social agencies in some states, perhaps a Department of Youth Services, might speak for children. But it is unclear to whom these agencies owe allegiance. They seem to exist in a murky area between the courts and the Executive branch with the Legislature intervening in times of crisis. Further, these agencies often lack credibility with the public. Private social agencies have performed marvelous services for children but their mandates are too diffuse, and their capability and credibility too uneven in different places, at different times, and with different audiences to expect that they can speak effectively, let alone authoritatively, for children and their needs.

I believe that a reconstituted juvenile court could best exercise the leadership necessary to hold society and its institutions responsible for seeing that children are empowered to attain full citizenship. The most significant aspects of a reconstituted court involve the relationship between the court and the community. The court must be open to the public and engaged in a continuing dialogue with the public regarding children, parenting, the responsibility of the institutions surrounding children, the responsibilities of the public, and how the court acquits itself of its own responsibilities. One could imagine the judge and officials of such a court actively seeking every opportunity to engage the public in discussion about children and the institutions surrounding them because it was a responsibility of the court to do so. That dialogue would take place at school board meetings, at P.T.A. meetings, on op-ed pages, at legislative hearings, on radio and TV talk shows, and so forth.

The conversation would enable the community to discuss with the court its opinions about values, and the court would discuss with the public the ways in which the community expresses its values. The court would be expected to take a long-range view about the society's obligations to its children, and to remind the community of how its values are expressed in law and in the constitution.

Unlike the alternative candidates for leadership around the issue of society and its children, the court would speak with a degree of authority and, one would hope, consequent courage. While the community is at times annoyed and angry with the court, by and large it listens when court officials speak because of the authoritative position of the court.

Benno Schmidt, when newly appointed as President of Yale, stated that one of the reasons that he welcomed the position was because it is a "bully pulpit," that is, a platform from which to speak and engage the attention of the public. The reconstituted court would speak from such a bully pulpit about children and their needs. It would play the crucial role in the construction of a vision for children and actively promote the public dialogue around society's expectations for and of its children. While the court would necessarily continue to interpret and apply statutory law, it also has a larger role to play regarding the norms of the community. This occurs not only through individual decisions, but through acquainting people with what is going on within the court and the juvenile system, arguing about the nature of obligations to and of children, and carrying on that debate in the most public manner possible.

Many of the persons now occupying the bench are disinclined or incapable of engaging the public. They were selected to meet a much narrower mandate. The reconstituted mandate would both attract those who want and are capable of a broader mission and empower those who are now constrained by the narrow mandate. While it is helpful for judges of the juvenile court to speak in concert and on national issues, the critical arenas in which they will be most effective are those within their geographical jurisdiction.

Here they can speak specifically and with the impact of an important local official. The society has given judges high social status which in turn produces capital, the capital to speak and be listened to by the public. That social capital should be expended on the issues of children.

Given the load already carried by the court, additional resources would be necessary. Exhortation, however powerful and necessary, would be insufficient without expanded resources. One of the goals of the hortatory effort would be the development of enhanced resources, both for the court and the institutions serving children.

The goal of the court within the juvenile justice system would be to foster the development of children as responsible citizens by setting standards for their care, for their responsible conduct, and by intervening in individual cases when those standards are not met and when that condition is brought to light. The court would not be a primary institution of socialization; it would continue in its role of line-backer, or place of last resort. Janet Fink, in chapter 15 of this volume, argues effectively for minimum state intervention into family life. In my conception, the court is to support other institutions, defend them, and speak for them to the community, and to reinforce the performance of duties and the meeting of obligations, both within the narrow framework of the law and in the broader context of a major normative force in the society.

The issue of moving children to citizenship is not one of having more children adjudicated. It is first of all one of providing a context within which other institutions can socialize children, and helping to strengthen and support this context aggressively and actively. Parents, families, neighborhoods, and schools should feel the supportive shadow of the court around their mission, and around their common mission mutually discussed and agreed upon.

The court has the role of holding these institutions responsible for fulfilling their mandate, and of making quick response to institutional failures regarding children. If it is to fulfill this role, it will be necessary to develop accountability measures for these institutions and to find ways of initiating action when necessary.

What does this court and this set of institutions look like? Judge William Gladstone, during the last meeting of the Executive Session, said, "It's certainly a different kind of creature from the traditional court. . . . It is a system of which the court is a part but not the focal point. Other agencies would have a true partnership with the court."

Lloyd Ohlin spoke to the issues of institutional form during the Executive Session.

The court becomes then a system for policing the relationships which exist among the agencies in the process of socialization. I find this a rather desirable and exciting concept . . . but I also see it as an awesome task for the court . . . it may be ill-equipped as it currently stands to discharge such a mission. I see several problems . . . One concerns the initiation of cases. How does the court find out about institutional failures? Another problem is fact-finding: How does it develop evidence about these failures? And finally there is the problem of what kind of sanctions the court is entitled to use in achieving this redistribution of responsibility among the socializing agencies. . . . There's an analogy that is not too remote. The federal courts have been involved very extensively in recent years in monitoring and restructuring institutions . . . but there have usually been constitutional grounds justifying the intervention. It seems that new grounds must be developed, perhaps through the legislative process or some other way to provide a basis for intervention in the network of supporting agencies. . . . The courts, to discharge this kind of function, would need supportive work by an agency responsible for overseeing the discharge of the socializing functions on a regular basis. . . . It would be possible to create in an umbrella agency a very strong unit with the obligation to monitor the agencies under its control.

Institutions need not be stagnant. One could imagine various institutional forms. In some ways, the court of which we speak is related to the juvenile court first constituted in Illinois in 1899, but with a broader focus in that it would mediate among institutions and operate with greatly increased accountability to the community. The issue is not one of what such an institution would look like, but whether the society has such a need and whether it will be met in the future.

A reconstituted juvenile court, attempting to address that need, will set standards and hold institutions responsible for their actions regarding children, and will do this in the context of an ongoing dialogue with the community about values. It will neither be a perfect instrument nor will it result in a perfect system. One will continue to be able to convene a group of intelligent, dedicated people around the problems of the system. But it will be a system operating with a vision about children which has been forged out of hard work and hard dialogue about what the community wants of and for its children.

Endnotes

1. Zimring, F. E. (1982). *The changing legal world of adolescence.* New York: The Free Press, p. 91.

Name Index

Subject Index

MIX
Papier aus verantwortungsvollen Quellen
Paper from responsible sources
FSC® C105338

If you have any concerns about our products,
you can contact us on
ProductSafety@springernature.com

In case Publisher is established outside the EU,
the EU authorized representative is:
Springer Nature Customer Service Center GmbH
Europaplatz 3, 69115 Heidelberg, Germany

Printed by Libri Plureos GmbH
in Hamburg, Germany